D1566313

RELIGION, REFORM, AND WOMEN'S WRITING IN EARLY MODERN ENGLAND

Long considered marginal in early modern culture, women writers were actually central to the development of a Protestant literary tradition in England. Kimberly Anne Coles explores their contribution to this tradition through thorough archival research in publication history and book circulation; the interaction of women's texts with those written by men; and the traceable influence of women's writing upon other contemporary literary works. Focusing primarily upon Anne Askew, Katherine Parr, Mary Sidney Herbert, and Anne Vaughan Lok, Coles argues that the writings of these women were among the most popular and influential works of sixteenth-century England. This book is full of new material and fresh analysis for scholars of early modern literature, culture, and religious history.

Kimberly Anne Coles is Assistant Professor of English at the University of Maryland.

*The order and manner of the burning of Anne Aſkew, Iohn Lacelles,
and others, with certayne of the Counſell ſitting in Smithfield.*

And thus ꝼ good Anne Aſkew with theſe bleſſed Martyrs, being troubled ſo many maner of wayes, and hauing paſſed through ſo many tormentes, hauing nowe
ended the long courſe of her agonies, being compaſſed
in with flames of fire, as a bleſſed ſacrifice vnto God,
ſhe ſlept in the Lord, an. 1 5 4 6. leauing behinde her a
ſinguler example of Chriſtian conſtancie for all men to
follow.

⸿Iohn

RELIGION, REFORM, AND WOMEN'S WRITING IN EARLY MODERN ENGLAND

KIMBERLY ANNE COLES

CAMBRIDGE
UNIVERSITY PRESS

PR
113
.C63
2008

CAMBRIDGE UNIVERSITY PRESS
Cambridge, New York, Melbourne, Madrid, Cape Town, Singapore, São Paulo, Delhi

Cambridge University Press
The Edinburgh Building, Cambridge CB2 8RU, UK

Published in the United States of America by Cambridge University Press, New York

www.cambridge.org
Information on this title: www.cambridge.org/9780521880671

First published 2008

Printed in the United Kingdom at the University Press, Cambridge

A catalogue record for this publication is available from the British Library

Library of Congress Cataloguing in Publication data

Coles, Kimberly Anne, 1966–
Religion, reform, and women's
writing in early modern England / Kimberly Anne Coles.
p. cm.
ISBN 978-0-521-88067-1 (hardback)
1. English literature – Women authors – History and criticism.
2. English literature – Early modern, 1500–1700 – History and criticism.
3. Religion and literature – Great Britain – History – 16th century.
4. Women and literature – Great Britain – History – 16th century.
5. Religion in literature. 6. Reformation in literature. I. Title.
PR113.C63 2002
809′.89287–dc22   2007033196

ISBN-978-0-521-88067-1 hardback

For Mark

Contents

Acknowledgments

I have two people in particular to thank: John Carey and Emma Smith served as joint supervisors to my Oxford dissertation. Both injected the important ingredient of indulgence into the thesis writing process. Both kept me honest, and approached my work with their customary care and intellectual rigour. Emma Smith, who directed the final stages of the dissertation, continued to council me long after it was completed. John Carey supplied me with both his remarkable scholarship and unstinting support.

Work on this book was made possible by a summer grant at the Folger Shakespeare Library and by a fellowship from the John W. Kluge Center at the Library of Congress. I wish to thank these institutions for their generous support. Others who supported this endeavour in a different way – by overlooking portions of the manuscript and offering insights and sound criticism – include: Thomas Betteridge, Elizabeth Clarke, Thomas Freeman, David Scott Kastan, Diarmaid MacCulloch, Peter MacCullough, Gerard Passannante, Ann Lake Prescott, Diane Purkiss, Nigel Smith, and Micheline White. In the final stage, Jane Donawerth and Theodore Leinwand read through the complete manuscript and purged it of infelicitous phrasing and errors in fact and judgment. Anne Coldiron kindly gave me her assistance on the French, where needed. Carole Levin provided the idea for the cover. The librarians in Duke Humfrey's, the Folger Shakespeare Library, and the Library of Congress also deserve my public thanks.

My family and friends are delighted at the prospect of this work's completion. They have been leaned on heavily throughout, and while I cannot attest that they kept me sane, they kept me on track – and helped to take me off it when necessary. Joyce Boro, Dana Gee, Sarah Halligan, Eva Ostergaard-Neilson, and Patrick O'Malley bear particular mention as people who often did no more, but certainly did no less, than to believe in me and in the project. By far the greatest debt is owed to my husband, Mark McMorris, who inspired, provoked, encouraged and read every word; and who wrote more pages than I can confess publicly. This book is dedicated to him.

An earlier version of chapter 1 was published (under the same title) in *Modern Philology* 99 (2002). A substantial portion of chapter 5 appears under the title 'The "difference . . . in degree": social rank and gendered expression', in *The impact of feminism in English Renaissance studies*, ed. Dympna Callaghan (London: Palgrave, 2007). I wish to thank the publishers for permission to reprint this material.

Abbreviations

ELH	*English Literary History*
ELR	*English Literary Renaissance*
HLQ	*Huntington Library Quarterly*
JEH	*Journal of Ecclesiastical History*
JMEMS	*Journal of Medieval and Early Modern Studies*
RES	*Review of English Studies*
SEL	*Studies in English Literature*
TLS	*Times Literary Supplement*

Introduction
Making sects: women as reformers, writers, and subjects in Reformation England

I have no difficulty in stating the central premise of my argument. It is that over a relatively short time – certainly no more than a generation or so – women have moved from being the objects of ... poems to being the authors of them. It is a momentous transit. It is also a disruptive one. It raises questions of identity, issues of poetic motive and ethical direction which can seem impossibly complex. What is more, such a transit – like the slow course of a star or the shifts in a constellation – is almost invisible to the naked eye. Critics may well miss it or map it inaccurately.

Eavan Boland, Object lessons

Our very reformation of Religion, seems to be begun and carried on by Women.

Bathsua Makin, An essay to revive the ancient education of gentlewomen

The sixteenth century saw the emergence of women in England as not just readers and writers, but as published authors.[1] Due to the important contributions of feminist scholars in the field of sixteenth- and seventeenth-century literary studies, we no longer ponder the 'perennial puzzle' described by Virginia Woolf. We now know that women were writing in the early modern period, and in numbers.[2] What has been less clear is how the literary products of these women should be mapped within their own historical context. The critical charting of women's texts within sixteenth-century English culture itself has still operated on the (however tacit) assumption that their literary products were devalued in that particular context. This book posits a different view of English literary history: that rather than the standard narrative of women writers as marginal within the operations of sixteenth-century English culture, some women writers were instead central to the development of a Protestant literary tradition.

The three most widely circulated versified works – Thomas Kyd's *The Spanish tragedy*, Samuel Daniel's *Delia*, and Shakespeare's *Venus and*

I

Adonis – probably sold fewer than 5,000 copies each by the end of the sixteenth century.[3] A single prayer book composed by Katherine Parr sold about 19,000 copies.[4] This hardly tells the whole story, but it does indicate that male literary production was not the sole prevailing force of sixteenth-century English culture. My research tries to demonstrate the effect of women's work. As a radically interior faith that insisted on the primacy of the Word, Protestantism offered a revolutionary soteriology – elevating the individual's immediate engagement with God above any mediations of the Church itself – that reformed a social universe, authorising the religious utterances of women. My argument is that some of these writings were among the most important and influential works of sixteenth-century England. This reconstruction stands on a number of grounds: publication history and book circulation; the interaction of women's texts with other (usually male-authored) texts of the period; and the traceable influence of women's writing upon other contemporary literary works.

In post-Reformation English poetics, the idea of the religious female became an authorising figure and a literary tool – one that could be manipulated by men and women alike. While I take up the formative pressures of religious language upon early modern English poetics, I am more interested in the formative pressures exerted by religious women. The terms of religion both empowered and controlled the conditions of female authorship. This study therefore examines women as writers, and women as written, during the period surrounding the crucial shift to Protestantism in England. Focusing primarily upon the writing of Anne Askew, Katherine Parr, Mary Sidney Herbert, Anne Vaughan Lok, and Aemilia Lanyer, I consider each work in juxtaposition to other contemporary writings in order to analyse some of the tensions that act upon its composition and production. My objective has been to understand how the construction of the religious female, as an abstract idea, is formed in literature – and in the process engage the question of how these pressures begin to affect the formation of the category of literature itself.

THE (RE)FORMATION OF WOMEN

The first and *The lattre examinacyon*[s] *of Anne Askewe* were printed in Wesel in 1546 and 1547, respectively.[5] The publication of two more editions in England by 1548 indicates the enormous success of the (by then combined) work.[6] Further, the fact that three of the five editions produced before 1560 are published without John Bale's voluminous commentary signals that it was Askew's testament itself that was of cultural interest, not his notations.[7] The incorporation of her text into John Foxe's 1563 *Acts and Monuments* made subsequent editions of the work unnecessary, but its formidable influence is evident even in commercial practices of the time.[8] The presentation of Robert Crowley's *Confutation of . . . N[icholas] Shaxton* was clearly an attempt on the part of the publisher, John Day, to yoke Crowley's text to the popular success of the *Examinations*.[9] The woodcut used to highlight Askew's narrative in the *Acts and Monuments* was originally designed as a fold-out illustration to Crowley's *Confutation* (Shaxton had been arrested with Askew and John Lascelles, but recanted at their execution).[10] The title page refers to the 'burning of mestres Anne Askue lively set forth in the figure folowynge'. But in spite of her prominence at the beginning, she is mentioned only once in Crowley's pamphlet.[11] Crowley writes of a number of 'true disciples . . . clapped in the chaynes of the syx Articles and . . . broughte to the slaughter house' through the confession of Shaxton; he does not focus on Askew, or any martyr, in particular.[12] By fixing Askew as a selling point to the inexpensive octavo booklet, Day hoped to attract an already identified (and large) audience.

A book that has a sufficiently prominent reputation to merit its use as a marketing tool certainly qualifies as an influential text; such commercial impulses locate its significance in the culture in which it participated. But the popularity of Askew's testament also registers, on some level, the importance of the figure of the religious woman in the emergent discourse of English Protestantism. The place of women was determined in theory – and to a great extent in practice – by a universal belief in their inferior capacity and by reference to the specific commands for their subjection found in Genesis and the Epistles of St Paul. But moments of religious dissent frequently forced a revaluation of this position. Anti-clerical movements in the Middle Ages often elevated the claims of both laymen and lay women within the Church. The Lollards, for example, encouraged reading of the Bible and recitation of scripture by women, and there is some evidence of female preaching.[13] Claire Cross even suggests that Lollardy survived in parts of East Anglia 'to merge with Lutheran ideas' due to the activities of women.[14] But Lollardy was never more than a minority movement; instead, this religious activity on the part of medieval women demonstrates the role that women could assume at times when orthodox church practice was under interrogation.[15] It also reveals (at least partially) the precedent for similar activity during the English Reformation.

Certainly reformers in England understood their project in the context of previous religious subversion – ranging from Lollardy to early

Christianity.[16] Equally clear is the manipulation of the female figure on the part of reformers like Bale in this construction. In *Lost property*, Jennifer Summit suggests that the figure of the 'lost' woman writer is used by Bale to 'redefine the cultural value of books for a society that appeared to him to be bent on their destruction'.[17] In the wake of controversies concerning the translation and transmission of The Book, the destruction of monastic libraries, and the burning of heretical texts, Summit claims that the 'recovery' of the writings of women signalled (for Bale) a reconstitution of English literary history.[18] But Bale edited two other narratives of martyrs, *A brefe chronycle concernynge the examinacyon and death of ... syr Johan Oldecastell* and *A treatyse made by John Lambert*, and notions of loss and recovery feature prominently in Bale's presentation of both of these works.[19] In the preface to his chronicle of the well-known Lollard martyr, Sir John Oldcastle, Bale writes of how he retrieves, and reclaims, Oldcastle's narrative from the 'brefe examinacyon' rendered by Tyndale, as well as the Latin *Fasciculi Zizaniorum*.[20] He frames this project as a restitution of the historical record, and advocates the undertaking of a full account: 'I wolde wyshe some lerned Englyshe mane ... to set forth the Englyshe chronycles in theyr ryght shape.'[21] Certainly Bale is not talking about chronicle histories that trace monarchs and political measures – he is speaking specifically of religious history (and presaging the project of John Foxe whose martyrology he actively supported). But the figures of men in these 'chronycles' signal the '[d]estruction and loss [that] are elementary to Bale's model of ... history' as much as those of women.[22]

The figure of the religious woman is used by Bale to imagine a history of opposition to religious orthodoxy.[23] What makes the figure particularly productive for Bale is not, or not simply, its utility in conflating different historical periods (the figures of men participate in this as well), but the crisis that is signalled by the participation of women in the struggle. The title page to Oldcastle's examination exhibits the knight in full armour, poised for battle. Oldcastle's martyrdom is equated with those who 'haue either dyed for theyr naturall contreye or daungered theyr lyues for a common welthe'.[24] In other words, Bale fuses the figure of the soldier-in-arms with that of the militant Christian of the Pauline epistles. He similarly renders Askew as a soldier of God, but emphasises the irregularity of a woman's bodily service in the cause.[25] Bale links contemporary reform with early Christian history by yoking the figure of Askew to that of the Christian martyr Blandina (and, by extension, attaches his own writing practice to that of Eusebius of Caesarea, the first major historian of the Christian Church). But in the exhibition of women's suffering bodies, his stress is upon how '[t]he strength of God is ... made perfyght by weak-enesse'.[26] He claims that '[m]anye were conuerted by the sufferaunce of Blandina. A farre greatter nombre by the burnynge of Anne Askewe.'[27] The figure of the female becomes, in Bale's text, the site of radical religious change.

Clearly, an emergent Protestant community also understood Askew's sacrifice as both an index of her faith and an expression of the urgency of the cause for which she gave her life. Neither of the narratives of male martyrs that Bale edits experienced anything like the commercial success of Askew's *Examinations*; this difference suggests that Bale's assertion of the number of converts initiated by Askew's example was correct. Certainly, she became an important figure under Edwardian reform.[28] But the power of the figure of the religious woman (in this case, Askew) in the project of reform can also be perceived in Bale's editing practices upon it. The most notable distinction, in fact, between Askew's *Examinations* and Bale's other edited texts is the nature and extent of his intervention. The revision that his 'elucydacyon[s]' perform upon Askew's text is the subject of chapter 1. But briefly, Bale's extensive explication of her text rewrites Askew's narrative as an exposition of early Protestant doctrine. It is precisely because Askew does *not* use the learned terms of the current theological debates – formulated by university men – that Bale tries to argue her case for her. In other words, he tries to make her behave like a man in print – and a magisterial Protestant at that. But his appropriation of her meaning speaks volumes. In one sense, Bale is borrowing his authority from Askew's voice. In a larger sense, his editorial activities demonstrate that he understood the importance of female advocacy on the part of the Protestant cause.

The figure of the religious woman exerted a shaping force upon the controversies in the period leading up to actual reformation in England. For Bale, the figure functioned as a symbol of radical religious dissent and change. For the conservative opposition, it was a sign of religious and political instability. If the debate between the two dominant positions in the religious controversy centred on (in John King's phrase) 'the relative merits of internal and external authority', then the religious woman provided a flashpoint for both sides.[29] Stephen Gardiner, the conservative Bishop of Winchester, nicely identifies the spectre of religious and political unruliness that the female figure raised: 'For if it be perswaded the understanding of Gods law to be at larg in women and children, wherby they may have the rule of that, and then Gods law must be the rule of all, is not hereby the rule of al brought into there hands?'[30] But it is precisely this disruptive potential that makes the religious woman – and the religious woman writer – such a powerful figure in reform.

'Trulye I am constrayned & forced to speake & write', Katherine Parr claims in her *Lamentacion of a synner*, 'to mine own confusion and shame: but to the greate glorye, and prayse of god.'[31] The conviction that 'con-strayn[s]' Parr to write that all souls dwell in the same fallen state (and are equal before God), and that every soul is individually accountable to God similarly compelled other women to bear witness to their faith. This assumption of authority was precisely what Gardiner perceived as funda-mentally corrosive to the social order. However, the agency of women in the interpretation – and dissemination – of scriptural and religious mean-ing communicated to an emergent Protestant community the underlying religio-political goal of the Reformation: individual apprehension of 'Gods law'. Of course, the expression partly traded upon cultural notions of female inferiority – the egalitarian impulses of reform are conveyed through the vehicle of women *because* of their status. Nevertheless, the circumstance in which women became ideal figures of political and reli-gious disruption opened space for the empowerment of women within the written culture of the Reformation.

One of the most productive features of feminist criticism of the past two decades has been the sustained attention on the cultural value of women's religious beliefs.[32] This recognition – that if women did not have a Re-naissance, they at least had a Reformation – not only asserts the proper historical chronology for England (acknowledging that the Reformation affected England before and arguably more deeply than the Renaissance did) but also identifies religion itself as the most pervasive idiom of early modern England. The writing of both men and women at the time was principally concerned with the subject of religion – about 45 per cent of printed material from this period treats the topic in some form.[33] The rather common assertion, then, that women were 'proscribed from com-position or publication in the genres considered to be serious', is simply wrong.[34] Rather, they were participants – insofar as woman wrote – in the most important cultural dialogue that was taking place.

But 'despite the groundbreaking work on early modern women writers produced in the past few years', Barbara Bowen observes, 'women's writ-ing still tends to be read as if it were less complex, smaller, than it is'.[35] Bowen goes on to say that 'a more useful sense . . . of the writings' – useful in both political and cultural terms – 'might follow from an expansion of the literary claims we are willing to make for them'.[36] I take Bowen to mean that we should extend our critical reach not only concerning the negotiation of cultural material *within* women's texts, but also regarding the cultural reception *of* women's texts. We speak of women's works as 'celebrated' rather than as influential (the underpinning assumption is that they are not). These articulations do not admit that the terms that directed social relationships might have been within the province of women's (at least partial) control. In fact, Gardiner's remark that 'the rule of all' could be 'brought into [the] hands' of women through the disruption of traditional religious belief, while tinged with paranoia, demonstrates his keen political awareness. Religion vitally – perhaps principally – informed both how individuals understood themselves and how they understood themselves in relation to their society. The extent to which women formulated the terms of the new religion therefore determined their influence upon the ideas that shaped cultural production.

Critical convention has it that women (with the notable exception of Queen Elizabeth) occupied a marginal position in key developments concerning early modern religious, political, and poetic reform. It has become clear to us that women appropriated the terms of religion for their own use; in fact, in the struggle against oppression, the terms of religion, properly negotiated, were among the most effective tools that women could employ. We also now acknowledge that in the course of the disruption in religious doctrine and practice, the participation of women in the project of reform threw the instabilities of the socially constructed category of 'woman' into sharp relief.[37] This recognition, however, has not led to a full appreciation of the extent to which women articulated the terms of emergent Protestantism for the larger English culture. The circulation of works by women examined here, as well as the manifest influence of these works upon the literary production of male thinkers and poets in the period, indicates that at a time of religious crisis, the voices of authority that emerge are not necessarily the ones that we would expect. This book argues that certain early modern women writers were far more fundamental to the development of Protestant consciousness, and later artistic identity, than has been previously acknowledged.

REPRESENTATION AND REFORM

It is my contention that the religious upheavals of the sixteenth century produced a period of heightened cultural agency for women. In making this declaration, I am speaking only of the tiny minority of literate women whose education was sufficient to take advantage of such an instance.[38] I am neither minimising the obstacles to the participation of women in

literary culture at this time, nor am I extracting women's cultural predica-
ment from its material conditions. But (and it has been said before)
evidence of early modern women's social experience is often not legible
in the objects of literary study – the social practices most representative of
female experience were usually rendered in terms that are no longer visible
at all.[39] For those few women whose education allowed them to engage
literary systems of representation, the status of the figure of the religious
female in early Reformation discourse enabled them to interrupt and
redirect existing patterns. The dominant ideology that they disrupted
was almost exclusively religious: the texts that I explore do not represent
a common female experience, nor do they offer (with the exception of
Lanyer's *Salve Deus*) a serious critique of patriarchy. But if the majority of
these works are not particularly oppositional (at least in relation to patriarchal design), they *are* culturally influential. The writing examined here
negotiated key points of contest and controversy during a time of overwhelming religious change: it conveyed central tenets of emergent Protestantism to a reading public that only imperfectly understood the
principles of the new religion; it mediated a changing national faith by
situating it in familiar terms; it helped to establish the early vernacular
forms of the Anglican Church; and when the tenets of English Protestant
culture came into conflict with developing notions of English poetics, it
opened channels through which devotional language flowed into lyric
verse.

Feminist critics have appreciated for some time that religious idiom was
potentially empowering for women of the early modern period. But this
awareness has been countered by the assumption that sociolinguistic codes
effectively thwarted the production of the female voice in public discourse.[40] However, as Elizabeth Hanson rightly observes, disrupting existing systems of language and representation is primarily a writer's problem
and a writer's task – one that only comes into play once the far more
pervasive problem of educational training (particularly for women) has
been overcome.[41] Hanson follows this observation with two questions
that, in many ways, describe the principal focus of my research: if the
problems confronting a woman writing in this period are not simply
'continuous with those facing the generality of women ... what exactly
is the relation between the global oppression of women and the unusual
position of the writing woman? Or to come at the problem somewhat
differently, how do we *construct* the task of writing in the effort to reveal
the operation of the sex/gender system upon it?'[42] I have been suggesting
that the effect of the gender system upon the religious woman writer in

this period is somewhat ironic: while Bale reinforces gendered assumptions, those very assumptions cause him to read 'woman' as a powerful sign in religious transition.[43] Thus the linguistic encoding of gender difference stood mostly firm; but the manner in which the figure of 'woman' was produced and deployed in the course of reform allowed women writers partial control over the terms of religious difference – and these were arguably as central to the operations of early modern culture and individual identity.

To return to Hanson's question, and to pose it slightly differently, how does one discover the activity of the gender system upon the composition, production, and reception of women's (religious) texts? Feminist criticism of the past few years has been particularly engaged with this question, and has sought to explore the issue of 'the relationship of woman and printed text in a historicism which offers a multidimensional approach'.[44] An enquiry of this kind must examine how gender operates both within and around texts: it must try to discern when (and whether) gendered encoding is consciously engaged within texts themselves; when the figure of the religious woman is deployed as a marketing device both within texts and in extra-textual apparatus; when it functions as a signifier between texts; and when the market of the book trade itself responds to these signs in its operations.[45] In trying to look at all of these issues, I have paid close attention to the production of texts in both compositional and material terms, and to their circulation within the marketplace. I have tried to account for the agency of editors and printers as well as authors in the mediation of cultural discourse. I have used straight publication numbers as well as stylistic patterns and verbal echoes in my attempt to demonstrate cultural influence.[46] But for the most part I reconstitute the materials from which these texts – by both men and women – are derived.

The practice of intertextuality – of reconstructing source material, of noticing how this material is redeployed within texts, and of understanding how a field of signs is activated among texts – is hardly new in feminist studies. The method has been refreshed by scholars such as Danielle Clarke who have insisted that women's writing be considered in the context of a cultural circulation of ideas – and that further, we understand 'woman' as one of these circulated, refractory ideas and not as a signature tied to a biological agent.[47] One of the benefits of such an intertextual approach is that it registers female voice in terms of representation. It recognises gender in women's texts – as in men's – as constructed. In scrutinising the exchange of signs between the texts of men and women, it captures a moment of gender construction. While a good deal of critical work has been done on how women were represented – in literature, conduct books, and on the English stage – there has been less analysis applied to how they represented themselves.[48] Clarke suggests that this circumstance occurs because 'the particular investments and aims of feminist criticism are such that there is little interest in assuming the reversibility or flexibility of [the] paradigm' that the gender of a text does not necessarily correspond to the author's biological sex.[49] Gynocriticism initiated a tendency to read women's texts for gender-inflected markings that affirm personal biography and biology, and while this strategy has proved its value in both critical and political terms, it has also proved hard to overthrow.[50] This is especially the case when dealing with texts that appear particularly amenable to gynocritical readings – when the sex of the author coheres with the speaker's gender. But in falling susceptible to such readings, we ignore the extent to which gender is performed within the text – part of a rhetorical strategy – for purposes other than self-expression.

A gynocritical reading strategy often overlooks the situation of the sign of 'woman' in material circulation – and how it might assist the commercial production and/or dissemination of women's texts.[51] John Day's use of the image of Askew's execution in advertising a book that does not really address her martyrdom is a case in point: it signals a cultural environment in which 'woman' has become a promotional device.[52] I am, of course, arguing that the milieu was ideologically and historically specific: not the sign of 'woman' absent the modifier; and not the 'religious woman' absent the cultural disruption that the Reformation caused. But I am further arguing that women who produce this figure within their texts frequently do so self-consciously, and with an eye toward the readership that will receive them. They deploy the figure in the service of their political intentions or their commercial objectives. Which is to say that it cannot be read as authentic – as a reliable index of 'real' expression. Its constructed nature must always be understood in terms of the cultural economy in which it was developed and circulated.

Figures are instances of representation. Insofar as one describes a figure, one is speaking of the already represented – of a moment of representation that relates to a larger sociolinguistic field that may not be straightforward. A figure might operate as part of a previously formulated category, but figures are not categories. A category organises its constituents: it provides a set of instructions that enable us to construe its members. Categories, then, activate networks of meaning, but they are not themselves embedded within texts. This means that the figure of the religious woman in early Reformation discourse accrues its power through the meanings that the category of 'woman' invokes. The figure relies upon the circumstance of religious transition – and the extent to which the pre-existing category of 'woman' can be used to articulate both the instabilities and ideals of the radical change that is taking place. This is precisely why the figure can trouble the existing terms of religion and politics but hardly disturb the system governing gender. Further, the figure tends to mediate the public reception of women's religious texts more than their authorial expression (this too explains why gynocritical strategies are not very productive in reading these texts). To take Askew once more as the illustrative example: the gender system crucially constrains her articulations (and a discussion of precisely how is central to my argument); but how she is constructed as a woman in the context of religious change – by both Bale and the wider English readership – informs the reception of her work. Katherine Parr, to take a different example, plays a central role in the reformulation of the terms of state religion. But part of her objective is to enunciate a shared Christian response to religious faith and practice – an aim that substantially (but not entirely) erases gender-inflected markings from her texts.[53] Parr is, however, sensitive to the potential of her own figure in the project of reform; she therefore uses herself as a character of conversion within her texts. The examples of Askew and Parr should indicate that the figure of the religious woman is itself not stable; it is under construction in the work of the women – and the men – examined in this book.

Because the figure is, in many ways, a device linked to the dissemination of texts, its use often expresses public (political, polemical, mercantile), not personal, intentions. But if the figure of the religious woman confers authority to the writing of women in this period, how women use this authority in their own writing performance is heavily inflected by class and/or commercial concerns. The reception of their texts is couched in the same set of concerns. Certainly one of the most complex problems facing feminist criticism that seeks to divulge a distant past is how different relationships of individual women authors to mechanisms of social power affect the production and reception of their work. It is only through careful unpacking of the internal operations of texts themselves – and the external effect of the energies that they deploy – that these kinds of distinctions become visible. The finer points of these observations get teased out in individual chapters. But Aemilia Lanyer serves as an effective index of just how complicated the problem can become. While Lanyer uses a female writing tradition to enforce the claims for her work, she is particularly sensitive to the fact that few women poets of the middling sort are housed within it. The alienation effect that this produces is evident in how Lanyer accesses the tradition – and particularly evident in the fact that she finally resorts to the works of other professional (male) poets for her models. Even so, Lanyer is herself unique; education was one of the primary registers of social power, and her standard of education was unusual for a woman of her status.

Lanyer's situation makes explicit why I try not only to examine the operation of the sex/gender system upon the writing and circulation of women's texts, but also to analyse how these operations respond to issues of class.[54] Through analysis of the cultural materials that men and women use in the composition of their work, I try to evaluate the objectives of their arguments; I notice how ideas (and materials) are exchanged; I observe the cultural controversies in which the work intervenes; I attempt to identify the audience for whom it is intended; and finally, I try to discern public reaction to it. Situating women's texts in the context of the circulation of discourse – paying close attention to the relationship between source, text, and reception – usefully throws light upon the contingencies of gender and class. It also permits a full interrogation of how a cultural dialogue concerning religion, and religious change, was conducted across gender and class boundaries.

This project has more to do with cartography than discovery. Feminist critics, doubling as archaeologists, have been exhuming the written materials of early modern women from the archives for decades. Much of the scholarship attendant upon this recovery has inadvertently marginalised the writing of these women by arguing for its cultural significance on the grounds of exceptionality. 'But the survival of these works in future school curricula', as John Guillory has pointed out, depends upon the recognition of 'their status as interesting and important cultural works that no intellectually responsible program of study can ignore'.[55] Assigning a different place to women's writing – at the centre rather than the margins of intellectual and literary exchange – revises the map by which we have been reading the culture of the early modern period. It does not merely include women in the diagram; it reveals that their absence has left gaps in our knowledge concerning crucial cultural developments. It adds an important component that has been missing from our evaluation and analysis of the dominant (male) writers and poets themselves, what Maureen Quilligan has termed 'Completing the conversation': incorporating 'the women to whom, in fact, [men] were in part speaking and to whom they may . . . well have been listening'.[56] Finally, it reorients our understanding of the literary output of men in the early modern period by exposing how – and how much – their production was informed by the interventions of women.

In the opening section of the book, I consider the role of women in the reorganisation of religious identity and devotion in mid-sixteenth-century England. The first chapter deals with *The first* and *The lattre examinacyon of Anne Askewe* and contemplates the construction of her martyrdom within the text(s) as redacted by John Bale and John Foxe. Because all manuscript copies of Askew's account have been lost, its only mode of transmission is through these edited forms. Askew's record of her defiance of Henrician civil and ecclesiastical authority marks the inner space of individual resistance. But the interior and unindoctrinated quality of Askew's discourse is eradicated in the editions of both Bale and Foxe for the purpose of religious polemic. While editorial intrusion into Askew's text goes a long way toward demonstrating the importance of the female figure to the arguments of early reformers, it is at least as revealing that English publishers removed all such interpolation after the initial printing of her testament. And it is certainly revealing that there were more editions of Askew's narrative produced in the sixteenth century than that of any other English martyr.

My second chapter examines Katherine Parr's formative role in the development of the devotional forms of the nascent English Church. I analyse both her *Prayers or meditacions* and *Lamentacion of a synner* in order to elucidate the complex way that Parr's adult apostasy registers in her devotional texts. The doctrinal exchanges of Parr's work render it pliable to the diverse devotional attitudes of English readers. But she also presses her own figure into the service of reform: by taking herself as the first example of the reformed evangelical Christian, Parr communicates – and negotiates – some of the more complicated issues of spiritual conversion. In order to structure her *Prayers*, Parr employs a prominent Catholic devotional text, *The imitation of Christ*. Through her use of the *Imitation*, she advances the ideas of her recent spiritual researches within a traditional framework; but the tactic also allows for some consistency within her own spiritual development. The design of the *Prayers*, then, serves the devotional needs of both its writer and its intended readers. The *Lamentacion*, by contrast, is an original narrative that relates Parr's personal experience of religious conversion. It is structurally organised according to Luther's *Preface to the Epistle to the Romans*, which outlines St Paul's epistolary strategy; Parr adopts this strategy in her own account of spiritual awakening. Her writing shows the influence of both prominent Catholics (such as John Fisher) and religious reformers (such as Thomas Cranmer). I discuss the eclectic nature of Parr's cultural borrowing in both important devotional works, and examine how the evident imprint of

Catholicism is turned to an evangelical purpose in her prose. I also explore how Parr's use of her own figure helped to formulate institutional notions of Protestant identity.

Having considered the contributions of women to the religious culture of Reformation England, I then take up women's contributions to the reformation of English literature. The third chapter examines the lyrical transcription of the Psalms by Mary Sidney Herbert, the Countess of Pembroke. I consider Herbert's psalm poems in the context of the anti-poetic convictions of Calvinist-inflected Protestantism. I first examine the case of whether or not a Protestant poetics is even possible – whether the theological doctrines of English Protestantism in the latter part of the sixteenth century could accommodate poetry within devotion. To establish a framework in which to understand the Sidney–Pembroke Psalter, I begin with a review of the history of Reformation hermeneutics in England. I then analyse Philip Sidney's *Defence of poetry* within the context of the larger frames that were current at the time: lectures on Aristotle's *Rhetoric* at Oxford; the rhetorical philosophy of Peter Ramus which was dominant at Cambridge; Calvin's own psalm-centred poetic theory; and the attitudes concerning aesthetics in devotion expressed by prominent English clerics. I subsequently demonstrate the particular objectives of the poetic Psalter translation that Herbert undertook – the project was, finally, her point of entry into the theoretical debate. The Sidney–Pembroke Psalter failed to achieve a revaluation of poetry within the Protestant theological system. This is because its intention – to elevate English lyric – was fundamentally at odds with Protestant ideals. In spite of this failure to change the devotional practices of the English Church, cultural recognition of Herbert's crucial role in revising secular poetic practice is later registered in how religious poets subsequently use her figure in licensing their own work.

In the fourth chapter, I consider the influence of the writing of Anne Vaughan Lok.[57] Lok is the author of a sonnet sequence – the first in English – that she appended to her translation of Calvin's sermons (1560).[58] The impress of the Sidney–Pembroke Psalter can be appreciated in the contemporary poetry of Barnabe Barnes, Nicholas Breton, Henry Constable, and Abraham Fraunce, as well as in the later devotional work of John Donne and Giles Fletcher. However, Henry Lok published his *Sundry Christian passions contained in two hundred sonnets* in 1593 – close enough to the circulation of the Psalter to have been developed independently. (It also seems clear that poets such as Barnes drew from Lok's work as well as the Psalter of the Sidneys.) As the son of Anne Lok, Henry's work must be seen in the context of her earlier composition. In spite of the early instances of lyric translations of the Psalms by Thomas Wyatt and Henry Howard, Earl of Surrey, there is virtually no imitation of their example from 1549 to 1591.[59] (I suggest that this has much to do with the induction of Calvin into English Protestantism.) A notable exception is Lok's sonnet sequence. She must have encountered the English sonnet form in Tottel's *Miscellany*; but her appropriation of it suggests that she had reservations about Surrey's evaluation (in 'The great Macedon') of Wyatt's psalm poems. In fact, her sequence aims to renovate these examples. The model that Anne adopts in her work is Calvin, not Wyatt – she imitates Calvin's rhetorical habit of dilating individual lines of scripture. The fundamental attitude of her work is Presbyterian, more collective than individual; but it is also a gender-inflected stance. Which is to say that the early development of Calvinist poetics owes much to a female exegesis. While his mother's model is evident in Henry Lok's first sonnet sequence, and particularly apparent in his subsequent work, *Ecclesiastes*, reformed writers such as Taylor, Vaughan, and Traherne also take something from her early example (which they encountered directly, or through her son).

The inclusion in the final chapter of a seventeenth–century poet, Aemilia Lanyer, clarifies and completes a project that aims to show how the conceptual notion of religious womanhood enabled the writing performance of women in the Reformation. Lanyer helps me to elucidate how that figure could be controlled and directed by members of both sexes. In her long poem, *Salve Deus Rex Judæorum*, Lanyer turns to a religious subject for the purposes of seeking patronage. This is not to claim that Lanyer held no religious conviction, but rather to propose that she self-consciously affiliated herself – and her work – with a female religious writing tradition. Certainly one of the things that this tactic suggests is the visibility of that tradition at the start of the seventeenth century. But it also exposes how the figure of the religious woman could itself be used to license professional work. Lanyer navigates her entry into the professional literary sphere through the figure of Mary Sidney Herbert, herself a useful mediator precisely because of her intervention in the rhetorical and theological debates concerning devotional lyric. The extent to which male writers try to use the figure of Herbert to authorise their religious work testifies to the shared cultural awareness of her place in the controversy. Lanyer trades upon the poetic achievements of Herbert – and by extension, those of a female tradition – in order to promote her own standing as a professional religious poet.

The figure of the religious female became a powerful mediating symbol through which women could engage the public role of authorship, and through which they themselves would be read. Their negotiation of that symbol enabled written work that contributed significantly to the development of both the devotional and secular forms of an emergent Protestant written culture. In describing the interventions that account for shifts that ultimately revolutionise religious and artistic practice in England, critics have inevitably reserved these inroads for the traffic of men. This book argues that, in the process of cultivating forms for a new Christian sect, certain women in England reformed its cultural expression.

The death of the author (and the appropriation of her text): the case of Anne Askew's Examinations

> this is a personal matter,
> a private affair and God knows
> none of your business.
>
> Anne Sexton, 'Jesus dies'

In considering the theatrical nature of public executions in the early modern period, and the available spectacle of power for both the disciplinarians and the punished, Catherine Belsey has observed that these occasions afforded women 'the supreme moment to speak'.[1] But perhaps, in spite of the Foucauldian emphasis upon the scaffold, the moment came before. It was during interrogation that the statements of the condemned were most likely to be recorded – and transcriptions of these examinations (either produced by the state or the individual) were frequently published.[2] Of course, execution prevented their having any subsequent control over the production of their words.[3] This fact held special problems for the narratives of women, as the editors who generated the printed forms of their accounts were inevitably men.

The complications of such a textual encounter are graphically displayed in the edited versions of Anne Askew's *Examinations*. Askew's account of resisting religious authority participates in an emergent reformist discourse – one in which the available precedents were male-authored. While she worked from these models, her perspective was, obviously, unique. But her editors were used to revising the polemical, scholastically informed, accounts of men; neither understood the female-inflected argument. This fact produces an odd distortion of Askew's text in its various material forms. Askew's *Examinations* were printed in Wesel in 1546 and 1547. There were two more editions produced in England by 1548 (with continuous signatures), and a total of six before it was incorporated into the 1563 *Acts and Monuments*.[4] Askew's narrative, then, was available to a goodly portion of the English reading public during the crucial transition to Protestantism under Edward VI.[5] It has therefore secured for itself an important place in our analyses of the religious controversies of the period. What has received less attention, even from feminist critics, is how the shape of Askew's narrative changes depending upon the polemical intentions of her male editors. If we are to understand fully the conditions that governed the representation of women's speech in the early modern period, we should attend carefully to the editorial interventions that result in such radically different productions of Askew's text.

THE BODY OF THE TEXT

The woodcut of Askew's execution in John Foxe's *Acts and Monuments* is remarkable for its lack of a central figure.[6] The scene pictured is a bird's eye view of the site of her capital punishment at Smithfield: spectators swarm around a central ring in which four figures are bound to stakes, attendants move about them in preparation for their execution, and a preacher (Nicholas Shaxton) delivers a sermon from a pulpit in the north-west bend. The far left figure on the line, bound at the waist, presumably depicts Askew.[7] Although this illustration was not originally commissioned by John Day for the *Acts and Monuments*, its use here to punctuate Foxe's account of Askew's martyrdom is expressive: the woodcut maps the pattern of her corporal displacement which occurs within the text itself.

The story of Anne Askew's examinations and martyrdom is unique within the *Acts and Monuments* because she was a woman who wrote her own account of events (although the status of her autobiographical voice is troubled by the fact that it is redacted by John Bale[8]). What is perhaps most interesting in the account is the extent to which – and the places where – her voice and body are deliberately withheld. In the martyrologies of Thomas Cranmer, John Hooper, or Nicholas Ridley the verbal record of their bodies in the text is detailed (and often gruesome). Scholars have argued that the early modern understanding of physical torment was radically different from our own: because they bore witness to 'a new sense of the material location of truth', religious martyrs saw in torture the opportunity to objectify (or create) their truth.[9] In the *Acts and Monuments* Foxe tries to 'make [the] inward truth of the subject readable' – the inner truth of faith is objectified through a discourse of the body.[10] In contrast to these martyrologies, the instruments of Askew's corporeality – her voice and her body – are oddly decentred in her narrative. When questioned by the English authorities, Askew often offers silence as a form of resistance. At moments when the physical fact of her body registers in the text, she works to conceal it from public view. In this chapter, I explain this elision of her material subjectivity; I then explore the effect that this rhetorical manoeuvre produces within the context of the central works in which Askew's narrative appears: John Bale's *First* and *Latter examination of Anne Askew* and John Foxe's *Acts and Monuments*.[11]

In her article, 'Pain, persecution, and the construction of selfhood', Janel Mueller notices the doctrinal reformulations by which Marian martyrs articulate the experience of their bodies in pain. She argues that the process of trials for heresy – which denied silence as an alternative for the accused, and maintained the legally sanctioned mode of execution, burning at the stake, as a present threat during these exchanges – produced a rhetoric of embodiment that was an integral part of the religious debate.[12] Askew's account of her trials, however, refuses this construction. My argument is not an attempt to challenge Mueller's general outline of martyred identity, but to explore the very different construction of martyrdom that occurs when the subject is positioned at the edges of the debate.

Askew left her Catholic husband, Thomas Kyme, and two children, and migrated from her home in Friskney, Lincolnshire, to London for the purpose of seeking a divorce.[13] As a married woman who lacked the protection of her husband, Askew was extremely vulnerable when she was arrested 'for certeyn matters concernying the vi Articles'.[14] She was first detained in March 1545, and subsequently rearrested in June 1546. Although she may have suffered other detentions (Charles Wriothesley, the Windsor Herald, records another arraignment on 13 June 1545),[15] these two are the subject of her first and latter *Examinations*. She wrote her record of her trials either in separate instalments, or at one time in the days between her condemnation and execution. Unlike other (male) martyrs who recorded their ordeals (either in letters or as part of treatises), however, Askew refuses to 'publish . . . [her] mynde'.[16] In spite of the public act of authorship, her text registers a reluctance to exhibit the private precincts of belief. Askew's distinctive rhetorical habits need to be viewed in the context of her understanding of Protestant faith. This is not to say that her discourse is devoid of gender differentials – in fact, I will suggest the opposite. Her discursive practices, both in the course of defying Henrician religious authority and in how she records the procedure of her examinations, clearly register the convictions of Protestantism at an inaugural moment; but these convictions are inflected in her writing by her female position.

The only personal history written from prison during the reign of Henry VIII that bears resemblance to the *Examinations* is *The articles wherefore John Frith died* which is annexed to Frith's answer to Thomas More concerning the sacrament (1533). This is quite possibly the treatise that Askew was reading when Archdeacon John Wymesley warned her that 'Soche bokes as thys is, hath brought yow to the trouble ye are in.'[17] The *Articles* give some account of the examinations that Frith underwent, but they are mostly a point-by-point answer to the charges that condemned him. The publication of his system of belief, he himself observes, is sure to purchase him a 'moste cruell deth'.[18] It is precisely this kind of exposure that Askew's narrative refuses.

The first *Examination* is confined exclusively to public events; it witnesses the procedures that took place during the course of Askew's detention. Her defence during her interrogations takes two forms: silence or scripture. She manipulates the traditional role of her sex in order to avoid entrapment, and when this tactic fails, she resorts to a textual authority that cannot be assailed. When twice called upon to clarify her meaning concerning the scriptural passage 'god dwelleth not in temples made with hands' (Acts 17:24) – the answer to which could secure her conviction – she gestures in both directions. She first tells Doctor Standish, one of the theologians examining her, that it is 'agaynst saynt Paules lernynge, that I beynge a woman, shuld interprete the scriptures, specyallye where so manye wyse lerned men were'.[19] Then, when Edmund Bonner, the Bishop of London, probes her for a more satisfying answer to the question, she responds:

I beleue as the scripture doth teache me. Then enquired he of me, what if the scripture doth saye, that it is the bodye of Christ? I beleue (sayd I) like as the scripture doth teach me. Then asked he agayne, what if the scripture doth saye, that it is not the bodye of Christ? My answere was styll, I beleue as the scripture infourmeth me ... Then he asked me, whye I had so fewe wordes? And I answered. God hath geven me the gyft of knowlege. but not of vtteraunce. And Salomon sayth, that a woman of fewe wordes, is a gyft of God, Prouer. 19.[20]

Called 'tanswere to the lawe' for her 'obstinate' opinions in 'matiers of religion',[21] she uses the roles available to her – reformist or female – in order to open space for manoeuvre.[22] Rather than the usual interrogations that are played out in Foxe's 'Book of martyrs', in which both sides assert their contrary formulations of religious meaning, Askew's record of her trials transcribes the system of evasion by which she keeps her meaning indeterminate.[23]

Askew cannot enter the polemic into which John Frith inserts himself – she is barred by virtue of gender, education, and Pauline proscription.[24] Upbraided by the 'Byshoppes chaunceller' for 'utterynge the scriptures' counter to St Paul's directive, she tells him that she knows 'Paules mean-ynge so well as he, whych is, i. Corinthiorum xiiii. that a woman ought not to speake in the congregacyon by the waye of teachynge'.[25] Regardless of her willingness to instruct the members of the quest, her adherence to scriptural regulation would not have allowed her to enter into the public debate concerning transubstantiation being waged in numerous treatises. Rather, her authority rests on her power to interpret scripture for herself. She owns, and asserts her right to own, a private faith. 'I take the ... most mercyfull God of *myn*', she writes, 'to recorde, that I holde no opynyons contrarye to hys most holye worde.'[26] The structure of her faith is founded upon an individual grasp of scripture; it privileges local and positional truths. She does not use the occasion of her trial to assert the tenets of the early Protestant community. Unlike Frith, or even her fellow martyr John Lascelles, she does not use the platform of her interrogations to answer the articles with which she is charged.

Throughout the first half of the second *Examination*, she circumspectly refuses to fix her position concerning the sacrament. Then the course of the narrative abruptly changes: 'the Byshopp [Stephen Gardiner] sayd, I shuld be brente'.[27] Once her condemnation is pronounced, her voice becomes more expansive, and she begins to assert her faith. From the moment of Gardiner's judgment, she is willing to declare openly her opinion concerning sacramental ontology; her confessions of belief, how-ever, remain markedly different from those that appear in contemporary narratives (and from the testaments of the Marian martyrs that follow). Like the men who wrote accounts of the events that led up to their martyrdoms (or the faith that brought them there), her identity formation is laid on ideological ground; unlike them, it is stylistically privatised. 'I beleue', she writes in her confession of faith, 'we nede no vnwritten ver-ytees to rule hys churche with. Therfor loke what he hath layd vnto *me* with hys owne mouthe, in hys holye Gospell, that haue I with Gods grace, closed up in my harte'.[28] Askew does not enter the arena of sermonising where Frith or Lascelles, armed with masculine privilege, feel free to engage. When she articulates her belief, her disclosure takes the form of scriptural citation; her understanding of God's verity is individually appre-hended, and is 'closed up in [her] harte'. She writes from a singular, marginalised position – and the place from which she writes confirms the extent of her isolation: 'Truthe is layed in pryson.'[29]

NOT IN HIS IMAGE

Anne Askew appears to have been well educated, according to the standard of female education at the time. As Rosemary O'Day points out, early modern education was vocational in practice – and the vocation of women was marriage.[30] Juan Luis Vives wrote his treatise *The education of a Christian woman* as a manual of instruction for the general education of women, and his principal concern was with women in the upper ranks of society.[31] But even an educationalist such as Vives – with an eye toward the political life of Princess Mary Tudor – assumed that the vocation of women was domestic life. And female virtue – female chastity in particular – was at the heart of the curriculum: '[A]lthough rules of conduct for men are numerous, the moral formation of women can be imparted with very few precepts. A woman's only care is chastity; therefore when this has been thoroughly elucidated, she may be considered to have received sufficient instruction.'[32] The impulses of humanism led to the advocacy of education for women, but these attitudes were still restrained by assumptions of a woman's vocation and a preoccupation with her chastity.

In spite of the famous example of female erudition set by Thomas More's household, 'there is no record', Maria Dowling claims, 'of any father following his example in the early years of Henry's reign'.[33] For the daughters of gentry, such as Sir William Askew's, there were two prevailing options for female education: farming them out to the nursery of another socially elite family, or educating them at home. While Derek Wilson suggests that the three Askew sisters likely received private tuition at home, it is not clear which option was pursued.[34] Home tuition of the girls of affluent families could mean a better education for the young women involved. Tutors retained by noble families would sometimes educate the male and female children together – which, of course, meant that the girls received the same training as the boys (until the young men went to university). Wilson also states that the eldest son, Francis, was sent to Cambridge to complete his education.[35] There is, however, no record of Francis Askew's attendance at Cambridge. It is therefore unclear whether the Askew girls were instructed with their brothers, how many years of tuition they received, and whether they were tutored in languages other than English. It is also uncertain whether these women received added stimulation from Francis's exposure to university – and particularly to the religious researches that were a feature of Cambridge at the time.

What can be determined about the extent of Anne Askew's learning must be gleaned from her text. The picture that emerges is that of a woman who read deeply (but not broadly) in English, and who retained much of what she read. The evidence of scriptural reading in her discourse is absolutely plain; the traces of doctrinal tracts are less obvious, but nonetheless apparent. The treatise that seems to have had the greatest influence upon her thinking is John Frith's *A boke ... answeringe unto M. Mores lettur*. The impression that this work left upon Askew's rhetorical style and religious orientation is clearly visible in the *Examinations*. I will plot the points which demonstrate this influence; but finally, I want to emphasise the discursive differences which mark their very different points of entry into the religious debate.

The only book that Askew relates having in her possession is one 'of Johan frithes makynge'.[36] It is not explicitly indicated that this book was Frith's response to More – Frith was the author of seven treatises – but verbal echoes from this tract are evident in Askew's narrative. This correlation can be ascribed either to numerous readings of the text, or a recent reading that left details fresh in her mind. The fact that Wymesley takes the book from her when she is examined before Bonner (March 1545), and the prevalence of corresponding details in her account of her second examination (June 1546), argues for the former case. In his rehearsal of the articles that condemned him, Frith records his answer concerning sacramental presence:

I sayd ... that I thoughte that [the sacrament] was bothe christes body, and also our body ... In that yt ys made one brede of many graynes yt is our body sygnifying that we though we be many, are yet one body: and lyke wyse of the wyne in that yt is made one wyne of many grapes.
And agayne in that yt is broken, yt is Christes body, signyfyeng that hys body shulde be broken, that is to say suffer dethe, to redeme us from our iniquites.
In that yt was distributed, yt was christes body, sygnifyeng that as verely as that sacrament is distributyd vnto vs, so verely ys Christes body, and the frute of hys passyon, distributed vnto all faythfull men.
In that yt ys receauyd, yt is Christes body, sygnifiyng that as verely as the outwarde man receauyth the sacrament with his tethe & mouthe, so verely dothe the inward man, thorow faythe, receaue Christes body & frute of his passyon, and ys as sure of yt as of the brede that he eatyth.[37]

In his development of the parallel signification of the bread and wine of the altar and the body of the true church, Frith follows the written words of Cyprian: 'Euen as of many graines is made one bread, so are we one misticall bodye in Christ.'[38] Frith's innovation lies in his imaginative formulations of the model; he extends Cyprian's analogical example of the mystical body to encompass the sacramental elements, and then, by further extension, incorporates the breaking of Christ's physical body into his semiotic structure.[39] In her confession 'concernynge [her] beleve' Askew writes: 'I fynde in the Scriptures ... that Christ toke the breade, and gaue it to his dyscyples, saynge. Eate, Thys is my bodye, whych shall be broken for yow, meanynge in substaunce hys owne verye bodye, the breade beynge therof an onlye sygne or sacrament.'[40] Faint echoes of Frith can be heard frequently in Askew's narrative, but her yoking of the broken bread and the body of Christ is a direct inheritance. Frith's writing informs Askew's arguments beyond her assertions regarding sacramental ontology; his idiom is deployed by her as well.

Following Gardiner's pronouncement of death, William Paget visits her and asks how she can escape a literal interpretation of the words 'This is my body' (1 Cor. 11:24); she answers:

that Christes meanynge was there, as in these other places of the scripture. I am the dore, Ioan. 10. I am the vyne, Ioan. 15. Beholde the lambe of God, Ioan. 1. The rocke stone was Christ. 1 Cor. 10. and soch other lyke. Ye maye not here (sayd I) take Christ for the materyall thynge that he is sygnyfyed by.[41]

These assertions recall Frith's concerning the same words in Paul's epistle to the Corinthians:

And as touching the other wordes that Christe spake vnto his disciples at the last soup, I deney not but that he sayd so but that he so flesly ment as ye falsely faine, I vtterley deney. For I saye that his wordes ... were spiritually to be vnderstoden, and that he called yt his bodie. for acertaine propartie ... some textes are only to be vnderstood ... in the waye of an allegorye: As when Paule sayeth, Christ was the stone, and when Christe sayth hym sellfe, I am a very vyne I am the doore.[42]

Askew returns to the Privy Council the day after this interview and denies real presence in the sacrament in strenuous terms: 'And as for that ye call your God, is but a pece of breade. For a more profe therof (marke it whan ye lyst) lete it lye in the boxe but iii. monthes, and it wyll be moulde, and so turne to nothynge that is good.'[43] These terms are again Frith's: 'nature doth teache yow that both the brede and wyne contynewe in their nature, for the brede mouleth yf yt be kepte longe, ye and wurmes brede in yt'.[44] Frith's treatise lent an evident discursive structure both to Askew's argumentation and her written discourse; but Askew's disputation is, in fact, far more disruptive.

'The cause of my dethe is this', Frith writes in his *Articles*, 'because I cannot in consciens adiure and swere that our prelates opinion of the sacrament (that is, that the substaunce of brede and wine is verely chaunged in to the fleshe and bloude of our sauiour Iesus Christ) is an vndoubted article of the faythe, necessary to be beleauid vnder paine of dampnacyon.'[45] Askew again borrows his vocabulary to articulate the crux of her capital offence:

> But they both saye, and also teache it for a necessarye artycle of fayth, that after [the] wordes [of consecration] be ones spoken, there remayneth no breade. but euen the selfe same bodye that hynge vpon the crosse on good frydaye, both flesh, bloude, and bone. To thys beleue of theirs, saye I naye ... Loo, thys is the heresye that I holde, and for it must suffer the deathe.[46]

But Frith's rationale illustrates the fundamental difference between the two of them. He confirms his decision to die for an opinion that he admits is not an article of faith (either to hold or reject), 'because I will not bynd the congregacion of Christe (by myn example) to admitte any necessary article bysyde oure crede'.[47] Frith understands his activities (both written and performed) as a way of fixing doctrine for a community. Askew makes no such claims.

Frith disrupts the religious meanings established by Henrician authority, but his articulation of early Protestant tenets is detailed and exact. Because he aims to assert the doctrine of a group, he thinks globally and systematically. Askew's truth is set upon different ground. Despite her communal address (to the 'good people' of the first *Examination*, and the 'dere frynde in the lorde' of the second[48]) she makes no communal assertions. Her marginal position did not afford her a pulpit: the brake applied by Paul's strictures was sufficient to discourage her. But perhaps more importantly, the community that she addressed (as she would have been keenly aware) was fractured, marginalised, and at this particular political moment, under attack.[49] Askew's discourse is framed in isolation; it therefore marks the interior site of faith. Because Askew's belief is a privately erected system, it holds none of the semiotic stability that is exhibited in the work of Frith.

In a famous exchange of letters with Lord Protector Seymour (1547), Stephen Gardiner protested the 'lose disputacion' concerning matters of religion that he perceived to have taken hold in England:

> I haue seen of late 2. bokes [the *Examinations*] set forth in englysh by Bale very pernicious, sedicious & slaundrous ... to note, a woman to haue suffred vnder [my late soueraigne L. & maister] as a martyr, & the woman therwith to be ... boasted to be a sacramentary ... Certen printers, players, & prethers, make a wonderment, as though we knew not yet how to beiustified nor what sacraments

we shuld haue. And if the agrement in religion made in the time of our late soueraign lord be of no force in their iudgement, what establishment could any new agrement haue. And euery incertentie is noisom to any realme. And where euery man wilbe maister, there must needes be vncertainty.[50]

For Gardiner, the writings of dissidents such as William Tyndale, John Frith, and John Bale present a significant threat to order because they act as a powerful solvent upon what he assumes to be stable links between signs and their meanings.[51] The 1539 *Acte abolishing diversity in opynions* established sacramental meaning under the law, and forbade any English citizen 'by worde writinge ymprintinge cyphringe or in enye otherwise doe publishe preach teach saye affirme declare dispute argue or hold any opynion' contrary to His Majesty's government.[52] For Gardiner, the authorised signification is the only legitimate one: it is not the province of prelates or laymen to meddle in 'the setting out of the autoryty of the scripture' – these meanings must be institutionally assigned.[53] Further-more, prescribed sacramental belief during the reign of Henry VIII main-tained 'complete continuity between what materially signifies and what spiritually is signified by it'.[54]

But what is most interesting (in the context of the menace that Gardiner perceives) is the extent to which reformers like Frith reconceptualise or reconfigure continuity precisely at the point of disruption. While Frith holds that Christ is not to be taken 'for the materyall thynge that he is sygnyfyed by', he further develops, through an enlargement of patristic theology, a series of significations for the material components of the sacrament. His argument amounts to much more than a denial of Catholic doctrine concerning the Eucharist (adopted by the conservative Church of England); it sets out an alternative system of meaning by which the process of Communion (breaking, distributing, ingesting) can be understood. While there is no absolute equivalence between signifier and signified, there is, nonetheless, a good deal of stability in Frith's formulation. He not only firmly braces his structural framework, but also sets it upon an earlier foundation than Roman Catholic doctrine – the writings of the early Christian Fathers. He claims for his system of belief the primacy of both scripture and history.

There is none of this stability in Askew's text. In a letter to Captain Vaughan dated 3 May 1547, Gardiner laments the 'destruction of images' and of the political stability that he believes is inseparable from the outward ceremonial form. He uses the example of the King's seal, suggesting that the sign holds such power that 'an honest man' would revere the image as he would the King's real presence.[55] In his exchange with Askew, Secretary Paget similarly conflates spectacles of sovereignty and divinity:

Then he compared [Christ's presence in the sacrament] vnto the kynge, and sayd, that the more hys magestees honour is set forth, the more commendable it is. Then sayd I, that it was an abhomynable shame vnto hym, to make no better of the eternall worde of God, than of hys slenderlye conceyued fantasye. A farre other meanynge requyreth God therin, than mannys ydell wytte can deuyse, whose doctryne is but lyes without hys heavenlye veryte.[56]

What Askew articulates here is radical and fundamentally fractious to prescribed religious order. She is willing to accept faith's demand that we renounce the terms and relations by which we reckon value in the world. Her correction of Paget recognises that there is, in Luther's terms, a 'distinction between God preached and God hidden, that is, between the Word of God and God Himself'.[57] Askew maintains the inscrutability of divine will, which can only be glimpsed through scripture. Her insistence that authority over meaning does not lie with the Church has deeply subversive implications. The only guide to the obscure will of God is his scriptural word. Implicit in Askew's assertion that God's 'meanynge' is beyond the understanding of man (and cannot, therefore, be determined by institutional directives) is the conviction that the only legitimate interpreter of the word is individual conscience. '[W]here every man wilbe maister, there must needes be vncertainty': Gardiner rightly grasps the disruptive potential, in political terms, of such a view.[58]

JOHN BALE: THE VOICE

And one thing is maruelous, that at the same time it is taught that al men be liers, at the selfe same time almost euery man would be beleued. And emongest them, Bale when his vntruth apereth euidently in setting forth the examination of Anne Askewe which is vtterly misreported. (Stephen Gardiner)

The question of the foundations upon which Askew could have established her belief system is a complicated one. She was clearly informed by the theological teachings of reformers other than Frith: when a priest examining her (at Bonner's request) offers her confession, she answers that she will speak to 'one of these iii. that is to saye, doctor Crome, syr Gyllam, or Huntyngton ... bycause I knewe them to be men of wysdome'.[59] At another time, when she is profoundly ill, she asks to speak with Hugh Latimer. As she professes an acquaintance with the learning and insight of these men, she has presumably heard them speak. But in spite of her evident familiarity with the sermons of leading reformist clerics, the patterns of their preaching do not appear in her prose. Her vernacular resembles Frith's writing alone.

The voice that emerges from Askew's text is unadorned. Her argumentation is stripped of the syllogism that shapes the discourses of university men. When Bonner's unnamed priest asks her 'if the host shuld fall, and a beast ded eate it, [did] the beast … receyve God or no?' she refuses to follow the protocol of disputation:

I answered, Seynge ye haue taken the paynes to aske thys questyon, I desyre yow also to take so moche payne more, as to assoyle it your selfe … And he sayd, it was agaynst the ordre of scoles, that he whych asked the questyon, shuld answere it. I tolde hym, I was but a woman, & knewe not the course of scoles.[60]

Askew will not debate in the codified terms of university scholars. In his extended commentary to her *Examinations*, John Bale cannot resist an argument:

Where God is eaten, it is of the sprete, and neyther of mouse nor ratte, as Wynchestre and Peryn, with other lyke popysh heretykes haue taught now of late … *Oure* God is in heauen, and cannot fall nor yet be eaten of beastes. If they haue soche a God, as maye fall, and so be eaten, as thys preste here confesseth, it is some false or counterfett God of their owne makynge.[61]

Bale's own prose is more irascible than syllogistic. He reasons by antithesis. Protestant truth is asserted negatively – by what it is not – and emerges as a systematic opposition to conservative doctrine (and conservative clerics).[62] This process of refutation, however, stabilises his writing. Meanings defined in opposition are still anchored within the system that serves as the comparative figure. Rather than setting out (as Frith does) an alternate system of meaning, the closure of Bale's text is achieved by contradiction.

Bale also clearly understands his assertions as a collective truth. He claims a common God – and a common belief – for a community of faithful. But the belief that he outlines is not the same (in spite of its apparent similarities) as that of Anne Askew. The God of Askew's faith is indefinable, even in oppositional terms. Meaning must be verified by a God whose meaning is beyond human intelligence. Truth is attainable only through a personal engagement with scripture. Amidst ideological clash, she will not frame her truth to fit the needs of either side. When she does answer, it is in the form of a statement: 'Then wolde they nedes knowe, if I wolde denye the sacrament to be Christes bodye and bloude: I sayd, yea.'[63] She speaks for herself alone.

The singular character of Askew's prose is exposed in sharp relief when it is contrasted with that of her partner at the stake, John Lascelles. In a letter written during his detention, Lascelles also tries to articulate his reasons for choosing to die rather than to subscribe to the sacramental belief that the Six Articles made law:

Wherfore, as at Gods hand the breakyng of the most innocent & immaculate bodye and bloude of Christ, is the quietnes of all mens consciences, the onely remedye of our sinnes, and the redemption of mankynde . . . so the Masse whiche is the inuention of man (whose author is the Pope of *Rome*, as it doth appeare in *Polidore Virgill* and many others) is the vnquietnes of all Christendome . . . I think that if men will looke upon S. Paules wordes well, they shalbe forced to say, as S. Paul sayth: the Lord Iesus sayd it, and once for all, which onely was the fulfiller of it. For these woordes: *Hoc est corpus meum*, were spoken of his naturall presence (whiche no man is able to deny) because the acte was finished on the crosse, as the story doth playnly manifest it to them that haue eyes.[64]

Lascelles writes to persuade. He first contrasts the divine action with worldly mimicry; he then cites the historical reference that warrants his claim that the sacramental ceremonies of Rome are Rome's invention. He suggests that if men were to examine (rather than peruse) the words of Paul, they would arrive at the same conclusions that he himself has drawn. He then goes on to explain the meaning of the Latin phrase that is the crux of the matter in an erudite, tightly argued thesis.

And *S. Paule* following the same doctrine [of Christ], doth playnly shew the dutie of the Minister, and also of them that shall receiue it: *As oft as you shall eat thys bread, and drinke this cup, ye shall shewe the Lordes death vntyll he come.* Here I do gather, that the Minister hath no farther power and authoritie, then to preach & pronounce the Lordes death, or els to say the Lord Iesus sayd it, which did fulfill it on the crosse.[65]

'[Y]e shall shewe the Lordes death' supports the reformist conviction that priests do not have the power to channel miracles, and that their sole function in the ceremony of the Mass is to preach the story of Christ's sacrifice and to proclaim the coming of the Lord. Lascelles does not simply state what he finds in the Bible, but analyses the text in order to prove his beliefs by scripture. Over the course of ten paragraphs, he marshals considerable reading to exhibit the foundation of his belief.

By contrast, Askew's only tactic is to demonstrate: 'Then I shewed hym the vii. and the xvii. chaptre of the Apostles actes, what Steuen and Paule had sayd therin.'[66] For her, the Bible holds final authority; she need only cite the text. Askew's discernible convictions do not differ greatly from those that Lascelles outlines; it is the form of her articulation that is different. Her beliefs are framed as declarative statements.

[T]he breade is but a remembraunce of [Christ's] death, or a sacrament of thankes geuynge for it, wherby we are knytt vnto hym by a communyon of Christen loue. Although there be manye that can not perceyue the true meanynge therof, for the vayle that Moses put ouer hys face before the chyldren of Israel, that they shuld not se the clerenesse therof. Exo. 34. and 2. Cor. 3. I perceyue the same vayle remayneth to thys daye.[67]

Precisely for this reason, Bale feels compelled to tell us what she means:

Not without the holye place (sayth Christ) is that abomynacyon, but in it, Math. 24. Antichrist (sayth S. Paule) shall sytt, not without, but within the verye temple of God. 2. Thessalon. 2. The papacye is not without, but within the verye churche of Christ, what though it be no part therof, Apoca. 11. Therfor it shall be mete that we be ware, and separate our selues from them at the admonyshmentes of hys holye doctryne, least we be partakers with yow in their promysed dampnacyon, Apoca. 18. By the vayle ouer Moses face, she meaneth the blynde confydence that manye men yet haue in olde Iewysh ceremonyes and beggerlye tradycyons of men, as S. Paule doth call them, Gala. 4. Wherby the veryte of God is sore blemyshed.[68]

Bale quotes Christ, then St Paul, then St John the Divine. Each voice is marshalled to prove the truth of his claim. (Like most reformed commentators, Bale feels that his position is tenuous unless tethered to the teachings of the Gospels or patristic theology.) Once he has anchored his meaning to his satisfaction, he then goes on to describe hers. Where Askew merely points to a scriptural passage, Bale must explain it. Bale's gloss does nothing to clarify 2 Cor. 3:13-14, but only supplies us with an alternate interpretation of the text – his.

Protestant doctrine's insistence upon the primacy of scripture as the word of God drove the commitment to vernacular scriptures; however, central to the Protestant project of biblical translation was the inclusion of critical apparatuses which controlled the interpretation of that word. In their rejection of the religious authority of the Catholic Church, early reformers maintained the plain truth contained in the biblical text; accumulated traditions (and accepted scriptural interpretations) must be rejected unless 'playnlye expressyd in the sacred scriptur of God'.[69] But as the reformers themselves were forced to admit, scripture is subject to figurality. Reformers like Frith argue that Christ's directives at the last supper cannot be taken literally, that certain scriptural 'textes are only to be vnderstood ... in the waye of an allegorye'. But this is to concede the necessity of mediating scriptural meaning – allegory requires interpretation. Trying to maintain both positions produced a kind of spasm in reformist arguments that can be clearly perceived in Bale:

> The disciples of antichrist with their bifurked ordinaries must violently pluck from the true Christian church . . . the eternal word of the Lord. Then must they take from [the common people] the consuming fire that Christ sent down into the earth of men's hearts, to dry up all malice and sin . . . the treasure that Christ hath left here to succour us they must hide under the ground, and the candle that he lit us to see over the house convey underneath the bushel . . . Already have they taken in England from the bibles the annotations, tables, and prefaces, to perform this their damnable enterprise.[70]

The 'disciples of antichrist' take away 'the eternal word of the Lord' when they exclude from the biblical text the mechanisms which explain its meaning; the text is baffled without its directing (Protestant) commentary. Lodged within this complaint is the tacit admission that, as David Kastan points out, the 'word of God is . . . available not plainly and immediately but, exactly as for their Catholic opponents, only in the mediations of their interpretive practices'.[71] The 'playn[ness]' of scriptural meaning can only be achieved by critical device. Indeed, its density seems to demand exposition. But it is the very density and complexity of its figures that permits scripture to notarise – through qualified readings – more than one ideological position. Reformist elucidations, then, attach specific meanings to a fundamentally opaque text.

The 'elucydacyon[s]' attached to Askew's text serve a similar function. Like the marginalia of the Protestant translations of the Bible, Bale's invasive annotations direct our reading of her. Bale revises and restates Askew's narrative to suit the purposes of Protestant polemic. 'Therfor it is mete', Askew writes, 'that in prayers we call vnto God, to grafte in our foreheades, the true meanynge of the holye Ghost concernynge thys communyon.'[72] Bale's interpretive commentary explicates the passage in the following way:

> By the fore heades vnderstande she the hartes or myndes of men, for so are they taken of S. Iohan, Apoc. 7. and 22. I can not thynke, but herin she had respect vnto the plate of fyne golde whych the lorde commaunded to be sett vpon Aarons foreheade, for the acceptacyon of the people of Israel, Exodi. 2. For here wolde she all mennys hartes to be endued and lyghtened with the most pure sprete of Christ, for the vnderstandynge of that most holye and necessarye communyon, the corrupted dreames and fantasyes of synnefull men sett a part. She knewe by the syngular gyft of the holye Ghost, that they are lyenge masters, procurers of ydolatrye, and most spygh[t]full enemyes to the sowle of man, that applyeth that offyce to the corruptyble lyppes, whych belongeth to an vncorrupted faythe, so settynge the creature that is corruptyble breade, in place of the creator Christ.[73]

The engraved plate set upon Aaron's forehead (Exod. 28:38) refers to the scene in the Bible when Aaron's priestly function is defined. The plate marks Aaron as the mediator between the Israelites and their Lord. But a mediated relationship with God does not seem to be what Askew is invoking at this moment; for her, scriptural meanings are assigned through personal faith. Askew solicits God for interpretive instruction.

While Bale's nominal belief approves Askew's denial of all non-scriptural authority, the conviction that he outlines is, in fact, fundamentally different. Rather than ignore the invention of 'mannys ydell wytte' and rely upon private apprehension, Bale recommends that only the wits of particular 'synnefull' men be set aside – in other words, only those who resist the reformist programme. But it is the way that Bale designs his commentary that matters here – he models it as Askew's belief. Bale appropriates her meaning and distorts it. He casts her as an opponent to conservative doctrine; in truth, she opposes the seizure of scripture for institutional purposes. She clearly holds reformist convictions, but her system of belief relies upon the immediate promptings of conscience (or soul). The unindoctrinated quality of Askew's discourse, which asks only that God direct her meaning, is eradicated for the needs of the religious polemic.

Anne Askew's record of her defiance of Henrician civil and ecclesiastical authority marks the inner space of individual resistance. Alert to her position in the religious controversy that was taking place, her account of her trials for heresy assumes the privatised shape of the outsider. Her execution under the Act of the Six Articles, however, guaranteed that she would not have the last word. Bale's commentary serves to stabilise her meaning in doctrinal terms. He interprets her written words and scriptural citations to fit the needs of Protestant opposition; he writes her voice into the persuasive idiom of the university men who dominated the debate.[74] Askew's narrative does not disappear entirely (in spite of the weight of Bale's voluminous explication), but her meanings are reassigned. This appropriation of her words is identified in Gardiner's complaint: he censures *Bale's* 'vntruth . . . in setting forth the examination of Anne Askewe'.[75]

JOHN FOXE: THE BODY

We shuld vnderstand the sacrament not carnally, but spiritually.

(Thomas Cranmer)

In Cranmer's formulation, Catholic doctrine affirmed a direct physical communion with God.[76] Protestantism recast the embodied presence of

Catholic belief into abstract terms. As Mueller observes, the activity of establishing an opposing ontology of presence to the Catholic formulation produced in the Protestant debate a pattern of complex figurative relations between the human and divine body.[77] Reforming churchmen who understood their disputation (both oral and written) as the mode of doctrinal formation, reconfigured the meanings of the Eucharist so that the process itself could be apprehended differently. The alternative system of meaning that they plotted is conceived through a rhetoric of the material body. In his disputations at Oxford, Thomas Cranmer articulates the Protestant formulation of sacramental presence from a chain of metaphors which he glosses for the faithful:

Christ saith not thus: *Thys is my body, eate ye*: but after he had bydden them eate, then he sayd: *This is my body which shall be geuen for you*. Whych is to meane, as though he should say: In eatyng of thys bread, consider you that this bread is no common thing, but a mysticall matter: neither do you attend that which is set before your bodely eyes, but what fedeth you with in. Consider and behold my body crucified for you: that eate and digest in your myndes. Chawe you upon my passion, be fed with my death. This is the true meate, thys is the drinke that moisteneth, wherewith you being truly fed and inebriate, shall liue for ever.[78]

Protestant figurations of the Mass replaced the Catholic story of communion with the divine – in which Christ's body miraculously inhabits the host and is subsequently ingested by the faithful – with a different method of absorption. The bread is digested, but the sacrament is not taken in except by an act of mental figuration; an understanding through faith of the signification of the sacrament allows the faithful member to receive its benefits. Nicholas Ridley outlines the way in which the sacrament is to be understood:

The Analogie of the sacramentes is necessary: For if the sacramentes had not some similitude or lykenes of the things whereof they be sacraments, they could in no wyse be sacraments. And this similitude in the Sacrament of the Lordes Supper, is taken three manner of wayes.
1 The first consisteth in nourishing: as ye shall reade in *Rabane*, *Cyprian*, *Augustine*, *Irenee*, & most plainly in *Isodore* out of *Bertram*.
2 The second, in the vniting and ioyning of many into one, as *Cyprian* teacheth.
3 The thyrd is a similitude of vnlike things: where, lyke as the bread is turned into our body: so we, by the right vse of this Sacrament, are turned through fayth into the body of Christ.[79]

Ridley's account of conversion focuses upon natural processes rather than supernatural intervention. Bread is no longer miraculously transformed but signifies a miracle once performed. The Protestant project of finding alternative material meanings for the Eucharist created a focus on the natural body. The absence of miracles necessarily carried the material facts of the process down to the level of physical experience (chewing bread, drinking wine, nourishing the body).[80]

It is at this level of experience that we witness the embodied constructions of martyred identity to which Mueller pays extended attention. A rhetoric preoccupied with sacramental ontology and the organic workings of the body was converted into a descriptive discourse of painful witness when human bodies burned. Perceiving themselves as examples to be followed, reformers also seem to have conceived of themselves as spectacles. 'Your cause is Christs gospell', William Tyndale tells Frith in a letter designed to encourage him, 'a light that must be fed with the bloud of faith. The lampe must be dressed and snuffed dayly, and that oyle poured in ... that ye light go not out.'[81] Tyndale plays upon metaphors of burning to emphasise the proselytising effect of his fellow reformer's death: Frith will be the light by which others see the meaning of the Gospel. Hugh Latimer invokes a similar metaphor in his famous exhortation to Ridley at the stake: 'we shall this day lyght such a candle by Gods grace in England, as (I trust) shall neuer be put out'.[82] These articulations stress the importance that early reformers attached to such spectacles in the project of spreading Protestant doctrine – but by the treatment of their bodies as wicks or raw materials for the consumption of the flames, they also express the hideous changes that the body will undergo during its trial by fire.

Anne Askew's account of her trials (as I have already indicated) is strikingly different. The acts of rhetorical self-enclosure that mark Askew's text carry over into her treatment of her body. Just after Gardiner's announcement of his lethal intentions, Askew writes that 'on the sonday I was sore sicke, thinking no lesse then to die ... Then was I sent to Newgate in my extremitie of sickenes: for in all my life afore was I neuer in such paine. Thus the Lord strengthen vs in the truth.'[83] What is remarkable about this recollection is her profound understatement. She does not concentrate on the natural fact of her bodily suffering, even at a time when illness threatens to carry her off. Pain registers for only a moment in the text; her focus quickly shifts to 'the truth' that allows her to endure it. The construction of selfhood that she articulates here has a dual aspect: a material element which can be tried, and a spiritual self-possession which sustains her in the midst of physical extremity. The body's torment becomes the means by which faith is fortified. This construction of her body is more pronounced at a later point in the narrative, when the body's physical limits are tested on the rack.

After Askew was condemned to death, Lord Chancellor Wriothesley and Richard Rich, hoping to gain information that would discredit Queen Katherine Parr, tortured her.[84]

Then they did put me on the racke, because I confessed no Ladyes or Gentlewomen to be of my opinion, and theron they kept me a longe tyme. And because I lay stil and did not cry, my L. Chauncellour and [master Rich], tooke paines to racke me with their owne handes, till I was nigh dead.[85]

The remarkable restraint of this passage is often noticed. I wish to call attention to its disembodied quality. We come at Askew's bodily experience obliquely: she does not observe her pain, only her response to it. Until she reveals that she was racked 'till [she] was nigh dead' we have no sense of the extent of her physical suffering. She relates her inability to stand up, and the experience of lying on the floor for hours as Wriothesley works to rob her of her belief:

Then the Lieftenaunt caused me to be loosed from the racke. Incontinently I swounded ... After that I satte ii. long houres reasonyng with my Lord Chancellor vppon the bare flore, wheras he with many flattering wordes, perswaded me to leaue my opinion. But my lord God (I thanke his euerlasting goodnes) gave me grace to perseuer.[86]

Her torture is imparted as a series of sensory events; she admits an awareness of her body's distress, but not the experience of it. Here (as in the episode of her illness), her consciousness divides into two parts: a corporal reality, and a realm of experience that she fixes as interior and private. Wriothesley applies physical torment in an attempt to probe and extract the inner recesses of her belief – to (in Elaine Scarry's resonant phrase) 'unmake [her] world'.[87] In denying her body she denies her tormentors access to the interior spaces that they are trying to dismantle; if she disowns the effect of her body-breaking – she lies still and does not cry – she retains the inner truth that torture is designed to discover. At moments of acute bodily suffering, Askew is 'strengthen[ed] ... in the truth', or endowed with 'grace': rather than her inner world crumbling during physical distress, she perceives in pain the opportunity for the 'making of [her] soul'.[88]

Following her racking, Askew writes that:

Then was I brought to an house, and laid in a bed with as werye and painful bones, as euer had pacient *Iob* I thanke my Lord God therof. Then my Lord

Chauncellour sent me worde if I would leaue my opinion, I should want nothing:
If I would not, I should forth to Newgate, & so be burned. I sent hym agayne
word, that I would rather die, then to breake my faith.[89]

She thanks God for her pain. Askew's conception of faith contains a
persecutory imagination similar to that of the male martyrs that I have
noted. She seems convinced that physical torment marks the members of
God's true church: that (as Tyndale writes) the faithful 'suffer with
[Christ] that [they] may also be glorified wyth hym'.[90] But she does not
conceive of herself in the spectacular terms of these prominent clerics. For
her, it is not a matter of serving as an example by which others will come to
comprehend the true meaning of the Gospel. It is an exclusively private
matter: 'I would rather die, then to breake my faith.' Askew's model of
witness depends upon maintaining the integrity of her soul against the
disintegration of her body.

   '[T]he houre commeth,' she writes, 'and is nowe, when true worshippers shall worshyp the father in spirite and veritie.'[91] This is incorporeal
communion whereby one's attention is concentrated entirely upon the
'sprite' which consumes the sacrament. Frith describes sacramental assimi-
lation in the following way:

And euen as ... the outward eyn doe see the breade, and yet the inward eyn doe
not regard that, or thyncke apon yt. So lykewise the outwarde man dygestyth the
breade, & castythe yt in to the draught. And yet the inwarde man dothe not
regarde that nor thynckе apon yt. But thynkyth on the thyng yt sellfe that ys
sygnyfyed by that breade.[92]

Or, as Askew herself writes: 'in spirite and fayth I [receive] no lesse, then
the body and bloud of Christ'.[93] Because it is the soul and not the body
that receives the benefits of the Passion, it is the soul and not the body that
draws her focus. Her denial of her body is conceptually linked to her
denial of presence. The body is no longer (with the repudiation of Catholic doctrine) the site where communion with God is achieved, for 'God
dwelleth in no thing materiall.'[94] Sacramental belief causes her to ignore
(or reject) her material body: 'The spirite is it onely that geveth lyfe.'[95] The
pattern of denial of the material facts of existence that emerges in her
narrative becomes more conspicuous when the integrity of her physical
being is jeopardised by torture and execution: her anxiety does not seem
related to the breakdown of her body, but to the possession of her soul.
Askew will not 'Labour ... for the meate that perisheth, but for that
that endureth into the lyfe euerlasting.'[96] The pliable (and assaulted)

boundaries of the body become the proving ground on which the inviolability of faith is established.

Mueller's study records Protestant reconfigurations of union with the divine that serve as a counterpart to Catholic conceptions of real presence. But Askew does not follow the figurations of male martyrs in which the unstable borders of their bodies give way to transformation; she envisions no alchemical process by which she will be organically converted into the body of Christ. Foxe, however, needs spectacular bodies. His history of the Protestant struggle against the Catholic Church required a kind of visual record: one that figured bodily sacrifice through verbal images. Askew does not understand herself as a public issue ('a singular example of Christen constancie for all men to folowe'[97]); her discourse is organised at the level of personal faith. It is her acts of self-enclosure that make Askew an 'eccentric subject' within Foxe's narrative in the *Acts and Monuments*;[98] such an inward self-construction does not fit the design of his project. Foxe needs to make the enigma of belief legible; his only means of doing this is to tell the story of the body that suffers for faith. Foxe, therefore, brings Askew's body back into the narrative. It is precisely Askew's gestures to an interiority that Foxe cancels in order to make her subjectivity a present textual fact.

In the 1570 edition of the *Acts and Monuments*, Foxe intrudes upon her account at the moment of her racking in order to emphasise the suffering that she will not concede. He describes, in an extended passage, how the rack was stretched 'til her bones and ioyntes almost were pluckt a sunder', and her body so mangled by the instrument that she had to be taken from the Tower in a chair.[99] Foxe feminises her at this moment as well; according to his scenario, the lieutenant in charge, Anthony Knyvett, 'tendering the weakenes of the woman', refuses to torture her further. After he defies their orders, Wriothesley and Rich grab the wheel themselves. This added moment serves to stress the horror of the scene, and the irregularity of torture performed upon a woman.[100] But Askew makes no mention of this; rather, she says that the two men tormented her because she *did not cry*. It was (according to her) her silent endurance, not her jailer's compassion, which so provoked her persecutors.

Foxe evokes her broken body as it is carried to the stake: 'the day of her execution beyng appoynted, she was brought into Smithfield in a chaire, because she could not go on her feete, by meanes of her great torments'.[101] He tells us that she 'was tied by the middle with a chayne' at the pyre in order to support her body.[102] Foxe's descriptions work to bring Askew's corporeality to the centre. Without a displayed carcass, Foxe has no means to demonstrate the enclosed sphere of faith; the subjects of his stories must be visible bodies. Askew purposefully denies her body and privileges a private realm of experience in her discourse. As his commentary frames her account, this results in a strange distortion of her appearance in the narrative. The effect of their conflicting rhetorical manoeuvres is that Askew's body is moved to the borders of her story; the tensions between the inward direction of her discourse and Foxe's aim to make inner truth plain and readable result in her body's actual marginalisation in the text.

Because Askew does not plot the points of Protestant sacramental meaning, her rhetoric does not assume the embodied terms visible in the writings of dissident scholars. She does not conceive of herself as either example or spectacle for the Protestant cause; her physical body, therefore, does not bear witness. John Foxe's purpose is to make her available to a popular audience. In the discourse of the body that marked the martyrology genre, Foxe must write Askew as a visible subject. These competing intentions produce a dislocation of her body within the text: she both appears, and crucially does not appear, in Foxe's edition of her narrative. As in the woodcut scene of her execution, Askew's bodily presence within the *Acts and Monuments* is incongruous – fractured, decentred, both exhibited and hidden.

SOWING THE 'SEED OF REFORMATION'

My objections to Jennifer Summit's argument concerning Askew, offered in the Introduction, are not grounded in any disagreement with her claim that the figure of the woman writer was 'instrumental to the production of England's . . . religious identity during the Reformation'.[103] But Summit's central contention is that the figure became the subject of wider debates concerning religious and cultural legitimacy; as such, the woman writer became a pivotal figure in Bale's reconstruction (and redefinition) of both England's past and its future. The problem with this reading is that it conflates too easily with Bale's larger practice of cultural reconstitution.[104] In his dedicatory epistle to Queen Elizabeth in the 1559 variant of the *Catalogus*, Bale outlines his project in the following way:

[I]t contains famous and illustrious noblemen and authors of the realm, by which at length emerges more justly a catalogue of the English than of England. For they are yours, most noble Queen, born and sprung in your realm, whom I have cited . . . and it is here that preachers, here that ministers will find their weapons, so that those who are assailed may defend themselves and slay their adversaries. Here are works of hidden and secret riches – here are seeds of divine and human doctrine, from whence shall come those more instructed for speaking and being wise.[105]

As J. Christopher Warner observes, 'Bale describes his recovery of books and recording their titles and authors as though he were saving *people* – that is, members of the "true" church.'[106] His excavation of 'works of hidden and secret riches' is tethered to a reclamation of a national past. He claims that his *Catalogus* is a roster of recovered writers who affirm that the Protestant identity that the English state was beginning to assume under Elizabeth (or, so Bale hoped) had long been embedded in the character of its people. (That Bale grossly misrepresents the bulk of his catalogue is beside the point – it is how he represents his project that matters here.) His practice of editing martyr-writings in the 1540s is cast in similar terms. He suggests a correspondence between his own activities in publishing the texts of English Protestant martyrs and the writings of the early Christian historians, in that both preserve the record of the true church.[107] But in spite of the fact that all of the martyr narratives that Bale edits serve his purpose of rewriting the English past as a struggle between the agents and opponents of church reform, the way that he handles Askew's narrative suggests that her importance to reform was unique.

Summit characterises Askew as a figure of loss, arguing that Bale's recuperation of her writing signals a reconstruction of English literary history. This reading renders his treatment of Askew indistinct from his treatment of every male writer whom he edits. Notions of the female play into the public reception of Askew's narrative, but to characterise her as a figure of loss – a figure of disappearance – fixes her importance to the tradition in terms, again, of her status as a marginalised figure. That Askew is marginal to the contemporary theological debates has been crucial to my discussion so far. But her place within the developing discourse of an emergent Protestant culture was central, not marginal. In fact, her figure – as both author and subject – was fundamental to ideas of Protestant self-consciousness and authority in this period of enormous religious change.[108]

John King has termed Askew's execution a *cause célèbre* in early Edwardian reform.[109] But even though the celebrity of Askew is widely recognised in critical discourse, the extent and scope of her influence has not been fully appreciated. Alec Ryrie, in a fine article that traces the slow beginnings of Protestant martyr-writing in England, places Askew's narrative 'four-square within [that] emerging ... tradition'.[110] In discussing the 'indispensable ingredient' of the martyred subject, however, Ryrie further declares that: 'If a Latimer or a Hooper could be found to fill the role, so much the better.'[111] Ryrie's point is partly that a Latimer or Hooper would clearly articulate the reformist position; but he is also suggesting that these male figures would necessarily carry more weight. While it is entirely logical to assume that the death of a prominent churchman would hold greater currency in the process of reform, the response of the market-place in Edwardian England suggests another possibility.[112]

There were more editions of Askew's narrative produced in the six-teenth century than that of any other English martyr.[113] This bald state-ment is, of course, reductive; but teasing apart the bibliographic evidence reveals not only a complicated history for the *Examinations*, but also the religio-political significance of this text at a key moment in the English Reformation. The most important continuity between the regimes of Edward VI was a consistent, if lurching, movement toward church reform. As Diarmaid MacCulloch puts it, 'The leaders of the Edwardian regimes set out to destroy one Church and build another.'[114] Exactly how the early reformers used the book-reading public for the dissemination of Protest-antism is an enormous topic, and beyond my scope here. However, the publication of martyr-writings in the early years of Edward's reign indi-cates that the emergence of the martyrological tradition in England was linked with an attempt to influence popular and political opinion under the new king.

All three of Bale's edited martyr-writings were published in the years 1547–8. What is immediately conspicuous is that his *Chronycle concernynge the examinacyon and death of . . . syr Johan Oldecastell*, which was initially printed in 1544, was reprinted in 1548.[115] In addition to Bale's martyr texts, *A boke made by John Frith*, which was previously published in 1533, was reproduced in Antwerp in June of 1546, and saw two more printings in England in 1548.[116] *The supplication made of doctour Barnes*, a well-known Henrician martyr, was reprinted in 1548 (the previous edition dates from 1534), and an imaginary *Metynge of doctor Barns and doctor Powell at paradise gate* was circulated in verse.[117] Crowley's *Confutation of xiii. articles wherunto N. Shaxton . . . subscribed*, with its assembly of English martyrs, was published in 1548, and the narrative of John Lascelles was added to the 1548 printing of *Wicklieffes wicket*.[118] We cannot assume from this information that martyr-writings were part of an organised campaign on the part of reformers to influence the new regime. But we can conclude from this profusion of texts that the reformers were aware of how persuasive this particular genre was in terms of public sympathy – and, further, how it could be used to criticise the increasingly embattled conservative guard.

'[T]he godlye sufferaunce of martyrs', Bale writes (quoting St Bernard), 'hath geuen as good erudycyon to the christen churche, as euer ded the doctryne of the sayntes'.[119] Clearly, the narratives concerning Oldcastle, Frith, and Barnes are reproduced in 1548 because of their status as Protestant martyrs (Oldcastle is appropriated as a proto-martyr in the Protestant cause). It is surprising, then, that twice as many editions of the *Examinations* were printed during Edward's reign than those of other martyr texts. While there is no straight equation between the popularity of a text and its influence, it is clear that Askew's narrative was purchased in greater numbers during the period of Edwardian reform than the martyr-writings of authoritative Protestants such as Frith and Barnes. What this suggests is that the economy in which Askew's text circulated, and through which it accrued its value, did not necessarily respond in the ways that we might expect to magisterial prestige. It further suggests that in the context of the reformist strategy to allow the sufferings of the faithful to serve as an argument, the English reading public found the figure of Askew particularly eloquent.

To return, then, to Ryrie's claim that male churchmen would have been more effective in transmitting the principles of reformist doctrine, he is, of course, correct. While Askew's testimony provides a vibrant – and clearly vital – exhibition of early Protestant faith, it pointedly fails to supply an exposition of Protestant doctrine. Bale's strenuous efforts to anchor Askew's text firmly within the tenets of early Protestantism betray his anxiety on precisely this issue. But the conveyance of Protestant ideology is a far more complicated and unwieldy matter than the communication of doctrine. In fact, the removal of Bale's commentary in the second continuous printing of the *Examinations* indicates that it was in no way necessary (and probably even counter-productive) to the commercial success of the book. King suggests that Bale's annotations were omitted to spare Secretary Paget, who is attacked in the commentary, political embarrassment.[120] But the most damning passages were removed from the first English printing, and the text could have continued to be published in this revised form.[121] Instead, the whole of Bale's comments are excised from subsequent editions.[122] The public response to Askew's work, then, clearly did not depend an unambiguously articulated doctrinal position, but upon the appeal of the martyred subject herself.

Askew's situation as an exceptional figure is based upon the fact that she is the only female author in the entire collection of martyr-writings produced in England in the 1530s and 1540s. But the circumstances surrounding the reception of her work (and its posthumous editorial reconstructions) indicate the broad political dimensions of the figure of the religious woman writer during the contentious period of early reform. There are specific components that make the female figure particularly serviceable to the objectives of the martyr-writing genre. The structure of the martyr narrative was ideally centred on the conflict between authority and the individual. The obstinate endurance of the martyr in the face of overwhelming pressure, and even violent death, was proof of the strength of his faith. These essential features of the martyr story were magnified when the martyr was female.[123] Cultural notions of the spiritual and physical weakness of women worked to heighten the isolation and the suffering of the martyr – not to mention the exhibited strength of faith. But any female martyr, regardless of the nature of her faith, would serve this purpose. Askew's figure bears significance specific to the Protestant cause.

That Askew resorts to scripture, not scholastic argument, in her confrontation with religious authorities exemplifies the Protestant ideal of individual apprehension. Her apparently private expression crucially fulfils both the needs of the martyr story, and the tenets of early reform. That she offers no formulation of religious doctrine reinforces the notion that she is a lone woman speaking in defence of her individual conscience.[124] In the drama that inevitably unfolds between the martyr and the inquest, the solitude of the martyr is essential: 'Unlike a simple execution, a martyrdom was an apocalyptic event, an echo of Calvary.'[125] The genre therefore needed, at its core, a victim who had no earthly assistance (to figure credibly as an imitation of Christ). In terms of how faith is registered in a martyr text, the extent of the victim's isolation speaks to the strength that faith provides at a moment of extreme duress. As a woman, Askew was obviously particularly useful in satisfying these generic conventions. That she frames her belief within the confines of a privately constructed system merely compounds the sense of her detachment from a worldly community. The expression that she offers in her written *Examinations* exhibits the Protestant tenet of reliance upon scripture alone – and must have been particularly resonant for a readership that was newly encountering the implications of this principle in spiritual life.

While Bale's editorial interventions demonstrate that he recognised Askew as a powerful symbol in terms of Protestant martyrology, he failed to completely grasp what an emergent Protestant community found principally compelling about her work. The publication history of the *Examinations* – with the disappearance of Bale's commentary – appears to confirm this. At a transitional moment when the institutional authority of the Church is under interrogation, a figure that has an ambiguous relationship to any doctrinal authority, however embryonic, holds greater appeal. It is, then, precisely the disruptive potential of Askew's text – that Gardiner abhors and Bale, to some extent, undermines – that is the source of its popularity. Despite the extreme politicisation (and polarisation) of the forms of religion at this time, the relationship between Protestantism and the English public was still vague at best; which is to say, that the principles of nascent Protestantism were only imperfectly conveyed and understood.[126] But if the energies and efforts of the reformers did nothing else, it was to arouse suspicion toward religious authority (particularly in the wake of the erratic course of the Henrician Reformation). This scepticism must also extend – equivalently, if not equally – to their own efforts to stabilise doctrine on their own terms. Askew's *Examinations* provide little insight into contemporary theological debates, but her arguments draw upon the one authority that remains uncontested – the Bible.

The figure of the woman writer both resides in Askew's text and stands apart from it: the martyr is both the author and the central character. It is clear, however, that the figure, separable from the text in which it first appeared, was potent and durable. In his sample of 'bestsellers and steady sellers' in the market of printed religious works, Ian Green lists a ballad based on the story of Anne Askew ('I am a woman poore and blind') that went into six editions between the years of 1624 and 1695.[127] However, as Tessa Watt explains, the 1624 entry in the Stationer's register represents a collection of 127 ballads consisting largely of old material which had been 'heretofore disorderly printed without entrance or allowance'.[128] It is therefore impossible to determine how much the ballad was in circulation prior to that time.[129] Nevertheless, the printing of the ballad as late as 1695 does tell us that interest in Askew as a Protestant hero persisted through the seventeenth century. The ballad reduces her to a caricature of female vulnerability and weakness pitted against a villainous Gardiner.[130] The representation emphasises (or rather, overstates) Askew's unschooled apprehension of a devious Bishop. (The pun on Gardiner's name allows for an extended conceit of how the seeds of true faith, latent within her, grow spontaneously.) Stock though this picture of Askew is, it retains elements of a contest between misleading syllogism and the truth of scripture. The representation of Askew in the broadside press probably tells us more about the needs of later generations of English readers than the earlier appeals of her text.[131] Still, it is at least suggestive that one of the enduring features of her martyr story is the victory of a generic or 'pure Protestant faith' over the machinations of university-educated clergy.[132]

Bathsua Makin, in her 1673 appeal for female education, asserts that 'the Seed of Reformation seemed to be sowed by [Askew's] hand'.[133] In the context of Makin's polemic, this assertion is, of course, suspect. Even so, it is important to remember that her polemical objectives could not have been served by a claim that was patently false, or that would have been received as improbable. Makin is partly talking about Askew's role in educating 'the Queen [Katherine Parr], and Ladies at Court', but she cites Askew's martyrdom as particularly instructive.[134] Feminist criticism on the subject of Askew has assessed how her private beliefs drew her into public conflict. But it is precisely the privatised nature of Askew's expression that made her such a public figure. Without the authority that university training would have allowed, Askew formulates her arguments in terms that, ironically, were more compelling to an English readership than learned exegeses of doctrine. The power of the figure of the female martyr is affirmed by the editorial practices of Protestant reformers upon Askew's text (and upon the figure itself). But while her bodily sacrifice signalled the urgency of religious reform, Askew's explanation of that action found a persuasive diction that magisterial Protestants could not muster themselves.

CHAPTER 2

Representing the faith of a nation: transitional
spirituality in the works of Katherine Parr

What matters, finally, in understanding emergent culture, as distinct
from both the dominant and the residual, is that it is never only a
matter of immediate practice; indeed it depends crucially on finding
new forms or adaptations of form. Again and again what we have to
observe is in effect a *pre-emergence*, active and pressing but not yet
fully articulated, rather than the evident emergence which could be
more confidently named.

Raymond Williams, Marxism and literature

You say that it's gospel, but I know that it's only church.

Tom Waits

At a moment when the English people were revaluating the merits of
internal and external authority, the seemingly private religious expression
of women could speak to newly urgent public concerns. But the way that
private expression resonates as public experience is markedly different
when the woman writer is herself a public figure.[1] The transitional spirituality in the work of Queen Katherine Parr reflects an England moving
tentatively between the old faith and new. Parr herself also functions
within her texts as a figure of transition. In *The lamentacion of a synner*,
she models her work according to Lutheran prescriptions outlined in the
Preface to the Epistle to the Romans. In so doing, she follows the pattern of
Pauline devotion (outlined by Luther) in an attempt to revaluate her
'wreched former lyfe' as a Catholic.[2] Using herself as an example of a
reformed evangelical Christian serves to parallel her private experience
with that of a nation; Parr's self-representation is a paradigm for a country
undergoing similar religious transformation.

Parr's configuration of herself as a model of reform plays upon the same
cultural assumptions that Bale exploits: '[t]he strength of God' can be
most 'perfyght[ly]' conveyed through the medium of a woman because
of her presumed spiritual 'weakenesse'.[3] But Parr is not, like Askew,
peripheral to the theological deliberations of the time – she is central to

their reformulation. Her use of her own conversion as a vehicle for religious change appears particularly appropriate once we recognise her crucial intervention in the development of vernacular forms of worship in England. What is striking about her reformation of devotional texts – in light of her conversion – is that she does not entirely discard the spiritual structures of Catholicism, but rather integrates them into the new religion. Parr was able to advance the ideas of a radically different theology within traditional modes of supplication. This tactic allowed some correspondence within her own spiritual history; her religious thought was changing, but it could be expressed in a way that was consonant with her lifetime practice. Further, Parr's was not the only private belief in a state of transition, and a search for consistency is the common impulse during moments of change.

The importance of Thomas Cranmer in the creation of the forms of worship for the Church of England is well known – but the role of Katherine Parr in this project has remained, for the most part, unexplored.[4] In fact, Parr's contribution seems even more revealing than Cranmer's in terms of understanding how the process of cultural reform in England was effected. The investigation of religious change in England in the early sixteenth century has been to some degree impaired by the categories that we use to describe it. While the ample critical work concerning the revisions or redactions of medieval literature in early modern English poetics has tried to appreciate change by first observing residual likeness, it has frequently been assumed that the doctrinal disruptions of the early Tudor period resist this kind of comparison. Literary critics and historians have alike tried to understand early modern devotional prose in terms of contrast rather than continuity. As Eamon Duffy observes: 'Whether the polarities employed are those of "medieval" as opposed to "Renaissance", or "unreformed" as opposed to "reformed", the temptation is to opt for a single ... descriptive category.'[5] The critical impulse has been, therefore, to locate a work in the frame of either antecedent or emergent forms of religious thought, or to try to tease out the elements of one or the other within a particular writer's output. This approach hinders our understanding of the complicated forms that straddle the faultline of literary and religious change. In our analyses of religious expressions at the beginning of the sixteenth century, we tend to search for the enduring accents of late medieval Catholicism or the anticipatory sounds of early Protestantism; but such analysis does not accommodate the mixed message of these locutions. Moments of radical change inevitably renovate available cultural forms. Emergent culture consists of formal reworkings and mixed compositions. Certainly this is true of Parr's religious writing, which consistently exposes the disadvantages of binary assessment. The doctrinal exchanges that take place in the organisation of her texts reveal the complicated spiritual negotiation that these works were designed to express. While we too often think in terms of the separation of Protestant and Catholic devotional attitudes, the writing of Katherine Parr shows us that effective reform of devotion in England depended upon cultural and religious integration.

NEW RELIGION

Parr was a considerable force in the early Reformation. Her compiled *Prayers or meditacions* went into seven editions between 1545 and 1550 alone (there were twenty editions by the end of the century);[6] her original piece of devotional prose, *The lamentacion of a synner*, went into three editions between 1547 and 1563, and was also included in Bentley's *Monvment of matrones* (1582); her patronage of the English *Paraphrases of Erasmus* (and possible translation of the book of Matthew[7]) led to the circulation of some 15,000 copies between 1548 and 1549.[8] Her significant contribution to the project of religious reform was made possible because of her position as queen consort to Henry VIII, but it was licensed by the trust that the king placed in her. Her activities in the religious area of public life, in fact, were enabled through her inauguration in the political one – Parr's first engagement with the issue of religious change in England was prompted by a war effort. Henry left his wife Regent of England from July to October 1544, while he led a campaign in France. But national exigency demanded the revision of available calls to worship, and while attempting to marshal the prayerful efforts of the English people in the face of threatening international circumstances, Henry apparently involved his wife – or, at least, permitted her involvement – in the project of advancing and shaping the devotional forms of the nascent English Church.

Janel Mueller was the first to hypothesise that Parr's *Prayers or meditacions* held 'a close complementary relation' to Cranmer's first English *Litany.*[9] An examination of all extant copies of the early *Litany* confirms that three devotional texts of this period – the *Litany*, the *Psalmes or prayers*, and the *Prayers or meditacions* – were quite literally bound together. The publication history of these three books exposes the complicated operations of a state programme designed and deployed by the collective agencies of the king, the queen, the archbishop, and the king's printer. It further shows the extent to which the queen assumed an active role in the reform agenda.

In order to understand Parr's involvement in the project of reform, we first need to review what that project entailed. On 11 June 1544 the king wrote to his Archbishop of Canterbury (in a letter no doubt drafted by Cranmer himself):

We greet you well; and let you wit that, calling to our remembrance the miserable state of all Christendom, being at this present, besides all other troubles, so plagued with most cruel wars, hatreds, and dissensions ... the help and remedy whereof, far exceeding the power of any man, must be called for of him who only is able to grant our petitions, and never forsaketh nor repelleth any that firmly believe and faithfully call on him ... being therefore resolved to have continually from henceforth general processions in all cities, towns, churches, and parishes of this our realm, said and sung with such reverence and devotion, as apperteineth, forasmuch as heretofore the people, partly for lack of good instruction and calling, partly for that they understood no part of such prayers or suffrages, as were used to be sung and said, have used to come very slackly to the procession, when the same have been commanded heretofore: we have set forth certain godly prayers and suffrages in our native English tongue, which we send you herewith.[10]

Thomas Berthelet, the king's printer, had already printed the *Exhortation vnto prayer ... to be read in every church afore processyons* with the appended *Letanie with suffrages to be said or song in the tyme of the said processyons* on 27 May. Cranmer accordingly issued a mandate to Edmund Bonner, Bishop of London and Dean of the province, to put the new English *Litany* into practice throughout the region.[11] This national effort of supplication was clearly designed to enlist God's aid on Henry's side in the war with France. The effect of the strategy was also to introduce, under royal sanction, devotional handbooks for the Church of England that departed from Catholic modes of worship. The movement toward Protestant formulations, however, was a tentative one, and (as Parr's work shows us) crucially reliant upon traditional spiritual modes.

In the *Exhortation*, Cranmer writes that 'it is verye conuenient, and moche acceptable to god, that you shuld vse your priuate prayer in your mother tongue, that you vnderstandyng what you aske of god, maye more ernestly and feruently desyre the same your hartes and myndes agreing to your mouth and woordes'.[12] But the *Exhortation* does not provide instruction in the form of private prayer. Rather, two separate vernacular prayer books were produced for this purpose – the *Psalmes or prayers* (1544), and the *Prayers or meditacions* (1545). The *Psalmes or prayers, taken out of holye scripture* was a collection – originally in Latin – made by John Fisher (Bishop of Rochester from 1504 to 1534) which had been published on the continent (c. 1525).[13] These prayers are compiled psalm citations knitted together with original text. The king's printer published the prayer book on 18 April;[14] a few days later (25 April), Berthelet printed the English translation.[15]

The first run of this English prayer book was evidently only a small number of copies commissioned by the king for distribution among his family and friends.[16] But evidence concerning the circulation of the *Psalmes* puts it in proximity (both physical and doctrinal) to the new English *Litany* – and judging from this history, it appears to have been part of the reforming scheme begun in the spring and early summer of 1544. Of the nine editions of the English *Litany* that were produced between 1544 and 1545, four were printed by Berthelet.[17] He enlisted two other English printers, Richard Grafton and Thomas Petyt, to print the remaining five editions. In the nineteenth century, Cambridge University Library and the British Library decided to separate bound bequests, and to bind their volumes individually. We therefore cannot determine from the editions held at these libraries the practices of sixteenth-century book buyers – which is to say, what books they were purchasing and binding together. But there are extant copies of the second (first full) print run housed in the Bodleian Library and the Library of Lincoln Cathedral.[18] Both of these are bound with the *Psalmes*.

This does not count as absolute proof of association, as both of the copies have been rebound. However, the book housed at Lincoln Cathedral has the monogram of Michael Honywood in its usual place in the top left corner of the first page – indicating that the works were already bound together when he acquired them. Honywood (1596–1681) was Dean of Lincoln from 1660 until his death (when he bequeathed his collection to the Cathedral). But far more compelling than this single instance is the fact that *all* other extant copies from other print runs by Berthelet are also bound with the *Psalmes*, and one of these, kept at the Huntington Library, is in its original temporary limp vellum binding.[19] Only one of the other surviving copies of the English *Litany* from this period – farmed out to Grafton and Petyt – is bound in this way.[20] If binding the *Litany* and the *Psalmes* together became the later practice of eighteenth-century collectors, we would not find this arrangement. Grafton and Petyt produced a still greater number of copies of the *Litany*, and there is no reason for collectors to have bound the *Psalmes* only to copies printed by Berthelet. This strongly suggests that the king's printer was urging the sale of the *Psalmes* as a companion to the English *Litany*.

Recent work of J. Christopher Warner details the extent to which Henry used Berthelet as a conduit for not only his own self-representation, but also the transmission of his political and religious agenda. Warner goes so far as to argue that Berthelet's imprint on any document (official or otherwise) would have signalled to Henry's subjects that the 'text was doing official service: proclaiming new laws [or] stating the king's views'. What is clear is that Berthelet became the 'official *representer* of the king and government'.[21] His activities, then, need to be seen as something more than a commercial impulse. If he was encouraging buyers to gather the *Litany* and the *Psalmes* into one collection, then he clearly considered these two works as parts of a single corpus. (There were, after all, other religious works in Berthelet's shop.) As handbooks that gave instruction on how to pray in public and private, the *Litany* and the *Psalmes* functioned as a unit to provide the community of faithful revised guidelines for worship within the new English Church. The practices of the king's printer indicate that he understood that he was supposed to disseminate these works as a single order of worship.

Whether Parr translated Fisher's *Psalmes* into English cannot be positively established, but there is evidence to suggest that she did.[22] In *Ecclesiastical memorials*, John Strype credits Parr with authorship – but this seems to be the result of a misreading of Nicholas Udall.[23] In his dedication to the 'Paraphrase of Erasmus vpon the Ghospell of Luke', Udall refers to the queen's 'Psalmes and contemplatife meditacions ... whiche ye haue set forth ... to the ghostly consolacion and edifiyng of as many as reade them.'[24] Udall is probably referring to the *Prayers or meditacions*, but his phrasing does not make that clear. In the dedication to the paraphrase of the Book of Acts he also writes that the queen 'deserueth ... to be estemed ... for dyuers moste godly Psalmes and meditacions of [her] owne penning and settyng foorthe'.[25] An entry in John Bale's 1548 catalogue of English writers gives us some insight into Udall's diction. Bale lists Parr's works as 'Meditationes psalmorum' and 'Lamentationem peccatoris'.[26] 'Meditations on the psalms' clearly refers to the *Prayers or meditacions* (which was printed in the versicle form of the Psalms), and the latter title refers to Parr's *Lamentacion of a synner*. Udall's consistent use of 'psalms' for 'prayers', then, might be a slippage in terms similar to Bale's. What is clear is that Strype understood Udall to mean that there were two different works.

The works that Strype describes are the two prayer books produced in 1544–5: the *Psalmes or prayers* and the *Prayers or meditacions*. Strype's misapprehension is both telling and instructive. The vast majority of the surviving editions of the *Psalmes* are also bound with the *Prayers*. There is no pattern indicating Berthelet's agency in this gathering (as no copies retain their original binding, it is impossible to say when they were put together).[27] What is certain is that by 1568 these books were printed together with continuous signatures under the title of *The king's prayers* and *The queen's prayers*.[28] The joint publication of the prayer books shows how linked they eventually became in the minds of the English public (or, at least, of English publishers); but their grouping as a collective set might result from their shared role in the crown project of devotional reform initiated with the publication of the English *Litany*.

Probably the most convincing evidence for Parr as the translator of the *Psalmes* into English is the appended 'praier for the king' and 'prayer for men to saie entryng into battaile' in all editions of the work.[29] Both of these prayers are also appended to the *Prayers or meditacions*, and Parr's composition of that work is certain. But the 'praier for the king' also appears in the 1544 *Psalmi seu precatio*. This might suggest that Parr ushered Fisher's original Latin text into print. Her Latin skills would surely have been equal to the task of translating the *Psalmes* (and, for that matter, writing the prayer in Latin).[30] But 'praier for the king' appeals to God to give the king 'strength . . . [to] ouercome all his and our foes', and summons the petitions of the community on Henry's behalf in his war with France.[31] The affixing of the prayer to these two prayer books, then, does more to situate them within the overall supplication scheme than to identify the translator/composer of the two works.

All of the evidence that might identify Parr as a translator of the *Psalmes* can be equally applied in support of an argument for her patronage. The case for her translation is based in part upon her active attempts to disseminate the work.[32] But the fact that the queen was so invested in the prayer book only confirms her involvement in the ongoing political process of church reform. It does not confirm her translation of the text. Still, the possibility cannot be denied. What is certain is that she was a participant in the plan to revise devotional practice – and, further, that her husband granted her power in this domain. Henry VIII was undoubtedly interested in the *Psalmes*; one of the rare surviving copies of the first print run bears a presentation inscription from the king to the queen.[33] But whether Henry's attention was motivated by pride in his wife's achievement or by his own political initiatives is impossible to say. Either way, her composition of the second prayer book in the reform programme, the *Prayers or meditacions*, was authorised – and quite possibly solicited – by the king. This prayer book, published a year after the *Psalmes*, differs markedly from the first in its theological grounding.

In her recent study, Judith Maltby has considered the *Book of common prayer* – the evolved version of Cranmer's English *Litany* – in the context of political propaganda. '[T]here was probably no other single aspect of the Reformation in England', Maltby observes, 'which touched more directly and fundamentally the religious consciousness . . . of ordinary clergy and laity, than did the reform of rituals and liturgy.'[34] While the reorientation of private prayer that attended these initiatives cannot be considered in quite the same terms, it is important to recognise its role as 'a means of [public] persuasion'.[35] Common prayer was intended as the public expression of communal belief, but private prayer was also (if not equally) crucial to the development of Protestant self-consciousness. The ubiquity of prayer books for private use – seen as supplements, not rivals, to the liturgy – establishes their prominent role within the religious life of the English community.[36]

In his discussion of the value of these collections, Ian Green particularly notes the 'very high levels of repeat editions' of these works. In situating the *Prayers or meditacions* among the survey of this material, one is imme-diately struck by the number of editions, as well as by the extended period of time in which they were produced. There were a total of twenty-four printed editions of the work over a period of sixty-eight years (1545–1613).[37] The number of editions puts the queen's prayer book among the best-selling works of the genre; but there is simply no parallel, among com-parable texts, for the longevity of its appeal.[38] Of course, the status of the work as part of the crown project for reform puts it in an unusual category – somewhere between an official text and a private devotional aid. In its very conception, the prayer book was intended as a supplement to public forms of worship. And it continued to be published well after the *Book of common prayer* was the established liturgical text of the Church of England.

Royal authorship obviously enhanced the early success of the *Prayers*; its title page prominently advertises the role of 'the moste vertuous and gracious princes Catharine, Quene of Englande, France, and Irelande' in compiling the text. This cannot account for the sustained public interest in the work, however. (If royal prestige alone were responsible for the prayer book's popularity, then the book nominally attached to the Supreme Head of the English Church – *The king's prayers* – would surely have seen more editions.[39]) As David Starkey succinctly puts it: 'its tone caught the moment'.[40] More accurately, the tone of the *Prayers* addressed the needs of a religious community over a series of shifting moments throughout the century. It proved compatible with religious identity and expression under both reform and counter-reform regimes. The value of such devotional flexibility cannot be underestimated in the context of the disruption caused by the erratic religious policies under Edward, Mary, and Elizabeth. While the expression of the *Prayers* corresponded to the attitudes of a community at a key moment of religious transition, it was also responsive to the '*de facto* religious pluralism' that was the result of the switchback course of England's long Reformation.[41]

It is believed that Parr underwent her conversion to Protestantism when her temporary sovereignty of the realm required her (at Henry's instruction) to have daily consultations with Cranmer, the ranking member of the regency council.[42] This raises an interesting speculation on the differences between the two devotional handbooks bound with the first English *Litany*. One might attribute the revision of late medieval Catholic mysticism found in the *Prayers or meditacions* – in contrast to the wholesale adoption of Catholic-inflected dogma in the *Psalmes* – to the change in Parr's personal faith that occurred between 1544 and 1545. While such an attribution of cause is pure conjecture, the devotional transitionality of the *Prayers* does correspond to the spiritual transformation of its author. Parr's conversion would have required considerable reorganisation of personal belief. Since Cranmer's own theological development at the time was leaning heavily towards Lutheranism, we may assume that her own early instruction was anchored in Luther's writings.[43] But it is highly unlikely that within a year she could have perfectly reconciled evangelical thought to a belief system that had its formulations in Catholic practice. The reorientation of Parr's faith would have been incomplete at the time of her composition of the *Prayers* – a faith which is itself a mixture of the old and new.

Critical arguments concerning the doctrinal commitments of the *Prayers* take both sides. Arguing that the theology of the *Prayers* 'is distinctly Catholic', C. Fenno Hoffman noticed years ago that the source of the extended meditation in Parr's text is Book 3 (chapters 16–55) of an English translation of *The imitation of Christ* (c. 1531), often attributed to Richard Whitford.[44] The *Imitatio Christi*, a celebrated book of English devotion, had remained virtually inaccessible to a vernacular audience until the printing of its second English translation (1504).[45] But Parr's emendation of the translated *Imitation* resists Hoffman's stark classification; doctrinal forms and ideas are intermingled in the body of her work in general. Her source text was a standard work of late medieval Catholic mysticism – one which Thomas More cited as essential to the 'encreace [of] devotion' in the traditional faith when confuting the 'new fangled heresies' of William Tyndale.[46] But Parr's excisions of the *Imitation* revise its theology to accommodate one of the 'heresies' which More firmly opposed – the doctrine of justification by faith alone.

Mueller (countering Hoffman) has argued for the almost complete reformation of Catholic spirituality in Parr's *Prayers*.[47] But even Mueller's attentive reading closes off crucial meanings that remain active in the text. Parr's changes indicate something more complicated than the remodelling of a Catholic source in order to advance Protestant conceptions. In both the *Prayers* and the later *Lamentacion*, her devotional work persistently registers the interdoctrinal impulses of a Catholic adult trying to reorder her faith. Parr uses the same method of cut and paste in the *Prayers* that Cranmer applied in the composition of the vernacular *Litany*. But Cranmer's exercises upon the Sarum rite were more thoroughly revisionist – if only because he needed to foreclose the possibility that the *Litany* would be used for saint worship.[48] As Green observes: 'The 1539 primer that Thomas Cromwell commissioned from Bishop Hilsey had a number of Protestant features in a work built up of essentially Catholic materials, while the one that Cranmer issued ... in [1544] was sufficiently different at a number of points from earlier primers to be deemed a Protestant work on balance.'[49] By contrast, while Parr's editing practices upon her source text revise its theological inflection, she significantly retains some of its most important spiritual components.

Because Mueller has thoroughly examined the departures from the source material that demonstrate Protestant revision, some repetition of her analysis is inevitable in my effort to point out the observable marks of Parr's changing spirituality within her edited text.[50] Parr begins with chapter 17 of the third book of the *Imitation*, 'A prayer that the wyll of god be alwaye fulfylled': 'Moste benygne lorde Jesu graunt me thy grace that it maye be alway with me and werke with me.'[51] Parr alters the line to 'worke *in* me', emphasising the impotence of man's will in the process of salvation. The denial of free will in Christian soteriology is subtly sustained throughout the mediation. 'Thy mercy is more profytable and more sure way', the *Imitation* claims, 'for me to the gettyng of pardon and forgyuenes of my synnes, then a trust in myne owne works ... And though I drede not my conseyence yet I may not therfore iustyfye my selfe, for thy mercy remoued & taken away: no man may be iustyfyed ne appere rightwyse in thy syght.'[52] Parr emends these lines in the following way: 'Wherfore to thy mercie I do appeale, seyng no manne maie be iustified ne appere rightuous in thy syghte, if thou examine him after thy iustice.'[53] According to Lutheran doctrine, the acceptance of the condition of predestination requires a saving awareness of our own sinfulness. Once we acknowledge our sinful nature, we understand that we are endowed with grace only through the mercy of God, and not through our own merit or works. It is then that we see the wisdom of God's prejudgement upon us, and come to terms with it. Parr's phraseology emphasises the incapacity of human nature to effect its own salvation. The variation is mostly achieved by verbal pruning, but Parr's reworkings of her source text consistently affirm this theological position.

While Parr only slightly alters her material to accommodate Lutheran doctrine, she does so consistently. She changes 'Lorde I wyll gladly suffre for the what so euer thou wylt shall fall vpon me'[54] to 'Lord, *gyve me grace* gladly to suffre whatsoeuer thou wilt shall fall upon me.'[55] The emendation stresses the inability of humankind, without the aid of God, to behave rightly (in this case, patiently). The struggle against the frailty of nature, the *Imitation* claims, 'is nat all unprofitable ... for therby I knowe the better myne owne infirmyties'.[56] Parr, by contrast, emphasises human powerlessness in the conflict, and claims that she 'muste seeke helpe onely at [God's] handes'.[57] Changes of this kind would be less striking if alteration were the common editing practice deployed in the *Prayers*, but it is not. While Parr frequently excises text – cutting the original by two-thirds – she modifies words with a purpose.

'Oftymes it is but a lytell thynge', the *Imitation* reads, 'that castyth me downe & maketh me dull and slowe to all good workes.'[58] Parr's text denies the role of works altogether, and the line is rewritten: 'maketh me dull and slow to serue the'.[59] She omits the reference to saints as examples for the Christian to follow.[60] She dispenses with the contemplative framework of the piece, and reforms the dialogue between 'Jesus' and the 'disciple' so that Christ does not address the human soul at all. The resulting monologue reinforces a Lutheran sense of alienation. From expurgation to amendment, all of these strategies serve to revise the spirituality which informs the *Imitation*, but they do not efface it altogether. As suggestive as Parr's erasure of what is conspicuously Catholic in the text is the extent to which she leaves the source intact.

A large proportion of the *Imitation* appears to have been consistent with Parr's evolving spirituality. Numerous long passages and even a few chapters in their entirety are reprinted with little or no modification.[61] In fact, over one third of the *Prayers* is an unbroken transcription of the human voice of the *Imitation*, the soul's petition to Christ. Clearly, the devotional language of the *Imitation* appealed to her own. Its theology must also have been, in many ways, compatible with her belief. The soul's persistent cry throughout the Catholic meditation is to be freed from the carnal attachments of the body so that it might follow Christ in all things. The aspiration of the soul is a total surrender to Christ, in order to be moulded according to his will: 'Lo I am thy seruaunte redy to all thinges that thou commaundest, for I desyre nat to lyue to my selfe but to the.'[62] This desire is echoed by Parr in one of her few original sentences: 'O lorde, grant me, that I maie wholly resigne my self to the, and in all thynges to forsake my selfe, and paciently to beare my crosse, and to folowe the.'[63]

The *Imitation* itself departs from the norms of Catholic spirituality in advocating that human will be shaped according to divine directives; the mystical understanding of spiritual perfection commonly demanded the *sacrifice* of the ego in order to be digested into deity. This idea of communion could not be adapted to fit a work which advanced a Lutheran-oriented conception of the Christian's relationship to God. But the notion of *subjugating* the ego to the will of Christ could be fitted to the theological frame of the *Prayers*. Which is to say that the *Imitation* was ideally suited for conversion and that Parr probably chose it for this reason. The text had the advantage of being both resonant within the tradition of English Catholic spirituality, and compliant to the emergent devotional forms of Protestantism. The combination of traditional and emergent forms would have been potentially meaningful for both the author and audience of the *Prayers*.

The compound structure of Parr's appropriated text allowed it to be pliable to the diverse devotional attitudes of a congregation that was potentially either conservative or evangelical – or commonly both. More importantly, it spoke to those members whose faith was undefined. The rhetorical design of the *Prayers* contains the spiritual accents of both Catholicism and emergent Protestantism; more to the point, it demonstrates that late medieval Catholicism is not always inconsistent with emergent Protestant logic. Parr's devotional work publishes her own spiritual enquiries and shows the religious transformation – and transference – occurring in people at the time of the early English Reformation. But it crosses the boundaries of what we as critics have come to regard as separate categories: Catholic and Protestant modes of religious devotion were clearly neither as starkly contrasted nor as completely incompatible as is usually assumed.[64] The *Prayers* was published under every Tudor reign, and remained popular beyond the end of the century – spanning three changes in official religion.

KEEPING THE FAITH

Just how complicated (and political) the process of conversion was in England – both for the individual and the nation – has been detailed by Michael Questier. While emphasising that the polemics of conversion necessarily caused clerics on both sides to highlight the contrasts between them, Questier reminds us that conversion 'did not inevitably and slavishly follow the logic of overt political oppositions'.[65] But if religious belief was not as compartmentalised as polemical discourse suggests, then the persuasive language of conversion was that of coalition rather than opposition.[66] Eric Jager has recently shown how the inward direction of late medieval Catholic practice increasingly set private prayer at the centre of public devotion.[67] If, as some critics have argued, the fundamental reform to religious consciousness in England was the communal worship of common prayer, then the expression of private prayer books served to replace what had once been a public mode of worship, privately experienced.[68]

In other words, the individual and inward turn of late medieval piety was susceptible to newly formulated notions of Protestant faith. Scholars such as Lee Patterson and David Aers have effectively dispatched claims that the radical separation between an interior and exterior world can be understood as a sixteenth-century development.[69] The practice of turning inward on the journey towards God finds its most powerful articulation in the *Confessions* of St Augustine. There, Augustine outlines a process of inner excavation through which we might hope to encounter God. This is not a matter of mining the soul where God is hidden, but of retiring to the inner recesses of the self where God might respond ('[God] is both the *light* and the *voyce* ... of my inner man'[70]). Of course the inward direction of this process relies upon the research of the soul – of self-knowledge that might allow God (conceived here as the 'inner man') to speak, or at least allow the penitent to hear. This theology of inwardness shapes the mystical tradition that characterises the books that Thomas More prescribes for the spiritual health of 'people unlearned' in particular: 'the lyfe of Christe ... the folowing of Christ and the devoute contemplative booke of Scala perfectionis'.[71] These ascetic works (*Vita Christi*, *The folowyng of Christe*, and *The scale of perfection*) articulate the ideals of modern devotional practice, which denied the value of worldly activity and instead advocated a retreat into the self – into the inner sanctum of the soul – where communion with God was possible: 'It is red that Moyses had alway recourse to the tabernacle of god for doutes & questions to be assoyled … So shuldest thou entre in to the secrete tabernacle of thyne owne hert and there aske inwardly with good deuotyon the helpe of god in al suche doutes & perylles.'[72] The inward apprehension of Christ is precisely what the disciple in the *Imitation* seeks. The text reflects the practice of inward-directed piety that became a model (by the end of the fifteenth century) for direct communication with God.

The devotional texts cited by More concentrate upon 'the dialectic between an inward subjectivity and an external world that alienates it from both itself and its divine source' that Patterson describes as 'fundamental [to the] economy of the medieval idea of selfhood'.[73] While Nicholas Love's translation of the *Meditationes vitae Christi* (attributed to Bonaventure) and Walter Hilton's *Scale of perfection* had a wider circulation in fifteenth-century England than any other comparable devotional texts, the English reputation of the *Imitation* derived from the successive editions of the work which appeared from 1504 onwards.[74] Its many vernacular printings were clearly intended to reach far beyond clerical communities, and within the space of about thirty years – as More's advice attests – it had secured its place among the significant texts of English spirituality. But More's emphasis upon the laity also demonstrates the particular influence that these modern devotional texts had upon lay piety. (Modern devotion is the term applied to the collective practice of the fraternal orders that thrived in northern Europe from the late fourteenth century onward.) Love's work was first printed by William Caxton in 1484, and subsequently went into seven more editions by 1530 (one more by Caxton, two by Richard Pynson, and three by Wynkyn de Worde).[75] *The scale of perfection* was first printed by de Worde at the request of Lady Margaret Beaufort in 1494, and saw four more printings by 1533.[76] The *Imitation* (or, *The folowyng of Christe*) was also ushered into print publication by Margaret Beaufort – and this time she also served as a translator of the fourth book.[77] The version produced by Atkinson and Beaufort went into seven printings, and the Whitford translation, which appeared in 1531, was reproduced five more times by 1545.[78]

Parr's selection of her source text might well have been a prudent nod to the contributions of Henry's grandmother to the history of English religious books – in any case, it aligned the new Tudor queen with that history. What is clear from the early publication history of the *Imitation* is its broad circulation among a vernacular readership. The popularity of the book among the laity reflects the religious changes in the late medieval period that, as Jager observes, 'encouraged laypeople to look to their own hearts as a center of spiritual life'.[79] While this process is revised in Parr's adaptation, it is not eschewed. Of course, there would be no possibility of the direct communication with God that is written into the *Imitation*: such a notion hardly coheres with Lutheran ideas of alienation. Consequently, Parr excises from her text 'the inwarde spekynge of Chryst to [the] faythful soule' that appears in the original.[80] But the *Prayers* vitally depends upon the inward contemplation of Christ expressed in the *Imitation*. In her appropriation of a text so central to late medieval English spirituality, Parr retains for private prayer the heart-centred practices of modern devotion that had become prevalent among the laity.

Modern devotional practice – articulated in books like the *Imitation* – held that the Passion was printed in the heart, and could be accessed there as readable matter. Indeed, the image of Christ in the heart was the essence of scripture itself, the good news of the Gospels. This immediate access to the Word of God was the organising conceit of Catholic notions of 'layman's books' and of the heart-centred practice of *imitatio*. The idea is imported into early Protestantism; but the way that the image is 'read' changes in that tradition. In his treatise *Against the heavenly prophets*, Luther writes:

I know for certain that God desires that one should hear and read his work, and especially the passion of Christ. But if I am to hear and think, then it is impossible for me not to make images of this within my heart, for whether I want to or not, when I hear the word of Christ, there delineates itself in my heart the picture of a man who hangs on the cross. [81]

Luther's faith is revealed as word-based in its apprehension of the image: 'verbal signifiers of Christ cast their signified in the form of an image [and] by saying that this image is how we ineluctably "think" Christ, Luther suggest[s] that, even for his faith without mediators, the reference of all references was a mediation still'.[82] The first resource in the Protestant tradition became the scriptural text – which would be read through the heart, but not accessed *in* the heart as the primary record.

In Luther's doctrine, then, the image of Christ appears as the signified of a scriptural message; and again, in turn, as a signifier pointing to the transcendental signified which is knowledge of God. This divine signified, however, remained unavailable to reason. The modern devotional tradition, on the other hand, held that such knowledge was present in the image. The inner picture of Christ was both information and utterance – it was knowledge of God that preceded scripture. Of course, for William of

Occam and the *via moderna*, true knowledge of God was not attainable to reason without revelation (hence, the emphasis in the *Imitation* upon the role of grace in apprehension). But Lutheran doctrine could not accept the conception of a God that, with the aid of grace, our reason is able to apprehend. Luther's declaration that we can only perceive God in his posterior is not simply an allusion to the humiliation of the incarnation – rather, it is a claim that God reveals himself to us even as he is hidden from our mortal sight (turned away from us). Any rational apprehension of him is inherently corrupting, because it is to mould him in our sinful image – in terms that we can understand. We can therefore only apprehend him through faith, which does not apply our terms. That the image of Christ 'delineates itself' in the heart suggests that it is the picture of faith, and not of cognition.[83] But Luther's doctrine of *dues absconditus* 'held that the crucifixion concealed God in order to designate his existence elsewhere'.[84] The inner crucifix, then, is no different: it is the sign of the hidden God.[85]

It is the orientation of late medieval religious practice, rather than a Lutheran point of reference, which is activated in the devotional mechanism of Parr's meditation for private prayer. Obviously, a Lutheran framework could not encompass Catholic practices such as *imitatio*, which turned upon the legible image. The practice of *imitatio* was a hallmark of late medieval affective piety. In the commemoration of the Passion, the penitent was enjoined to meditate upon Christ's suffering so as to participate emotionally in it; the believer would thereby be reminded to imitate Christ's example in the patient endurance of worldly affliction.

Blessed is that man, that for the loue of the lorde, setteth not by the pleasures of this worlde, & lerneth truely to ouercome hym selfe, and with the feruour of spirite crucifyeth his fleshe, so that in a cleane and a pure concience, he maie offer his prayers to the, and be accepted to haue company of thy blessed angelles, all erthly thynges excluded from his herte.[86]

The spirituality of the *Prayers* is not (in Hoffman's phrase) 'distinctly Catholic'; but neither can it be said to have been, as Mueller claims, 'wrenched from [a] perceptibly Catholic' spiritual framework.[87] This is the description of the practice of *imitatio*, where in an act of affective devotion the worshipper suffers with Christ ('with the feruour of spirite crucifyeth his fleshe') in an attempt to set his or her mind above material existence. The activity reconciles the devotee to God through the inward 'imitation' of Christ. The *Prayers*, then, is still partially situated within the modern devotional tradition from which it draws.

The meditation of the *Prayers* solicits God for the grace to follow the example that he supplied on earth:

For though this life be tedious, & as an heuy burdein to my soule: yet neuer-thelesse throughe thy grace and by example of the it is nowe made muche more easye and comfortable then it was before thy incarnacion and passyon.

Thy holy life is oure waye to the, and by folowynge of the, we walk to the, that arte our head and sauiour: And yet excepte thou haddest gone before, and shewed us the waye to euerlasting lyfe, who would endeuore hym selfe to folowe the? Seynge we be yet so slowe and dull, hauyng the light of thy blessed example & holy doctrine to leade and directe us.[88]

Parr retains the commitment of the penitent Christian to pattern his or her life after Christ – the essence of the tradition of *imitatio*. She does underscore the role of grace in the process in a subsequent line: 'O lorde Jesu, make that possible by grace, that is impossible to me by nature.'[89] But even this line is lifted from the *Imitation*, and it further serves to inflect the passages that follow which contemplate the weak ability of the disciple of Christ to undergo suffering. The power to sustain hardship resides, according to Parr's own diction, in the emulation of Christ: 'O lorde, grant me, that I maie wholly resigne my selfe to the, and in all thynges to forsake my selfe, and paciently to bear my crosse, and to folowe the.'[90]

Parr's adaptation does deny Christ speaking through the soul, but it recognises the role of grace in the illumination of it: 'Open my hert lorde, that I maie beholde thy lawes, and teache me to walke in thy commandementes.'[91] God's law is printed on the heart, if only the penitent had the clarity of sight to view it.[92] The *Prayers* persistently asks that Christ enter the recesses of the heart and provide the vision that human nature obscures: 'O euerlastyng light, farre passynge all thynges, sende downe the beames of thy brightnesse from aboue, and purifye and lyghten the inwarde partes of my herte. Quicken my soule, and all the powers therof, that it maie cleaue fast and be ioyned to the ioyful gladnes of gostly rauishynges.'[93] The unrelenting cry of the soul for visitation from Christ in the *Prayers* is, again, borrowed from the *Imitation*:

Come, O lorde, and visite me, for without the I haue no true ioye, without the, my soule is heuy and sadde.

I am in prison, and bound with fetters of sorow, till thou, O lorde, with thy gracious presence vouchesafe to visite me, and to brynge me agayne to libertie and ioy of spirite, and to shewe thy fauorable countenaunce vnto me.[94]

The disciple of Christ is promised inward instruction, but final apprehension is forestalled until the day of reckoning.[95] Parr's interventions in the text emphasise the distance between worldly experience and ultimate apprehension, but the penitent of the *Prayers* is still afforded the benefit of 'inwarde techynges': 'O lorde, only art he, that maist helpe me; and thou maiest so confirme and stablishe me, that my heart shall not bee chaunged from the.'[96] The possibility of God's withdrawal is certainly acknowledged ('And if thou withdraw thy comforte from me at any tyme, kepe me O lorde, frome desperacion.'[97]). But the interior promptings of the heart (or soul), illuminated by God, form the chief mode of instruction within the *Prayers*: 'Accordyngly as thou doest saie in thy gospel: where as a mannes treasure is, there is his herte.'[98]

What is evident in the *Prayers* is the very definition of what Williams terms 'pre-emergence': elements of Lutheran doctrine are 'active and pressing' upon its construction, but the principles of the doctrine 'are not yet fully articulated'.[99] The *Prayers* conflates the old and the new faiths – or rather, understands the terms of the new religion through older devotional practices. While such middle ground might at first seem unsatisfying, it does map out the space of transition. It helps us to see Protestant self-consciousness when it is under construction, and better to understand its course of development. Parr was reforming private prayer for a congregation that had not yet fully processed the implications of Lutheran doctrine. The *Prayers* allows us to appreciate how these doctrinal changes were assimilated – both by the individual and the culture. In the *Prayers*, a devotional exercise used in late medieval public worship is appropriated for private use. As Jager points out, the conception 'of the heart as a book containing God's word, a devotional memory, or a moral record of the individual's life' was an inherited notion – one pliable to emergent Protestant culture, but hardly its invention.[100] Parr's *Prayers* gives us some insight into how the transition was effected. The meditation of the *Prayers* does not imagine an immanent God; but it understands the secrets of the Crucifixion as encased in the heart; and the heart is treated as 'the ultimate devotional text'.[101]

'LOOKYNG INTO THE SPIRITUAL BOKE'

The devotional mode of the *Prayers* is highly unusual in the context of the generic conventions of sixteenth-century English prayer books.[102] The medieval precedents for these prayer books can be broadly divided into miscellanies and Books of Hours (which might contain miscellaneous prayers, but these are adjunct to the Hours themselves).[103] Susan Felch observes that many of the early printed primers began as versions of the manuscript Books of Hours, but these demonstrated increasing reformist tendencies in England after 1530 (Marshall's 1535 primer notable among them[104]). Certainly, the initial reformist primers all demonstrate a conscious shaping of Catholic materials in order to redefine – and reclaim – their use for a reformed community.[105] This impulse to emphasise what is common in Christian faith as opposed to what is distinctive is in evidence in the early reformist prayer books as well as the revisions on the Sarum rite in the vernacular Litany. It is also on display in Bale's insistent claims that the reformed Church had always been part of English history – both sacred and literary. Although Parr's impulse for reform parallels these attempts, I have been arguing that the *Prayers* occupies a unique intermediate position among devotional texts of this period. In fact, the equally persuasive critical arguments that situate the spirituality of the *Prayers* within either a Catholic or a Protestant framework do much to demonstrate the extent to which the text is transitional.

The interventions that account for the cultural transformations that enabled reform in England have most often been attributed to male clerics and scholars. The public reception of the work of both Askew and Parr, however, demonstrates the extent to which women's texts mediate principal questions of religious concern during a time of overwhelming religious change. Askew's text expresses the authority of scripture alone – and articulates the powers of individual apprehension to a reading public that was exploring reformist ideas. Parr develops the terms in which the public congregation can speak privately. But the two women figure very differently in their individual works, and this goes directly to the different manner in which they intercede in the religious debate. Parr's interventions are officially sanctioned, and she is writing for an established religious community.[106] Moreover, she clearly understands herself – and uses herself – as an example for the project of English reform.

In the *Prayers*, Parr's own voice merges with that of the English congregation. While the universal masculine is retained in the text ('Blessed is that man, that for the loue of the lorde, setteth not by the pleasures of this worlde, & lerneth truely to ouercome hym selfe'), the expression of the *Prayers* is principally personal address. In the process of purging the *Imitation* of God's response, Parr also eradicates the sex of the disciple (as God addresses him as 'my son').[107] The combination of strategies opens up the voice of the devotion. The diction of the *Prayers* denies a sexed soul, and instead permits each individual member of the congregation, regardless of gender, to identify with its terms. That Parr does this deliberately is indicated by her one modification of the default masculine position: 'I am but vanytye & nought before the a unconstaunt man and a feble' is changed to 'I am . . . an unconstant creature' in her text.[108] The term 'man' is allowed to serve in place of mankind, but the personal pronoun demands a specific amendment. The fact that she leaves the sex of the speaker undefined also crucially allows a point of entry for her own voice. As the title page of the *Prayers* declares her composition of the work, the personal pronouns collapse into her own expression. Parr becomes both a member of the communion of faithful and its example.

As the royal author of an instruction in private prayer, Parr also operates within the text as its primary speaker. It is entirely possible that the task fell to her in the first place because Henry regarded vernacular religion as a woman's domain. It was women and unlearned men who required vernacular translation; but Henry, of course, did not regard this as the proper tongue in which to conduct theological discussion.[109] The king's attitude partially reveals the reason why women's works could assume the status that they did in the early development of Protestant faith within popular religion. In the initial programme to revise the forms of worship of the Church of England, Parr functions as the advocate and exemplar for private devotion. What is also clear from the early reception of the *Prayers* – and the enduring public interest in the work – is the efficacy of the form she chose for a religious community that was engaged in the slow process of conversion.

The organisation of religious ideas in Parr's only piece of original prose, the *Lamentacion of a synner*, is far more complicated than that of her *Prayers*. The devotional work specifically treats her change from Catholic to Protestant faith. In her account of spiritual crisis, Parr again presses her own figure into service, but this time it is for the purpose of exfoliating the process of conversion itself. The *Lamentacion* describes the painful procedure of self-examination by which Parr was led to the new faith. It is not, however, simply an account of her own revelation, but an exposition of the steps by which such transformation is achieved. The purpose of its design, then, is not to convey personal experience, but rather to relate a spiritual formula. That the success of this objective is dependent upon Parr's status as both a woman *and* a public figure is made clear in the dedication by William Cecil:

Here mayest thou se one, if the kynde may moue the a woman, if degre may prouoke the a woman of highe estate, by byrthe made noble, by marriage . . . an excellent quene . . . forsakyng ignorance wherin she was blind, to come to knowledge, wherby she may see: remouyng supersticion, wherewith she was smothered, to embrace true re[lig]ion, wherwith she may reuiue.[110]

For Cecil, the figure of woman is a compelling vehicle for reform; and the combination of status and sex make Parr a particularly potent sign. Parr plays to cultural assumptions about women's spiritual weakness in order to emphasise the delusion of the Catholic faith, and to make her own deliverance more remarkable. But as Cecil declares: 'The fruit of this treatise (good reader) is *thy* amendement.'[111] In her text, Parr becomes literally a model to be copied – the very character of conversion.

The complications of the process are also part of her exposition (and are demonstrated in the speaker herself). In her testament of converted spirituality, Parr uses the odd metaphor of 'the book of the crucifix'. Consideration of how this metaphor operates within her devotional treatise exhibits the critical problems inherent in any bifurcated discussion of religious identity in early Reformation England. Parr's use of the metaphor has been understood in the context of the codex book and the Protestant emphasis upon vernacular scripture.[112] The focus upon one spiritual tradition has obscured the spiritual transaction that takes place at the site of the metaphor. Rather than indicating the early effects of Protestant book culture, Parr's deployment of 'the book of the crucifix' in her *Lamentacion* importantly reveals the complex way in which Protestant doctrine was being accessed and understood by its early adherents.

The women around the queen were advocates of the 'new learning' – scripturalists rather than traditionalists. Their ongoing deliberation on religious matters put them on the wrong side of the law more than once.[113] But the need for covert expression had passed (with Henry) by the time that the *Lamentacion* was published. The mixture of doctrinal forms and ideas that are a feature of the text must therefore be a function of Parr's own spiritual researches, not a means of navigating dangerous political waters. Early ideas of scriptural sufficiency (emanating from theologians such as Wycliff) appealed to the interior process of apprehension that was characteristic of late medieval devotional thinking:

A case in point is the position taken by ... Wyclif in a series of Oxford lectures delivered around 1378. Wyclif defined Scripture in terms of a five-level hierarchy ranging from the Trinity down to the physical text. The fourth, or next-to-last, level is the 'truth as it is believed, as it is inscribed in the book [*libro*] of the natural man, which is his soul' – as distinct from the fifth level of Scripture, the material codex consisting of mere parchment and ink.[114]

The process relied upon the Christian's inward reception of Christ (and his Gospel) written in the book of the human heart (or soul). The interior inscription of the Word ultimately arbitrates the exterior, material expression of scripture. As Jager observes, this account is not particular to Wycliff; even Wycliff's opponents advocate similar conceptions of the soul as the store of scriptural truth (although they advance them to different ends).[115] This emphasis upon the internal book is also apparent in the *Imitation.* Christ tells his disciple to: 'write my words therfore in thy herte diligently and ofte thynke thou vpon them & they shalbe ... moche necessary vnto the[.] that thou understandest nat whan thou redest it [,] thou shalt understande in the tyme of my visitacyon'.[116] This returns us to the conception of the heart as a devotional text. The meanings that remain elusive to the reader of the material text are discernible when the penitent examines the book of her heart. Early reformers alter this interpretive model, so that the reader absorbs scripture through the heart (or soul, as these are almost indistinguishable terms at this time), but they make an important distinction between the heart and text as readable matter. The material codex has primacy. One can see this construction in Askew's confession when she claims that the words of the printed text – *written* 'verytees' – are received by and 'closed up in [her] harte'.[117] By contrast, Parr's construction envisions the laws of God as a record of the soul: 'Open my hert lorde, that I maie *beholde* thy lawes.' Parr's 'book of the crucifix' relies upon pre-reform ideas of scriptural sufficiency; the picture of the Crucifixion is contained in the heart where the devotee can 'read' it – a practice very similar to that of *imitatio.* Certainly these ideas do not evaporate after reform (early modern English poets, in particular, made good use of the scripture of the heart – as John Donne's Holy Sonnet 9 or George Herbert's 'Jordon II' attest).[118] In Parr's work we can perceive an early instance of the appropriation of the idea.

One possible source for Parr's exact phrase 'the book of the crucifix' is Bishop John Fisher.[119] Fisher stretches this metaphor into a whole sermon concerning the Passion preached upon the occasion of an (as yet) unidentified Good Friday.[120] His central conceit is that Christ is the scroll – a recasting of Ezekiel's scroll – and that the Crucifixion is a book. From this metaphor, Fisher enlarges the conception to take in the emblems related to the Passion: the intersecting poles are the boards by which the text is opened and spread, Christ's skin is the parchment, the scourge-marks the writing, his five wounds the illuminated capitals, and so on. Affective devotion to the Passion of Christ and its connected symbols was the locus of late medieval spirituality, and Fisher's specific configuration taps into a rich vein of traditional topoi. The idea draws upon an extensive history in the medieval English religious tradition: from the widespread notion that images in general are 'laymen's books', to more specific precedents in devotional writing. It is important to bear in mind that the intended effect of these devotional models was to activate the internal image of Christ inscribed in the heart of the individual devotee.

The middle English Passion complaints known as the Charters of Christ are one such model, in which the charter endowing man with the kingdom of heaven is written on the parchment of Christ's skin with the ink of his blood.[121] Such religious writing – both lyric and prose – which imagines Christ's body as a book predates the Charters by some 200 years: for example, William Herebert's *Ave Maris Stella*,[122] or Richard Rolle's *Meditations on the Passion*.[123] The Crucifixion is treated as an educational aid in these conceits; the reader of Christ's body is instructed in the knowledge necessary for salvation:

> Wo-so wil ouer-rede this book,
> and with gostly eyen ther-on loke,
> to other scole dare he not wende,
> to saue his soule fro the fende.[124]

The image, therefore, is frequently conceived in the pedagogical (as opposed to legalistic) mode; it serves as an instrument for instructing schoolchildren in a number of ABC poems on the Passion.[125]

I am not trying to trace the metaphor in medieval spiritual writing (and my examples are by no means exhaustive). 'Conceits of this kind', as Rosemary Woolf claims, 'were already commonplaces of devotional litera-ture.'[126] Certainly, the metaphor of the crucifix as a book appears with ever more regularity in religious lyrics and sermons through the fifteenth and up to the early part of the sixteenth century (as Fisher's sermon attests).[127] Fisher is therefore more an illustrative example of how the image was used than a confirmed source. His sermon was rightly celebrated, but was not published until around 1578. Parr may well have been acquainted with his phrasing, but she had access to the idea of the crucifix as a readable book of the heart through countless other means (including the *Imitation*). The way that she uses the metaphor in her *Lamentacion* reveals the mixture of old and new faith that grounds her belief; it graphically describes the spiritual response of a late-in-life apostate. More importantly, it demon-strates how emergent notions of internal authority are being understood – and expressed to an English readership.

If we assume that Cranmer was Parr's early teacher, we can expect that her evangelical education would be based on Luther's writings. Of the titles by Luther that Cranmer is known to have owned (one being the collected Latin works), two important books were probably already part of his library at this time: the *Annotationes in aliquot cap. Matthaei* (Wittenberg, 1538); and a copy of the *Preface to the Romans*, in the Latin version of Justus Jonas (Mainz, 1524).[128] Luther's *Preface* was a seminal work for the Protestant understanding of justification by faith alone. Luther cites the Epistle to the Romans as the most instructive book in the Bible for the new faithful:

For as moche as this pistle is the principall and most excellent part of the newe testament and most pure Euangelion ... & also a lyghte & a wayein vnto the hole scripture I thynke it mete that euery Christen man not only knowe it by rote and with oute the boke but also exercise hym selfe therin euermore continually as with the dayly brede of the soule.[129]

Parr does more than learn the book by rote; she adopts it as the model for her work. Luther structures both the religious and formal conception of her devotion: the *Lamentacion*, I will argue, is organised according to Paul's letter as outlined by Luther. But I will further argue that the image of the Crucifixion is treated as an interior devotional mechanism, and displaces Luther's 'theology of the cross' as the central and controlling meditation of the piece.

Cranmer was not above loaning his copies – at least one book by Luther in Henry's library came from Cranmer.[130] Parr also had access to the 1534 vernacular *Newe Testament* in which Tyndale's *Prologe* to Romans closely follows Luther's text (and it is not clear whether she used the Latin or English version).[131] The *Preface* first considers Romans as an ideal model and then proceeds to outline Paul's rhetorical strategies chapter by chapter. Luther's analysis opens:

for as moche as it becometh the precher of Christes glad tydinges first ... to rebuke all thinges & to proue all thinges synne that procede not of the sprit and of faith in Christe & to proue all men synners ... and therwith to abate the pryde of man and to bringe him vnto the knowledge of him selfe and of his miserye and wretchednes that he myght desyre helpe.[132]

Parr's *Lamentacion* begins:

When I considre in the bethinking of myne euill, and wreched former lyfe ... I am partly by the hate I owe to sinne ... partly by the love I owe to all Christians, whome I am contente to edifye, euen with thexample of myne owne shame, forced and constrayned ... to confesse and declare to the world, how ingrate, negligent, unkynde, and stubberne, I have bene to god my Creatour ... beyng suche a miserable, and wreatched sinner.[133]

Parr's introduction is standard for the late medieval period (one need only look at Marguerite de Navarre's *Miroir de l'ame pécheresse* for confirmation[134]), so her phrasing cannot really be very suggestive here. But Parr continues to follow the structure of Romans, exploring its proposals chapter by chapter, throughout the narrative unfolding of her devotion.

The *Lamentacion* is far longer than Luther's consideration of sixteen chapters. But there are distinctive shifts of topic in Parr's devotion, where a new paragraph also signals a change in the logic of the prose. Paragraph breaks are infrequent, and, at least in the early stages of the book, the narrative focus tends to shift at about every second one. According to this breakdown, Parr appears to adopt the arguments of chapters 1–5 chronologically until she reaches the spiritual locus of her work. For example, the second chapter of Paul's letter, according to Luther

rebuketh all those holy people ... [who] lyue well outwardly in the face of the worlde & condempne other[s] gladly as the nature of all ypocrites is to thinke them selues pure in respecte of open synners & yet hate the lawe [of God] inwardly ... These are they which despise the goodnes of God ... accordinge to the hardenes of their hertes.[135]

The section that I have identified as corresponding to chapter 2 in the *Lamentacion* begins in the following way:

And I most presumptuously thinkyng nothyng of Christ crucified, went about to sette foorth myne owne righteousnes, saiyng with the proude Pharisey. Good Lorde I thanke the, I am not like other men. I am none adulterer, nor fornicatour, and so foorth, with such like wordes of vaine-glory, extollyng my selfe, and dispisyng others ... neyther did I considre how beneficial a father I had, who did shew me his charitie and mercy ... But my harte was so stony and hard, that this great benefite was never truly and liuely printed in [it].[136]

I do not expect correspondences like these to be convincing on their own; the language can still be attributed too easily to the conventional rhetorical strategies of religious writing at the time. However, the consistency with which the discursive pattern of the *Lamentacion* matches the form delineated by Luther is unmistakable. Luther states that Paul's objective in chapter 3 is to show 'the right waye vnto rightewesnes' and to expose that way as only 'thorowe fayth in Christ'. It concludes that: '[God's] lawe is holpe & ordered thorowe fayth though that the workes therof with all their boste are brought to noughte & proued not to iustifie.'[137] The related part of Parr's work also reasons that the only way of salvation is faith in Christ, and ends confirming that 'Sainct Paule sayeth, we be iustified by the fayth in Christ, and not by the dedes of the lawe' (Romans 3:28).[138]

The fourth chapter of Romans, in Luther's description, takes up the issue of Christian conduct when works provide no justification ('shall men do no good workes, ye & if faith only iustifieth, what nedeth a man to stody for to do good workes?'[139]). The thrust of his argument is helpfully sectioned off in the *Newe Testament* for emphasis: 'For we are iustified and receaue the sprite for to doo good workes, nether were it otherwyse possible to do good workes excepte we had first the sprite.'[140] In the fourth section of the *Lamentacion*, Parr also claims that good works follow from the right faith: 'This dignitie of fayth is no derogacion to good woorkes, for out of this fayth springeth al good workes.'[141] Of course, this idiom is common in early Reformation writing; however, this specific idea concerning 'good workes' is repeated only two other times in the text (and the phrase itself is repeated only once).[142]

None of these examples clinches the case; but I do think that a persuasive instance occurs in chapter 6 (or what I have identified as 6 in my conception). At this point, Paul's letter (according to Luther) addresses the 'principall worke of fayth the batayll of the sprite agaynst the flesshe'.[143] Even after justification, sin and lust still reside in the impulses of our body: 'as ... Adam made vs heyres of synne thorowe ... bodely generacion'.[144] But we are redeemed so long as our faith stands in opposition to our nature: 'yes there is synne remayninge in vs but it is not rekened because of fayth and of the sprite which fighte agaynst it'.[145] The corresponding section in the *Lamentacion* is preoccupied with the same issues. But it is Parr's phrasing that draws my attention here. Her words of comfort concerning faith's power over original sin sound remarkably like Luther: 'And although the dregges of Adam, do remaine, that is our concupiscences, whiche in dede be synnes: neuerthelesse they be not imputed for sinnes, if we be truly planted in Christ.'[146] (Concupiscence frequently takes the name 'old Adam' in Luther's text.) In this example, Parr not only duplicates Luther's assertion, but mimics his (albeit familiar) analogy. The *Lamentacion* both copies the argumentative form ratified by Luther, and (in limited instances) imitates Luther's language at the local level. This does seem to me sufficient evidence to suppose that Parr employed the rhetorical scheme summarised in the *Preface* in drafting her own chronicle of spiritual conversion.

But Parr's account is personalised. As is clear from the quotations, she cites herself as the example of a fallen Christian. She writes her devotion as an experience of her own religious life. After chapter 5, Parr reaches the meditative focus of her work (before resuming sequence with the rest of the chapters). This is when she uses the metaphor of the 'book of the crucifix'. In order to explain why this happens, I have to return again to Luther. For the first half of the chapter description in the *Preface*, Luther builds an argument for the need for predestination (the *Lamentacion* also works up to this point). He then digresses to plot the points of the argument, which he condenses in this way:

> But folowe thou the order of this pistle & noosell thy selfe with Christ & lerne to vnderstonde what the lawe and the gospell meane and the office of both two that thou mayst ... knowe thy selfe & how that thou hast of thy selfe no strength but to synne ... And then se thou fyghte agaynst synne & the flesshe ... After that when thou arte come to the viii chapter and arte vnder the crosse and sufferinge of tribulacion the necessite of predestinacion will waxe swete & thou shalt well fele howe precyouse a thing it is. For excepte thou haue borne the crosse of aduersite and temptacion and hast felte they selfe brought vnto the very brymme of desperacion ye and vnto hell gates thou canst neuer medle with the sentence of predestinacion without ... secret wrath and grudginge inwardly agaynst God.[147]

Luther makes clear that in order to gain theological knowledge, and to come to an awareness of Christ, one need only search the cogent structure set down by Paul in the Romans.[148] In her *Lamentacion*, Parr first proves all men sinners, proves that the only way to righteousness is through Christ and not through works, and then takes up the weakness of the flesh. When she has brought herself to the 'brymme of desperacion', she contemplates the cross.

Meditation on the Crucifixion is the activity that reconciles the Christian to predestination. As man's sinful nature makes it impossible for him to see rightly, he must rely upon the tolerance of a merciful God. Luther regards true knowledge of God as unattainable by reason. God must appear to us in a way that confounds our rational expectations – to surprise us into understanding him. For Luther, God's righteousness is revealed in the paradox of the Crucifixion. The glory of God is shown to us through the humiliation of Christ. Our salvation is revealed through the apparent triumph of evil in Christ's death. God is revealed through his hiddenness – a revelation that is visible to faith alone. This conception has come to be known as Luther's 'theology of the cross' (which formed the core of his Heidelberg Disputation).[149] When Parr, however, tries to access Luther's theology at the centre of her own work, she uses a metaphor in the model of Fisher to evoke the scene at Calvary.

The 'book of the crucifix' is marshalled in the *Lamentacion* to move the reader beyond the 'dead, humain, historical faith, and knowlage' which is acquired through 'scholastical bokes'.[150] I am not suggesting that Parr opposes Bible reading (the structure of her own thesis would refute this); but she clearly sees academic knowledge – the doctrines of men – as an obstruction to faith. She therefore argues that contemplation of the crucifix yields a greater understanding to those who muse upon it and marvel at it than is attainable through any ordinary book. But in arguing this, she emphasises the internal book of the heart upon which the Gospel is inscribed. The soul 'is appoynted for the uery tabernacle' of God where the Christian may retreat and study the secrets of the Crucifixion.[151] What is crucial to my discussion is that she uses the image of the Crucifixion as a book in a way that is very similar to Fisher's conception ('This booke may suffice for the studie of a true christian man, all the dayes of his life. In this boke he may finde all things that be necessarie to the health of his soule'[152]).

'Therefore inwardelye to beholde Christe crucified vpon the crosse', Parr writes, 'is the best and godlyest meditacion that can be ... better then all the bokes of the worlde.'[153] The inward apprehension of Christ is necessary to bring the reader to an awareness of his/her own sinfulness. In this way, it operates in the text according to Luther's directives: so that the Christian 'shal well fele howe precyouse a thinge [predestination] is'. But the manner of apprehension that Parr employs runs the risk of fallible translation. Like Fisher, she privileges the image of the heart to any other study: 'Then this crucifix is the boke, wherin god hath included all thynges, and hath moste compendiouslye written therin, altruthe, profitable and necessarye for our salvacion.'[154] Every book, even the Bible, is subverted to the value of the image. An awareness of our own sinful state, and a true understanding of God's mercy, is achieved through a meditative exercise reminiscent of Catholic practice. Parr presses all the points of Lutheran paradox in her consideration of the metaphor. But her emphasis here is on a mode of access that relies upon the heart, and what God has written there, not upon the scriptural text. Thus the metaphor of the 'book of the crucifix' looks simultaneously in the direction of antecedent and emergent forms of religious thought. It is the metaphor in context – inflected by the material around it – which alters its meaning.

Of course the reformers retained the reciprocity between heart and book; the *New England primer* declares that 'My *Book* and *Heart* / Shall never part.'[155] But the distinction between the heart and book (once the tenets of Protestantism are codified) represents a shift. In answer to how 'the Word [is] to be Read . . . that it may become effectual to Salvation?' the *Primer* outlines the following procedure: 'we must tend [to the Word] with diligence, Preparation & Prayer, receive it with Faith & Love, lay it up in our Hearts, & practice it in our Lives'.[156] For Parr, the Book *is* the heart: the Gospel, which is Christ's Crucifixion, 'is inscribed in the book . . . of the natural man, which is his soul'. It is there that the news of our salvation may be witnessed. This apprehension of the soul has primacy over and above the material manifestation of the Word. More important to my discussion is that the emphasis here is upon the image that the heart contains.

Surely, this stress upon the image and not the text produces some inconsistency with Luther's doctrine; but it also usefully exposes the necessary slippage in a converted faith. Fisher's trope is invoked by Parr to discourage the busyness of scholastics, not to deter Bible reading in the laity. But she is, in any case, describing a 'layman's book'. She uses the emotive quality of an image to describe the organising conceit of her faith (visual aids had been the habit of her devotional life until her late twenties). The *Lamentacion* is marked by the transition in faith that was occurring at the time – both within and outside of its author. 'I . . . neuer knew myne own miseries and wretchednes so wel by booke, admonicion, or lernyng', Parr writes, 'as I haue done by lookyng into the spiritual boke of the crucifix.'[157] Even though the Crucifixion is described as text, Parr's emphasis is upon reading an image ('lookyng'), not scrutinising the characters of movable type.

In the discourse of the *Lamentacion*, the doctrines of men are unnecessary because the primary location of scriptural truth is within the soul of the individual Christian. God has enclosed in the human heart the secrets of the Crucifixion – and therefore all knowledge necessary to mediate scripture. This hierarchy of scripture is already an accepted idea in the Catholic faith (certainly the reason that Wycliff makes good use of it). That Parr can be said to be following a Wyclifite model of scriptural sufficiency might seem to make any further distinction irrelevant. But Parr (like Wycliff) is searching for an explanation of internal authority that relies upon familiar terms. She appropriates a concept central to Catholic faith in order to make radically different religious ideas accessible. (However heart-centred later Protestant practices became, the usual direction of the Word was from the external to the internal expression.[158]) This helps us to appreciate not only how the process of conversion was effected in England, but also how internal authority was initially understood.

The *Lamentacion* embraces two different devotional conventions, producing an imaginative and sensitive expression of changing faith. Luther's doctrine shapes Parr's belief, but the emotive and iconic mode of Catholic practice is found at its centre. Parr moves beyond the method of scissors and paste (employed so often by Cranmer) in her *Lamentacion*, and instead draws from textual models to invent her own dissertation of spiritual crisis. The result is a formally ingenious work that was responsive to the religious equivocations of its age. Parr presses key spiritual elements of the old religion into the service of the new. Crucial to this operation, however, is her reproduction of the terms by which her own religious identity was undergoing reform. The *Lamentacion* circulated widely, particularly for the genre of a personal account (there were probably about 2,500 copies produced – excluding the *Monvment of matrones*[159]). The *Prayers or meditacions* was a principal work in the early forms of supplication of the Church of England (a conservative estimate puts its circulation at some 19,000 copies by the end of the century[160]). Parr's literary achievements matter most, however, in the context of significant developments in mid-sixteenth-century English spirituality. She mediates many of the crucial questions of an emerging religious identity – and employs her own figure in the operation. She gives the English congregation the words of private prayer, conceived in terms of the heart-centred practices of familiar devotional mechanisms. She provides a blueprint for the difficult process of self-examination that leads the Christian to religious conversion. But in her excavation of an inner world, Parr takes herself as the first example. As Questier has observed, the arguments for conversion that were ultimately persuasive did not emanate from the polemical books of theology; instead, the Protestant cause found its most effective expression in personal testament.[161] Parr constructs both of her devotional texts within this privatised framework. In doing this, she provides – and becomes – a model for religious change.

CHAPTER 3

'[A] pen to paynt': Mary Sidney Herbert and the problems of a Protestant poetics

In a theological system which drove such a wedge between grace and (fallen) nature, and thus undermined the place of secondary causes in the economy of salvation, it was difficult to establish a cogent reason for setting ... great store by the pursuit of eloquence.

Richard Rex, *A Reformation rhetoric*

Poesie is a study fit for [women's] purpose; being a wonton, ammusing, subtill, disguised, and pratling Arte; all in delight, all in shew, like to themselves.

Michel de Montaigne, 'Of three commerces or societies'

The writing of women exerted formative pressure upon not simply what it meant to be an English Protestant, but also what it meant to be an English Protestant poet. This study has thus far assessed how the figure of the religious female lent authority to the writing of women, and how, in turn, women used this authority in the arena of religious polemics. This is not to say that women were not participants in what we regard (in post-Romantic terms) as literary production. On the contrary, women were crucial agents in the development of a religious literary tradition in England. The influence of martyr narratives and private prayer upon later literary language has been widely researched and described.[1] It is impossible to trace that influence to a single work – it is only possible to demonstrate the prominent place of certain women's works within these generic conventions. But one woman writer in particular was instrumental at the moment when religious debates concerning figurative language drove the definition of the literary category itself.

Our modern conception of the literary history of the early modern period is based upon a set of anachronistic assumptions that have especially costly consequences for the writing of women.[2] Indeed, our contemporary classification of literature as works of fiction leaves out the most common mode of expression in the sixteenth century – the religious mode. Men's and women's writing was overwhelmingly preoccupied with the subject of religion, and most of the published work of women was in the religious vein.[3] Hence, feminist criticism focused on mechanisms of social repression in the sixteenth century rather than the religious forms of women's expression has incorrectly located the problem of women's cultural exclusion in the early modern period rather than in our own.[4] It seems useful, then, to explore the emergence of the modern literary category (rooted in the sixteenth century even if it did not achieve its full flowering until the eighteenth), and particularly enlightening to address the significant role of a particular woman, Mary Sidney Herbert, in the development of our present construction of literature.

This construction finds virtually its first voice in Philip Sidney's *A defence of poetry* (published posthumously in 1595). As the tenets of Protestant culture became codified, competing notions of what it meant to be an English Protestant interacted with emergent notions of what properly constituted the literary. A defence needed to be mounted precisely because works of the imagination were suspect in the context of a Calvinist-inflected Protestant society. But it was not, ultimately, Sidney who intervened in the cultural controversy; it was Mary Sidney Herbert. The theoretical project of the *Defence* can most crucially be tested not in Sidney's secular verse, but in the Psalter that he began and that his sister, the Countess of Pembroke, completed and revised in the years following his death. A complete manuscript of the Sidney–Pembroke Psalter was circulated at least one year prior to the initial printing of Sidney's treatise (for which Herbert was also responsible). The internal agreement of the two works – as well as their synchronised public release – was not accidental. The publication of both projects was an orchestrated effort on the part of the Countess of Pembroke to situate lyric poetry within a Protestant cultural context.[5] The Sidney–Pembroke Psalter was largely her literary creation, and it was clearly designed to initiate a rethinking of poetry's place in devotion. It was, in fact, the technical demonstration of Sidney's *Defence*.

REFORMING HERMENEUTICS

Since Israel Baroway's influential essay on 'The Bible as poetry in the English Renaissance', a number of critics have considered both Sidney's *Defence* and the Sidney–Pembroke Psalter in relation to the antipoetic debates of early Protestantism.[6] I revisit this enquiry because no analysis, it seems to me, has dealt quite adequately with the failure of both projects to resolve the controversy, let alone with the implications of this failure. It is the question of whether or not a Protestant poetics is even possible – whether the terms and conditions of devotional lyric are inherently at odds with the tenets of English Protestantism – that I want to reconsider. Barbara Lewalski positions the Sidney–Pembroke Psalter as a 'secure bridge to the magnificent original seventeenth-century religious lyric in the biblical and psalmic mode'.[7] But her situation of the Psalter in English culture concentrates on artistic conventions – the precursors to devotional lyric.[8] I address the permit and purview of poetic forms in relation to devotion. For the bridge joins traditions that are radically at odds with each other, and the irresolvable nature of the conflict is one of the distinctive features of the Psalter translation.

To establish a framework in which to understand the Sidney–Pembroke Psalter, we need to begin with the history of Reformation hermeneutics in England, and then move to consider mainstream Protestant thought as it bears upon rhetoric. The theologians of the early Reformation were not kind to poetry. In 1530, William Tyndale published *An answer to Sir Thomas More's Dialogue* (concerning heresies). More casts his polemic in a fictional mode: the conversation of the *Dialogue* takes place in More's home, its family setting reinforced with references to members of his household. Literary effects of this kind allowed More to translate wider social issues into a local and particular context.[9] But it was precisely the literary component of More's arguments that so outraged reformers.[10] For his part, Tyndale does not relieve the tedium of his theological disputation with any kind of rhetorical invention. The difference is wholly intentional on Tyndale's part. For Tyndale, the fabrications of More's work go to the heart of their disagreement: he sees fiction as emblematic of everything wrong with both More and the Church he is defending. Tyndale understands his chosen career of biblical translation and interpretation as one of purging the text of the taints of human authorship. He consistently accuses the Roman Catholic Church of corrupting not only the Bible, but also the writings of Church Fathers, in order to advance its own doctrine above the primacy of scripture.[11] So Tyndale frequently calls More a 'poet' and vilifies Catholic theology as the substitution of 'false imagination' and 'deceitful poetry' for scripture: the term 'poet' becomes a slur.[12]

The religion of Protestants was suspicious of the corruptive powers of language and certain of the debased status of the human imagination. In c. 1536, Thomas Swynnerton wrote the first English rhetoric of the Reformation. His treatise, dedicated to Cromwell, was entitled *The tropes and figures of scripture*; in it, he outlines the forms and uses of figurative language for the purpose of understanding scripture. He describes first the occasions when the literal sense in scripture is to be adhered to (except when to do so entails absurdity, blasphemy, heresy, or immorality) and when it is not. He then goes on to detail every form of rhetorical trope. Swynnerton's exercise shows the comprehensive approach that early Protestant hermeneutics took towards policing language. It is 'a matter desyred of so muche necessitie', Swynnerton claims, 'that withoute it can not easely be avoyded the daunger of heresy'.[13] But the exposition mostly serves us as a record of the cultural anxiety that took hold in England with the translation of a vernacular Bible and the advent of Protestantism.

Swynnerton's treatise is specifically concerned with the application of rhetoric to scriptural interpretation, but he was not alone. There were five rhetorics (besides Swynnerton's) produced by the mid-seventeenth century that were devoted largely or solely to the Bible: Dudley Fenner's (1584); John Barton's (1634); Thomas Hall's (1654); John Smith's (1656); and Bishop John Prideaux's (1659).[14] Textbooks using examples of the figures of grammar and rhetoric in scripture multiply throughout the sixteenth century and into the seventeenth.[15] Leonard Cox (1532), Richard Sherry (1550, 1555), and Henry Peacham (1577) all analyse biblical style in the same way that they interrogate classical models.[16] Both Sherry and Peacham cite the 'better vnderstanding of the holy Scriptures' as a primary objective of their work.[17]

The attitude of the early English reformers concerning rhetoric – that tropes and figures distorted the true meaning of scripture (and that they had been used by the Catholic Church to do so) – is carried over into a general cultural suspicion towards figurative language. Metaphor was open to misinterpretation (and manipulation), and the rhetoric handbooks that I have noted sought, if not to close down meanings, at least to contain them. Sherry writes that a knowledge of rhetoric is necessary 'in the readinge of holye scripture, where if you be ignoraunte in the fyguratiue speches and Tropes, you are lyke in manye great doubtes to make but a slender solucion: as ryght wyll ... testefy[s] ... the noble doctor saint Augustine'.[18] Augustine is frequently invoked as the patristic authority in discussions of rhetoric in early modern England. Indeed, Swynnerton claims the tenets of Augustine's *De doctrina christiana* as the model for his particular project:

[B]y certayne rules, of the moost famous doctor, S. Augustyne, is declared, when the literall sense of any Scripture ought to be embraced, and when to be refused, When the lettre kylleth (as they saye) and when it kylleth not. These rules of the blessed doctor, well and groundely vewed, neuer fayle ...

AFTER THESE RULES of Augustyne, ensueth immediately the Definicion of a Trope with the descripcion of his menbres, required of necessitie to thunder-standynge of Goddes worde . . .

LASTE OF ALL, It is made playne, howe to behave oure selfes, in placies of Scripture importynge great clerenesse, but in dede beinge darke, how to behave oure selfes in placies semynge to dissent.[19]

But what is far more telling than Swynnerton's adoption of Augustine is the extent to which he misinterprets him.

Augustine acknowledges the opaque nature of scripture and develops a theory based upon two levels of scriptural meaning – the literal and the figurative. He sees two ways in which the text operates on the figurative level: he speaks of 'figures of speech' and 'figures of things'. By 'figures of speech' he refers to rhetorical devices; by 'figures of things' he means something that prefigures or is emblematic of something else. He per-ceives two significant dangers in scriptural interpretation: taking a figu-rative expression as a proper one; and mistaking a proper expression for a figurative.[20] Both accidents corrupt the sense of scripture – but clearly, the ambiguities of scriptural metaphor are a particular con-cern, and require the most deliberate explication.[21] Roland Teske has observed, however, the (apparent) conflict between the minimalist theory of Augustine's commentary on Genesis (*De Genesi contra Manichaeos*) and the maximising theory posited in *De doctrina christiana*.[22] The minimalist theory asserts that scripture must be interpreted literally except when the literal sense is either absurd or blasphemous; this relies on what Teske has dubbed the 'absurdity criterion'. But Augustine's later work adopts a more expansive criterion of figurative language in scripture. *De doctrina christiana* classifies that which 'cannot be related either to good morals or to the true faith . . . as figurative'.[23] This is because the essential message of scripture is contained in the creed and the commandments. But since nothing in scripture is superfluous, that which does not directly relate to this core of scripture must be interpreted for a Christian readership figuratively.[24] This maximises the bulk of scripture that operates on the figurative level. Indeed, figurative interpretation, by these lights, is not called for when logic will not serve, but rather when the subject of the text demands it.

My concern is not with Augustine, but with how (and why) Protestant programmes of scriptural interpretation depart from him. In spite of Swynnerton's confidence in his understanding of Augustine's method, the mode of scriptural interpretation that he outlines is, in fact, radically different. While Swynnerton's criteria for scriptural analysis would have been widely accepted within scholastic circles, his is a 'highly modern, and at this time essentially Protestant', standard.[25] In his dedication to Cromwell, Swynnerton mounts the usual argument of the reformers against the Catholic side:

> When it lyketh them, the lettre kylleth, the Scripture is figurate, it includeth a Trope, thoughe it be neuer so playne and simple, neuer so clere withoute trope. When it lyketh them, then the lettre kylleth not, then the Scripture is not figurate, then there is no Trope, all thoughe the lettre be infarced with tropes, no lesse then the firmament with sterres.[26]

Protestant reformers charged their Catholic opponents with interpreting God's word according to their convenience (although, as I have noted in chapter 1, both sides could be painted with the same brush). Accordingly, many reformers insisted that only the literal sense of scripture would serve as proof in doctrinal disputes. Swynnerton adopts this guideline:

> [I]n any article of the faithe, it is and must be only the literall sense, that proveth. I call it the literall sense, when euery worde retayneth his owne naturall significacion, gyven hym by the firste authours of that toungue . . . As touching this literall sense, it is also requyred, that there be but one only sense apon one texte, that it be certayne and agreed apon, that it be simple and playne, and voyde of all obscurite.[27]

Swynnerton's treatise, therefore, leans heavily toward the literal sense in scripture–asserting that literal interpretation must be employed except when to do so violates reason, decorum, or morals. He further asserts that in all places where there is no scriptural figure under scrutiny, 'euery word therein ought to be taken in his owne proper and naturall significacion, yea to alter but one worde in it from his natyfe propertie, who coulde iuge it lesse then sacrilege?'[28] Reformers such as Tyndale would obviously have ratified this method of scriptural interpretation, but it bears little resemblance to the interpretive model that Augustine advances in *De doctrina christiana.*

   How did this body of theological/cultural opinion make itself felt in England at the time of Sidney's composition of the *Defence of poetry?* And what, precisely, was Sidney defending poetry against? It is frequently assumed that Sidney was responding to Stephen Gosson's *The school of abuse* (1579), which Gosson unwisely dedicated to him.[29] (The correspondence between Gosson's charges and Sidney's answer certainly make this seem likely.[30]) It has become something of a critical tradition to characterise Gosson's work as negative and uncompromising – to stigmatise him as 'Puritan'. What is less often acknowledged is the extent to which Gosson's opinions were part of mainstream Protestant thought.

'[T]HE ZODIAC OF HIS OWN WIT'

Although there were a number of attacks on poetry penned (both in England and on the Continent) in the early sixteenth century,[31] the latter part of the century saw an explosion of these criticisms in England: John Northbrooke's *Treatise where in vain plays or interludes are reproved* (1577); Henry Denham's *Second and third blast of retreat from plays* (1580); Philip Stubbes's *Anatomy of abuses* (1583); George Whetstone's *A touchstone for the times* (1584); William Rankins's *A mirror of monsters* (1587); Dudley Fenner's *Treatise of lawfull and unlawfull recreations* (1587); and John Rainolds's *Overthrow of stage plays* (1599) are among the works which took aim at literature.[32] There were also efforts mounted in poetry's defence,[33] but the dissenting opinions far outweighed (on paper at least) those in favour. As Alexandra Walsham points out, Northbrooke's treatise went into a second printing within two years, and Stubbes's *Anatomy of abuses* was not only republished in its first year, but its popularity prompted a sequel. Such demand for these tracts indicates that they 'did not articulate the grievances of an over scrupulous few'.[34]

But the pervasiveness of a particular mode of thought is not easily established through tracts and pamphlet wars: such materials are never impartial. It is instead more revealing to look at the theory of discourse imparted in university lectures. (In other words, rather than test Gosson's opinions, we should examine Gosson's teacher.) John Rainolds was a 'leader of advanced protestant opinion' in late sixteenth-century England, and a ruling force in the intellectual life at Oxford University.[35] As the Greek Reader at Corpus Christi (1572–8), he delivered a series of lectures on Aristotle's *Rhetoric* that established his reputation: 'as Jewel's fame first grew from the rhetoric lecture, which he read with singular applause, and Hooker's from the logic, so Reinolds' from the Greek, in the same house'.[36] The lecture notes survive in Rainolds's copy of the *Rhetoric* (Paris, 1562), currently installed in the Bodleian.[37] These lectures present a careful and critical examination of Aristotle's major positions in the *Rhetoric* – often dissenting, but always evaluating. Rainolds admires Aristotle's theories of how men reason in discourse ('We believe that Aristotle has carefully ordered the subject of eloquence'), but Aristotle's observations are limited, in

Rainolds's mind, by their lack of Christian awareness ('But we ourselves must add to his masterpiece').

> For philosophers have many excellent things, but they are mixed with the lowest dregs. True, but we read profane writings that we may be eloquent, and we meditate on sacred writings that we may go forth good men ... We see that our intellect is corrupted by blindness, and our will by perverseness. Let us seek both wisdom and righteousness from sacred writings.[38]

What Rainolds adds to Aristotle is Christian *ethos*.[39] The particular *ethos* that he applies is Calvinism.

Rainolds's participation in what Russell Fraser has called *The war against poetry* seemingly marks him as a biased source for mid-sixteenth-century opinion concerning rhetoric; however, as Laurence Green has noted: 'the contemporary acclaim for his lectures and the institutional context in which he delivered them indicate a broadly and securely based reception for his views.'[40] More to the point, Sidney's *Defence* is grounded in a neo-Latin academic tradition that Rainolds specifically interrogates. This is one reason that we can profitably analyse Sidney's *Defence* through the lens of Rainolds's Oxford lectures. Rainolds's scholastic instruction allows for a full reckoning of how (and how much) an Italianate humanist tradition (which Sidney's *Defence* draws upon) conflicts with English Protestant thought. I am not suggesting here that the Florentine humanists were not proper Hellenists – or that Rainolds held this position. I am speaking of the specific strands of humanism that Sidney plucks, which quite starkly conflict with Calvinist-inflected English Protestantism.

In *Plays confuted in five actions* (1582), Gosson refers to the university wits who 'beare a sharper smacke of Italian deuises in their heades, then of English religion in their heartes'.[41] Gosson is specifically impugning Thomas Lodge, but Sidney himself is vulnerable to the charge. The elements of Sidney's argument in the *Defence* have been scrupulously researched, and their provenance in Renaissance intellectual thought has been traced to four major sources in particular: Aristotelian theory,[42] Neoplatonic theory,[43] mannerist art theory,[44] and Calvinism.[45] But the Calvinist stem of Sidney's argument is artificially grafted on to its Aristotelian trunk – creating what D. H. Craig has termed 'A hybrid growth'.[46] Which is to say that in spite of his determined effort in the *Defence* to marry his religious beliefs and his humanist training, Sidney fails. The precise ways these philosophical positions come into conflict under Sidney's handling reveal the problems inherent in a Protestant poetics.

'The bulwark of Sidney's defense of poetry', Peter Herman writes, poetry's ability to teach virtue, 'consists of a three-step process that begins with the poet's imagination and ends with the reader.'[47] Sidney maintains that the poet's independent imagination fashions ideal models:

Only the poet, disdaining to be tied to any ... subjection, lifted up with the vigour of his own invention, doth grow in effect another nature, in making things either better than nature bringeth forth, or, quite anew, forms such as never were in nature, as the Heroes, Demigods, Cyclops, Chimeras, Furies, and such like: so as he goeth hand in hand with nature, not enclosed within the narrow warrant of her gifts, but freely ranging only within the zodiac of his own wit.[48]

Next, the poet inscribes these idealised images, 'in such excellency as he had imagined them', without any corruption or misapprehension.[49] Finally, the reader transforms the Idea of the poet into deeds. The problem with Sidney's narrative of the transmission of ideas into action is that Protestant moralists and theologians would have regarded every step of the process he outlines as 'at best dubious and at worst blasphemous'.[50]

In the *Institutes of the Christian religion* Calvin asserts 'that the human soul consists of two faculties, understanding and will'.[51] Sidney's division of 'wit' and 'will' imitates Calvin's distinction. While both agree on the compromised state of human will in a postlapsarian world, their understanding of the range and capacity of the human intellect is vastly different.[52] Calvin allows man a limited ability to understand earthly things, but he denies a place to man in the area of understanding where Sidney claims the most for his poet.[53] The 'erected wit' of man 'maketh us know what perfection is', Sidney maintains; the imagination of the poet figures forth the images of this ideal realm.[54] By contrast, Calvin insists that

[E]ven though something of the understanding and judgment remains [after the Fall] as a residue along with the will, yet we shall not call a mind whole and sound that is both weak and plunged into deep darkness ... Since reason, therefore, by which man distinguishes between good and evil, and by which he understands and judges, is a natural gift, it could not be completely wiped out; but it was partly weakened and partly corrupted, so that its misshapen ruins appear.[55]

Calvin does not concede to the human intellect the power to perceive the perfection of supernatural things, let alone to frame them.[56]

The very point upon which Sidney would erect his thesis – poetry's ability to move and to teach – puts him in conflict with mainstream Protestant thought. Sidney conceives of the effect of poetry as more than the mere rousing of emotions – rather, its virtue lies in its ability to impel the will to specific action. In other words, he conceives of poetry as a form of persuasion. There is nothing unusual about the position that poetry is a form of rhetoric. But in examining a passage in Aristotle concerning the mechanics of persuasion, Rainolds considers the effect of man's compromised reason upon the transmission of ideas:

> We can be taught by the authority of the ancients what we ought to have learned from our own experience: not only are the arts difficult, but the wits we use to perceive and study the arts are feeble. It needs to be said, in all fairness, that striving for the heights is a mark of ... considerable good fortune; learning many things is very noble; understanding everything, superhuman; and not to know something, unavoidable for a man confined as he is in his body, as if in a jail.[57]

Sidney perceives an entirely different 'scope' for poetry, which is 'to know, and by knowledge to lift up the mind from the dungeon of [man's] body to the enjoying [of] his own divine essence'.[58] While Rainolds agrees with Aristotle – and, by extension, Sidney – that there is a place for the passions in the motivation of virtue, he does not recognise poetry as the vehicle for such stimulation: 'ecclesiastical eloquence is proper when it impels something which ought to be done; that not only does it teach in order to instruct, and delight in order to hold listeners, but it also bends the wills of the listeners in order to vanquish them'.[59] Sidney's construction, then, positions the poet in the place of the preacher.

This is a deliberate manoeuvre. Early in his treatise, Sidney aligns – but does not equate – the Elizabethan poet with the Roman *vates* (due to the 'heart-ravishing knowledge' that both impart) precisely because he is attempting to establish a place for poetics within Protestant devotion.[60] But in raising the human imagination above the faculties of reason, he steps beyond what Protestant theological (and philosophical) opinion will allow. Rainolds patently rejects poetry, on these grounds, as part of the field that he is teaching:

> Whereas rhetoric was correctly defined as the faculty of seeing what may be suitable for producing belief in any subject whatsoever; and since many things produce belief besides just signs and probabilities; moreover, since those things which produce belief do so by proofs, and since the proofs of rhetoricians are called enthymemes; it would necessarily follow, certainly from the authority of Aristotle himself, that by nature the enthymeme embraces not only signs and probabilities, but any kind of material, all sorts of arguments, whether they be probable or necessary. I ... have no desire to disagree ... with Aristotle ... But truly, in this respect the custom of Plato makes me bolder to put truth before all

authorities. Plato used to protect the sacred truth against the *vates* (who get their name from their care for the gods); he taught that falsehoods should be rooted out from among the learned and that, despite the opposition of the epic poets, among wise men the best things must be proven.[61]

Reason was the means 'by which man distinguishe[d] between good and evil' – the seat of his judgment and the natural gift which remained 'as a residue' even after the Fall: '[I]n man's perverted and degenerate nature some sparks still gleam. These show him to be a rational being, differing from brute beasts, because he is endowed with understanding.'[62] Reason is therefore privileged among theologians as the instrument of humanity's limited comprehension – the means by which human knowledge is acquired.[63] Indeed, the concomitant demonisation of the imagination by the early reformers established something of a tradition. We have already seen how Tyndale handled the imagination, and Elizabethan clerics clearly held the faculty in similar esteem. William Perkins, for example, declares categorically in his *Treatise of mans imaginations*, that 'The imagination and conceite of euery man is naturally euill.'[64] Divines of the previous generation, such as Edward Dering and William Alley, would have supported this assertion.[65]

But while Protestant theologians might have found Sidney's claims for the status of the imagination suspect, they would have deemed his assertions regarding its nature and function sacrilege. 'Neither let it be deemed too saucy a comparison', Sidney writes,

to balance the highest point of man's wit [the imagination] with the efficacy of nature; but rather give right honour to the heavenly Maker of that maker, who having made man to His own likeness, set him beyond and over all the works of that second nature: which in nothing he showeth so much as in poetry, when with the force of a divine breath he bringeth things forth surpassing her doings.[66]

Protestant doctrine minimised the sufficiency of natural human powers, and insisted that 'the knowledge of all that is excellent in human life is . . . to be communicated to us through the Spirit of God'.[67] The notion that poetry was a product of divine inspiration was common in classical literature, but it was something that few sixteenth-century Englishmen were willing to claim for themselves (or their contemporaries).[68] Andrew Weiner makes the case that this nevertheless is precisely the paradigm that Sidney follows: 'That "the Poet hath that *Idea*" is manifest proof that he sees "with the eyes of the minde, onely cleered by fayth" . . . that he can bring them forth "with the force of a diuine breath" argues that he, like

David, merely follows the promptings of the Holy Spirit.'[69] With his evocation of the *vates* and of David as a divine poet, it does appear as though this is what Sidney is advocating – but it is not. In fact, Sidney explicitly states that the ancient philosophers 'attributeth unto poesy *more than myself do*, namely, to be *a very inspiring of a divine force*, far above man's wit'.[70] Weiner acknowledges that the 'infected will' of man would interfere with divine inspiration.[71] But Sidney's 'divine breath' is not the intervention of the Holy Spirit. Rather, Sidney is asserting a 'divine essence' in man that is both the source of the poet's insight, and the spirit to which the didactic powers of the imagination appeal. This argument is unacceptable in the strict interpretation of Protestant doctrine. Calvin writes that '[a]s it was the spiritual life of Adam to remain united and bound to his Maker, so estrangement from him was the death of his soul'; thereafter, 'the heavenly image was obliterated in him'.[72] Protestant theology simply does not admit the 'divine breath' that is the source of Sidney's model of inspiration – the corrupted nature of man's imagination guarantees that what proceeds from it must also be corrupt.[73]

The image of God is restored in us, according to Calvin, only through the grace of God: 'Therefore it remains that men seek elsewhere for that which they shall never be able to find within themselves.'[74] The new nature to which Calvin refers is the transformation wrought by the Holy Spirit, not the 'second nature' that Sidney's poet summons by his 'own invention'.[75] Further, Sidney's nature of the mind is communicated to the reader in ways that are troubling to Protestant theology. The knowledge to which the poet has access elevates the reader 'to the enjoying his own divine essence'. This declaration of the devotional power of poetry seems to assume that the 'speaking picture' of lyrical language can inspire the mind of the reader to a form of grace – that poetry can move man to understand himself in relation to an imminent God. But Protestant doctrine denied that such a relationship was possible under the terms and conditions that Sidney suggests: 'words have no power to imbue men's minds with divine matters, unless the Lord through his Spirit gives understanding'.[76] Man cannot apprehend his relationship to God through rational means; this salvific knowledge was only possible through the divine inspiration of the Holy Spirit. The speaker of Du Bartas's *The divine weeks*, as Craig observes, resembles Sidney's visionary poet in that he is able to glimpse perfection in the world beyond, but 'unlike Sidney, du Bartas requires of his prophet that he deny his own human powers and rely entirely on faith and prayer'.[77] Sidney is in the untenable position of trying to pose an argument that would apply to the composition of both secular and sacred verse. (While his Psalter translation serves as a demonstration of how lyric poetry can be put to theological use, his objective in the *Defence* is an ethical recuperation of the bulk of literature.[78]) He is therefore unable to invoke the 'holy fyre' that inspires Du Bartas's divine poetry.[79] Sidney denies his poet this particular muse because it would be arrogant to claim it – and impossible to claim it for all (secular) poets.[80] But in so doing, he claims too much for the poet's wit, and he problematises, in Protestant terms, the poet's Idea both in its nature and its instruction.

'Philosophers grant far more than they ought to human nature', Rainolds writes, 'because they do not know it is depraved.'[81] Sidney also awards too much to human capacity because he does not effectively delineate, as Craig points out, the crucial difference between classical and Christian conditions 'for the beatific vision'.[82] This, I would argue, is less the fault of Sidney than the effect of Protestantism. The Protestant context in which Sidney was contained did not allow scope for his argument; the best that he could do was to mount his *Defence of poetry* by interlacing classical models and English Calvinism. These traditions do not always fit easily together – as Rainolds's careful revision of Aristotelian theory reveals – and Sidney's thesis is an excellent example of the philosophical ruptures that can occur when one attempts to mesh them.

'SCHOLEMENNES CONTROUERSIES'

Not every writer in England – male or female – was Calvinist. But as Lori Anne Ferrell succinctly puts it:

After decades of revisionism, Calvinism's success [in England] no longer goes without saying. Current wisdom on the sixteenth century holds that England's reformations did not occur because of the decline of late medieval Catholicism, and social historians keep teaching us the humbling lesson that the great majority of English people were neither theological adepts nor daring cultural ideologues, but semi-pelagians and pragmatists. These caveats notwithstanding, most historians agree that after 1580 a malingering late medieval society saturated in dramatic and pictorial religious representation was radically reconstructed, England becoming – as even Christopher Haigh concedes – a Protestant country. What accounts for this about-face? Simple: it took Calvinism to Protestantize England.[83]

Or, as she continues, 'it took Calvin*ists*'.[84] These reforming energies grabbed particular hold at the university level. Rainolds became a 'spokesman

for a younger generation of divines ... who had not assumed the unwel-
come and uncompromising burdens of episcopacy under Elizabeth,
and who were altogether more radical than the passing generation'.[85]
But it is important to remember that Rainolds was himself a moderate.
Indeed, as Peter Lake has asserted: 'Claimed as [one of] their own
by both presbyterians and conformists, [Rainolds] undeniably stood
at the centre of the spectrum of contemporary religious opinion.'[86] (If
Rainolds produced a Gosson, he also created a Hooker.) Further, the
rhetorical training at Oxford, with its emphasis on Aristotle, was far less
radical than the education offered at Cambridge – with the introduction
of Ramism – in the late 1570s and early 1580s. It is worth beginning with
Rainolds precisely because his brand of Calvinist-inflected Aristotelianism
represents the moderate form of instruction that young men could receive
at university. It is also worth starting here because numerous critics, following arguments put forward by Lewalski, have traced one route for the
licence of religious lyric poetry through sanctions of eloquence in preaching.[87] But Rainold's denial of poetry as part of rhetorical training makes
the point: he allows 'ecclesiastical eloquence' for the purpose of persuasion; but following Aristotelian divisions, lyric poetry – which expresses
matters more possible than probable – is flatly rejected.[88] As J. P. Thorne
observes, it is 'the Aristotelian theory of poetry – that of idealistic distortion – that Sidney, alone in the England of his time, was trying to put
forward'.[89]

Sidney is unusual in his eclectic use of both Aristotle and Plato; this,
however, produces an obvious conflict, as Plato cited such distortions – of
both the real and ideal world – as the basis for banishing poets. Sidney's
reason for borrowing Platonic terms is to respond to others' conflation of
the rationale for Plato's censure of poets with Protestant admonitions. But
if one hears echoes of Christian Platonic thought in the *Defence*, they are
decidedly Sidneian echoes. For example, the Idea of the poet seems to
reflect the concept of universal principles that is central to Christian
Platonism: '[T]he skill of each artificer standeth in that *idea* or fore-conceit
of the work, and not in the work itself. And that the poet hath that *idea* is
manifest, by delivering them forth in such excellency as he had imagined
them.'[90] In its implication of a divine order that the logic of the author
intuitively captures, Sidney's assertion sounds vaguely Platonic; that is,
until we acknowledge the role the imagination is being asked to play. The
universal idea is at large in nature. Natural logic is the mechanism that
apprehends it – not the imagination, which according to Sidney's articulation, is 'not enclosed within the narrow warrant of [nature's] gifts'.[91]

Sidney's argument, that poets are superior to philosophers, is premised upon the capacity of the imagination to improve nature: 'Her world is brazen, the poets only deliver a golden.'[92] The purpose of Sidney's treatise is to advocate an ethical role for the imagination in the context of a Protestant culture that increasingly understands reason as the sole source of man's moral activity. That he must reformulate classical philosophy (not to mention Protestant theology) indicates the extent of the breach he is opening.

The most explicit expression of this cultural emphasis upon reason – and the attendant need to order discourse – is the rise of Ramism at Cambridge. Ramist logic is grounded in Christian Platonism, as is evident in its most fundamental premise: 'If the art of logic is to be conceived as an imitation of nature, the rules of logic and such notions as universal concepts must be embedded in nature herself and are not merely artificial constructions of the human intellect, invented in order to facilitate discourse.'[93] Universal concepts are accessed intuitively, and their accurate description forms the basis of the Ramist system. Ramus attacks Aristotle on the ground of his divisions. For Ramus, 'the operation of the intellect is of one character' (as opposed to Aristotle, who identifies particular operations with their attendant forms of expression).[94] All forms of discourse are treated in the same manner, and the only thing that distinguishes poetry from other forms is its versification. Of course, this means that poetry can be treated with the same order of logic that governs any other rhetorical form. Given the cultural environment in England, it is not surprising that certain advocates of poetry, satellites of Sidney, seize upon Ramism as the method to defend it.[95]

Sidney is himself caught up in the movement – although his composition of the *Defence* predates his acquaintance with Ramist philosophy. William Temple presented a copy of his 1584 Latin edition of Ramus's *Dialecticae libri duo* to Sidney, and Sidney responded enthusiastically, appointing Temple his personal secretary.[96] For Sidney, a system that could logically dispose of poetry held obvious appeal. His own *Defence*, however, fundamentally conflicted with Ramism – at least insofar as it was interpreted in England – as Temple's response to his treatise confirms.[97] Sidney supplied Temple (a leading Ramist in England at the time) with a manuscript copy of the *Defence* precisely so that Temple could evaluate its arguments.[98] Temple counters Sidney at almost every crucial point. Temple's analysis reveals an essential difference between the two men concerning the origins and objectives of lyric poetry. For Temple, the form of the argument is irrelevant; however, what is important is the conceptualisation of the subject.[99] Sidney claims that the poet can apprehend universals, and it is this (Platonic) conception that prevents his fictions from being 'wholly imaginative'.[100] Temple does not accept this account of apprehension:

> For it can be objected that a work of nature exists in fact, while the work of the poet exists only in the image of a thought ... You refute this objection when you identify the subject in which the artist's preeminence and worth inhere. They inhere (you say) in the idea of the work, and not the work itself. But how would you show that this delivering forth of an idea is not fictional in every part?[101]

For Temple, the relationship between image and Idea cannot be assumed: 'Only if Ideas have been derived by the proper precepts of rational thought – the rules of dialectic – can one be assured of their truth.'[102] Temple's meaning becomes clearer when he transposes 'fiction' for Sidney's 'imitation':

> *Poetry is an art* of imitation, or of fiction-making (*fictio*), with the end of teaching and delighting.
> This is the definition ... that holds the whole controversy, and on which ... this treatise *On Poetry* that you teach almost entirely stands ... You want the essential nature of poetry to be understood as a certain kind of fiction-making. But can it be that such a making is anything but the invention of something that has never existed?[103]

For Temple, 'invention' simply means argument. He is not disparaging poetic creation, but simply situating poetry in terms of logical argument and arrangement. He goes on to claim that 'feigning causes, effects, subjects, adjuncts and all the other arguments, is nothing other than inventing causes, effects, subjects, adjuncts.'[104] The process by which a fiction is described rests upon the same order of language and categories of thought that make up dialectic. Poetry therefore achieves sense through logical disposition.[105] Temple grants that there are such things as true fictions – just as there are true universals – but identical processes of rational thought must attain these. His substitution of 'fiction-making' for 'imitation' exposes the problem that Sidney's diction elides: 'To define poetry as a "speaking picture" implies the existence of objects it can be a picture of, and if that implication is allowed, one can easily underestimate or even overlook the questions of how one conceives of these objects in the first place.'[106]

If Temple is troubled by the way Sidney gets from Ideas to images, he simply cannot accept Sidney's arguments concerning poetry's didactic appeal. Sidney quotes Aristotle when he claims that the purpose of poetry is to teach and delight.[107] Temple responds that this fails to describe the essence of poetry: teaching is the end of logic, and poetry teaches insofar as it is logical; delight proceeds from many causes (particularly logical arguments) – too many to be unique to poetry.[108] But when Sidney declares 'that moving is of a higher degree than teaching',[109] Temple contradicts him outright:

> Certainly you will never be taught just by moving; yet that would be the case if moving were the cause of teaching. We are only taught by that which brings about some sort of knowledge in the mind; yet this does not happen by any 'moving', but only by the force and illumination of an argument, ordered through rules of judgement.[110]

Temple is doing more than simply subordinating the emotions as the effect of teaching. He is also highlighting the subordinate position of the affections in the instruction of virtue. As John Webster observes:

> Sidney's aesthetic for Temple simply does not place enough importance on the conceptual problems of understanding ... [he] is willing to grant poetry a power to move us to action, but his concern is in what precedes moving. Thus he keeps reminding Sidney of problems of knowing, learning and inventing, and through these 'logical' issues he repeatedly suggests his sense that the formulation of an aesthetic must begin not with the will, but with the understanding.[111]

In other words, while Temple is not preoccupied with theological issues *per se*, his objections finally focus on the same concerns that exercised Sidney's original opponents.[112]

The natural method of Ramus moved from the general to the particular; but there was another approach, the prudential method, that worked in the opposite direction. It was, theoretically, applied if the audience was unlearned: by starting with specifics, the speaker (or writer) could capture the attention of the uneducated.[113] Kees Meerhoff points out that this method allows for the 'inventive freedom of the creator', and could be applied 'in the course of logical analysis which escapes regular didactic exposition'.[114] But this method is not adopted in England. Instead, the attitudes of Ramus's first English translator, Roland MacIlmaine, ultimately prevailed. MacIlmaine dispatches this 'craftie and secrete methode' in a single short chapter, citing its primary purpose as the deception of the auditor.[115] The effect of this editorial presumption was 'to give support to the view that Ramus had only proposed the natural [perfect] method'.[116] Certainly, other translators of Ramus, such as Fenner, recognise the different applications of both techniques – but even those who sponsor the prudential method hardly seem to promote it. Fenner calls it 'the hiding or concealing, or crypsis of Method'.[117]

In his *Sheapheardes logike* (c. 1585), however, Abraham Fraunce does apply the prudential method – or, at least, he creatively applies its terms – to his defence of poetry:

[The] preceptes of artificial Logike both firste were collected, and alwaies must be conformiable to [the] sparkes of natural reason ... manyfestlie appearinge in the monumente and disputacons of excellent autors: and thier is this of art more certaine then that of nature, because of manye *particulars* in nature, *ageneral* and infallible constitucon of Logike in art is put downe.[118]

In his movement from the particular to the general, Fraunce seems to be describing a discursive practice in which the minor precedes the major premise; the second step of analysis is 'the reduction of the creative devi-ation, which is there for reasons of oratorical prudence, to the logical norm'.[119] But here Fraunce deviates from Ramist procedure. It becomes clear that he is arguing that the 'particulars in nature' make it susceptible to imperfection that is not present in art, precisely because of the integrity and order of logic:

[A]rt which first was but that scholer of nature, is nowe become that mistresse of the same, and as it were atable of glasse, wherin shee seinge & vewinge herselfe, maie washe out those spotes & blemishes of natural imperfection: for ther is no nature so constant & absolute but by loking & perusinge her owne force it maye be best red: no nature so weake & imperfecte, which bie the holpe of art is not confirmed.[120]

That this argument echoes Sidney ('[Nature's] world is brazen, the poets only deliver a golden') is not surprising: Fraunce claims that he began the treatise when he 'first came in presence' of Sidney.[121] But the argument itself founders on many of the same rocks as the *Defence*. Fraunce tries here – as he does later in *The Arcadian rhetorike* (1588) – to 'dignify [poetry] by relating it to rule and precept'.[122] In Ramism, however, logic must follow nature; the notion that poetry, or any other art, could improve upon nature is incompatible. As Temple writes: 'any art considers its subject matter – that which it wants to treat through its precepts – abstracted from singulars to the universal by means of the mind and understanding'; therefore, abstraction or the 'general consideration of things, does not result either in metaphysics'[s] differing from natural philosophy, *or in its being said to be raised above the natural*'.[123] However difficult this process might be, Temple avers that it is the obligation of any art to investigate 'matter and the forms of things' and to describe 'them through its precepts'.[124]

This is the very difficulty that Sidney sidesteps and Fraunce subverts. Sidney's 'imitation' of nature – implicit in Fraunce's 'glasse' held up to nature – evades the issue of how the truth in the image is assured. Like Sidney, Fraunce seems to assume that 'our erected wit maketh us know what perfection is': he asserts that the 'ingravin gifte and facultye of wytte and reason [shines] in the peticular discoursinge' of poets.[125] These 'sparkes of natural reason', he declares, are manifest in the works themselves. But this argument is fundamentally tautological: poetry teaches virtue because man innately knows what virtue is. The formulation adapts Ramism to the service of Sidney: 'In the last analysis no poet or orator has the power to destroy the immutable order of logic, and no one can, nor wants to, evade the empire of syllogism which commands the human mind: Ramist logic is indeed a *logica naturalis*.'[126] But the logic that Meerhoff describes does not answer, or even address, the critical objections to poetry raised in England – that the poet might mislead, or that poetry can teach vice as easily as virtue. Fraunce does not recognise the emotions as the cause of the didactic process that poetry performs.[127] But he also does not subject poetry to the practices that would evaluate its truth claims. Rather, he forecloses, as Sidney does, 'the more truly Platonic sense of complexity and difficulty in attaining to a vision of the perfect Idea that the dialectical view of poetry presupposes'.[128]

'Discrepancies between one Ramist and another are always in evidence', Wilbur Howell declares, 'and they are to be accepted only as a reminder that they can exist and flourish without thereby creating any serious divisions within Ramism as a movement.'[129] Howell's assertion papers over actual fissures. Gerard Passannante points to such a breach in his analysis of Gabriel Harvey's intertextual practices in *Three proper, and wittie, familiar letters*. Whereas digression in Ramist logic can always be said to be teleological – beneath the ornaments of language, the argument is, and must be, reducible to syllogism – Harvey's reading of classical texts in the *Letters* disrupts the possibility of such reductive analysis.

For Ramus, beneath the surface, will always be an underlying order ... depending on how deep you look. For Harvey, who deploys the intertextual politics of ancient poetry, underneath the smooth surface of a Renaissance Virgil or Ovid is volatility and strife ... In the end, Harvey seems to imply that there are some digressions that cannot be contained – the kind that force us to reexamine the conventions within which they arose.[130]

Harvey's ironic use of ancient texts reveals the 'active or reactive force' of literature.[131] His intertextual practice, Passannante argues, forces a disruption of logic in the manner of metaphor – where reorientation itself compels a revaluation of the terms and relations by which logical order was initially achieved. Although he was one of the first lecturers on Ramism at Cambridge, Harvey ultimately suggests that poetry cannot be reduced to a system of order. He describes a commotion similar to the earthquake that is the subject of his letter; the tremor begins at one textual site, but it radiates through a series of texts. This convulsion reveals the refracted meanings of any literary text that makes the reduction to a single chain of argument impossible.[132] 'All of the riches of the literary text' cannot, as Meerhoff would have it, '[be] absorbed by the analytical machine.'[133] Harvey intends to deliver a defence in logical packaging. Instead, like Fraunce, Harvey's interpretive practice attests to the problems of method in the exposition of poetry.

CALVIN AND THE CONTROVERSY

Sidney mounted his *Defence* precisely because 'poetry ... [was] thrown down to so ridiculous an estimation' in England.[134] But none of Gosson's charges would have pinched Sidney quite as hard as his allegation that poetry was essentially an un-Christian activity. Sidney's Protestant convictions are well established.[135] His intention was to find a place for lyric poetry within a theological system that denied its value. Sidney was not alone in his attempt or his failure to solve the problem.[136] Calvin himself tried to reconcile his particular strain of Protestantism and poetic expression, and – for all intents and purposes – failed to do so.

The philosophical quandary does not begin with poetry, but with the Psalms themselves. In his *Confessions*, St Augustine admits to the troubling passage of temptation through his ears. This temptation arises when he listens to the singing of the Psalms in church service. While he is aware of the affective power of music, it is the very nature of its persuasions that cause his conflict. Augustine is anxious about the aesthetic in devotion. He is aware that his own mind has been excited to a more ecstatic sense of religious zeal through church music, but he also knows that aesthetic pleasure diverts attention from the doctrinal value of scripture. Form inevitably distracts from content: 'the sence goes not so respectfully along with the reason, that it can with any patience endure to come behinde it'. The result is that, in the very act of devotion, the listener is lured unawares into sin: 'yea very fierce am I sometimes, in the desire of hauing the melody of all pleasant Musicke, (to which Dauid's Psalter is so often sung) banished both from mine owne eares, and out of the whole Church too'.[137] Augustine goes on to acknowledge the spiritual benefit of affective devotion, but, Annabel Patterson observes, the ability of the sung Psalms to animate worship resides precisely for Augustine 'in the spiritually dangerous enjoyment which is always in danger of invalidating their use. This "perplexity" is of course not limited to the Psalms as sung, but is transferable to ... any other aesthetically pleasing form of devotional expression.'[138]

One can see Calvin wrestling with this same problem in his preface to the Geneva Psalter. Calvin's introduction is so careful in its deliberation that it is worth quoting at length:

if [one] must indeed move to moderate the use of Music, to make music serve for all honesty, and so that it be not at all an occasion to unleash any dissolution, or to feminise ourselves in disorderly delights; & that music be not at all an instrument of laziness, nor of any shamefulness ... for there is hardly anything in this world that might turn or divert here and there the morals of men, as Plato prudently thought: & in fact, we experience its secret, nearly incredible virtue or power to move hearts one way or another. For this reason we must be even more diligent to govern it so that it might be useful to us, and in no way pernicious. For this reason the old doctors of the Church so often complained of what the people of their time were given over to, unchaste and shameful songs, which, not without cause, they esteem and call mortal and Satanic poison to corrupt the world. For speaking of Music, I understand two parts: that is, the letter or subject and matter: second, the song or melody. It is true that every bad word (as St. Paul says) perverts good morals: but when melody accompanies it, it pierces the Heart so much more strongly, & enters into it: just as wine is shot into a vessel by a funnel: thus venom and corruption are distilled right down to the bottom of the heart, by melody. What, then, must one do? [One must] have songs that are not only chaste, but also holy, those that may be like needles to incite us to pray and to praise God, to meditate on his works, in order to love, fear, honour, and glorify him. For what St. Augustine says is true, that no one can sing a thing worthy of God unless he has received it from God. For this reason, when we [shall] have gone all around everywhere searching here and there, we shall not find better songs, not righter ones for this than the Psalms of David, those the Holy Spirit said and made for him. However, when we sing them, we are sure that God puts the words in our mouths, as if he himself were singing it in us, to exalt his glory. For this reason Chrysostom exhorts man [sic] as well as women and little children to get used to singing them, so that it might be like a meditation to associate oneself with the company of Angels. For the rest, we must recall what St. Paul says, That spiritual songs can only be sung by heart. For the heart demands understanding. And in that (says St. Augustine) resides the difference between man's song and bird's song.

For a sparrow, a nightingale, a linnet, or a popinjay will sing well: but it will be without understanding. For man's own gift is to sing in knowing what he says. After understanding, the heart and affection necessarily follow, which cannot happen unless we have the Canticle imprinted in our memory.[139]

Calvin's poetics is wholly psalm-centred, prompted by the puzzle of exactly how the Psalms figure in the reformed church service. The French poet Clément Marot translated fifty Psalms of the Geneva Psalter – twenty of them at Calvin's explicit request – and it was finished by Calvin's successor in Geneva, Theodore Beza. But Calvin's lengthy clarification justifying the Psalms in music tells us precisely the place he perceived for such translations. He specifically addresses Augustine's concerns regarding aesthetic ecstasy (and attendant doctrinal neglect) and feels compelled to warn the world that the psalm translations that follow are devoid of human vanity, and, indeed, are for one purpose in particular – memorisation. Augustine raises the spectre of 'float[ing] . . . betweene perill of pleasure, and an approoued profitable custome'.[140] Calvin tries to achieve a compromise that would allow the senses patiently to pursue reason rather than to lead it. The poetic praise of God is permissible when it serves to imprint the Psalms in the mind. If the Psalms are fixed in memory, the heart and affection can follow the intellect ('After understanding, the heart and affection necessarily follow, which cannot happen unless we have the Canticles imprinted in our memory'). Even with this allowance, the psalm translations executed by Beza are far less lyrical than Marot's, and far more unambiguously devotional in nature – indicating the true objectives of the work (or, at least, the objectives of Beza).

Further, Calvin's position is contradicted by his own psalm commentaries. These voluminous notations treat the Psalms line by line, carefully defining each word of the scriptural text, and explicating its figurative language in rational terms. Whatever poetry Calvin would permit for the benefit of recollection, his deeply ambivalent attitude toward figurative language in a devotional context is evident in this extended exegesis that seeks to weed it out.[141] The doctrinal value of scripture is his main concern, and he obviously perceives the poetic effects of the Psalms as an impediment to their being properly understood. Theodore Beza makes his own contribution to psalm commentary – the English translation of Beza's biblical annotations claims to clarify the text 'according to the right sense of euery Psalme. With large and ample Arguments before euery psalme, declaring the true vse therof.'[142] If magisterial Protestants accepted that there were rhythmical (and poetic) books of the Bible – a widely held notion among scholastics – they were also clearly troubled by the fact.[143]

The limited scope that Calvin allows for poetry – as a mnemonic device for spiritual texts – was adopted in England. It is, in fact, the one allowance that Gosson grants in his overall dismissal of poetry's value: '[T]he beginning of poetrie in the bookes of Moses, & Dauid, was to sett downe good matter in numbers, that the sweetenesse of the one might cause the other to continue, and to bee the deeper imprinted in the mindes of men.'[144] The Sternhold–Hopkins Psalter (1562) assumed the status of a quasi-official liturgical text in England. *The forme of prayers and ministration of the sacraments* (1556) used by the English exiles in Geneva includes the first fifty settings of this Psalter (and bears Calvin's approbation).[145] The Psalter frequently employs common metre – the standard ballad form of alternating lines of four and three iambic feet.[146] Its aimed to make scriptural text accessible and easy to recollect – and its popularity can be directly attributed to its memorable lyrics. But while the ubiquity of the Sternhold–Hopkins Psalter prompted other attempts at metrical translation, it clearly did not assuage the cultural (and theological) angst concerning scriptural versification.[147] Calvin's psalm theory legitimised metrical translation, but translators of scriptural text were still anxious to affirm that they did not stray from his restrictive purview.

Archbishop Matthew Parker is a case in point. He published his own translation of metrical Psalms in 1567. While this Psalter appears to have been neither widely circulated nor particularly influential, its value to us lies in the textual apparatus that prefaces his translation. Parker rehearses the problems of aesthetic delight in church music (what Augustine calls the 'delectation of the eares'[148]), and answers with thirty-seven pages of patristic authority (including Athanasius, Basil, and Chrysostom) in defence of the Psalms as sung poetry. Parker marshals a tradition (descending from the Greeks) that recognises pleasure as a devotional tool. As Basil writes:

For where as the holy ghost perceiued that mankind was hardly trayned to vertue, & that we be very negligent in thinges concerning the true life in dede, by reason of our inclination to worldly pleasures & delectations: What hath he inuented? he hath mixte in his forme of doctrine the delectation of musicke, to thintent that the commoditie of the doctrine might secretlye steale into vs, while our eares bee touched with the pleasauntnes of the melodie.[149]

But even as this tradition is invoked, it is undermined by the inclusion in full of Augustine's objections. For example, Athanasius is cited as a source of support, but he is later undercut by the claim that he 'caused the readers of the quier to recite the psalms in such euen equalitie of the voyce, that it appeared to bee more like a reading then a singing' in order to prevent the 'suttle deceit of [the] senses' that Augustine warns will cause the hearer to 'offend mortally'.[150] The back-and-forth gestures that mark Parker's preface serve as an index of the anxiety that surrounds the practice of metrical psalm translation – even among those who would endorse it.

Sidney's declaration, then, that 'holy David's Psalms are a divine poem', is not a polemical claim.[151] Hebraists, rhetoricians, theologians, even Stephen Gosson would have agreed with him. But if the poetics of David's divinely inspired text were admitted, poetic inventiveness that altered the Text was considerably more problematic. When a psalm translation went beyond the compass of common metre (and was therefore clearly marked for a purpose other than congregational song) it exceeded the warrant for poetry which was permissible in a Protestant theological context. This may seem to be a minor distinction (and, therefore, a minor transgression) – but it is not. Calvin writes that if

we ponder how slippery is the fall of the human mind into forgetfulness of God, how great the tendency to every kind of error, how great the lust to fashion constantly new and artificial religions. Then we may perceive how necessary [is scripture], that it should neither perish through forgetfulness nor vanish through error nor be corrupted by the audacity of men.[152]

We need only recall the special contempt the early reformers reserved for Catholic manipulation of biblical text (or Swynnerton's assertion that 'to alter but one worde in [the Bible] from his natyfe propertie, who coulde iuge it lesse then sacrilege?') to imagine the provocative nature of a lyrical interpretation of scripture. The polemical gesture on the part of Sidney and Mary Sidney Herbert was to translate the Psalms with the primary intention of elevating poetry.

PSALM POETRY

In her conclusion to the Sidney–Pembroke Psalter, Herbert uses the standard vehicle for praise of a beloved.

> O laud the Lord, the God of hoasts commend,
>   exault his pow'r, advance his holynesse:
>   with all your might lift his allmightinesse:
> your greatest praise upon his greatnes spend.

Make Trumpetts noise in shrillest notes ascend:
    make Lute and Lyre his loved fame expresse:
    him lett the pipe, hym lett the tabrett blesse,
him Organs breath, that windes or waters lend.

Lett ringing Timbrells soe his honor sound,
    lett sounding Cymballs so his glory ring,
that in their tunes such mellody be found,

As fitts the pompe of most triumphant king.
    conclud: by all that aire, or life enfold,
lett high Jehova highly be extold.
        (Psalm 150)[153]

This is, in fact, the sonnet form that Sidney most often employs in *Astrophil and Stella.* The literary form that lauds the celestial love of Sidney's secular verse is put to the service of love of God. The aesthetics of courtly philosophy are not eschewed here, but celebrated: the transference suggests the Neoplatonic conception that the love of an earthly ideal leads, through a series of steps, to love of the divine. While this allusion coheres with Sidney's description of David as 'a passionate lover of that unspeakable and everlasting beauty [of the divine]', it, like the *Defence*, nonetheless muddles the difference between the Platonic and the Christian requirements for a pure and unobstructed vision.[154] David's clear eye is the result of the divine working through him (as Calvin writes, his Psalms are poems that 'the Holy Spirit said and made for him'). But the Sidney–Pembroke Psalter champions the virtues of human wit and of earthly inspiration. Its conveyance of David's Psalms through the conventions of Elizabethan lyric poetry amounts to a rewriting of scripture.

The theological and cultural opposition to poetry has long been recognised by scholars who have written about religious lyric.[155] But it has also been widely asserted that the 'innovative forms' of the Sidney–Pembroke Psalter 'were sanctified by the content'.[156] Such assessments are based on two assumptions: that the imitation of biblical models was accepted, at this time, as an antidote to the immoral uses of poetry; and that the influence of the Greek tradition, which emphasised pleasure in devotion, provided a counter-weight to the problems concerning figurative language and the primacy of scripture. But the internal workings of English metrical psalm translations themselves reveal that Augustinian anxiety prevailed at this time over and above any pleasures of the text. In spite of the example of the adventurous psalm translations of Wyatt and Surrey – both of which predate much of this psalm theory – there are conspicuously few poetic imitators between 1550 and 1590.[157] (Indeed, I have been arguing that sanctified subjects themselves rendered poetic innovation problematic.) Further, these frequently compelling critical arguments do not engage the nature of rhetorical training at the university level, and it is at this point that the pressures against figurative language generally, and poetry in particular, are most fully revealed. The opinions of Rainolds at Oxford, and the influence of Ramus at Cambridge, suggest a prevailing view among the educated class – both secular and clerical.

The literary activities of Mary Sidney Herbert need to be understood as a deliberate intervention in this debate. Since Barbara Lewalski and Louis Martz have positioned the Sidney–Pembroke Psalter within a developing tradition of devotional lyric, its influence upon the artistic forms of the seventeenth century is not a case that needs to be made.[158] I am instead arguing that those forms themselves were made possible by the cultural revaluation that the Psalter activated. This is to argue something very different from the account that makes Du Bartas the progenitor of religious lyric in England. The assumption that biblical topics were widely accepted as the superior subjects for lyric poetry descends from Lily B. Campbell.[159] Lewalski certainly recognises the problems of 'art and the sacred subject' in religious lyric (concerns widely noticed in the work of John Donne, George Herbert, and John Milton), but follows Campbell's lead in tracing another route for the licence of religious lyric descending from Du Bartas's poem, *L'Uranie* (1574). *L'Uranie*, however, was not published in England proper until 1589.[160] In the earlier English translation, published in Edinburgh, James VI implies an ignorance of the work of Du Bartas in Britain generally.[161] Robert Ashley's 1589 Latin translation seems to affirm this circumstance in England (five years later). In his dedicatory address, Ashley claims to have enjoyed the poetry of Du Bartas as a boy at Oxford.[162] Ashley's intended audience, however, was obviously the university educated – which suggests that Du Bartas was not widely accessible even among those who attended university.[163] A translation would be produced if a need could be perceived, and a Latin text would hardly be required if the French were available (Ashley, in fact, provides both languages so that readers can compare his translation with the original). While one cannot discount the influence of Du Bartas's Christian muse upon the overall development of the devotional poetic tradition in England, Harvey laments that his verse had *not* spawned imitation as late as 1593.[164] Rather than the publication of *L'Uranie*, the watershed event for devotional lyric in England was the concurrent circulation of the Sidney–Pembroke Psalter and the published *Defence*.

Sidney's *Defence* was clearly not intended as a public statement – he himself admits that his 'arguments will by few be understood, and by fewer granted'.[165] The available evidence suggests that there were, perhaps, only four manuscript copies produced, and that they were given to people within an intimate circle: his brother, his sister, his secretary, and a close friend, Penelope Rich.[166] It was the Countess of Pembroke who first released the *Defence* into the public arena that we now take to be its natural habitat.[167] 'It is not easy', Henry Woudhuysen writes, 'to judge the immediate effect of [the] appearance [of the *Defence*] in print: what to modern eyes appears to be one of [Sidney's] most important and brilliant works may have been passed over by his contemporaries with a certain amount of puzzlement'.[168]

The critical focus upon Sidney's place in literary history frequently fails to recognise Herbert's contribution to the development of her brother's poetic theory. Any consideration of the collaborative undertaking of the Sidney–Pembroke Psalter must necessarily include not only Herbert's engagement with her brother's literary ideals, but the often neglected extent to which she advances them. The Psalter was itself an argument – a volume developed in co-operation with the *Defence* that was intended to highlight the moral and religious application of lyric poetry. Herbert releases the two texts at roughly the same time because of this close complementary relationship. But her decision to circulate the Psalter in manuscript is an index of the sensitivity of the material, as Debra Rienstra and Noel Kinnamon have shown.[169] Rienstra and Kinnamon acknowledge that the Psalter 'strained conventional understandings of what it was appropriate to do with Scripture', but they maintain that the approach could be justified through Reformation notions of individual apprehension of the scriptural word.[170] Restricting the Psalter's circulation, they argue, protected it from being 'misunderstood by a wider public' and circumscribed its use for private devotion.[171] But the fact that the translation operates within the space of individual interpretation is precisely what makes it controversial in the context of the culture in which it was produced. More to the point, its intentions were decidedly public. Herbert holds the Psalter back from the press, but seems to have circulated the work widely (in contradistinction to Sidney's activities).[172] Her co-ordinated publishing strategy suggests that this was a calculated attempt to redeem a devotional aesthetic practice – and such an objective was inevitably involved in a voluble public controversy.

Sidney composed the initial versions of the first forty-three Psalms, but internal evidence suggests that (as J. C. A. Rathmell has surmised) he then simply stopped.[173] Sidney worked closely with the Marot–Beza Psalter, and his use of its verse forms is particularly apparent in the versification of his last ten Psalms (34, 36, 38, 39, 40, 41, and 42 all imitate forms found in the Geneva Psalter).[174] In his mimicry of Beza's Psalm 42, Sidney discovered a technique that he was to employ heavily in *Astrophil and Stella*: combined trochaic metre and feminine rhyme. By following the French pattern precisely (including the unaccented end syllables) he created a musicality that he clearly enjoyed – enough to follow the Psalm with an experiment of his own using the same elements (this time with a trimeter variation). The fact that he then breaks off the sequence, only to use his technical discovery in six of the eleven songs of *Astrophil and Stella*, indicates that Sidney's psalm translations were probably antecedent.[175] It further indicates that Sidney was experimenting with verse translations of the Psalms around the same time that he was writing his *Defence*.[176] This strongly suggests a link between the two projects in Sidney's mind.

Of course, it was Herbert who revised her brother's verses, and translated the remaining 107 Psalms, following the compositional method established by Philip. The Sidney siblings both compared the versions of the Psalms found in the Prayer Book Psalter and the two current vernacular Bibles, the Geneva Bible of 1560, and the Bishops Bible of 1568. They also referred to the extensive commentaries of Calvin and Beza (in the English translations of Golding and Gilby). Such attention to the translations of scholarly editions signals their commitment to producing a distinctly Protestant text. But this dedication is matched by the impulse to extol the virtues of English verse.[177] The very range and technique of the Sidney–Pembroke Psalter is unparalleled in sixteenth-century English poetry – there are only three instances in the entire collection where a formal structure is repeated (the metrical pattern and rhyme scheme of Psalm 8 is the same as 118; 32 is duplicated by 71; 60 by 119[S]).[178] Such prolific variety itself asserts the acclamation of poetic form as one of the central objectives of the work.[179]

The integrity of the translation of the Psalter is as crucial to its aims as its artistic expression. Protestant culture in England devalued the imaginative exercises in which the poet engaged: it called poets 'liars' and poems 'sinful fancies' (in fact, two sections of the *Defence* address these specific charges). In their attempt to find a place for lyric poetry within a devotional tradition that sought to deny it, the Sidneys had first to situate their poetics within a specifically Protestant context. But the poetics of Protestants is not the same as Protestant poetics: however much they aligned their translation with authoritative texts, they still violated the principles of Protestant devotional practice. The Sidney–Pembroke Psalter was not designed for congregational use – its complicated stanzas do not conform straightforwardly to music, nor do they stick easily in the mind. In exploring the emotive possibilities of the Psalms, the Sidneys provoke an engagement which is far more erotic than it is meditative – far more sensuous than spiritual. This appeal to the experience of the language of the Psalms distracts attention (in the Protestant conception) from their doctrinal value. If the profit of scripture is confined to its doctrine, then emphasis upon the aesthetic pleasures of scripture undermines its use.

Herbert begins her lyric translations with a glance toward her brother as a model. Psalm 44, the first in the Sidneian collection attributed to Herbert, is a close, but not exact, imitation of Sidney's Psalm 42 (both have eight-line trochaic tetrameter stanzas with feminine rhymes).[180] But she abandons her brother's dependence upon the Marot–Beza Psalter – only 20 of her 128 poems follows a stanzaic pattern in this Psalter[181] – and develops her own poetic style. 'By recreating the Psalms as Elizabethan poems', Rathmell writes, 'the Countess compels us to read them afresh.'[182] This is, of course, part of the problem. Herbert exploits the poetic potential of the Psalms' metaphoric language through frequent expansion of biblical images. The Geneva Bible begins Psalm 44:

> We haue heard with our eares, O God: our fathers haue told vs the workes that thou hast done in their dayes, in the old time:
>
> How thou hast driuen out the heathen with thine hand, and planted them: how thou hast destroyed the people, and caused them to grow.
>
> (PS 44: 1–2)

Herbert's reworking of the opening is stunning:

> Lorde, our fathers true relation
>   often made, hath made us knowe,
> howe thy pow'r in each occasion
>   thou of old for them did'st showe.
>   how thy hand the Pagan foe
>   rooting hence, thie folke implanting,
>   leavelesse made that braunch to grow,
>   this to spring, noe verdure wanting.
>
> (1–8)

Herbert develops the horticultural images of her source text, and enlarges them into a fine poetic passage. The heathen is now violently weeded from the land and God's chosen are fostered. She goes on to expand the parallel in the next two sentences, where the 'braunch' of the 'Pagan foe' is cut off and fruitless, while God's people flourish in a green season. If the effect is beautiful, it is because Herbert conspicuously embellishes the passage of scripture.

In Psalm 55 (as another example), a Psalm principally concerned with the deceit of men, the ninth verse in the Geneva Bible reads simply: 'Destroy, O Lord, and diuide their tonges: for I haue seene crueltie and strife in the citie' (*PS* 55: 9). Herbert renders the line:

> but swallow them ô lord in darknes blind,
> confound their councells, leade their tongus astray,
>   that what they meane by wordes may not appeare.
>   for Mother Wrong within their towne each where,
> and daughter Strife their ensignes soe display,
> as if theie only thither were confin'd.
>   (19–24)

Herbert's text, while richly conveying the meaning of the Psalter's line, reconceives the Word of God. She employs the word-music of poetry – the personifications, metaphors, metres, and rhymes of poetic language – not only to register the emotional experience of the Psalm, but also to reproduce that experience in the reader. Herbert's verses are composed to accomplish what Sidney claims is the project of poetry: 'to teach and delight'.[183] But Augustine's objections are centred upon the spiritual perils of such enjoyment. It is at this level of aesthetic delight that the reader abandons the doctrinal seriousness that magisterial Protestants deem necessary to an encounter with scripture.

Calvin's compromise sought to minimise the dangers presented by the realm of the senses (the fleshy world of the emotions) through an emphasis upon reason. He agreed that emotions could excite one to virtue, but stressed that they could as easily (or more easily) incline one to vice. Consequently, the Psalms had to be committed to memory, so that understanding would always precede affection. Obviously, the Sidney–Pembroke Psalter is crafted according to a different set of directives. Of the 171 poems in the collection, 93 are isometric, 46 are in two measures, 23 in three, and 1 in four (Psalms 120–7 are composed in unrhymed quantitative verse). The metrical cadences of the Psalter are various: they punctuate, extend, and contract according to emphasis. While the poems are musical, they do not fit easily to music – they instead celebrate the musical possibilities of the poetic line.[184] As Seth Weiner observes, the Psalms that Sidney adapted from the French Psalter do not always even correspond to their tune, and he concludes that 'Sidney was interested more in appropriating the measure of the music than in the music itself.'[185]

> From the lyers trace,
>> from falshoods wreathed way,
>>> ô save me lord, and graunt I may
> embrace
>> the law thou dost commend.
>>> for the path ay right,
>>>> where truth unfained goes,
>>>>> my tongue to tread hath gladly chose:
>>> my sight
>>>> thy judgmentes doth, as guides, attend.
>>>>>>> (Psalm 119D, 21–30)

This poetic passage translates the biblical line: 'Take from me the way of lying, and grant me graciously thy Law' (Geneva Bible, *PS* 119: 29). It is obviously badly formed for musical accompaniment, but its strophic construction complements its content. Indeed, Susanne Woods has noted the way this poem uses structure to enforce its rhythms.[186] The Psalm deals with the problem of finding the way to righteousness. Its meandering lines on the page emphasise our confusion in a crooked world. The words of the stanza reinforce the impression: rather than the simple diction of 'Take from me the way of lying', the 'lyers trace', and 'falshoods wreathed way' impress the reader with the perils and perplexities of locating the straight and narrow path. '[M]y tongue to tread' picks the path that pursues God's Word, and greatly improves upon the lines in the Parker Psalter: 'Due sence geue me: to understand: the wayes of thy precepts / Demure I will: then take in hand: to talke thy wondrous steppes.'[187] It is the deliberate breaks that make this stanza both unmalleable to music and poetically dynamic. The strong sense of the word 'embrace' (as opposed to Parker's 'take in hand') is buttressed by a long pause – imposed by the shape of the stanza itself. The eyes that are watching God are similarly isolated for effect. Herbert's poetic syncopations would have found no suitable accompaniment in early modern music.

Martz has remarked that the Sidney Psalms represent 'the closest approximation to the poetry of [George] Herbert's *Temple* that can be found anywhere in preceding English poetry'.[188] Martz's observation is at

least partly based upon the complexity and variety of the metrical forms
found in the Sidney–Pembroke Psalter.

> You that Jehovas servants are,
>   whose careful watch, whose watchfull care,
>   within his house are spent;
>   say thus with one assent:
>   Jehovas name be praised.
>   then let your hands be raised
>   to holiest place,
>   where holiest grace
>   doth ay
>   remaine:
>   and say
>   againe,
>   Jehovas name be praised.
>   say last unto the company,
>   who tarrying make
>   their leave to take,
>   all blessings you accompany,
>   from him in plenty showered,
>   whom Sion holds embowered,
>   who heav'n and earth of nought hath raised.
>   (Psalm 134)[189]

Here is a stanzaic pattern typical of *The temple*: verse formed of asymmet-
rical lines. The parallelism (which acts as a refrain), the variety of measures,
and the way in which the contractions of the poem serve the sense, all
closely correspond with George Herbert's later poetic experiments. The
pattern of the stanza stresses a feeling of communal praise – it sounds like
an address and answer that might take place in a church service. (But while
the linguistic patterns of the poem mimic a church custom, this is certainly
not a congregational hymn.) What is remarkable is the way in which the
arrangement of the poem reinforces the words. The middling lines are a
preamble to the repetition of God's praise: the contractions serve to underscore the refrain. The lines, 'Jehovas name be praised / then let your hands
be raised' are aligned on the page with the subsequent echo. Lagging
behind, are those 'who tarrying make / their leave to take'. The poem then
swells again to encompass the 'blessings' and 'plenty' of heaven and earth.
The material form of the poem, then, is self-reflective. While its formal
coherence is not as obvious as 'Easter wings' of *The temple*, its structure
nonetheless compounds its sense. We see Herbert here – and again and
again in her poems – striving to fit the content to its vehicle.

Herbert employed 126 different stanzaic patterns (she repeats herself only once). The variety of forms is intended to do more than exercise the metrical possibilities of the English language – she is struggling to make sound, sense, and structure concur. Psalm 55 is a good example of this approach. The Psalm is made up of six stanzas of twelve iambic pentameter lines. The last three stanzas reverse the entire rhyme scheme established by the first three, forming a perfect palindrome.[190] The first half of the Psalm concentrates upon the present threat posed to God's servant through the deceit and evil of other men – it focuses upon the fears of the psalmist in a treacherous world. The second half of the Psalm meditates upon the strength of God's protection, and reverses the former circumstance. The rhyme scheme, then, imitates the logic of the text. There are numerous other instances in the collection where the metrical or rhyming patterns have been fashioned to mimic the narrative of the poem: rhyme royal is used to express the translation of the important penitential Psalm 51, 'Miserere mei, Deus'; a perfect Elizabethan sonnet (the medium of praise) fills out the slender five lines of Psalm 100; Psalms 120–7 (Psalms that were particularly resonant in the Genevan community because of their theme of exile) are experiments in the quantitative verse of Latin poetry; and the familiar complaint of Psalm 137 is rendered in ottava rima. Herbert's capacity to rephrase the Psalms with a kind of personal conviction, coupled with her ability to fit her phraseology into stanzaic patterns of enormous complexity, produces a dazzling poetic performance. But it is an exclusively *poetic* performance. The ornate settings of the Sidney–Pembroke Psalter are evidently not designed to achieve a more adequate liturgical text – they are wholly intended to execute a more expressive form of psalm poetry. As Herbert's Psalm 45 declares:

> My harte endites an argument of worth,
> the praise of him that doth the Scepter swaie:
> My tongue the pen to paynt his praises forth,
> shall write as swift, as swiftest writer maie.
> (1–4)[191]

'I have not sought to please, unless in so far as I might at the same time be profitable to others', Calvin writes in the preface to his commentaries, 'therefore, I have . . . observed throughout a simple style of teaching.'[192] Clearly, Herbert does not use plain diction for the purpose of elucidating the Psalms. In fact, she creatively reinterprets Calvin as well. In Psalm 139, for instance, which is preoccupied with the creation of man, the fifteenth line in the Geneva Psalter reads as follows: 'My bones are not hid from thee, though I was made in a secret place, and fashioned beneath in the earth' (*PS* 139: 15). Calvin gives extended attention to this line: concentrating upon the Hebrew verb which means *to weave together*, he expands the metaphor, and compares the mother's womb to what he calls the 'dark cave' of the artisan's workshop.[193] His insight into the Hebrew original produces the metaphors in Herbert's startling interpretation:

> Thou, how my back was beam-wise laid,
>   and raftring of my ribbs dost know:
>   know'st ev'ry point
>   of bone and joynt,
>   how to this whole these partes did grow,
> in brave embrodry faire araid,
>   though wrought in shopp both dark and low.
>   (50–6)

The power of the Countess's version derives from her sense of involvement. The body is first evoked as the skeletal frame of a built structure. Its assembly appears to be a male occupation – the beams and rafters of the body are laid and jointed in a housing-plot or shipyard. But as these parts knit together, the images of the stanza move into the female domain. Unlike Calvin, Herbert is not referring to the commercial profession of the tailor, but to the privatised and feminine activity of embroidery.[194] The architecture of God the father is not being denied here, but neither is the woman's contribution which provides the covering of flesh. As a mother herself, the Countess has reinserted woman into the process of human creation where the Bible has left her out.

She draws similar inspiration from Beza's commentaries on the Psalms. In his argument, Beza calls Psalm 104 a 'heauenly poeticall inuention'.[195] Taking her cue from this remark, Herbert composes one of the finest poems in her collection. The Psalm contemplates the ample benefice of God towards man – from the creation of the world to the sustaining of its life. The thirteenth and fourteenth lines of Beza's Psalter (translated by Gilby) read:

But on the other side, euen from heauen, thou waterest the mountaines, powring downe rayne from thy chambers, and by that thy benefit it commeth to passé, that the earth as it were, drinking drinke to the fill, doeth not deceiue the hope of the husband man. That self same power bringeth foorth of the bowelles of the earth grasse, and many kyndes of hearbes to nourish the beastes, which are necessarie for the vse of men: finally, it bringeth all kinde of nourishment.[196]

Herbert executes these lines with ingenuity and compression:

> Thou, thou of heav'n the windowes dost vnclose,
> dewing the mountaines with thy bounties raine:
> Earth greate with yong hir longing doth not lose,
> the hopfull ploughman, hopeth not in vayne.
> the vulgar grasse, whereof the beast is faine,
> the rarer hearbman for him self hath chose:
> all things in breef, that life in life maintaine,
> from Earths old bowells fresh and yongly growes.
>
> (41–8)

Two biblical passages are elegantly rendered in eight lines. She picks up on the biblical reference to God's 'chambers' (used in the Geneva Psalter as well) and expands it into an image of heaven's window opening to rain life upon the world. She particularly exploits an idea found only in Beza's Psalter. Instead of the Geneva 'he may bring forth bread out of the earth', Beza describes the 'bowelles of the earth' which produce nourishment. Herbert enlarges the metaphor into an extended allegory of the earth's fruitfulness: the pregnant planet bears her 'yong' to 'the hopfull plough-man'. The way in which she has extracted from Beza's image the idea of the earth's interior as a womb that constantly reproduces is arresting – Herbert has again imagined female fecundity as central to the productive processes of life. In fact, she frequently conceives of woman as central to the most basic creative activities. This repeated conception would be less striking if she did not consistently impose it in places where female production is not the issue.

I am not suggesting that Herbert was resentful of male dominance in either the theological or creative domains. (She may well have been, but such a supposition is too much to draw from single instances.) But she clearly has involved herself in the text – her process of creative engagement is highly subjective. Herbert assumed her brother's poetic project after his death, but the execution of that project is essentially hers. The brilliant achievements of the Sidney–Pembroke Psalter – its muscular word choice, its insistent verbal play, its vigorous rhythms, and stylistic inventiveness – are finally to her credit, not his. As Rathmell admits, 'Sidney's share in translating the Psalms, most critics have agreed, is decidedly inferior to that of his sister.'[197] It is easy to see why Herbert's translations attracted so much contemporary admiration. (In his verse miscellany *Bel-vedére*

(1600), John Bodenham lists her alongside Sidney, Spenser, and Shake-speare as a writer of merit.[198]) Consider her verse transcription of the biblical line: 'O Lord God of my saluation, I cry day and night before thee' (Geneva Bible, *PS* 88: 1):

> My god, my lord, my help, my health;
> to thee my cry
> doth restles fly.
> both when of sunn the day
> the treasures doth display,
> And night locks up his golden wealth.
>   (Psalm 88, 1–6)

Versification such as this is as controlled and artfully expressed as anything one finds in George Herbert's poetry.

The Countess of Pembroke had probably finished the entire Psalter by 1593; Samuel Daniel praises her psalm translations in his dedication of *Cleopatra*.[199] Certainly, a complete manuscript was circulating by 1594, as Henry Parry at that time, in a tribute to young William Herbert, refers to 'that sacred poetical work of King David' that 'has at long last received its final polishing'.[200] Other writers who commend Herbert's Psalms include John Davies, John Donne, Sir Edward Denny, Michael Drayton, Sir John Harington (who sent three verse translations to the Countess of Bedford), and Aemelia Lanyer. The widespread circulation of the Sidneian psalm translations in manuscript clearly reformed secular poetic practices.[201] Evidence for this argument lies in the contemporary undertaking of devotional lyric composition by Barnabe Barnes, Nicholas Breton, Henry Constable, Francis Davison, Giles and Phineas Fletcher, and Abraham Fraunce[202] – as well as the impress the Psalter translation left on the religious poetry of Donne, (George) Herbert, Vaughan, and Milton.[203]

But the revaluation of the separation between poetry and devotion that the Sidney–Pembroke Psalter instigated took place outside of the church, not within it. In his praise of the collection, Donne writes that he 'can scarce call [the English Church] reformed until' the English Psalter is 'reformed'.[204] Donne's comment tells us that by c. 1621, it had not been (at least not to the extent that Donne wanted). The reason for this is partly alluded to by Donne himself: he calls the Psalms 'well attired abroad, [and] ill at home . . . well in chambers, [and] in . . . church so ill'.[205] Donne decries the fact that the text of private devotion has surpassed the one intended for the congregation of the church. But regardless of Donne's desire to see the Psalter adopted in church, the Sidneian Psalms were not appropriate for public devotion. The Sidney–Pembroke Psalter failed to introduce poetry into the devotional exercises of the English Church precisely because it was so involved in the conventions of secular English poetics. In *A briefe and necessary catachisme or instruction* (1572), Edward Dering seethes against such conventions:

but as though the wickednes of our forefathers were not yet full, we wyll make up their measure, and set up Shrines to the word of God, and the wrytinges of all of hys Saintes . . . To thys purpose I trow we haue multiplied for our selues so many new delightes that we might iustify the idolatrous superstition of the elder world . . . to this purpose we haue gotten our Songes & Sonets, our Pallaces of pleasure . . . and such lyke Sorceries.[206]

Dering's yoking of works such as Tottel's *Miscellany* and Catholic idolatry nicely exemplifies the associations that lyric poetry held for many (or most) English Protestants. The Sidney–Pembroke Psalter did not achieve a revaluation of poetry within the Protestant theological system because the principles behind its design were fundamentally at odds with Protestant ideals.

Retrospectively, scholars have read Sidney's claims for poetry as privileging the imaginative achievements of poets. In fact, he was simply trying to assert that the poetic imagination *had* a moral (and potentially theological) purpose. His sister greatly advanced his theoretical project both by bringing his thesis to public view, and completing the Psalter that established its central point. In so doing, she carved out a place for works of the imagination within a secular Protestant tradition. Herbert's position as a primary motivator in the shift from secular to devotional lyric registers within the operations of contemporary religious lyric production and circulation itself. She becomes a key figure over which subsequent struggles concerning religious poetry were carried out (an issue that I explore at length in chapter 5). Lanyer uses the figure of Herbert to negotiate her own entry into professional poetic circulation. The way that she employs her figure – literally conducting the business of poetry over it – speaks to the importance of the Countess of Pembroke within the context of a religious lyric tradition. That contemporary male poets also make use of the figure of Herbert to authorise their religious writing points to her recognised prominence in Protestant literary activity.

Precisely because the terms of the argument were developed in opposition (Sidney elevated works of the imagination *because* they were devalued), the ensuing literary history, particularly in the eighteenth century, has tended to reverse the model – esteeming works of the imagination and denigrating religious prose. Neither Sidney could have anticipated the consequence of their attempts to vindicate poetry's place within Protestant culture. Protestant poets perceived in these two extraordinary works a licence to write religiously; the Psalter in particular worked to legitimate the use of poetry in the treatment of religious subjects. But poetic works were subsequently appreciated as the literary products of value. Martz has claimed that the Sidney Psalms are an 'attempt to bring the art of Elizabethan lyric into the service of psalmody'.[207] My reading of the cultural intervention of the Psalter translation inverts this claim: I argue that it is instead an attempt to bring psalmody to the defence of English lyric.

CHAPTER 4

A new Jerusalem: Anne Lok's 'Meditation' and the lyric voice

Western lyric discourse can be seen to operate dialectically between the ritual and fictional modes, asking us both to re-experience its statements from the inside and to interpret them from the outside, but often to do one of these things at the expense of the other ... [I]nnovation within the lyric genre often occurs through such a reweighing of these phenomena against each other; and ... the English Psalters show the cooperation and tension of these modes in unmistakable relief – show themselves, in fact, to operate as indirect theoretical statements about the nature of lyric.

Roland Greene, 'Sir Philip Sidney's *Psalms* ... and the nature of lyric'

It is ironic that I have been using the term 'lyric' in the modern sense, when the origin of the word declares its associations with song. But the distinction that I have been making – between merely metrical compositions set to music and intended for ritual, or collective, use, and those conceived as lyric poems to excite the imagination of individual readers – is evident both in the exercise of sixteenth-century psalm translation and the contemporary discussions of the practice. Greene recognises the distinction, but he underestimates the rupture that occurred between these aims in connection to devotion. His argument charts the emergence of devotional lyric as an outgrowth of psalm translation: a recalibration of the ritual and subjective elements involved in the transmission of scriptural language. But it does not appreciate the extent to which these elementary modes of poetic production came into conflict over the issue of religious expression.

Nonetheless, Greene's argument is a useful place to begin a discussion of these issues precisely because he is alert to the different theoretical positions concerning poetry that individual Psalter translations of this period declare. Moreover, his account of the progressive reorientation of psalm translation – that metrical Psalters over time begin to 'reorganize the relations of ritual and fiction' until, like a shelf phenomenon, they tip over to devotional lyric poetry – betrays a basic critical assumption regarding the emergence of religious lyric as an English Protestant form.[1] This assumption is that licence for a devotional aesthetic was at large in sixteenth-century culture – and particularly visible in ubiquitous metrical Psalters. If metrical psalm translations were a feature of the English Protestant service, how is it possible to assert that the faith, even once it becomes Calvinist-inflected, was opposed to poetry? On one level, it is not. But if Sidney accepted metrical versions of the Psalms as part of the category of poetry he was defending, he could hardly claim that poetry stood in peril of being 'scourged out of the Church of God' (and his case concerning the Psalms themselves would have been gratuitous).[2] It must be that Sidney was speaking of verse that had no collective orientation – verse that operated outside of a collective, or ritual, imagination. This definition of poetry, then, approximates a modern understanding of lyric (even though modern subjectivity must be inherently problematic in any poetry that takes the Psalms as its source).

It is when religious poetic expression begins to trace the outlines of an individual imagination – and at the same time appeal to the emotive experience of an individual reader – that it becomes troubling in the context of Calvinist Protestantism. We recognise this conflict in the work of seventeenth-century lyric poets. The same anxiety, however, is widely evident in Elizabethan metrical translations of the Psalms.[3] Most English divines at this time – of both high and low Church sympathies – considered themselves Calvinists.[4] While it obviously would be wrong to suggest that this identification produced a uniform faith and practice (in light of the debates concerning practice), the effect of Calvinism upon rhetoric in England – particularly the high rhetoric of poetry – is conspicuous. And yet the conflict that this caused is barely visible in critical narratives that marry the Book of Psalms with Petrarchan models. Barbara Lewalski writes that 'A long tradition of more or less free paraphrases of the Penitential Psalms reaches from Dante's terza rima paraphrase, to Petrarch's almost total transformation of the Psalms into religious meditations adapted to his own circumstances, to George Chapman's highly paraphrastic and ornamented verse descant on Petrarch.'[5] Lewalski's articulation does much to reveal both the source and the underpinning logic of these narratives. Her appraisal swiftly traverses religious ideology, national identity, and hundreds of years of history. It is the expressed purpose of Lewalski's project to account for the development of a religious literary tradition over centuries – and from the wide view that she takes, her assessment is accurate. The problem is that such a perspective tends to elide the tensions that are indigenous to a particular time and place.

Hannibal Hamlin's recent study of how the Psalms inform the literary culture of early modern England is a useful index of the force that these narratives have exerted upon critical thinking. Since Louis Martz noticed an affiliation between the Psalms of Philip Sidney and George Herbert's *The temple* more than fifty years ago, and J. C. A. Rathmell pointed out an even closer relationship between the translations of Mary Sidney Herbert and the same work ten years later, the role played by the Sidney Psalms in the expansion of poetic forms of devotion has been part of mainstream critical commentary. Hamlin, however, whose central point is that these lyric poems emerge as part of the development of a psalm culture, questions the extent to which the Sidney–Pembroke Psalter is 'original'.[6] Although superb in its detailed analysis of how certain Psalter translations influence particular literary outcomes, Hamlin's book does not address the challenge posed to these developments – failing even to register an awareness that significant obstacles existed. A progressive freedom in verse translations of the Psalms and other scriptural materials is starkly apparent, and cumulative, up to 1591. There are, however, important distinctions to be made between the devotional compositions of William Baldwin, William Byrd, Michael Drayton, Dudley Fenner, George Gascoigne, and William Hunnis, and those of Abraham Fraunce, Nicholas Breton, and Henry Lok, in the early 1590s – distinctions that are often not addressed.

Calvin's psalm theory is not perceived, in critical terms, as ultimately obstructive to religious lyric in part because Protestants wrote devotional poetry.[7] Examples such as the continental Marot–Beza Psalter, and George Buchanan's lyric Latin paraphrase in Great Britain itself, seem to stand as proof that significant impediments did not exist.[8] But the histories of these translations, and the convictions that support them, are anything but straightforward (as I hope I have shown in the case of Beza's contributions to the French Psalter). Even less simple is the history of their influence in England. For it is precisely because devotional precedents were available – and clearly read – in England that the absence of imitation is so remarkable.[9]

The principal reason that the current accounts of the emergence of religious lyric (as a relatively unproblematic outgrowth of the practice of metrical psalm translation) are unsatisfying is that they do not explain the dearth of devotional lyric production over an approximately forty year period.[10] Thomas Wyatt's verse adaptations of the seven penitential Psalms (modelled on the prose paraphrases of Pietro Aretino and Jan van Campen[11]) first appeared in 1549.[12] The translation of Psalm 88 (and the possible translation of 31 and 51) and the verse transcriptions of *Ecclesiastes* I–III by Henry Howard, Earl of Surrey, were appropriated under the name of Thomas Sternhold at approximately the same time.[13] (The three psalm poems in this volume were subsequently plagiarised by Francis Seager.[14]) Archbishop Parker quotes Surrey's *Ecclesiastes* I as a motto for his Psalter.[15] At large in the culture, these English examples of lyric verse translations of scriptural materials were rarely copied. It is not until the 1590s, with the appearance of Fraunce's *Countesse of Pembrokes Emanuel* (1591), Breton's *Pilgrimage to paradise, ioyned with The Countesse of Penbrookes loue* (1592), and Lok's *Svndry Christian passions* (1593), that devotional lyric begins to emerge in England as something more than an occasional – and frequently private – practice.

I am not unique in setting this demarcation. Studies that trace the emergence of the religious sonnet sequence in England frequently take Henry Lok as a starting point.[16] But they also frequently assume that Lok and his contemporaries were 'writing within the context of sixteenth-century religious poetic trends' – naturalising the rather abrupt appearance of these lyrics.[17] Yet the devotional work of Fraunce, Breton, and Lok is not an organic product of sixteenth-century English culture; it is enabled – and indeed, activated – by the work of women writers. Breton and Fraunce themselves promote their associations with the poetic project of Mary Herbert (a point that I will address in the next chapter). Growing critical attention has also turned to the 1560 sonnet sequence of Henry Lok's mother, Anne Vaughan Lok, as the significant English precedent.[18] What I want to throw into relief is precisely how the cultural interventions of these women caused the emergence of these identifiably Protestant lyric collections – and influenced the devotional production in England that followed in their wake.

Such an endeavour requires that we revise our understanding of the obstruction that the Protestant theological system presented to the operations of individual creativity that Sidney celebrates. Although the Sidney–Pembroke Psalter does not by itself resolve the conflict, its circulation does serve to release poetic energies that we can see accumulating in the late 1580s. We can further witness contemporary poets invoking either the *Defence* or the religious work of Herbert to lend authority to their own devotional enterprise. But the poetry of Henry Lok has a different origin (he had no proximate relationship to Herbert, and there is no evidence that he would have had access to her manuscript prior to 1593). If the devotional sonnet sequence of Anne Lok is '[s]ituated at an all but unexplored crossroads of genre and religion', this intersection is central to the issues that I have examined in the previous chapter.[19] Anne Lok is probably the ideal example to lend nuance to the preceding discussion of the antipoetic convictions of post-Reformation English Protestant culture, for her poetic work declares its religious affiliation with Calvin (the sequence is appended to her translation of Calvin's sermons).[20] It responds to Wyatt's verse transcription of the Psalms – and is the only example of such poetic engagement after Surrey. It is also undeniably a lyric sequence.

DEVOTIONAL PRECEDENTS

The project of reform exploited the tradition of psalm-singing for the purpose of making scripture accessible to the unlearned. A significant anxiety, however, was inducted with the gesture. The paradox is, of course, that music appeals to the senses, which distracts from the devotional value of the Psalms (and lures the listener to sin); but it also allowed the Psalter to be easily memorised – and better for the unlettered to know the Psalms, than for congregants to be ignorant of all scripture. Erasmus articulates these levelling impulses in the preface to his 1516 translation of the New Testament (*Novum Instrumentum*), and subsequent preface to the chapter of Matthew.[21]

I wolde to god thy plowman wolde syng a texte of thy scripture at his plowbeme. And that thy weuer at his lowme with this wolde dryue awaye the tedyousnes of tyme. I wolde the wayfaringe man with this pastime wolde expell thy werynes of his jorney. And to be shorte I wolde that all the communicacyon of thy christen shulde be of thy scrypture for in a maner suche are we our selves as oure dayly tales are.[22]

The Erasmian aspiration that scripture might be incorporated into the daily lives of all Christians clearly underwrites the first complete metrical Psalter in English, translated by Robert Crowley and published in 1549.[23] Crowley's Psalter contains an address to the lay 'Christian Reader' as well as a Latin epistle to Owen Ogelthorpe, president of Magdalen College, Oxford. Here was a text conceived for scholastic and layperson alike. In his address to 'the Christian Reader', Crowley very specifically outlines the procedures for use:

Thou hast also in this boke, a note or song of iiii. partes, which agreth wyth the metre of this Psalter in suche sorte, that it serueth for all the Psalmes therof, conteynynge so many notes in one parte, as be syllables in one meter, as appeareth by the dyttie that is printed wyth the same.[24]

Crowley fits all of his Psalms to the same vehicle, and while he claims that his project is to 'moue [his audience] to delyte in the readynge and hear-ynge of these Psalmes', the translation itself affords few pleasures.[25] Indeed, the principal intention of this Psalter is to make 'open and playne, that whiche in other translations, is obscure and harde' (and his letter to Ogelthorpe asserts the reformist credentials of the translation that he followed).[26] Crowley's presentation of his work betrays the central pre-occupations of English metrical psalmists: fidelity to the text (in this case the Latin translation of Leo Jud from the Hebrew) and an unadorned style suited to the simplest congregational member.

The early reformers emphasised pleasure in psalm-singing, but even at the outset of their project, they tried to police the affective experience of the singer. We can see an expression of this in the introduction of Miles Coverdale's *Goostly Psalmes and spirituall songes* (1535):

[T]hou mayest perceaue, what spirituall edifienge commeth of godly Psalmes and songes of Gods worde ... And yf thou felest in thine hert, that all the lordes dealynge is very mercy and kyndnes, cease not then to be thankfull vnto hym therefore: *but in thy myrth be alwaye syngyng of him,* that his blessed name may be praysed now and euer.[27]

Coverdale emphasises the delight in songs taken from the Psalms because he, like Erasmus, wants to replace secular ballads with scriptural texts ('By this thou mayest perceaue, what spirituall edifienge commeth of godly Psalmes and songes of Gods worde: and what inconuenience foloweth the corrupt ballettes of this vayne worlde'[28]). But while stressing the pleasure of scriptural songs might entice the ploughman to sing, the benefits of the practice are undermined if the song distracts him. Cover-dale therefore warns that the singer's enjoyment does not come from the music, but from contemplation of God. The substitution of the Psalms for popular ballads, then, was not an uncomplicated endeavour. The inherent paradox of the reformer's strategy is made visible by Coverdale, who encourages the practice of psalm-singing even as he tries to regulate its uses.

It would be wrong to claim that magisterial Protestants in England saw no merit in works of the imagination. In *Philargyrie of greate Britayne* (1551), Crowley points to his poetic occupation as an avenue to truth. He further admits that he has 'feyned / and wrytten a lye', but the lie allows him to veil the truth 'vnder a straynge name'.[29] Plays that drama-tised the struggles of the Reformation were performed under Edward VI, and Paul White has shown just how vital a role theatre played in reform.[30]

The Erasmian project of popularising scripture clearly produced some flexibility in relation to the metrical – and dramatic – rendering of biblical themes. John Bale used his own troupe (under the patronage of Thomas Cromwell) to perform his propaganda.[31] Martin Bucer advocates the use of scriptural subjects in drama – and Bucer's objective is clearly the dissemination of scripture to the unlearned.[32] With similar didactic intentions, Crowley defends the pedagogical use of poetry by appending his own metrical 'Praiers and graces' to the 1582 edition of Seager's instruction for children, *The schoole of vertue*.[33] But if a literary imagination animated the conduct of popular reform in England, the attitudes that attended the poetic treatment of scripture itself were highly ambivalent.

It is ironic that Bale, with his expressed opinion against the corruption of scripture, should be among the few to publish metrical psalm translations absent musical accompaniment between 1545 and 1550.[34] However, his three psalm poems composed in rhyming couplets of unvarying eight syllable lines are caste in the form of popular song. Furthermore, the text that precedes two of the translations – one is appended to *The first examinacyon of Anne Askewe*, and the other concludes *A godly medytacyon of the christen sowle* by the (then) princess Elizabeth – attaches them to female Protestant heroes, thereby encouraging their popular transmission.[35] William Hunnis translates the Psalms at roughly the same time, and his six paraphrases are straightforwardly ballad compositions.[36] The potential constraints of this form, for which Hunnis seems to apologise, are also evident in John Hall's execrable verse translations of the Proverbs. The first edition of these, printed by John Case, also contains Surrey's verse psalm(s) and *Ecclesiastes*; but Hall corrects the misattribution of the material in his 1550 edition, and reprints only his own metrical versions.[37] He would have done better to disown them:

> How can you saye (oh mortal men)
> that wisedome doeth not crye
> And prudence eke exalt aloude
> her voice incessauntlye:
> . . . . . .
> In common places, and nigh the same
> in churches and in stretes,
> And in the gates of Cities great
> where many people metes.
> The mightie word, the son of god
> doeth call vnto mankyde,
> Which was before the heauens were made
> and vttreth . . . his mynde.[38]

Still, Hall's translation, while certainly not improving upon chapter eight of Proverbs, does accomplish his asserted goal. He intends to provide ballads within the frame of the 'dayly tales' that Erasmus prescribes. Hall's preface encourages the reader to 'doo thou also exercyse thy selfe in syng-ing, ryming, and talking of the Pouerbes of Salomon, and the Psalmes of Dauid, and other Chapters of the holy scripture'.[39] His metrical verse therefore demonstrates similar objectives to that of Bale and Hunnis. While none of these translations shows a particular concern regarding the affective response of the reader/singer, equally clear is that none is preoccupied with the execution of the poetic line.

William Baldwin's *The canticles or balades of Salomon* (1549) is the most inventive interpretation (apart from poems by Wyatt and Surrey) of scrip-tural material at this time. An excerpt of scripture, and an argument that explains the scriptural text, precedes each of Baldwin's poems. Each is therefore couched in terms that direct the reading of the individual poems. Baldwin claims to have undertaken the project because the scriptural text is itself inscrutable:

No doubt but it is an hie and misticall matter, and more darkely hyd than other partes of the scripture, by meanes of wanton wordes: which also cause many to deny it to be Gods wurde. Whose errour to redresse is the chief cause why I haue medled with the matter. And because the redrest way was to make a paraphrase, I haue attempted it: and that in meter, because they bee balades.[40]

Baldwin's intention is clarification of scripture; by rendering the text in ballad stanzas, he asserts that he is returning it to its proper form. But while many of the poems are written in measures that conform to popular song, Baldwin also departs from balladry. The speakers of his poems are imagined as singers, but the verse itself is not always adaptable to simple tunes. Rather than confine himself entirely to common metre, Baldwin plays with form, opting for poems composed of recurring lines of three, four, or five iambic feet. His poems are also populated by refrains that break the metrical patterns he establishes. Baldwin is unusual in his contemporary context for displaying a poetic inventiveness that moves beyond the merely met-rical. Of course, part of what distinguishes his work is simply talent. (Surrey proved that poulter's measure does not necessarily produce bad poetry.) He is careful, however, to provide biblical text in order to circumscribe the meanings in his verse, and to present his work as a ballad collection.

The paraphrases of Baldwin, Bale, Hall, Hunnis, Surrey, and Wyatt constitute the extant English examples of scriptural verse printed between 1545 and 1550 that is not explicitly composed for song. Other metrical translations of scripture from the period unambiguously declare this intention – and are often published with musical settings to make the point.[41] Cultural reticence is discernable from the limited number of printed works produced purely as lyric poems: the translations of Wyatt and Surrey can alone be confidently placed in this category. (While publication is not limited to printed works, as in the case of the Sidney–Pembroke Psalter, the issues surrounding scriptural verse concern audience and reception – and are therefore situated within the public domain.[42]) But if ambivalence concerning poetic transcription is evident in cultural practices that moderate the interpretations of scripture – and regulate affective responses to it – this attitude calcifies with the return of the Calvinist exiles from Geneva.[43]

'It is easy', Lewalski warns, 'to over-state the role played by the suspicion of the senses in seventeenth-century Calvinist-Puritan aesthetics.'[44] While this is certainly true, it also seems possible to under-state this role, particularly in the sixteenth century. The Puritan 'war against poetry' is a critical commonplace, but it has long been assumed that the redirection of the secular tradition of ballad-singing for the purpose of scriptural edification provided a natural conduit through which devotional language could issue into lyric poems. It is also commonly presumed that Calvinist concerns emerge as a feature of seventeenth-century religious poetics. Ramie Targoff has recently countered these critical narratives, arguing that the application of lyric forms in religious expression would have posed significant problems for sixteenth-century religious culture.[45] (She also cites the Sidney–Pembroke Psalter as the important development in the cultural shift to devotional lyric.) But while Targoff notices the phenomenon, she omits the principal cause: she does not recognise the strain that the advance of Calvinism in England places upon products of the imagination, and how this development stymies invention in scriptural verse.

Targoff importantly understands the Psalter of the Sidneys in terms of its polemical, rather than aesthetic, intervention. But her argument stumbles on taxonomy. She writes that

Once Sidney assigns the label of poetry to this body of devotional texts [metrical Psalms], he forces a new attention to the relationship between poetry and liturgy, a relationship that was formerly unproblematic precisely because no one had demanded that David's Psalms – however elaborately versified – be recognized as anything other than texts of praise and prayer.[46]

This rather confuses the case, for these devotional texts had long been regarded as poetry prior to Sidney's *Defence*; at issue was the purpose of their metrical forms. As Stephen Gosson declares, the aim of poetry in scriptural translation 'was to sett downe good matter in numbers, that ... one might cause the other to continue, and to bee the deeper imprinted in the mindes of men'.[47] Elaborate versification, then, is refused in these works. When Sidney rejects merely metrical translations as poetry, he calls our attention to form (and the formal variety of the Sidney–Pembroke Psalter makes this objective plain). What is at stake for him is not a minor distinction; it is the very ground of the controversy.

When Calvin sanctions the Marot–Beza Psalter, he explicitly considers how poetry may be employed in devotion. A passage in his introduction considers Plato's arguments in relation to psalm-singing:

> if [one] must indeed move to moderate the use of Music, to make music serve for all honesty, and so that it be not at all an occasion to unleash any dissolution, or to feminise ourselves in disorderly delights; & that music be not at all an instrument of laziness, nor of any shamefulness ... for there is hardly anything in this world that might turn or divert here and there the morals of men, as Plato prudently thought: & in fact, we experience its secret, nearly incredible virtue or power to move hearts one way or another. For this reason we must be even more diligent to govern it so that it might be useful to us, and in no way pernicious.[48]

Calvin's conflation of music and verse makes clear that he understood the metrical Psalms as poetry. Precisely for this reason, they require government. Reason must set limits; translations must appeal to the rational mind so that the pleasures of devotion proceed from contemplation of the scriptural word. Such governance grew in importance when Psalter collections expanded to include metrical hymns and canticles based upon scripture. While the tradition enlarges to take in new materials, the verse forms become more controlled and codified. William Whittingham's metrical version of the Song of Simeon (Luke 2:29–32), for example – which is modelled after Marot's (7.6.7.6.6.7) – is dropped from the canticles included in the 1561 edition of the *Psalmes of Dauid,* and the 1562 *Whole booke of Psalmes,* printed by John Day.[49] Rather, Day's collection records a remarkable obedience throughout to a prescribed set of metrical forms.[50]

It is this compliance that distinguishes, for example, Thomas Whythorne's *Triplex, of songes* and *The first booke of ayres* by Thomas Campion (even though both are set to music).[51] If music signalled the inclusion of a metrical translation in the ritual mode, its operation within this framework also depended upon the restriction of its form. Hall's 1565 collection of scriptural translation and ballad verse continues his project of trying to transpose scripture for the 'lecherous Ballades' of *The court of*

Venus.[52] While the metrical psalms in *The courte of vertue* are not situated within musical settings, their metrical forms correspond with those of the *Whole booke of Psalmes* – and all of them fit tunes printed in other sections of the work.[53] Many poems explicitly direct the singer to these musical arrangements. Other works, such as Hunnis's *Seuen sobs of a sorrowfull soule* (1583), are wholly composed in common metre, and further print the psalms themselves within musical settings.[54] Fenner's *The song of songs* (1587) contains voluminous commentary on the biblical text, and each translation is attached to a particular tune in the metrical church Psalter.[55] Numbers by themselves inevitably require further explication, but they usefully expose cultural patterns: between 1558 and 1590, there are two works of vernacular metrical translation of scripture printed in England without musical settings (or explicit direction to a tune in the Sternhold–Hopkins Psalter): Anne Lok's sonnet sequence based upon Psalm 51, 'A meditation of a penitent sinner'; and Gascoigne's translation of Psalm 130, *Deprofundis*.[56]

'PAINT[ING] THE LIUELY FAITH'

Given that the debates concerning poetry ultimately proceed from seats of higher learning, it seems improbable that women could intercede in the controversy at all. But it is precisely their placement outside of formal institutions that affords them a point of entry. Although the interventions of Herbert and Lok are not at all similar, both exhibit an indifference to the pressures that impede university men. The evidence of this pressure is graphically displayed in the treatises and published letters (of Sidney, Fraunce, and Harvey) that seek to overcome it. It is also discernable in the preceding survey of extant poetic materials based on scripture. Certainly, Herbert is aware of the controversy – her close association with both Sidney and Fraunce would have provided full disclosure. Her engagement of the issue, however, does not show Sidney's reticence. This difference is attributable in no small measure to cultural developments in the decade between their activities, and to Herbert's own political and financial capital.[57] It also partly rests on the fact that her training has not persistently emphasised the challenges to poetry. Sidney and Fraunce proceed defensively (indeed, Sidney neither prints his work, nor commits it to scribal publication); Herbert's defence is the circulated Psalter.

Anne Lok enters the arena from a very different place. Her intervention is not the calculated effort of Herbert; she displays a very different attitude toward lyric poetry. She is, nonetheless, interested in the renovation of form. In a richly complicated analysis of her work, Christopher Warley argues that Lok writes against the cultural evaluation of the sonnet form as an aristocratic luxury item.[58] Rather, he claims, Lok uses the form to package Calvin's message for delivery to an urban, non-aristocratic English readership. His concentration upon the social implications of the sonnet, however, causes him to overlook the most important feature of Lok's formal intervention. 'English Protestant poetry [like Lok's] emerged', Warley claims, 'out of native traditions of verse that were generally non-aristocratic; early Reformers, and especially Edwardians, took over native, medieval traditions of plain, didactic verse and applied Protestant messages to them.'[59] Such an easy transition from ballad to lyric verse forms (the process favoured by many analyses of religious poetry in the period) neglects the considerable tension that the use of the sonnet form in religious translation would have produced at this time.

The 'Meditation of a penitent sinner' conjoins a collective and an individual voice, scriptural text and its poetic interpretation, and ritual and lyric modes of poetic production. Lok's lyric poetry has proven resistant to critical terms precisely because her sonnet sequence is not spoken from the position of a unique subject.[60] A confluence of factors related to gender and class accounts for the posture of the speaker of the 'Meditation'. The figure of the religious woman, perceptible in Lok's poem(s), is not self-consciously developed or deployed as a poetic device (as it is, for example, in Lanyer's *Salve Deus*). Instead, a gender-inflected attitude – one that cannot be separated from class position or religious ideology – is a prevailing and, indeed, important characteristic of Lok's verse cycle. In this case, the figure of the woman assumes a Presbyterian position – more involved in collective than individual agency.[61]

Lok was influential in the promotion of Calvinism in England – but she largely exercised both her social and cultural power through the vehicle of men. She became an intimate friend of John Knox, and at his prompting, left London in 1557 to join him in Geneva (taking her two infant children).[62] The value of her support to Knox cannot be underestimated – their friendship leaves a bequest of some thirteen letters written from Knox to her between the years of 1556 and 1562.[63] The letters reveal, if nothing else, the extent to which Knox relied upon her.[64] Lok's second husband was the prominent Calvinist preacher Edward Dering, whom she married in 1572. But her own contributions to religious reform were largely of a supportive nature, and her publication of religious texts assumes a similar role. Lok uses the arguments of men to advance her own religious or religio-political opinions; but she positions herself marginally within the texts themselves. Her activities within the arena of publication are not obeisant – but they are deferent.

Part of the difficulty in analysing Lok's work derives from the fact that it is so deeply embedded in male discourse. While her translation of Calvin's *Sermons . . . vpon the songe that Ezechias made after he had bene sicke* (1560) is dedicated to another female religious reformer (and fellow exile), Catherine Brandon Bertie, the dowager Duchess of Suffolk, its impulse and organisation are directed toward the dissemination of Calvin's words:

[W]e se dayly, when skilfull men by arte, or honest neyghbours hauyng gathered vnderstandyng of some specyall dysease and the healing therof by theyr owne experiment, do applie their knowledge to the restoring of health of any mans body in any corporall sicknesse, howe thankfully it is taken, howe muche the releued patient accompteth him selfe bound to him by meane of whose aide and minis- tration he findeth him self holpen or eased. What then deserueth he, that teacheth such a receipt, wherby health both of body and mynde is preserued . . . This receipte God the heauenly Physitian hath taught, his most excellent Apothecarie master Iohn Caluine hath compounded, and I your graces most bounden and humble have put into an Englishe box, and do present vnto you.[65]

Lok's dedication does not deny the significance of her role as apothecary's assistant. The 'Englishe box' in which Calvin's message is contained is undeniably important to its transmission. Moreover, Calvin himself is merely a conduit: he receives knowledge from God, and mixes it with the requisite words to convey the meaning. Lok's service is at an additional remove because she packages the material in English. But the expression is crucial, as her own articulation of the project describes: 'Concernyng my translation of this boke, it may please you to vnderstand that I haue rendred it so nere as I possibly might, to the very wordes of [Calvin's] text, and that in so plaine Englishe as I could expresse.'[66] Her concern to render the text with care is echoed by other translators of Calvin's work; in his dedication to *The institvtion of Christian religion*, Thomas Norton writes that he laboured 'to folow the wordes so nere as the phrase of the English tong would suffer me'.[67] The distinction lies in the situation of the two translators within their respective texts. All editions of Norton's *Institvtion*, with the exception of the first, are outfitted with a lengthy preface from the translator – which swells with each successive edition. These prefaces reveal the control that Norton exercised over the orienta- tion of the text – including compelling a corrected edition when 'the evil maner of my scribbling hand, the enterlining of my Copy, and some other causes . . . made very many faultes to passe the Printer'.[68] By contrast,

Lok's considerably more original contribution to Calvin's *Sermons*, her sonnet collection, does not bear her name.[69]

It is impossible to determine definitively who tailored the presentation of the sequence. It is printed under this peculiar disclaimer: 'I haue added this meditation folowynge vnto the ende of this boke, not as parcell of maister Caluines worke, but for that it well agreeth with the same argument, and was deliuered me by my frend with whom I knew I might be so bolde to vse & publishe it as pleased me.'[70] Some critics have assumed that Lok included this headnote. The more credible explanation, however, is that it was affixed by the printer, John Day.[71] The sonnets were probably composed between March 1559 and their publication in January 1560; the 'deliuer[y]' of the 'parcell' suggests that Day might have received the collection sometime after the initial manuscript, and decided to include it. But his diction also suggests that Lok ceded the decision to him. Day's editorial practice is not entirely unique – Reyner Wolf and John Harrison similarly identify Norton as a 'frende of oures', whose translation they commissioned, in the first edition of *The institvtion*.[72] But once Norton becomes actively engaged in the publication of the text, he provides lengthy accounts of his process and procedure in translation. In other words, he asserts ownership over his work. What is striking, then, is Lok's composition of an original text that she does not declare as her own. She provides Day with a copy of the work, and leaves its publication to his discretion. We cannot know if Lok's name was suppressed through her own initiative or his; but we can be reasonably sure that Day would have attached her name had she made the request.

This situates Lok's sonnet sequence somewhere between a private exercise and a public text. Her equation of the circumstances of 'two moste excellent kinges, Ezechias and Dauid' in the dedication suggests that she intended to include her translation of the *Miserere mei Deus* with the *Sermons*.[73] Further, as Rosalind Smith has observed, the psalm translation serves to expose a political dimension to Calvin's oration – and to direct it toward England.[74] All of this points to public activity. But Lok also seems to have permitted the possibility that her sonnets never see print. We do not know how the sequence was attributed in subsequent editions of the *Sermons*; but its initial publication carries an ambivalent message.[75]

The ambivalence is attributable in part to gender. Lok self-consciously enacts the restricted role of her sex in her 1590 translation of Jean Taffin's *Of the markes of the children of God*:

Euerie one in his calling is bound to doo somewhat to the furtherance of the holie building; but because great things by reason of my sex, I may not doo, and that which I may, I ought to doo, I haue according to my duetie, brought my poore basket of stones to the strengthning of the walles of that Ierusalem, whereof (by grace) wee are all both Citizens and members.[76]

She does not assume, however, that all women are subject to the same regulation. She means for her dedications to influence those noble women 'whom the Lord ... hath set vp, as it were a light vpon an high candlesticke, to giue light vnto manie'.[77] Patriarchy is never monolithic, and factors such as economics, education, class, and religious affiliation complicated women's relationship to the social arrangements of sixteenth-century England.[78] Certainly there was a social ethic in place that demanded women's subordination to men; but the ethic was modified by class position.[79] In Lok's case, the subordinate position that she assumes is part of a gendered performance. Indeed, her strategy is to undermine boundaries appropriate to her sex and status while never appearing to do so. The marginal place that Lok assumes appears to be her own construction. But there is a kind of agency at the margins that a central location does not afford.

In his account of the process of translation, Norton (speaking from the centre) makes the handling of religious texts sound something akin to bomb-making: 'If I should leaue the course of words, and graunt my selfe liberty after the natural maner of myne own tong, to say that in English which I conceiued to be [Calvin's] meaning in Latine, I plainly perceiued how hardly I might escape error: and on the other syde in thys matter of fayth and religion, how perilous it was to erre.'[80] Norton's diction exhibits his sense of the explosive energies released by crossed wires. Lok does not register the same level of concern. The comparison partly reveals the different attitude engendered by her placement outside of the 'scholemennes controuersies' that so consume Norton.[81] Her attempt to revaluate the use of lyric in religious expression, and revise the application of its forms, demonstrates a similar confidence that only an outside position would allow. The fact that Lok does not claim the experiment as her own once it is produced suggests a lapse in her assurance when the project reaches print. Perhaps Lok's tentativeness in relation to the publication of her sonnets corresponds to her deepening awareness of the controversy in which she was involving herself. This too, I would suggest, could have motivated her behaviour. If Lok deliberately placed herself at the margins of her textual production, discretion could deflect criticism.[82] But the situation further serves the aim of the project as a whole. Generally stated, this aim is the recuperation of the sonnet form for a Presbyterian purpose.

Lok's sequence is an answer to the *Songes and sonettes, written by the ryght honorable Lorde Henry Haward late Earle of Surrey, and others*, commonly known as Tottel's *Miscellany*. As Michel Spiller surmised nearly a decade ago, Surrey is the likely source of the sonnet form that Lok adopts. Aware of Petrarch as the forerunner of the sonnet, the poets who employed the form in English tended to observe the octave/sestet break. Surrey's 'The great Macedon' uniquely (even for Surrey) overruns this break – a practice that Lok implements in seventeen of her twenty-six sonnets.[83] The only place where Lok could have encountered the poem is in Tottel's. Spiller incorrectly assumes that 'The great Macedon' prefaces the translations in Wyatt's printed *Certayne Psalms chosen out of the Psalter of Dauid*, as it does in the Blage manuscript. Lok worked from a copy of Wyatt's translation of Psalm 51, as Spiller has shown, but she very likely used the version of the poem in print.[84] (In her movement from England to Frankfurt to Geneva, books would have been preferable cargo.) Even if she did not, unless she followed a manuscript variant of the Blage, she could not have seen Surrey's poem prior to its publication by Tottel.[85] Warley suggests that she could have obtained a copy of the *Miscellany* when she returned to Frankfurt in March 1559.[86] It is also entirely possible that Lok read Tottel's on her return to England in June 1559, and wrote her sonnet sequence in the intervening six months before it was published.

The poem in the *Miscellany* that draws her concerted attention is Surrey's 'Praise of certain Psalmes of Dauid, translated by Sir. T. W. the elder' (this is the title given to 'The great Macedon' in Tottel's collection). If Lok already possessed a copy of Wyatt's *Certayne Psalms*, there is good reason for her attraction. But Surrey's homage also stands out among the poems in Tottel's for its promotion of lyric verse as a vehicle for moral and religious redemption. Wyatt's translation is treated as a portrait of Christian struggle:

> Where he doth paint the liuely faith, and pure,
> The stedfast hope, the swete returne to grace
> Of iust Dauid, by perfite penitence.[87]

The representation has vivifying powers: the capacity to wake Christians, and Christian kings, 'out of their sinfull slepe'.[88] Lok pursues the suggestion of poetry's ability to represent penitence (and Smith's sharp analysis of her sonnet sequence traces the political element of this idea). She further accepts that lyric poetry can cause the reader to 're-experience its statements from the inside'.[89] But the 'Mediation' consists of a reframing of the lyric that she finds in Tottel's – and a reconstitution of its materials for a sacred purpose.

Lok's sonnet sequence can be understood as an active contemplation of the lyric mode. She borrows Surrey's suggestion that lyric can force its claims upon the individual reader; but she also tries to engage a collective, as opposed to an individual, voice in her poem(s). In other words, her poetry operates in both the ritual and lyric modes. Just as Lok allows Calvin to carry her message in the translation of the *Sermons*, her own penitent cry is subsumed in the voice of David in the 'Meditation'. Warley rightly identifies a 'question of the gendered authority of the speaker'.[90] But multiple voices form part of the poem's ritual mode – the collective voice is part of its narrative strategy. The speaker is David *and* Lok; it is also the English congregation that Lok leads in prayer. Presbyterianism asserted the authority of individual members to lead the religious communion. In this sense, Lok's poetic sequence is both a depiction of Christian penitence and a prayer for individual church members to follow.

The rhetorical model that predominantly informs the 'Meditation', in fact, is not a poetic one at all. Lok appropriates Surrey's sonnet form, and borrows Wyatt's diction; but the dilation of scripture that produces the sequence imitates the rhetorical practice of Calvin. The 'Meditation' is a collection of twenty-one sonnets, each loosely based upon a single line of the source text (there are also five prefatory sonnets to the sequence). Lok's original translation of Psalm 51, scored in the margin, is based upon the Latin Vulgate; each sonnet corresponds to the biblical verse printed at its side (although she splits verse one and four).[91] Greene reads this enlargement of the Psalm text as a gendered convention: 'the speaker's gender ... is implied by the symbolic association with a postmedieval context of feminine copiousness and dilation'.[92] But the sonnet sequence, as its headnote declares, 'well agreeth with the ... argument' in Calvin's *Sermons*, and it follows the same discursive practice. The *Sermons* themselves are a dilation of Isaiah 38. Like the sonnet sequence, each sermon begins with a citation of the lines of biblical text that it will treat. Calvin starts at Isaiah 38:9, and exfoliates between three and four verses in each address. Throughout his oration, he repeats the verses that are the subject of his sermon, explaining the terms and expounding upon the themes, but always organising his speech around the Text. Lok, in turn, imports Calvin's rhetorical strategy of dilating scripture into a poetic practice: he enlarges four lines into a sermon, she expands a single verse into a sonnet.

That Lok's poetic production is modelled upon a particular strain of sermonising seems to support Lewalski's theory that lyric poetry was sanctioned through the licence allowed for preaching. But Calvin serves Lok as a model of restriction:

Therefore if one would make an arte of Rethoricke of the praiers of the faithful, it is a great abuse: for our lord humbleth vs to this end, that we shold not imagine to obteine any thing at his hands by any fair tale: he had rather that we were so confused, that we had not only one word a right in oure praiers, but that nowe we shoulde cast out puffynges, and blowinges, and anon that we should abide styll with silence: alas my God, alas what shal I do? and when we shall mourne so, that we should be so wrapped in, and tangled, that there should neither be begynnynge nor ending. Then when we shalbe brought to that point, our lord knoweth this kind of language, although we vnderstande it not, and although our perplexities hinder vs, that we can not bringe forthe one perfect sentence, so that men also vnderstande not what we say: yet God ... wyll heare vs well ynoughe.[93]

Calvin's 'arte of Rethoricke' suggests a specific referent. While Thomas Wilson's *Arte of rhetorique* (1553) takes aim at the 'tediousnesse' of contemporary preaching, this book does not seem to be Calvin's target.[94] Rather, he seems to be referring to Leonard Cox's extended treatment of the oratory that should serve preachers. Cox's *The arte or crafte of rhetoryke* (1532), loosely based upon Philip Melanchthon's *Institutiones rhetoricae*, aspires 'to make som proper werke of the right pleasaunt and persuadible art of Rhetorique whiche ... is very necessary to all suche as wyll ... be techers of goddes worde'.[95] Calvin certainly places a high premium upon preaching. But the oration, as Calvin himself demonstrates, should be in as plain a style as possible. When Calvin claims that 'we shold not imagine to obteine any thing at [God's] hands by any fair tale', he is referring the rhetoric of preachers as well as the faithful: 'that all the imagination of men when they trust in their own strengthes is nothing but a dreame, bicause they loke not vpon God, and do not there stay themselues, that they mighte be spoiled of all vayne ouerwening of themselues'.[96] For Calvin, ornamental language only adorns the preacher; the right way to address God, emphasised in his *Sermons*, is to stutter.

This *absence* of eloquence is central to the formal choices of Lok's work. Her genius lies in the conscious application of Calvin's principles to poetics. She was probably not fully cognisant of the arguments concerning the hierarchy of reason above the imagination – the functions of the wit, particularly as they related to rhetoric, were largely parsed in 'scholemennes controuersies'. But she was certainly aware of Calvin's attitudes concerning language. David is consistently invoked in the *Sermons* as a paradigm – along with Hezekiah – of the penitent sinner:

from [penitence] ... procede[s] al these complaints that we see in the Psalmes. They that ar not exercised in these batails and perplexities, think that Dauid meant to make his trouble greater than it was ... but when we come to the profe, we fele that there is not one word to much for the stormes that the faythfull fele when God searcheth them earnestly and to the quicke, surmount al that may be expressed with mouth.[97]

True penitence, according to Calvin, stuns reason and makes language an impossible performance. While Lok clearly did not sanction the secular uses to which lyric poetry had been put in Tottel's, she was nonetheless arrested by the idea that poetry could truly depict penitence. At issue was how to reconcile the formal and elegant expression of lyric and the impaired expression that Calvin claimed was appropriate to the penitent sinner.

Lok's tortured syntax in the five prefatory sonnets '[p]oure[s] forth' in a 'piteous plaint' and resolves in prayer.[98] These sonnets enact the exploration of an internal state, where the sinner encounters horror at the soul's condition (and fear of God's inevitable retribution).[99] The anguish of the opening sonnets then gives way to the 'Meditation ... vpon the 51. Psalm'. Calvin explains the reason for this structure:

For whan oure Lorde sheweth vs a terrible countenaunce, oure mouthes are stopped, we are fylled wyth suche anguisshe, that it is impossible for vs to blesse hym. Rather contrariwise there shall be nothynge but gnashynge of teethe, when the wrath of God shall so astonishe vs ... On the other syde, when God sheweth hym selfe mercyfull towarde vs, and vttereth some signe of hys fauor toward vs, he openeth oure mouthes, as it is sayde in the li Psalme.[100]

Once the penitent is brought low by consideration of '[t]he hainous gylt of my forsaken ghost', the direction of the lyric sequence changes to contemplation of God's mercy.[101] Calvin claims 'that we can not pronounce one worde to his prayse, whiche procedeth from a good hartie affection, except we be thoroughly perswaded in this, that God is mercyfull vnto vs'.[102] As the focus of Lok's sequence changes from an inward to an outward direction, the sonnets become more melodious, and confidence in God's mercy is reinforced by repetition:

> Haue mercy, God, for thy great mercies sake.
> O God: my God, vnto my shame I say,
> Beynge fled from thee, so as I dred to take
> Thy name in wretched mouth, and feare to pray

> Or aske the mercy that I haue abusde.
> But, God of mercy, let me come to thee:
> Not for iustice, that iustly am accusde:
> Which selfe word Iustice so amaseth me,
> That scarce I dare thy mercy sound againe.
> But mercie, Lord, yet suffer me to craue.
> Mercie is thine: Let me not crye in vaine,
> Thy great mercie for my great fault to haue.
> Haue mercie, God, pitie my penitence
> With greater mercie than my great offence.[103]

The first sonnet of the 'Mediation' proper performs the process by which Calvin claims the sinner's mouth is opened: alienation from God makes the penitent afraid to pronounce his name, but his mercy permits the necessary boldness to speak. This process is enacted several times throughout the sonnet sequence, as though the speaker must repeat it each time expression fails:

> Lo straining crampe of colde despeir againe
> In feble brest doth pinche my pinyng hart,
> So as in greatest nede to cry and plaine
> My speache doth faile to vtter thee my smart.
> Refreshe my yeldyng hert, with warming grace,
> And loose my speche, and make me call to thee.[104]

Lok presents her text as an addendum to Calvin's work, an illustrative example of his message: 'So here this good soules Physician [Calvin] hath brought you where you maye se lyinge before youre face the good king Ezechias, somtime chillinge and chattering with colde, somtime languishing and meltynge away with heate, nowe fresing, nowe fryeng, nowe spechelesse, nowe crying out.'[105] In her own 'liuely' depiction, Hezekiah, as much as the poet, experiences the 'straining crampe of colde despeir' that causes his/her 'speache [to] faile'. The individual voice that emerges from the 'Mediation' joins with the voices of David, Hezekiah, and Calvin. Identity is inherently multiple in psalm poetry, where the speaker's voice and David's inevitably fuse. But Lok deliberately constructs such a collaborative voice. This construction is partly intended to bypass the theoretical problems that Sidney encounters: Sidney assumes that the 'speaking picture' of poetry can itself transport the mind. Calvin insists that 'words have no power to imbue men's minds with divine matters, unless the Lord through his Spirit gives understanding'.[106] Lok therefore follows the procedure that Calvin outlines for revelation in her 'Meditation'. The emphasis upon the interruption of speech indicates that in the act of penitence, 'the Holy Spirit has taken over the plea for mercy when the resources of the human tongue fail (Rom. 8:26)'.[107] The sequence, in other words, is imagined as a re-enactment of the process that prompted David's song. This explains the discordant sounds of the prefatory sonnets that then give way to a more melodious voice at the cry for mercy. It also accounts for the marginal psalm verses that control the 'Mediation' itself. The sonnet sequence collaborates between scriptural text and interpretation precisely because it is reproducing a method. If words cannot illuminate the mind without the intervention of the Holy Spirit, Lok's poetry manufactures the process by which the Spirit is summoned. The speaker of her poems, then, is any Christian who calls upon the help of God within the framework that Calvin (and David) prescribes. Lok is not simply employing the persuasive powers of lyric poetry in order to compel the experience of penitence in the reader; rather, the act of reading the poem(s) causes the individual to perform it.

The subjective mode that Lok encountered in Tottel's obviously would not facilitate such a project. But Wyatt is the poet whose work Lok primarily revises. Wyatt's invention is to appropriate the Penitential Psalm 51 for emergent evangelical thought; Lok's innovation is its appropriation for Calvinist Presbyterianism. Throughout the 'Meditation', we can witness Lok taking language and metaphor from Wyatt, while dismantling the unified subject that speaks his verse. The most obvious means of cancelling individual subjectivity in the 'Meditation' is the reproduction of the verse Psalm at the margin:

For lo, in sinne, Lord, I begotten was,   *For loe, I*
With sede and shape my sinne I toke also,   *was shapen*
Sinne is my nature and my kinde alas,   *in wicked-*
In sinne my mother me conceiued: Lo   *nes, and in*
I am but sinne, and sinfull ought to dye,   *sinne my*
Dye in his wrath that hath forbydden sinne.   *mother con-*
Such bloome and frute loe sinne doth multiplie,   *ceived me.*
Such was my roote, such is my iuyse within.
I pleade not this as to excuse my blame,
On kynde or parentes myne owne gilt to lay:
But by disclosing of my sinne, my shame,
And nede of helpe, the plainer to displaye
Thy mightie mercy, if with plenteous grace
My plenteous sinnes it please thee to deface.[108]

The first four lines of the sonnet are a close paraphrase of the biblical text, while the subsequent ten meditate upon the idea expressed (not every sonnet in the sequence follows this pattern). In dilating the Text, Lok borrows a suggestion from Wyatt:[109]

> For I my selfe, loo thinge moste vnstable,
> Formed in offence, conceaued in lyke case
> Am nought but synne from my natyuytie
> Be not these sayde, for myne excuse, ah alas
> But of thy helpe, to shewe necessite inwarde.[110]

Lok's declaration, 'I am but sinne' follows Wyatt's 'Am nought but synne from my natyuytie.' But she elaborates upon Wyatt's evocation of the origins of sin. 'Such was my roote, such is my iuyse within', invokes the first parents, who are not then held ultimately to blame (lines 9–12 obviously take directly from Wyatt). In developing the concept supplied by Wyatt, Lok emphasises the condition of all Christian souls – the 'kynde' with whom she shares her sinful state. There is no precedent for this depiction of a shared Christian condition in the scripture, or in other translations of Psalm 51.

Lok returns to this strategy in her description of the remedy for sin:

> With swete Hysope besprinkle thou my sprite: *Sprinkle*
> Not such hysope, nor so besprinkle me,   *me, Lorde,*
> As law vnperfect shade of perfect lyght   *with hisope*
> Did vse as an apointed signe to be   *and I shal-*
> Foreshewing figure of thy grace behight.   *be cleane:*
> With death and bloodshed of thine only sonne,   *washe me*
> The swete hysope, cleanse me defyled wyght.   *and I shal-*
> Sprinkle my soule.[111]   *be whiter*
>   *then snow.*

Again, these lines draw from Wyatt:

> And as the Iewes, to heale thee lepper sore
> Wythe Isoppe clense, clense me and I am cleane
> Thou shalte me washe, and more then snowe therfore
> I shalbe whyte, howe fowle my faulte hath bene
> Thou of my health, shall gladsome tydinges bringe
> When from aboue, remission shalbe sene
> Discende on earth.[112]

Lok eschews Wyatt's allusion to an ancient Hebrew practice; but she pursues his evocation of the 'gladsome tydinges' of the Gospels. The hyssop serves as a sign of Christian salvation, and converts to the cleansing agent of Christ's blood. If Wyatt alludes to Christ's coming in the 'remission' that '[d]icende[s] on earth', Lok develops the theme to incorporate a description of the means by which the Christian soul is cleansed ('wash thee in Christ's blood, which hath this might / That being red, it dyes red souls to white'[113]). Lok's 'Meditation' is organised as an encounter with the biblical text; but unlike Wyatt's psalm poem, it is not an individual encounter that is depicted. Rather, Lok endeavours to describe a shared condition – and to produce a meditative practice for Christians to follow. Hers is the psalmic 'I' in the truest sense: the 'I' of David that speaks for all Christians.

The juxtaposition of Fall and Resurrection, suggested by Wyatt's poem and enlarged in sonnets 7 and 9, inspires Lok to continue to put the universal Christian themes of original sin and saving grace in apposition throughout the 'Meditation'. Her imagination persistently returns to the garden of the Fall in sonnets 14, 15, and 16:

> But render me my wonted ioyes againe,
> Which sinne hath reft, and planted in theyr place
> Doubt of thy mercy ground of all my paine.
> . . . . . .
> So shall the profe of myne example preache
> The bitter frute of lust and foule delight:
> . . . . . .
> Assoile me, God, from gilt of giltlesse blod,
> And eke from sinne that I ingrowyng haue
> By fleshe and bloud and by corrupted kinde.[114]

But once the speaker's 'yeldyng hert' is revived 'with warming grace' (the entry of the Holy Spirit), sonnets 17, 18, and 19 turn to the sacrifice that paid for sin:

> Ne can I ryse, ne can I stande alone.
> . . . . . .
>   But thy swete sonne alone,
> With one sufficing sacrifice for all
> Appeaseth thee, and maketh the at one
> With sinfull man, and hath repaird our fall.[115]

Christ's Passion is the chief index of God's mercy toward 'sinfull man'. The refreshed Christian soul therefore turns to it. This movement from perplexity to assurance of God's mercy parallels the trajectory of the Psalm itself. But the speaker of the sonnets has been, by this time, completely absorbed into a collective Christian identity. The amplification from the particular to the general Christian condition propels most devotional poetry. Lok departs from poets such as Wyatt and Surrey when she revaluates the claims of an individual speaker. The 'Meditation' is so invested in multiple voices that it is difficult to perceive an individuated experience at all.

Greene characterises the 'Meditation' as 'a poetry of matter – of the received text made still more substantial, more material – by a fruitful but decidedly unoriginal intelligence'.[116] This underestimates Lok's complicated strategies. The pressure that Wyatt's translation exerts upon her composition betrays a highly productive poetic imagination. She does, however (as Greene observes), inhibit invention in terms of figurative language. Hers is a poetic application of Calvin's rhetorical discipline. Calvin vivifies the figures of Hezekiah and David by the graphic description of their physical suffering. Lok gives the suffering an agonised voice. But the fullness of Christian anguish cannot flow into the language of the courtly love lyrics that populate Tottel's *Miscellany*. It is an affliction that (Calvin claims) renders speech in 'broken wordes'.[117]

The 'Meditation' must be evaluated in relation to the cultural context that produced it.[118] If Lok does not exhibit the elaborate play of language that we have come to identify with sixteenth-century lyric verse, she nonetheless brilliantly reconceives the frames in which lyric poetry can operate. Indeed, her sonnets operate within individual and collective frames simultaneously. The displacement of a female voice on to an array of male voices is an index of a biographical reality. The deference to male voices in Lok's poem(s) is a gendered position that she assumes in all of her work; but from a gender-inflected speaking position she produces a polyphonic text. The collaboration of the voices of David and Hezekiah establish scripture as the primary source of poetic inspiration. The rhetorical habits of Calvin organise the verse. The 'Meditation' itself is ultimately conceived as a devotional exercise that simulates the voices of the Calvinist faithful. Lok's principal innovation is the inscription of polyphonic subjectivity – a multiplication of voices that allegorises the Presbyterian congregation.

NORTON'S AFFLICTION: THE *MISERERE MEI DEUS*

Lok's novel strategies partly resolve some of the issues that afflict religious lyric poetry at this time. Where the 'Meditation' fails, finally, is in its incomplete habitation of the ritual mode. The religious expression of the sequence retains one foot in the frame of individual subjectivity.

But its sonnet form is also inherently problematic in terms of ritual (as the metrical forms in the translations of men attest). That Lok's poetic experiment did not achieve a resolution of the prevailing cultural conflict is confirmed by the only contemporary response to her work: Norton's metrical translation of Psalm 51. And Norton is probably our best index to the complex attitudes concerning religion and lyric verse. He does not register any anxiety in connection with his composition of the first three acts of *Gorboduc* (and his 'Epitaph of maister Henry Williams' is printed in Tottel's[119]). But as soon as he embarks on the translation of religious texts – whether prose or poetry, Calvin or the Bible – the activity becomes fraught with peril.

Norton's translation of Psalm 51 appears for the first time in the 1562 *Residue of all Dauids Psalmes in metre*, which Day published to supplement the 1561 edition of the metrical English Psalter.[120] It was subsequently printed, along with Whittingham's translation, in *The whole booke of Psalmes*. Since other works by Norton appear in the 1561 Psalter, his translation of the *Miserere mei Deus* was probably completed sometime between the publication of this edition and the *Residue*. There is no reason, in spite of their similar religious commitments, to assume that Norton knew Lok, or even to assume that he knew the identity of the translator of Calvin's *Sermons*. What we can be sure of is that any translation of Calvin's work would have attracted his eye (and his entrenchment in the London book trade would have certainly brought the *Sermons* to his attention). The most persuasive evidence that he read the 'Meditation', however, is legible in the translation itself.

What is immediately striking is how closely Norton seems to have followed Lok's original translation of the biblical Psalm. Of the ten different vernacular prose versions of Psalm 51 collated by Susan Felch, Norton's translation most often echoes the first authorised English primer of 1545, and, secondarily, the Great Bible of 1539.[121] There are numerous instances where a particular phrase employed by Norton is not in *The primer*, but can be discovered in *The Byble in Englyshe*, and vice versa. There are also a few examples of language absent in both versions, but found in other Psalters. Significantly, however, in almost every instance Norton's phrasing is available in Lok's translation.[122] Norton could have followed the same Vulgate version of the text (the Gallican Psalter) that Lok used; but two translators conceiving of the same words to convey the Latin seems extremely unlikely. Additionally, there are verbal echoes from Lok's poem that are not suggested in any other source – either in prose or metrical translation. Setting Norton's

metrical version next to Lok's psalm translation is the most persuasive
method of comparison:

NORTON	LOK
Haue mercy on me, God, after	*Have mercie vpon me (o God)*
thy great abounding grace:	*after thy great merci. And accord-*
After thy mercies multitude	*ing vnto the multitude of thy*
doo thou my sinnes deface.	*mercies do away myne offences.*
Yet wash me more from mine offence	*Wash me yet more from my*
and clense me from my sin:	*wickednes, and clense me from*
For I beknow my fautes, and still	*my sinne. For I knowledge my*
my sinne is in mine eyen.[123]	*wickednes, and my sinne is euer*
	before me.[124]

The first two lines most closely resemble the Great Bible's 'haue mercy
vpon me (O God) after thy (greate) goodnes', but bear no direct resemblance to any prose version (indeed, 'abounding grace' does not echo any
text).[125] Norton's 'thy mercies multitude' also finds a correlative in *The
Byble in Englyshe* ('according vnto the multitude of thy mercyes'). The
subsequent line, however, 'doo thou my sinnes deface', does not resemble
any prose text, and echoes Lok's 'My plenteous sinnes it please thee to
deface' (184).[126] Since a similar line is also included in Whittingham's
Psalm 51, 'My sinnes deface, my fautes redresse', there is still no reason
to think that Norton had to have relied upon Lok.[127] But Norton's next
line, 'Yet wash me more from mine offence' diverges from the Great Bible
and corresponds mostly closely to the wording of *The primer*. And it
strongly echoes Lok ('offence' is drawn from Lok's previous line).

There are also correspondences between Norton's metrical translation
of Psalm 51 and Lok's poetic 'Meditation'. In Norton's third stanza, he
confesses:

> Beholde in wickednes my kinde and
>   shape I did receyue:
> And loe my sinnfull mother eke
>   in sinne did me conceiue.[128]

The Great Bible is a possible source for this: 'Behold, I was shapen in
wickednesse, and in synne hath my mother conceaued me.'[129] So is Lok:

For lo, in sinne, Lord, I begotten was,	*For loe, I was shapen in*
With sede and shape my sinne I toke also,	*wickedness, and in sinne*
Sinne is my nature and my kinde alas,	*my mother conceiued me.*
In sinne my mother me conceiued.[130]	

Norton's 'kinde and shape' recalls Lok's 'sede and shape' – and he seems to compress Lok's conception of sin residing in the nature of humankind. Furthermore, the verbal echoes persist and accumulate. Norton writes:

> With hysope, Lorde, besprincle me,
>   I shalbe clensed so:
> Yea wash thou me, and so I shall
>   be whiter than the snow.[131]

His first line sounds very close to the opening of Lok's sonnet 9, 'With swete Hysope besprinkle thou my sprite' (the term 'besprinkle' appears nowhere else), and his subsequent lines resemble her conclusion: 'Wash me, O Lord: when I am washed soe, / I shalbe whiter than the whitest snowe.'[132] Since 'thou shalt wash me, and I shalbe whiter then snowe' does not vary much among the prose versions, this could easily be a coincidence.[133] But the final lines of Norton's stanza also cite the 'broosed bones' of Lok's sonnet 10; while this phrase can be found in *The primer* (and in Hunnis's translation of Psalm 51[134]), the succession of correspondences to Lok's work is telling.

There are also examples of language in Norton's translation that appear to have no source other than Lok. Norton renders the tenth verse of Psalm 51 in the following way:

> O God creat in me a hart   *Create a cleane hart within me,*
>   vnspotted in thy sight.   *O God: and renew a stedfast*
> And eke within my bowels, Lorde,   *sprite within my bowels.*[136]
>   renew a stable sprite.[135]

Lok converts 'stedfast' from the translation to 'constant sprite' in her poem. The phrase 'stable spirit' is used in George Joye's 1534 *Dauids Psalter* – but there is no comparable description in the prose versions that sets the spirit deeply within the bowels of the body.[137] Norton's 'comfort of thy sauing help' (43) is identical to the biblical text aligned to Lok's sonnet 14 (the closest analogue in the prose versions is Joye's 'gladnes of thy sauinge helth'[138]). The final lines of Norton's sixth stanza also borrow from Lok's prose:

> And I will teache therfore,   *I shal teach thy waies vnto the*
> Sinners thy wayes, and wicked shall   *wicked, and sinne[r]s shall be*
>   be turned vnto thy lore.[139]   *tourned vnto thee.*[140]

Certainly the sense is conveyed in other versions, but not the diction (for example, 'turned' does not appear in other texts). At this point in Norton's poem, echoes occur at virtually every line. There is also an echo of Wyatt that Norton appears to have taken from Lok. In the seventh stanza, Norton struggles to call to God: 'My lippes that yet fast closed be, / doo thou, O Lorde vnlose.'[141] The conventional cry is for God to 'open [the] lippes' of the sinner, or 'Touch thou my lippes, my tonge vntye.'[142] Lok borrows the terms of Wyatt ('Thou muste, oh lorde, my lippes fyrste vnlose'[143]) for her expression: 'Lord loose my lippes, I may expresse my mone.'[144] Only Wyatt, Lok, and Norton use this phrasing in English.

If we are to assume that Norton did not read Lok's work, then we have to assume that he read the Great Bible, the English primer, Joye's Psalter, and the translations of Psalm 51 by Hunnis, Whittingham, and Wyatt. This is possible; he almost certainly read *The Byble in Englyshe* and *The primer*.[145] What seems impossible is that he adopted the same terms from these works, at identical moments in the biblical text, without reference to Lok.[146] If we accept that Norton read Lok's 'Meditation', we can arrive at some important conclusions: the first is that he did not adopt her form; the second is that he is far more interested in her translation of the biblical Psalm than in the sonnet sequence itself. The first observation might be tempered by the fact that Norton's translation was composed for the English metrical Psalter; its form was regulated by the requirements of collective worship. But Norton at no time (so far as we know) attempted a translation of scripture in lyric verse. However compelling he found the language of Lok's 'Meditation', he finally rejects the sonnet form as an acceptable vehicle for its transmission. Further, he appears to have been drawn to the Text far more than to its lyric interpretation. Norton's metrical version of Psalm 51 is a genuine example of what Greene calls poetry 'of the received text': poetry that attempts to mimic the terms and structures of scriptural verse, and to restrict invention to the extent that it is possible in poetic translation. Rather than follow Lok's initiative, Norton returns her poem to the appropriate expression and prescribed form.

Lok was probably not aware of the dimensions – or, at least, all of the components – of the controversy concerning religious lyric poetry. Whether she became fully cognisant of the issues, through the tutelage of Day or some other person, prior to the publication of her sonnet sequence is an open question. At some point, however, she seems to have been made aware of the consequences of form (marriage to Dering would have certainly provided this education).[147] Lok adds an original poem to her translation of Taffin's *Of the markes of the children of God* entitled, 'The necessitie and benefite *of affliction*', that is properly couched in common metre.[148] While this poem adds something to the developing tradition of religious verse – insofar as it is an individual contemplation of religious life, rather than a received text – it is nonetheless expressed in a form that declares its ritual intent. In this sense, it participates in the cultural developments that we can perceive in the 1580s – from the acrostic poem of Frances Abergavenny in *The monvment of matrones* to the original metrical verse of Byrd, Drayton, and Hunnis.

SVNDRY CHRISTIAN PASSIONS

Clearly, a more experimental and more subjective religious poetry could be imagined in England before the 1590s; but there were significant obstacles to its production and publication. As Gascoigne explains in his epistle 'To the reuerende Diuines' which prefaces his *Posies*: 'the depth and secrets of some conceytes, which (being passed in clowdes and figuratiue speeches) might ... be offensiue to your grauitie, and perillous to my credite'.[149] Potentially the most offensive 'flowre' of his collection was his lyric translation of Psalm 130, *Deprofundis*.[150] Gascoigne draws his authority from the example of Calvinists such as Theodore Beza, who 'after they haue both reformed their liues, and conuerted their studies ... did not yet disdaine too suffer the continued publication of such Poemes as [they] wrote in youth'.[151] Statements such as this do more to expose the intense pressure against the use of lyric poetry in religious expression than to suggest its relief. English poets had (by 1575) continental as well as vernacular examples of religious lyric poems.[152] Moreover, while Beza and Buchanan both wrote lyric compositions when their spirituality was identifiably Catholic (however reform-minded in its orientation), they do not, as Gascoigne points out, block the publication of their poems once their faith reformed.[153] In other words, there was precedent on which to build. But English poets did not, for the most part, act upon it.

Gascoigne's original lyric translation also did not provoke broad imitation (although his *Posies* was printed in two editions in 1575, and *Deprofundis* was reprinted in his 1587 *VVhole woorkes*[154]). Indeed, one of the few to follow his model was Mary Sidney Herbert.[155] What we see instead of the published initiatives of poets at this time is the impetus of printers. Thomas Vautrollier, in particular, was instrumental in the production and dissemination of religious lyric in England during the late 1570s and early 1580s. His first effort to motivate a cultural conversion came in the form of the 1577 printing of Buchanan's *Baptistes* and the English translation of Beza's *Abraham sacrifiant*.[156] His most significant attempt at the reform of English poetics, however, was the first publication of Buchanan's *Psalmorum Dauidis* in Great Britain. Vautrollier published two editions of the Latin Psalter – with an annexed edition of Buchanan's *Jephthes* – in London in 1580 and 1583.[157] (Richard Field, who married Vautrollier's widow and inherited his printing licences, subsequently printed the work in 1592.[158]) In the case of Buchanan's *Psalmorum*, Vautrollier did not act independently – although he appears to have taken his own initiative in other instances.[159] The force behind the publication of Buchanan's Psalter in England seems to have been Daniel Rogers (son of John Rogers), acting on behalf of the Sidney circle.[160] Rogers provided Vautrollier with a letter recommending him to Buchanan, and Buchanan himself probably collaborated on the edition.[161] The elaborate versification of Buchanan's Latin lyric Psalter – the paraphrase has an appended taxonomy of twenty-nine different metrical patterns that he employed – makes evident why it was a work that so interested the literary circle around Sidney.[162] A Latin paraphrase of scripture occupies a different context from vernacular religious lyric verse since its audience would have been members of the educated elite exclusively. Nevertheless, the publication of the text in England can be understood as an attempt to influence vernacular lyric poets.

Defences of poetry by Sidney and Harvey that cite the precedent and authority of 'such famous preachers and teachers as Beza and Melanchthon', and 'so piercing wits as George Buchanan', suggest that this activity was part of a strategy.[163] The publication and promotion of poetry by Buchanan and Beza may well have constituted an attempt by the coterie around Sidney (which included Harvey, Rogers, and Spenser) to provoke a reconsideration of devotional lyric – and, by extension, the moral utility of lyric poetry generally. If so, this gambit did not involve the public release of their own vernacular religious verse. Indeed, it appears as though Sidney and members of his circle waited for a cultural revaluation to occur before committing their devotional work to public criticism.[164] This would account for the failed publication of Sidney's translation of Du Bartas's *Premiere sepmaine* and his abandoned lyric translation of the Psalms.[165] It would also explain why Spenser executed (presumably lyric) translations of *Ecclesiastes, The Song of Solomon,* and the Penitential Psalms – as well as several original devotional poems – without publishing the material.[166]

The appearance of Buchanan's Latin lyric Psalms did not realise its intended aim; as I. D. McFarlane observes, 'Buchanan's hour in England was not yet at hand.'[167] Vautrollier next tried to reach England through Edinburgh. He published two vernacular translations of Du Bartas's devotional poetry in the same year: *The historie of Iudith in forme of a poeme*; and the translation of *Vranie* by James VI.[168] James's promotion of devotional poetry, not to mention his flexible religion, must lead us to understand the developments in Scotland as a separate case. Certainly, production of religious poetry expanded when he came to the English throne (as James Doelman has demonstrated).[169] But *The essayes* of the King of Scotland defending *the divine art of poesie* had no discernable effect on English cultural practice in 1584.[170] This is not to say that there was no shift: the increased number of defences of lyric poetry in England – from William Webbe's *Discourse of English poetrie* (1586), to Thomas Nashe's *The anatomie of absurditie* (1589), to George Puttenham's *Arte of English poesie* (1589) – is a clear sign of the ground moving.[171] But religious metrical verse – the target of Vautrollier's publishing campaign – registers only minor tremors.

The first of these is discernible in the 1582 *Monvment of matrones*. Among the prayers, narratives, translations, and other materials that Thomas Bentley uses to record female religious identity – and activity – in England, he includes an original poem by Frances Abergavenny. While this poem does not appear to have been composed for a public purpose, its public transmission is nonetheless anomalous.[172] There is nothing unusual about the poem's verse form: eight syllables in alternating rhyme. But the fact that it transcribes a subjective religious experience (underscored by the fact that it is an acrostic of Abergavenny's name) marks a departure from devotional poetry that was printed for an English readership. Indeed, this is not a lone departure. The metrical verse of Byrd, Drayton, and Hunnis indicates tentative cultural movement in the direction of the lyric mode. Hunnis's *Handfull of honisuckles*, *The poore widowes mite*, and the *Comfortable dialogs betwene Christ and a SINNER* – all appended to the *Seuen sobs of a sorrowfull soule* – reveal a restive creative impulse that he nonetheless struggles to contain.[173] The same can be said of Byrd's *Psalmes, sonets & songs of sadnes and pietie* (1588) and *Songs of sundrie natures* (1589), and Drayton's *The harmonie of the Church* (1591).

One sign of this agitation lies in the wealth of original material that makes up these collections. Of course, Hall's *courte of vertue* was similarly comprised of scriptural translation and created text, so this does not, of itself, establish that metrical poets aspired to more experimental religious verse. Still, there is a perceptible strain against forms of convention in the religious poems of Hunnis and Byrd. Hunnis employs an odd innovation of alternating lines of two and three iambic feet in a few of his poems.[174] This is not a particularly adventurous form: it reverses the arrangement and shortens the line (by one metrical foot) of common metre. It is the limited nature of the invention that suggests he was forced to operate within restriction. The dialogues that begin the final section are entirely composed in common metre, but they nonetheless dramatically represent the discourse of the individual soul with Christ, and the personal struggle between the spirit and the flesh.[175] (Interestingly, it is at this point that musical settings are again introduced into the collection to reinforce the ritual intention of the poetry.) Byrd's *Psalmes, sonets & songs of sadnes and pietie* presents a more visible example of cultural tension. All of Byrd's poetic material – comprised of psalm translations, religious songs, and pastoral poems – is set to music. However, Byrd abruptly breaks out of the lockstep of ballad arrangement in two of his pastoral love lyrics.[176] The gathering of sacred and secular verse into one collection is itself unusual. But the situation of these models of poetic tradition side by side provides confirmation of their different formal requirements: as soon as Byrd concludes his collection of translated Psalms, he is able to abandon the confines of common metre. Neither Hunnis nor Byrd, however, produces a recognisably lyric religious expression. On the contrary, what is notable about their collections is the extent to which each poet affirms the ritual organisation of their work when expressing a religious theme.

Drayton's metrical verse in *The harmonie of the Church* is more adventurous.[177] His collection does not contain musical accompaniment; its title page asserts only that the 'English Meeter [is] meete to be read or sung.'[178] There is at least a suggestion here that the ground has been prepared for the devotional lyric poetry written for the aesthetic pleasure of the reader that emerges in the same year. The poetry of Henry Lok is not first among these collections; the works of Fraunce and Breton precede him (works influenced – and very likely commissioned – by Herbert). But his *Svndry Christian passions* is the second English sonnet sequence to take religion as its subject.[179] Lok's place within the development of an English Protestant literary tradition has been thoroughly rehearsed, so there is no need to revisit the case. Lewalski asserts that his expanded 1597 sonnet sequence (appended to his lyric translation of *Ecclesiastes, othervvise called The preacher*[180]), 'pioneered strategies which were to be refined and perfected in the seventeenth century'.[181] The critical work of Lewalski and of Thomas Roche has established the importance of *Svndry Christian passions* for contemporary poets such as Barnabe Barnes, as well as later poets such as Donne, (George) Herbert, Henry Vaughan, Thomas Traherne, and Edward Taylor.[182] What seems important to underscore, then, is the extent to which Lok's strategies are a maternal inheritance.[183]

Lok's *Svndry Christian passions* is entirely subjective in its organisation. The purpose of the sonnet cycle, he tells the reader, is graphically to render his own penitence for 'passed afflictions'.[184] His representation sounds strikingly similar to the 'straining crampe of colde despeir' that his mother depicts as the proper Christian attitude. Lok's sonnets function, like the Psalms themselves, 'as ... a glasse' in which the Christian may read a lively example of 'the state of a regenerate soule, sicke with sinne, sometimes (Ague-like) shiuering with cold dispaire, straight waies inflamed with feruencie of faith and hope'.[185] The two separate collections of 100 sonnets are structured according to the process of penitence and restoration described in Psalm 51 (and the 'Mediation' that takes the Psalm as its source). To repeat Calvin:

[W]han oure Lorde sheweth vs a terrible countenaunce, oure mouthes are stopped, we are fylled wyth suche anguisshe, that it is impossible for vs to blesse hym ... On the other syde, when God sheweth hym selfe mercyfull towarde vs, and vttereth some signe of hys fauor toward vs, he openeth oure mouthes, as it is sayde in the li Psalme.

The first part of the *Svndry Christian passions* contains sonnets of 'meditation, humiliation, and prayer' that suffer under the burden of sin; the second section describes the 'comfort, ioy, and thankesgiuing' that attends the assurance of God's mercy.[186]

The speaker of the first 100 sonnets (as both Lewalski and Roche have shown) sees himself reflected in a series of Old Testament types, 'their experiences recapitulated in his own'.[187] This multiplies the strategy of the 'Meditation', in which David and Hezekiah variously figure as paradigms for the poet's expression. The *Svndry Christian passions* repeats, in little and in large, the procedure followed in the 'Meditation':

> My bodie Lord infected long with sin,
> Whose running issue is almost past cure,
> Which helpe by humane phisicke cannot win,
> And without comfort cannot long endure,
> By viewing mercies thine becommeth sure,
> If but thy gratious hem my hand may reach,
> That loue in Christ my pardon shall procure,
> And reunite in stregth healths former breach.
> Through presse of worldly lets, faith shall me teach,
> To seeke my safetie in thy promise true,
> Vouchsafe thou eke repentance so to preach,
> That I no more offending, health insue
> Thy vertue Lord, which bidding me be cleane,
> To yeeld me health of soule is readie meane.[188]

Roche has shown how, by using the parable of Christ related in Mark 12, Lok's sonnet 50 meditates upon the cause of the Crucifixion prefigured in the allegory.[189] This central sonnet transcribes both the sinful state that is the source of Christian anguish and its cure. The structure of *Sundry Christian passions* is not as tightly conceived as that of the 'Meditation' (this is understandable in the array of 200 poems). The poem at the centre of the first cycle, however, enacts the cause for penitence, and subsequent salvation, that loosely organises the arrangement of the entire sequence. Consequently, in the conclusion to the first cycle, the speaker's torment is soothed by consideration of God's mercy: 'Mourne thou no more my soule, thy plaint is hard, / The bill is canseld of the debt it owes.' Redemption is the final thought of the first 100 sonnets, then the speaker's 'plaint' is converted 'into more pleasant song'.[190]

Like his mother before him, Lok's is 'a poetry of matter'. His lyric rhetoric is not tempered with acoustic or visual surprise. Lok instead exploits the 'complexities of Christian allegory'.[191] The capacity of the poetry to startle us lies in its inventive application of Christian typology to personal experience. The speaker is the dead Lazarus, 'Voyd of true life, and buried in the graue' of sinful flesh. His sisters, who appeal to Christ, become 'sister virtues [who] to dispaire begin, / Of euer seeing once my lifes restore.' The stone that Christ rolls back becomes the 'hard stonie heart', and he bids the soul 'arise, / Who slaue to sin in earthly coffin lies.'[192] This is a different approach to enlarging scripture than what we witness in the 'Meditation', but it nonetheless executes a similar intent. Lok enacts a performance of penitence and praise, conveyed through the vehicle of biblical allusion, which he claims is 'not ... altogether vnprofitable for others to imitate'.[193]

Then too, the versification in *Sundry Christian passions* is complex: Lok chooses an elaborate form for each section, and then sustains it over 102 sonnets (including 'preface' and 'conclusion').[194] His emphasis upon intricate form, and insistence upon plain speech, represents an effort to achieve invention without compromising the matter of the verse. This programme is set out more clearly in his only attempt at scriptural translation, *Ecclesiastes.*

[T]hat you might truly consider of the cariage of the matter, according to the scope of the Text, I haue caused the same to be quoted in the margent, reducing for memorie sake into two abstract lines of verse set in the top of euerie leafe: the substance of euery pages content ... is paraphrastically dilated page by page, in the plainest forme I can deuise.[195]

The lyric translation virtually duplicates the formal structure of the 'Meditation'; instead of expanding each biblical verse into a sonnet, however, Lok opts for two stanzas of seven lines in iambic pentameter (rhymed ababbcc). That Lok borrows both structure and strategy from the poetry of his mother is self-evident. Equally clear is the fact that certain developments in the English devotional lyric tradition that Henry Lok is understood to have promoted – such as the self-definition of 'the poet as embodiment of certain biblical metaphors and types' – draw upon the example of Anne Lok.[196] The impress of Henry's lyric poetry is itself evident in the 100 religious sonnets that Barnes publishes two years later;[197] it also, as Greene points out, serves as an example to '[e]very reformed poet who thinks of poems as material to be disposed for penitence or praise'.[198]

It is important to mark the distinction between causing the emergence of religious lyric in England and lending expression to its aesthetic development. In some senses, Anne Lok's influence inhabits the latter category. Henry's tenure at the Scottish court provided him with a model of how the composition of religious lyric could serve political ambition.[199] No doubt, this (at least partially) prompted his venture into print. Certainly, Henry does not cite Anne's early effort among the analogues for his work offered in *Ecclesiastes*; instead he resorts to the religious authority of figures such as Beza and Tremellious, and the poetic example of continental Latin poets such as Joannes Vivianus.[200] But the explanation for this omission might not conform straightforwardly to gender: just as Gascoigne cites Beza (and implicates Buchanan), Lok might be trying to operate under the shield of unassailable names. (Furthermore, if his mother's name was indeed suppressed with a purpose, Lok would not reveal it now.) All of this suggests that there was reason to proceed with caution in England; it further suggests that Lok was alert to the potential difficulties. We should not discount, then, in this context, the confidence that Anne's precedent gave to her son's endeavour (particularly as Henry might not have seen similar poetic projects by Fraunce and Breton by the time of his initial publication).

None of what I have been advocating for the agency of women in the development of religious lyric verse devalues the activities of men. Chief among these is the effort of Sidney. But if we make a distinction between cause and expression, we must admit that while Sidney provokes a confrontation, he does not actually bring it to fruition. He obviously gave important discursive and artistic expression to the origins of devotional lyric; but the language of causation is not entirely appropriate in connection to activities that he ultimately aborted. Du Bartas presents a similarly nuanced case. The accretion of translations of Du Bartas's poetry throughout the 1590s had an observable effect.[201] But while Du Bartas's footprint is deep in English devotional poetics, the early initiatives of English poets (that find their way to print) seem principally to derive inspiration from vernacular models.[202] Even with these caveats, the role of Sidney or Du Bartas – not to mention Fraunce, Harvey, Rogers, and Spenser – in the renovation of religious lyric in England should not, and indeed cannot, be excluded. What I am suggesting is that if we fail to notice the impress of the writing of women upon this particular moment in cultural history, the sudden appearance of religious lyric verse in the 1590s – after decades of resistance – has no direct explanation. The devotional production of Byrd, Drayton, and Hunnis in the 1580s does not account for it. Even Gascoigne's lyric verse does not explain the materialisation of a devotional tradition after such a long interruption. What these examples show is a cautious and indefinite movement toward lyric expression. But if the emergence of a religious lyric tradition is evidenced by the wing-case showing on the pupa, the initiatives of women allow for full metamorphosis.

CHAPTER 5

'A Womans writing of diuinest things': Aemilia Lanyer's passion for a professional poetic vocation

There are but fewe of many that can rightly judge of Poetry, and yet thear ar many of those few, that carry so left-handed an opinion of it, as some of them thinke it halfe sacrilege for profane Poetrie to deale with divine and heauenly matters.

> Giles Fletcher, *Christs victorie, and triumph in heauen, and earth*

Come all the worlde and call your wittes together,
borrowe some pennes from out the Angells winges;
Intreate the heauens to send the muses hether,
to holpe your soules to write of sacred thinges.

> Nicholas Breton, *The Countesse of Penbrookes passion*

In her dedication 'To the Queenes most excellent majestie', Aemilia Lanyer asks her 'to view that which is seldome seene, / A Womans writing of diuinest things.'[1] Lanyer's claim notwithstanding, divine things were the most common subjects of literary (and, in post-Romantic terms, extraliterary) treatment by women in the early modern period. While Lanyer's long poem, *Salve Deus Rex Judæorum* (1611), is ostensibly religious in nature, a number of critics deem the religious content of the work peripheral to its central intentions.[2] Such assertions are subject to question; what is clear is that religious conviction was not Lanyer's sole – probably not even her prevailing – motivation.[3] She published her poem on the Passion of Christ to solicit patronage. What makes this gesture so compelling in the context of women's cultural history in England is the extent to which the figure of the religious female has become at this point a critical – and self-consciously constructed – means of negotiating the professional literary sphere. Since the influence of sixteenth-century women writers upon an English Protestant literary tradition has been my topic, it makes sense to conclude by exploring how the tradition of female-authored religious texts inflected the self-representation of a seventeenth-century woman poet.

While the proto-feminist appeals of *Salve Deus* are compelling to modern feminist readers, we need to be alert to the artifice of the voice that emerges from the poem. A number of articles have considered the gendered inscriptions of Lanyer's text, but few have examined the gendered performance within the work itself, either in the context of poetic circulation or competition.[4] The critical work which depicts Lanyer as a '17th-century feminist voice' is positively abundant.[5] But we cannot regard the proto-feminist voice of *Salve Deus* as authentic; we must instead understand how it is constructed in relation to a commercial economy. The argument of the poem stands in opposition to patriarchy, and it is seductive to view this poetic positioning as representative of a personal stance; but the simulated nature of poetic composition at least suggests a verbal pose. My reading sees the pro-feminine expression of Lanyer's poetic text as a rhetorical tactic – one developed in contradistinction to male poets with whom she was in direct financial competition – that amounts to a marketing device.

Of course the biological subject makes claims on the *Salve Deus*. But there are other pressures – market forces – that drive its formulations.[6] We benefit considerably from reading Lanyer's work in the context of the marketplace – and against the poets with whom she was competing. To do so is to locate the strains of cultural discourse to which Lanyer's text responds. It is to remind us of the sorts of imitative gestures that were the stock and trade of literary circulation. And it is to measure the gap between the poem and its paradigm (or source text), hence to see more clearly a specific instance of transmission and transformation.[7] Concrete examples of such transfers reveal a good deal about the fashioning of the gendered voice itself, for the creation of that voice occurs in the transaction between source (male) and text (female). Moreover, such an example provides an object lesson in how the circumstances of class position can actually compel the performance of gender within a text at this time. Perhaps most importantly (at least for my purposes), it shows how the vehicle of religion serves such a performance.

THE 'PAINEFULL BEE': NEGOTIATING PATRONAGE

The most unusual feature of Lanyer's literary engagement is not, in fact, her subject but her subject-position. Her pursuit of a professional writing career is contingent upon her class status, and enabled by her educational training. Exactly how Lanyer acquired her education is something of a vexed question, and so I need to spend some time on a rehearsal of the arguments. Lanyer calls Susan Bertie, the dowager Countess of Kent, 'the Mistris of [her] youth' in a dedicatory poem addressed to her.[8] This phrase has caused a good deal of conjecture as to how the Countess of Kent featured in Lanyer's tuition. What is clear, from the last testament of Margaret Johnson Bassano (Aemilia Lanyer's mother), is that her family was closely connected with that of Stephen Vaughan, the only brother of Anne Vaughan Lok. Stephen Vaughan is appointed as the primary overseer of Margaret's will, and 'Ms Vaughan' is also bequeathed 'a ringe of twentie shillings'.[9] Susanne Woods speculates that Lanyer (then Bassano) might have entered the service of Susan Bertie through the influence of the Vaughan family when her father, Baptista Bassano, died in 1576.[10] Leeds Barroll raises a number of objections to the theory,[11] but an entry in one of Simon Forman's diaries (whose astrological advice Lanyer sought) does appear to support the claim that Lanyer was brought up 'w the contes of Kent'.[12] If this, in fact, occurred, very likely Lanyer would have been educated in the Countess's nursery between the years of 1576 and 1581 when Susan Bertie is presumed to have lived at Elizabeth's court. This would have provided her with a Protestant humanist education from the years of seven to twelve.[13]

However theoretical, this account squares with other information that we have about her. Simon Forman writes that 'She hath bin fauoured moch of her mati [majesty] and of mani noble men & hath had gret gifts & bin moch made of. and a noble man that is ded hath Loued her well & kept her and did maintain her long.'[14] Lanyer was the mistress of Henry Carey, Lord Hunsdon until 1592 when, pregnant with Hunsdon's child, she was married to Alfonso Lanyer.[15] Henry Carey was Elizabeth's Lord Chamberlain from 1583 to his death in 1596. Whether her acquaintance with Queen Elizabeth began as Hunsdon's mistress, or her acquaintance with Hunsdon began when she was herself at court, we cannot determine. But Simon Forman (for any number of personal failings) was neither politically or socially naïve. It makes little sense that he would have accepted a report that could not be reconciled with the facts as he knew them. Given what Forman knew of Lanyer, he must have found her claims credible.

Even if her operation within the intellectual and cultural environment of the Elizabethan court cannot be counted as proof of her high standard of education, her establishment of a grammar school later in life can. Lanyer founded a school to 'educate the children of divers persons of worth' in the wealthy suburb of St Giles in the Field in 1617.[16] There are some conclusions that we can draw from this. In order to make such a venture a going concern – which she did for two years before a dispute with her landlord caused her to shut down – Lanyer would have had to have been prepared to offer an education sufficient to prepare well-heeled young men (as presumably most of her students were) for university. Even if she retained male tutors for the purpose, she would have had to review their qualifications. Further, the language of her petition to the court suggests that she trained the pupils herself.[17] No matter which scenario is correct, or how young her charges were, educational training of this kind would have required knowledge of the classics, and some reading ability in Latin and Greek.[18]

Which is to say that Lanyer was fairly anomalous (even by late sixteenth-century standards): a woman of middling class position with a good education. She also appears to have been a voracious reader of contemporary literature (a habit that access to Hunsdon's library would have easily sated). Her long poem explicitly invokes the writing of Samuel Daniel, Michael Drayton, and William Shakespeare, and additionally exhibits an intimacy with the works of other writers such as Nicholas Breton and Mary Sidney Herbert. While verbal echoes are insufficient to positively prove Lanyer's use of a particular text, there is nonetheless persuasive evidence to suggest that her work was informed by specific textual models. Her engagement with this discrete body of work exhibits a calculated construction of her own currency within a certain literary economy.

The dedicatory apparatus of *Salve Deus Rex Judæorum*, if one includes its appended country-house poem, 'The description of Cooke-ham' (a homage to Margaret Clifford and her daughter Anne), accounts for over two-thirds of the text.[19] Lanyer's insertion of herself into the patronage system is not subtle. But the sorority that she depicts in the collection of poems to aristocratic women that preface the work is fictitious; what is more, Lanyer is acutely aware of the social divisions that the poems themselves elide.[20] The ideal female community that she imagines is, rather, a clever means of self-promotion. As Lorna Hutson argues, 'patron–client relations cannot be forged without the competitive self-advertising that an open market of intellectual ability demands'.[21] Lanyer chose to carve out her own space within this marketplace by invoking a network of female patronage. But in order to garner the favour of rich women, she needed to prove that her own poetic services were indispensable. The nature of her service and the way that she represents it are matters to which I will return. For now, I want to consider the literary models that she followed and the literary circles that she was trying to infiltrate.

John Rogers claims that 'nearly all of Lanyer's critics ... have attempted to understand the dynamics of [her] extraordinary assumption of authority'. He goes on to argue that Lanyer legitimates her work through the invocation of a female writing '"tradition" whose filiations – whose very existence, in fact – it is the obligation of the *Salve Deus* to call into being'.[22] Rogers locates Lanyer's long poem on the Passion within evolving generic conventions among male poets, but he cancels the debt that *Salve Deus* owes to a female writing tradition. Rogers's contention is not unusual. But his example is useful precisely because he so carefully reconstructs the formal context for Lanyer's work. The problem with his reconstruction is that it is premised on the assertion that Lanyer's volume of poems was 'the first significant book of original poetry published by an English-woman'.[23] Whether we accept this premise turns on what we count as 'significant' (Isabella Whitney's two printed volumes of poetry predate Lanyer's[24]), and what we count as 'published'.[25]

One might be tempted to say that the most productive approach to the *Salve Deus* is to describe the way that Lanyer's works occupies a liminal space between male and female traditions. But even this is to create a rigid and artificial distinction. I have been asserting all along that though a female tradition existed in England, women writers of this period did not understand themselves or their work solely within the restricted pur-view of female authorship. What is more, the work of male writers and editors – such as Bale, Foxe, Sidney, and (Henry) Lok – engaged with the fact of significant female authors in both material and ideational ways. *Salve Deus*, as a site of cultural production, in many ways reproduces the complex interplay between male and female writers that was characteristic of early modern English culture.

The mediating figure in this exchange is Mary Herbert. The role that Herbert plays in authorising Lanyer's long poem has been well rehearsed, and widely revised. Barbara Lewalski set out the claim which has since been interrogated and contested in numerous arguments.[26] Both Rogers and Kari Boyd McBride have examined the complications that Herbert's priority creates for Lanyer's work. McBride argues that Lanyer fuses Pembroke's 'poetic person to that of her dead brother' in an attempt to dislodge Herbert's primacy altogether, and to construct her own 'poetic vocation on the corpse/corpus' of a predecessor who is written-off.[27] Rogers similarly claims that Lanyer 'is planning to profit poetically from the countess of Pembroke's own final sacrifice', even as he maintains that she takes no literary inheritance from her.[28] This apparent contradiction nicely illustrates just how unwieldy the problem of Herbert's precedence is in connection to Lanyer. Lanyer's relationship to the literary legacy of the Countess of Pembroke is troubled by her own point of entry into literary circulation. As a woman of middling status seeking professional status as a writer, she occupies a social position that is radically different from that of the illustrious poet whom she praises. Nor is this simply a matter of decorum. Lanyer is offering her services to Herbert; it is therefore in her interests to maintain – and, indeed, to invoke – the separation between patron and client. When Lanyer uses the work of Giles Fletcher, Abraham Fraunce, and, most explicitly, Nicholas Breton, as poetic models, this serves strategically to situate her within a system of patronage.[29] Breton and Fraunce, after all, are part of a Protestant literary coterie centred on the Countess of Pembroke. The way in which Lanyer calls attention to Herbert as a figure who lends authority to her own work also underscores the extent to which Herbert's literary efforts have licensed the devotional lyric poetry of these men.

As Debra Rienstra has observed, 'The authors dreame' in which Herbert appears to Lanyer signals that she 'presides over Lanyer's imaginative world'.[30] (This parallels the inspiration for the title of the work: Lanyer claims that it was 'delivered' to her 'in sleepe'.[31]) But the poet whom Lanyer figures as her Muse ('earthly goddesse') is credited with only one work – even though Herbert could have been praised for several.[32] Lanyer is not claiming inspiration from a female poet *per se*, but from the particular poetic achievement of the Sidney–Pembroke Psalter. What this suggests is that she recognises the role of the Psalter in enabling the devotional mode that she is now engaging.

The claim might at first appear exaggerated: that Lanyer was conscious of the hard-won achievement of religious lyric poetry in the context of a Calvinist-inflected Protestant society; and that she was further aware of the intervention of the Sidney–Pembroke Psalter in that effort. The assertion gains plausibility, however, when we consider Fletcher's introduction 'To the Reader' in *Christs victorie, and triumph in heauen, and earth* (1610).

Theare are but fewe of many that can rightly iudge of Poetry, and yet thear ar many of those few, that carry so left-handed an opinion of it, as some of them thinke it halfe sacrilege for profane Poetrie to deale with divine and heauenly matters, as though *David* wear to be sentenced by them, for vttering his graue matter vpon the harpe: others something more violent in their censure, but sure lesse reasonable (as though Poetrie corrupted all good witts, when, indeed, bad witts corrupt Poetrie) banish it with *Plato* out of all well-ordered Commonwealths.[33]

Fletcher's line of thought closely shadows Sidney's in the *Defence*.[34] Defences of poetry became more numerous toward the end of the sixteenth century; however, the trajectory of Sidney's argument is distinct among these treatises, and appears to be reproduced in miniature here. Either Fletcher had read Sidney's *Defence*, or the latter's arguments had become part of the intellectual environment. Fletcher's close literary association with Spenser gives him an approximate relationship to Sidney – and it seems likely that he would have been familiar with Sidney's treatise. (Certainly his brother, Phineas, was indebted to the Sidney–Pembroke Psalter.[35]) Either way, Giles Fletcher's short defence of his own poetic project establishes two things: that the cultural/religious complications for poetry were clearly perceived (and keenly felt) even in 1610; and that the arguments that Sidney traces in defence of poetry were at large in the culture.

While Fletcher does not make explicit the connection between Sidney's *Defence*, or the Sidney–Pembroke Psalter, and his own devotional poetry (except to highlight the Psalms as poetry), it seems to me that Lanyer does. Sidney is figured as the heroic Protestant poet, 'whose cleere light / Giues light to all that tread true paths of Fame.'[36] His sister is his soul made flesh on earth – the heroic female poet who, interestingly, is credited with the sole authorship of the Psalter.[37] The sibling relationship of the two Sidneys was often invoked – usually to produce a doubling effect in which Mary Sidney Herbert brought Sidney's literary activities to fruition. But I do not see this configuration here: rather Sidney becomes the doppelganger, and Herbert, the woman artist 'Directing all by her immortall light.'[38] It is the 'holy Sonnets' of Herbert that Lanyer hears sung in her sleep: the word-music of the Psalter inspires the project that Lanyer is about to undertake.[39] When the god Morpheus steals her dream vision from her, she resolves to retain the 'rare sweet songs' that she has heard through her own recreation of them.[40] She tells him that he cannot bar inspiration from her waking mind: 'For to this Lady now I will repaire, / Presenting her the fruits of idle houres.'[41] The *Salve Deus*, then, will remedy this loss of 'heauenli'st musicke'.[42] To reproduce the effect (and to present the fruits of her labours to the Countess of Pembroke) is to take ownership of the musicality of the songs/Psalms in her newly awakened imagination.

While much of the rhetoric of Lanyer's dedicatory verse is conventionally encomiastic, she does construct a fantasy in which her own work continues the music of the Psalter. Fletcher's induction demonstrates just how available the arguments concerning devotional poetry were. If we assume that Lanyer read Fletcher's verse narrative of *Christs victorie* (as a number of critics have[43]), then we have no reason to deny that she was familiar with these arguments. But even if we cannot positively establish Fletcher as a source, Fletcher's defensive manoeuvre makes clear that the controversy was in the public domain. Lanyer's use of the Psalms – and specifically the Sidney–Pembroke Psalms – as the composition that authorises her own religious verse testifies to her awareness of a devotional tradition that the Sidney–Pembroke Psalter explicitly sanctions.[44]

Lanyer, then, self-consciously situates her own poetic project in the context of a religious literary tradition that Herbert enabled. Because this literary tradition is female-identified in terms of Herbert's participation, Lanyer is quite obviously trying to take poetic licence from the identification. And yet, try as she might to align herself with a distinguished female poet, Lanyer remains alert to her different social place in poetic circulation.

> Though [Pembroke's] sugar be more finer, higher priz'd,
> Yet is the painefull Bee no whit disgraced,
> Nor her faire wax, or hony more despiz'd.[45]

Herbert's refined status here entirely alters her relationship to other authors producing verse ('hony'). She is instead imagined as the queen bee for whom Lanyer will work. But the metaphor also locates Lanyer's place within the literary hive of male writers of a similar social caste who are pursuing Pembroke's patronage. 'The authors dreame' does something more complicated than cite Pembroke's example as precedent. It acknowledges the role of the Countess of Pembroke – and, by extension, a female writing tradition – in the development of English devotional literature. And Lanyer may insinuate her own work into this context, but she very well recognises the limits of that tradition (largely pursued by upper-class women writers) to facilitate the writing performance of a woman in service.

MARKET STRATEGY

Lanyer's market savvy can be fully appreciated when we notice how she positions herself against other devotional poets similarly engaged in the pursuit of patronage. Her unusual circumstance (a woman possessed of much education and few means) left her with only male competitors. The two most obvious ones were Breton and Fraunce. Breton was perhaps the most popular contemporary poet of the late sixteenth and early seventeenth centuries – he certainly was the most prolific.[46] Fifteen of his religious works were printed, and, of these, ten are versified.[47] Of the eight poetic works that bear dedications, four are dedicated to noble women, and two to women of upper rank (although the presentation of the *Countesse of Penbrookes passion* changes in print[48]). Breton clearly saw women as his most viable audience for devotional verse, and noble women as his most likely patrons. With nine prefatory dedications to noble women, and one to 'vertuous ladies in generall', Lanyer exceeds Breton's example (although she does have a precedent in Lok's *Ecclesiastes*, with which she may well have been familiar[49]). But the generic form in which she was writing – devotional poetry – was associated with women in terms of the marketplace. Further, it was closely aligned with the Countess of Pembroke – the dedications of Breton and Fraunce make this clear.[50]

It is also clear that Lanyer was trying to contend with this specific body of devotional material. Internal parallels between her work and particular poems of Breton make her acquaintance with (at least one of) these contemporary writers apparent.[51] Her tactics for positioning her poetry within the traffic of literary exchange expose the braided nature of gender and class.[52] Lanyer is hindered as a woman in a man's profession; she can, however, exploit the figure of Herbert. 'The authors dreame' shows Herbert's example working through her, as part of her imaginative world. The implication – which Lanyer develops throughout the poem – is that writing 'of diuinest things' is more accessible to her *because* she is a woman. But while she invokes a religious writing tradition – explicitly identified as female in her text (and embodied in the figure of Herbert) – she draws upon the poetic precedents of Breton, Fletcher, and Fraunce, with whom she is in direct competition.

Unless we regard religious versification at this time as a fraught enterprise, the function of Herbert's figure in the poetic works of Breton and Fraunce – not to mention Lanyer – remains unclear. For them to yoke their devotional texts to a patron and poet whose own work sanctions religious poetry is to borrow authority from her example. Herbert's patronage obviously compromises our ability to discern precisely when and how her figure is employed for the purpose of artistic licence. Mary Ellen Lamb has argued, for example, that Breton's exclusive focus upon Herbert's support of religious activities deliberately obscures her role as a poet.[53] But the use of the figure of Herbert within devotional texts by men is far more complex than straightforward appeals for her financial aid. After all, Breton's writing exhibits an acute awareness of the contemporary debates concerning poetry in which Sidney's *Defence* and the Sidney–Pembroke Psalter intercede ('And such a Poet as the Psalmist was', he declares, 'did the world in

Musique passe'[54]). Breton's use of Herbert as a 'religious muse' (in Lamb's phrase) might therefore function in a way similar to Lanyer's representation of her as an 'earthly goddesse'. In other words, Breton is not attempting to undermine Herbert's secular writing, but rather to underscore her part in licensing religious lyric poetry. This is confirmed by the fact that the devotional works by men dedicated to Herbert are often overtly involved in arguments concerning the nature of poetry.[55]

Breton and Fraunce were both within the ambit of Pembroke's literary circle.[56] While Fraunce was not the first English poet to publish lyric translations of the Psalms that are disposed for a reading audience – Anne Lok, George Gascoigne, and Richard Stanyhurst precede him – he is the first to publish an original devotional poem that is unambiguously situated in the subjective mode.[57] Unlike William Hunnis's *Seuen sobs of a sorrow-full soule*, Dudley Fenner's *Song of songs*, William Byrd's *Psalmes, sonets, & songs of sadnes and pietie*, or Drayton's *Harmonie of the Church*, Fraunce's *The Countesse of Pembrokes Emanuel* does not straddle the faultline between ritual and subjective models of poetic reception. Fraunce himself cites a reading list of suggestive analogues for his work: 'Reade *Homer*, reade *Demosthenes*, reade *Virgill*, reade *Cicero*, reade *Bartas*, reade *Torquato Tasso*, reade that most worthie ornament of our English tongue, the *Countesse of Penbrookes Arcadia*.'[58] Such a roster of male examples seems to undercut my claim that these initiatives in devotional verse emerge from the writing of women. But if the work of Sidney or Du Bartas informs Fraunce's poetic collection, he most closely binds his project to Herbert.

In the overwrought dedication to *The Arcadian rhetorike*, Fraunce writes that Herbert fills the temple of Sidney with the celestial honey ('cælesti melle') of words.[59] The term 'honey' is often employed in connection to verse (as in the instance of Lanyer's metaphor); since this is the English rhetoric in which the verse of Sidney and Du Bartas is first enshrined, it is likely that Fraunce is praising Herbert for similar poetic gifts. It also suggests that Fraunce had read a version of the Sidney–Pembroke Psalter by 1588. His quantitative verse Psalms – affixed to a narrative poem concerning 'Natiuity, Passion, Buriall, and Resurrection of Christ' – exhibit a debt to Herbert's experiments.[60] Fraunce did have other possible sources of inspiration for his poem in English hexameters: Stanyhurst's hexameter translation of the *Aeneid*, with its appended translation of Psalms 1–4 in quantitative metres, is one obvious example. (Stanyhurst is cited in Harvey's 1592 *Foure letters* – along with Sidney, Spenser, and Fraunce – for his achievements in the verse form.[61]) In spite of their different religio-political affiliations, Fraunce would not have disdained to use Stanyhurst as a model. But Protestant attitudes against religious lyric poetry would not have impeded an Irish Catholic like Stanyhurst.[62] Fraunce, on the other hand, is clearly susceptible to these cultural pressures. Like Sidney, his repeated defence of poetry itself shows the strain; and, like Sidney and Herbert, his use of lyric poetry in the treatment of a religious subject is as much a theoretical intervention as an artistic one.

Herbert might well have tasked Fraunce with the composition of a devotional poem.[63] Whether he wrote on her initiative or his own, Fraunce's employment of hexameter verse in his description of the life of Christ takes inspiration from the Sidney–Pembroke Psalter. As Isreal Baroway has shown, 'Renaissance criticism did attribute to certain heroic portions of the Old Testament the metre of the classical epic.'[64] Stanyhurst exploits the supposed metrical variety of the Psalms to expose the potential for the English appropriation of classical verse forms.[65] By contrast, Sidney's adaptations of the hexameter, Hannibel Hamlin has observed, are usually used in the service of a heroic or royal subject. In other words, the use of classical form corresponds to the content of the poem. Herbert adopts the strategy, and her hexameter translations of Psalms 76 and 141 highlight the epic nature of the struggles of ancient Jerusalem.[66] But Herbert's contributions to the Psalter, far more than Sidney's, demonstrate a concentrated effort to fit structure to sense. Fraunce's application of epic form follows her example. The hexameter highlights the epic structure – absence, return, reconciliation – in the life of Christ. In the case of Fraunce's *Emanuel*, it is man who is alienated from, and ultimately reconciled to, God. But the verse itself imposes a frame in which the poem should be read. This strategy closely parallels the poetic practice of Herbert, whose employment of classical verse – or any verse form – inevitably inflects the meaning of the poem.

Fraunce uses Herbert's compositional method to good effect; he also calls explicit attention to the connection between the Sidney–Pembroke Psalter and the *Emanuel*. The psalm translations appended to his narrative poem declare (if the title of the work is not sufficient) the collection's affiliation with Pembroke's poetic project. Fraunce is not, or not only, flattering a patron with this presentation of his poem: he is advertising her influence and her sanction. There are reasons why both are required. The Sidney–Pembroke Psalter was clearly in coterie circulation by the early 1590s – both Fraunce and Daniel had access to a version of the manuscript – and public reaction to its wider distribution is conspicuous by 1595. In *Piers Gaveston*, Drayton asks that his patron, Henry Cavendish,

'lend [his] eyes awhile, / From *Meridian's* sun-[b]red statele straine'
(1735–6).[67] Jean Robertson has credibly claimed that this is a reference
to Herbert and her *Psalmes* (as Drayton uses *Meridianis* – an anagram of
'Mari Sidnei' – to identify her in *Idea's mirror*).[68] Drayton's special plead-
ing suggests an intense cultural interest in the work only one year after the
'final polishing' of the manuscript. Fraunce's presentation of his collection, then, is a promotional device. *The Countesse of Pembrokes Emanuel*
proclaims that it is a work written for her, and he dedicates it in the
following way: 'Mary the best Mother sends her best Babe to a Mary.'[69]
Fraunce conceives of Herbert as both the mother and Magdalene figure
who receives his 'Babe'. But the mother 'Mary' confuses author and
patron, and seems to conflate them as creators of the poem. Fraunce both
credits Herbert's inspiration and places his verse under her protection.
Since it is the product of her labour, she will preserve it. Together, with
Fraunce, she will promote his poetic activities in the devotional mode – for
which she, after all, is responsible.

The second lyric collection similarly affiliated with Herbert is also the
second English devotional composition in the fictional (and subjective)
mode: Breton's *Pilgrimage to paradise, ioyned with The Countesse of
Penbrookes loue.* While Fraunce's connection of his work to Herbert is more
straightforward, Breton's is, in some ways, more revealing. In terms of
influence, Breton also had other precedents to follow: as the stepson of
Gascoigne, he was certainly familiar with his lyric version of *Deprofundis.*[70]
Still, Breton uses the figure of Herbert to usher his work into print. In his
dedication 'To the Gentlemen students and Scholers of Oxforde', which
prefaces *The pilgrimage to paradise*, Breton claims that the reason he undertook his composition 'was to acquaint the honest mindes of vertuous
dispositions, with the heauenly Meditations', of the Countess of Pembroke.[71]
Lamb argues that Breton juxtaposes Castiglione's service to the Duchess
of Urbino to his own service to the Countess of Pembroke, thereby
'adapt[ing] elements of the Neoplatonic ideal – by which the lady inspires
the suitor to spiritual progress – to create a model of patronage'.[72] This is
to relegate Herbert to religious patronage alone. But is Breton referring to
Herbert's written meditations or to her pious mind? That Breton terms his
own sonnet sequence 'Meditations' in *The soules harmony* suggests that he
is referring to the *Psalmes.*[73] In Breton's Neoplatonic representation, then,
Herbert's example becomes the means by which religious lyric is produced. In fact, in the appended *Countesse of Penbrookes loue* – a verse
narrative that ventriloquises Herbert's voice in a moment of private penitence – she becomes the very instrument of the poem.

For Suzanne Trill, the format of *The Countesse of Penbrookes loue* points to Breton's unease concerning his own poetic gifts. Trill argues that 'Breton's inability to represent the heights of spiritual ravishment in a male voice betrays an anxiety about the value of both poetry per se and his own writing in particular.'[74] It is my sense that this is not a case of anxiety; rather, when Breton uses two voices – Herbert's and his own – he is trying to link their identities as religious poets. In *The pilgrimage to paradise*, Breton, as author, is the implied speaker (although his *Pilgrimage* traces Pembroke's steps). In the appended narrative poem, however, he conjures a scene in which he overhears Herbert's secret contemplation ('Her selfe alone, saue but my selfe vnseene').[75] If in Breton's *Pilgrimage*, the poet transfers his affections from goddesses such as Venus and Diana to Christ, the appended meditation, *Penbrookes loue*, demonstrates the poetic felicity of Christian inspiration. Herbert, as a character in Breton's work, speaks its verses – and becomes the ideal example for other poets to imitate.

The Countesse of Penbrookes loue is the only verse narrative where she is explicitly represented as the speaker.[76] Breton employs the strategy at the inaugural stage of his engagement with the devotional mode. Herbert is represented as both Muse and model in Breton's work. In his appropriation of her figure, Breton is not simply appealing for her patronage; he is using her figure as a form of protection. In Breton's construction of his poetic project, he deliberately does not write by his own initiative: instead, he claims that Pembroke's example incited him to write in this way, and he causes her to speak in the devotional register after he has described its lyric uses. As Trill observes, 'other critics argue that Breton's depiction of Pembroke mistakenly situates her as one who denies poetry and explicitly abjures the practice of writing for herself'.[77] But Trill points out that it is only the value of secular poetry that Herbert refutes in this representation. The portrayal does elide Pembroke's poetic activities in the secular realm, but it also fixes her importance in relation to religious verse. Herbert's primary significance in cultural terms is her activation of the devotional mode – and these early collections of devotional lyric put this awareness on display. Clearly, certain poets saw the production of religious lyric as a means to circumvent competition, and to gain her financial support. But as Breton's appropriation of Herbert's voice reveals, the use of her figure in devotional lyric production exceeds any application for funds. It is a means of authorising religious verse that declares no collective intention.

Breton continues to dedicate his devotional works throughout the decade to Herbert; a subsequent breach with her probably explains his later dedications to other noble women.[78] While Breton frequently asks female patrons to identify with the speaker of his poems, he does not situate them within the works themselves.[79] Rather, it is the soul, gendered female, which conjoins the speaker of the poem – usually associated with Breton – and his dedicatee. Through this poetic tactic, Breton tries to collude with his female patrons. Breton's almost exclusive dedication of his devotional verse to women underscores the extent to which the genre becomes gender-identified (a point that I have argued elsewhere[80]). But the emergent tradition is itself closely associated with a woman poet – a fact that the targeting of women as *patrons* for religious verse sometimes obscures. Lanyer throws these different operations into relief precisely because she is doing both things: seeking female patrons, and making good use of the alignment of devotional lyric with a woman writer.

'The authors dreame' demonstrates her double strategy: Lanyer represents herself as one of a collection of writers producing verse for Pembroke (as patron); she also figures herself as a woman whose access to Herbert's inspiration is more immediate than that of her male competitors. The complex gesture in many ways imitates the appeals of male poets to Herbert as both writer and patron. But it also highlights Lanyer's precarious position as a professional woman poet. Lanyer's insertion of her work into a female writing tradition must contend with the problems that very tradition holds for a woman poet of the middling sort. Her social status requires her to reinvent (or rewrite) the tradition. It is not enough for her to use the model of male devotional poets in the service of noble women; she also must assert the superiority of a female poet in professional circulation.

A PASSION FOR THE COUNTESS OF PEMBROKE

Fletcher and Fraunce both composed verse narratives on the subject of the Passion, but the poem with which Lanyer is most obviously engaged is Breton's *Countesse of Penbrookes passion*.[81] Precisely how Lanyer gained access to Breton's work is not clear. The poem was in circulation prior to 1599, when Thomas East prints it without attribution.[82] The surviving evidence is thin, but what remains does suggest that the poem was ascribed to Breton in manuscript circulation: of the two extant copies, one bears witness to Breton's authorship;[83] the other bears Breton's title.[84] (A third manuscript, now lost, seems to have contained no information of the poem's origin, but we do not know when it was produced.[85]) The Sloane MS further indicates that contemporary circulation was fairly wide: the owner, John Botterill, was a Scholar at Caius College, Cambridge, in 1600 when he transcribed his copy.[86] Lanyer appears to have known that Breton was the author of the poem – if nothing else, her choice among the available competition is extremely telling. Of all contemporary poets, Breton was the most occupied with devotional poetry as a career strategy. Fletcher and Fraunce also composed versified passion narratives, but only Breton's applies a Calvinist reading.[87]

The correspondences between *Salve Deus* and *The Countesse of Penbrookes passion* are striking, and unlikely to be accidental. While verbal echoes and stanzaic patterns are insufficient to establish Breton's *Passion* as a source text, there is one reverberation worth exploring. Breton's poem begins in a melancholy vein:

> The dayes like night all darkned in distresse,
> pleasure became a subiect all of payne,
> the spyritt ouerprest with heuynesse,
> while hopelesse horrour vexeth euerye vayne,
> death shakes his dart, greife hath my graue preparede,
> yet to more sorrowe is my spyritt sparde.[88]

Continuing the extended metaphor of days shadowed by hopelessness and sorrow, Breton speaks of his 'owlye eyes that not endures the light'.[89] Since Breton is treating the natural world as an index of his own internal one, the 'owlye eyes' refer to his own eyes occluded by passion – in other words, he is blind to the light of faith. Melancholy is the consequence of loss of faith, and his despair is partly prompted by this awareness. Here is Lanyer's vocative address to Caiphas:

> To thee O *Caiphas* doth [Christ] answere giue,
> That thou hast said, what thou desir'st to know,
> And yet thy malice will not let him liue,
> So much thou art vnto thy selfe a foe;
> He speaketh truth, but thou wilt not beleeue,
> Nor canst thou apprehend it to be so:
>   Though he expresse his Glory vnto thee,
>   Thy Owly eies are blind, and cannot see.[90]

Caiphas's 'Owly eies' express a vision obstructed by passion, unable to perceive with the clear eye of the faith. Of course, owls have difficulty seeing in light, and Breton and Lanyer may merely share a commonplace for those who cannot see the light of God. However, the OED cites a single use of the phrase before 1630; it appears twice in Sidney's 1593 *Covntesse of Pembrokes Arcadia*. In both instances, it refers to individuals who are 'blind to the light of vertue' (Cecropia), or unable to perceive the hopeful prospect of Christian salvation.[91] The use of this odd expression in both poems only hints at a link between them. But if Breton borrowed the phrase from Sidney, which seems likely, it does usefully remind us that poetic imitation was a signal of a writer's inclusion – or desire for inclusion – within a particular coterie.

While Lanyer's *ottava rima* does not duplicate Breton's stanzaic pattern (six iambic pentameter lines rhymed ababcc), it certainly follows this structure more closely than that of other contemporary textual models that treat the subject of the Passion (Fletcher, for example, uses an *ottava rima* stanza, but the rhyme scheme of abacccdd is very different). There are also poetic moments in these two works that seem to mirror each other. Similar occasions sometimes elicit comparable images. For example, at the start of his passion narrative, Breton's search for inspiration quickly leads him into a 'night' of sorrowful contemplation ('darkned in distresse'). Lanyer begins her passion in deep midnight as well – in the garden of Gethsemane – but her depiction of 'sad blacke fac'd Night, / Whose mourning Mantle covered Heavenly Light' evokes a mood as well as a moment.[92] Both poets render faltering inspiration in physical terms.[93] Lanyer appears to adopt Breton's rhetorical patterns at times as well. Breton often uses anaphora in the quatrain of his stanzas. In describing those who refused to recognise Christ as their Saviour ('Unseene he came'), Breton decries:

> To hate a loue, must argue loathsome nature,
> To wronge a freinde, must proue too foule a deede,
> To kill thy selfe, must show a cursed creature,
> To slay thy soule, no more damnation neede,
>   Thou spoyle the fruite whereon thy spyrite feedeth,
>   Oh what a hell within thy soule it breedethe.[94]

Lanyer depicts the 'High Priests ... Scribes, and Elders of [Jerusalem]' who order the arrest of Christ in similar terms:

> How blinde were they that could not discerne the Light!
> How dull! if not to vnderstand the truth,
> How weake! if meekenesse overcame their might;
> How stony hearted, if not mov'd to ruth:
> How void of Pitie, and how full of Spight,
> Gainst him that was the Lord of Light and Truth.[95]

That these instances coincide with similar occasions in the poems makes it less likely that they are random. Rather, they seem to reveal the pressure of Breton's poem upon Lanyer's imagination.

Most suggestive of all is the correspondence between how the two works handle their subject. Breton's poem is part of a group of texts – ranging across genres, from printed sermons to literary works – that demonstrate a debt to Calvin's reading of the Passion in his *Harmony of the Evangelists* (1584).[96] *The Countesse of Penbrookes passion*, therefore, provides the segue to other Calvinist passion narratives with which Lanyer's long poem, Barbara Bowen observes, 'is in dialogue'.[97] The rhetoric of identification, in which the trials of the elect are conflated with the sufferings of Christ – in much the same way that Margaret Clifford, Lanyer's chief patron, is invited to commune with Christ in *Salve Deus* – is one feature of the narratives that are explicitly informed by Calvin's representation of the Passion in his biblical exegesis.[98] Of course, this is classic Protestant typology. But the passion narratives that draw upon Calvin depict a difficult relationship between suffering and responsibility. The reader/author, who is situated in the text as a form of Christ, also participates in his torture:

[T]he texts make it clear that if the torturer is the demonic other, he is also the reader. The reader must *identify* with the torturer. The notion that since Christ died for our sins we are all responsible for the Crucifixion originates early in Christian thought, but the Calvinist passion narratives intensify this complicity by merging the position of the reader with that of the torturer. Our sins become not simply the antecedent cause of Christ's sacrifice; rather, we find ourselves sucked into the scene as participants in the acts of cruelty.[99]

Identification becomes self-flagellation. One can immediately perceive the psychomachia of Donne's Holy Sonnet 7 ('Spit in my face you Jewes') in such a reading. But Breton's poem participates in this psychology as well:

> I saw [Christ] faultlesse, yet I did offend him,
> I saw him wrong'd and yet did not excuse him,
> I sawe his foes, yet sought not to defend him,
> I had his blessinges, yet I did abuse him.
>> but was it myne, or my forefathers deade?
>> whose ere it was, it makes my hart to bleede.[100]

The allocation of blame is at the heart of Lanyer's radical reinterpretation of the Passion. She takes the central question of the Calvinist narratives ('was it myne, or my forefathers deade?') and answers it squarely: the responsibility lies with men. As Bowen notes, Lanyer's text is in dialogue with the passion narratives, not in concert with them. Which is to say that Lanyer both co-opts the form and counters it.

In the *Harmony of the Evangelists*, Calvin is absorbed by the psychosis that produced Christ's torments.[101] He focuses upon the irrationality of the crime: the participants in the Crucifixion are 'more stupid than brute beasts', having been gripped by the 'giddiness with which God intoxicates the reprobate, after having long contended with their malice'.[102] Consequently, Christ's enemies are rendered in inhuman terms, as animals overcome by fury: they are in the 'darkness of ... rage', 'bewitched', and 'intoxicated'.[103] They are 'filled with a malicious hatred', 'seized with astonishing madness', and consumed by an 'insatiable cruelty'.[104] This depiction is imported into Breton's poem:

> Shall I not curse those hatefull hellishe feindes,
> that led the world to worke such wickednesse?
> and hate all them that had not bene his freindes,
> but followed on that worke of wretchednesse?[105]

But the terminology also pervades Lanyer's representation of Christ's trial and execution.

> The Iewish wolues, that did our Sauiour bite;
> For now they vse all meanes they can deuise
> To beat downe truth, and goe against all right.
> . . . .
> The chiefest Hel-hounds of this hatefull crew,
> Rose vp to aske what answere he could make.[106]

Calvin focuses on the insane malevolence of Christ's persecutors because he wants to underscore that they *knew* who Christ was – they recognised him as the Saviour – and crucified him anyway.[107] 'The circumstances of *an armed multitude* having been sent by *the chief priests*', Calvin writes, 'and of *a captain and band* having been obtained by request from Pilate, make it evident, that an evil conscience wounded and tormented them, so that they did every thing in a state of terror.'[108] This emphasis upon the collusion of the Jews in a sin against God serves Calvin in his displacement of responsibility. The depictions of a reprobate rabble whose 'minds were darkened [by Satan], so that, *seeing they did not see*' are transposed by Calvin on to present-day Christians: 'for this will excite in us deeper horror at our sins'.[109] The implication is that this spiritual blindness possesses us all, and our sins make us complicit in Christ's death: 'All sins resolve into reenactments of the Passion's sadistic violence.'[110] As Breton claims, 'my deede was causer of his deathe'.[111] Lanyer obviously complicates this theory of shared responsibility, even as she exploits it.

The Calvinist narratives, as Debora Shuger observes, 'dwell repeatedly on the shamefulness of Christ's sufferings'.[112] In Calvin, the image of

Christ's agony becomes the locus of our shame and guilt – literally the picture of our sin.

> For if we are desirous to profit aright by meditating on the death of Christ, we ought to begin with cherishing abhorrence of our sins, *in proportion to the severity of the punishment which he endured.* This will cause us not only to feel displeasure and shame of ourselves, but to be penetrated with deep grief, and therefore to seek the medicine with becoming ardour, and at the same time to experience confusion and trembling.[113]

Works influenced by Calvin duly emphasise the humiliation of Christ. They render Christ's loss of control over his body and the breakdown of his physical integrity. Bodily fluids become the symbols of Christ's shame.[114] Lanyer highlights the 'whipping, spurning, tearing of [the] haire' of Christ, and the 'bloody sweat' of his dying body.[115] Breton emphasises his subjection, his bleeding injuries, and the tears on his face.[116] Attention to wounds and gore produces grotesque images on which the poems nonetheless compulsively fix. Breton writes:

> To see the feete, that trauayled for our goode,
> to see the Handes, that brake that liulye breade,
> to see the Heade, whereon our honor stoode,
> to see the fruite, whereon our spyrite fedd,
> > feete pearc'd, handes bored, and his Heade all bleeding,
> > who doth not dye with such a sorrowe readinge.
> . . . . . .
> His faultlesse members nayled to the crosse,
> his holye heade was crowned all with thornes,
> his garmentes giuen by lotts to gayne or losse,
> his power derided all with scoffes and scornes,
> > his bodye wounded and his spyrite vexed,
> > to thinke on this, what soule is not perplexed[?][117]

And Lanyer:

> > His joynts dis-joynted, and his legges hang downe,
> > His alablaster breast, his bloody side,
> > His members torne, and on his Head a Crowne
> > Of sharpest Thorns, to satisfie for pride:
> > Anguish and Paine doe all his Sences drowne,
> > While they his holy garments do divide:
> > > His bowells drie, his heart full fraught with grief,
> > > Crying to him that yeelds him no reliefe.[118]

The degeneration of Christ's body to flesh and fluid is the necessary circumstance for our renewal. Understanding Christ on the cross as the site of our salvation is, obviously, Christian history and not particular to Calvin. What is specific to Calvin is the proximity of the images. The representation of the abject body gives way to the description of our own transformation:

The object of all these expressions of contempt [spitting in Christ's face] was to show that nothing was more unlikely than that he should be a prince of prophets, who ... was not able even to ward off *blows*. But this insolence was turned by the providence of God to a very different purpose; for the face of Christ, dishonoured by *spitting* and *blows*, has restored to us that image which had been disfigured, and almost effaced, by sin.[119]

The face of Christ – bruised, bloodied, and spat upon – is suddenly reconfigured here as the restoration of God's image in us. It is because of this construction (which is employed repeatedly in the *Harmony of the Evangelists*) that the narratives modelled on Calvin tend closely to juxtapose the radically different images of the man of sorrows and the lover of the Canticles.[120] Like the migration in Calvin's passage from mutilation to splendour, 'by mapping the erotic body onto the disfigured one', Shuger writes, these texts 'fuse the two images'.[121]

They also fuse, by extension, the two ideas. In Breton's *Passion*, therefore, Christ's broken body is displaced by a lover's looks:

> Meethinkes I see, and seeinge sighe to see,
> how in his passion patience play'd his parte,
> and in his death, what life he gaue to me,
> in my loues sorrowe to releiue my harte.
> . . . . . .
> And lett me see how sweetelye yet he lookes,
> euen while the teares are tricklinge downe his face,
> and for my life how well his death he brookes,
> while my deserte was cause of his disgrace.[122]

Lanyer also re-presents the scene at Calvary in 'A ... description of [Christ's] beautie vpon the Canticles.'

> This is that Bridegroome that appeares so faire,
> So sweet, so louely in his Spouses sight,
> That vnto Snowe we may his face compare,
> His cheeks like skarlet, and his eyes so bright
> As purest Doues that in the riuers are,
> Washed with milke, to giue the more delight;
> His head is likened to the finest gold,
> His curled lockes so beauteous to behold.[123]

The similarities between Breton's poem and *Salve Deus*, however, cannot be entirely accounted for with reference to Calvin. While both works respond to Calvin's interpretation of the Crucifixion, the internal parallels between the poems appear to be the result of Lanyer's use of Breton's *Passion* as a paradigm for her own. Of all of the contemporary passion narratives, in fact, none even remotely bears the likeness to *Salve Deus* as does Breton's passion for the Countess of Pembroke.

As Shuger notes, relatively few poetic narratives that concentrate on the Passion were produced in England between the mid-sixteenth century and the civil war (and even fewer which employ a Calvinist reading).[124] The problems concerning religious poetry aside, Protestant devotional practice privileged introspection over visualisation. Breton is therefore unusual in his repeated treatment of the topic.[125] In following his example, then, Lanyer is engaging this set of devotional narratives. Obviously, this circumvents rivalry with secular poets. But it also puts her in direct competition with Breton. The similarities between *Salve Deus* and the *Countesse of Penbrookes passion* are sufficiently pronounced, it seems to me, not to go unnoticed by noble patrons familiar with Breton's work (such as Pembroke herself). In fact, the resemblance between the two poems invites the comparison – which is to say that it was probably deliberately drawn. By signalling her connection to Breton's work, Lanyer indicates the point of departure for her own.

JESUS AS WOMAN

Lanyer offers female patrons who support the endeavours of devotional poets (particularly the Countess of Pembroke, and her primary dedicatee, the Countess of Cumberland) a response to the religious writing of men. *Salve Deus* reconsiders the evaluation of women within the Calvinist passion narratives. Male descriptions of the Passion tend to write women out of the story; Lanyer's service to her female audience is that she includes them as part of it. In fact, she privileges the female perspective in her revision. The elevation of women as witnesses of Christ in Lanyer's poem goes to the heart of her own self-construction as a professional religious poet. The different moral vision of men and women is a theme developed within the *Salve Deus*, and becomes the argument for its value. The poem is premised upon the superior capacity of women to perceive Christ.[126] By advocating the devotional faculties of women, Lanyer also promotes the abilities of the female poet in the devotional mode.

Similarly, in 'An invective against outward beuty unaccompanied with virtue', Lanyer does not really inveigh against outward beauty at all, but rather against the systems of male exchange in which women are pawned:

> That pride of Nature which adornes the faire,
> Like blasing Comets to allure all eies,
> Is but the thred, that weaves their web of Care,
> Who glories most, where most their danger lies;
> For greatest perills do attend the faire,
> When men do seeke, attempt, plot and devise,
>   How they may overthrow the chastest Dame,
>   Whose Beautie is the White whereat they aime.[127]

The physical beauty of women marks them as prey; but Lanyer is not simply decrying the objectification of women. She goes on to cite specific examples of women who are overthrown:

> Twas Beautie bred in *Troy* the ten yeares strife,
> And carried *Hellen* from her lawfull Lord;
> Twas Beautie made chaste *Lucrece* loose her life,
> For which prowd *Tarquins* fact was so abhorr'd:
> Beautie the cause *Antonius* wrong'd his wife,
> Which could not be decided but by sword:
>   Great *Cleopatraes* Beautie and defects
>   Did worke *Octaviaes* wrongs, and his neglects.[128]

The unusual grouping of Helen of Troy, Lucrece, and Cleopatra alerts us to the fact that Lanyer is aiming at something other than compromised chastity. Even though Cleopatra contributes (in Lanyer's representation) to her own demise, the list is comprised of women usually assumed to be at different ends of the moral spectrum. Lanyer's addition of Rosamund and Matilda to the list of female figures spells out her true intentions. These women are all the subjects of recent literary treatment by men: Shakespeare's non-dramatic poem (1593) and Thomas Heywood's *The rape of Lucrece* (1608); Daniel's *Cleopatra* (1593) and Shakespeare's *Antony and Cleopatra* (1606–7); Daniel's *Complaint of Rosamund* (1592); and Drayton's *Matilda* (1594).[129] When she cites these women in a section that ostensibly reclassifies the terms of feminine beauty, Lanyer is not simply rejecting the system of male rivalry in which these women are traded; she is developing a tactic by which they are removed from male literary circulation. She is declaring a new definition of female beauty – one that relies upon inward, not outward, construction, and one that is developed by a woman, not by men. The strategy is an extremely clever assertion of the place of the

professional woman poet in literary activity. It affirms the need for a new
(female) perspective in poetic representation.

Lanyer, then, is creating her text as a counter-narrative. Breton's *Passion*,
like other poems that employ a Calvinist interpretation, is consumed by a
sense of shared responsibility with the past ('was it myne, or my forefathers
deade?'). Lanyer's revision of these stories of crime and punishment similarly focuses upon this question, but yields a very different answer. The
arrest, trial, and execution of Christ is enacted in *Salve Deus* as a series of
mistakes, misnomers, and misreadings of the event. What is particular
about Lanyer's depiction is that it is only the men who misapprehend the
scene. The women of the poem recognise Jesus as Christ. It is Pontius
Pilate's wife who has a dream (Matt. 27:19), and it is she who sues to Pilate
for 'her Sauiours life'.[130] When Christ is led through the streets of Jerusalem:

> First went the Crier with open mouth proclayming
> The heauy sentence of Iniquitie,
> The Hangman next, by his base office clayming
> His right in Hell, where sinners neuer die,
> Carrying the nayles, the people still blaspheming
> Their maker, vsing all impiety;
> > The Thieues attending him on either side,
> > The Serjeants watching, while the women cri'd.[131]

The names of the offices of men give way in the stanza to the only human
voices – the cries of distressed women.[132] While the men exhibit incom-
prehension, the women experience the full horror of the sin that is taking
place.

Pilate's wife 'speakes for all' women.[133] For her, Christ's death was a
crime of men, not a crime of humanity. Rather, she says that Eve's Fall was
a minor stumble in comparison to the second Fall of man that is about to
occur. If Eve's action purchased the subordination of women to men,

> Then let vs haue our Libertie againe,
> And challendge to your selues no Sou'raigntie;
> You came not in the world without our paine,
> Make that a barre against your crueltie;
> Your fault beeing greater, why should you disdaine
> Our beeing your equals, free from tyranny?
> > If one weake woman simply did offend,
> > This sinne of yours, hath no excuse, nor end.[134]

The killing of Christ releases women from their subordinate position. Her
argument is that men were granted power over women, but have proved

inadequate in their use of it. Their moral blindness in this instance is a case in point.[135] If introducing knowledge into the world was women's fault, the Crucifixion is men's – one sin erases the other. But the indeterminacy of the narrative voice is such that it is difficult to tell if it is Pilate's wife who delivers the brief for the end of male domination, or if it is Lanyer as omniscient author. (Difficult enough that more than one critical analysis of the poem has suggested that it is Lanyer's voice.[136]) In fact, as Janel Mueller has observed, this collapse is part of the poetic effect.[137] Lanyer claims that Pilate's wife speaks on behalf of all women; by leaving the voice that petitions Pilate so undefined, she opens the possibility of other female voices – or all female voices – arguing in concert.

This produces the effect of all women, regardless of specific time and place (except insofar as it is Christian), suing for their release on the basis of men's greater sin.[138] It further makes the demarcation between past and present unstable. As we have seen, Christ's tormentors merge with present-day sinners in Calvinist passion narratives. Our complicity in Christ's death is sealed by our actual involvement. In Lanyer's diction as well, the sins of the past are ongoing. Lanyer may not place contemporary men at the foot of the cross, but she nonetheless suggests that they 'Crucify [Christ] daily' by other means.[139] The case for the role of men in the crime of Christ's execution is revisited precisely because the need to argue for women's delivery persists. Lanyer further implies that the political violence that men practised upon Christ continues to be exercised upon women.

Throughout *Salve Deus*, women have a special affiliation with Christ:

> To speake on word, nor once to lift his eyes
> Vnto proud *Pilate*, no nor *Herod*, king,
> By all the Questions that they could deuise,
> Could make him answere to no manner of thing;
> Yet these poore women, by their pitious cries
> Did mooue their Lord, their Louer, and their King,
> > To take compassion, turne about, and speake
> > To them whose hearts were ready now to breake.[140]

Christ is depicted in the poem in feminised terms. Elaine Beilin argues that 'in her direct praise of Christ, Lanyer actually reveals Him as the true source of feminine virtue'.[141] His 'owne profession' is described in terms of conventional feminine ideals: 'patience, grace, loue, [and] piety'.[142] His demeanour during interrogation has a feminised aspect: '[Lanyer's] Christ, like the ideal woman of the Puritan manuals, is silent except when induced to speak, and modest and taciturn when he does.'[143] He has a special association with women because his relation to male authority is similarly constructed as submissive. He is an impoverished, marginalised, and subordinate figure, and as such shares an experience common to women. The suggestion in Lanyer's poem is that women are able to recognise Christ because his earthly circumstances resonate with their own.[144]

Calvin's exegesis mentions women only once as Christ is led to the site of his execution.[145] Even in Calvin, these women exhibit some signs of faith:

And though [their] faith ... was weak, yet it is probable that there was a hidden seed of piety, which afterwards in due time produced fruit. Yet their *lamentation* served to condemn the wicked and shocking cruelty of the men, who had conspired with the scribes and priests to put Christ to death.[146]

He goes on, however, to use them to presage the destruction of Jerusalem. Unsurprisingly, women tend to be ignored in the treatments of the Passion which follow Calvin, or they serve only to highlight God's retribution. Lanyer turns this passing mention in Calvin into an extended episode (in fact, the implication here that women resisted the deadly operations of men forms the basis of her argument). The manner in which the voices of women overcome the administrative noise of men has already been noticed. But Lanyer further develops Calvin's hint of their superior spiritual insight:

> Most blessed daughters of Ierusalem,
> Who found such fauour in your Sauiors sight,
> To turne his face when you did pitie him;
> Your tearefull eyes, beheld his eies more bright;
> Your Faith and Loue vnto such grace did clime,
> To haue reflection from this Heau'nly Light:
>   Your Eagles eyes did gaze against this Sunne.[147]

The 'Eagles eyes' of the women stand in contrast to the 'Owly eies' of Caiphas, and the blindness of the men. Women not only possess a clearer moral vision, but also unfailingly recognise who and what Christ is. Such certain sight is inevitably given through faith.

Obviously, this acuity of understanding holds special privileges for the female poet. Like the voice of Pilate's wife that 'speakes for all' women, knowledge of Christ is not confined to a historical time and place. If the logic of Lanyer's poem insists upon the superior spiritual awareness of women, then she, as a woman, is able to perceive (and depict) the Passion of Christ with greater clarity than her male counterparts. This is not simply a logical inference: this conclusion is explicitly drawn in the body of the text. Lanyer offers Christ's emblematic body to the female readership of her poem. 'This', she tells the Countess of Cumberland, 'with the eie of Faith thou maist behold', and proceeds to unveil the scene:[148]

> Blacke as a Raven in her blackest hew;
> His lips like skarlet threeds, yet much more sweet
> Than is the sweetest hony dropping dew,
> Or hony combes, where all the Bees doe meet;
> Yea, he is constant, and his words are true,
> His cheeks are beds of spices, flowers sweet;
> > His lips like Lillies, dropping downe pure mirrhe,
> > Whose loue, before all worlds we doe preferre.[149]

Given the emphasis throughout the poem upon the different capacity of men and women to behold Christ, the requisite 'eie of Faith' seems to omit the male gaze. In her address 'To all vertuous ladies in generall', Lanyer instructs them to 'Put on your wedding garments euery one, / The Bridegroome stayes to entertaine you all.'[150] Such erotic messages, modelled on the Song of Songs, are a common feature in passion narratives (whether produced by Calvinist piety or not). It was also not uncommon to imagine Christ as a handsome young man (as is evident from Breton's depiction). But it is the feminised body of Christ that is made available here.[151] Lanyer's *ottava rima* stanza renders Christ in the mode of a Petrarchan beloved. Wendy Wall was first to notice Lanyer's use of the conventional female blazon to display the broken figure of Christ's Passion. Understanding the blazon as a means of inscribing authority and control, Wall asserts that Lanyer's employment of it serves as 'a tool . . . to proclaim, to publish, to unfold to view'.[152] What she is publishing is not simply the erotic body of Christ as a desired subject, but also her own desires for authorial recognition and patronage. Like the strategy by which she wrested the terms of feminine beauty from male circulation, Lanyer here assumes the Petrarchan mode of commodification and display in order to circulate the body of Christ to other Christian women.

The text's insistence upon a female gaze permits acceptable channels for female desire, but as Jonathan Goldberg points out, the figure of the Passion that Lanyer constructs participates within a female–female exchange.[153] Breton also imagines a scene of execution in which the religious passion of the penitent speaker coincides with same-sex eroticism – having dedicated his poem to Herbert, however, he allows the female reader to participate in the erotics of the moment as well. By contrast, in Lanyer's poem, the body of Christ is inscribed as female and is witnessed – at least within the text itself – by an audience of women. Her reconceptualisation of the blazon is an act of literary enclosure: Christ is imagined as a woman for women. This fits neatly with the particular network of female patronage Lanyer is trying to serve. It also effectively cordons off male intrusion. I am not suggesting that Lanyer is putting herself forward as a kind of pander within a female Christian community; but she is, on some level, establishing herself as a purveyor of Christ's favours.

In her dedication to Queen Anne, Lanyer asks (in diction that suggests domestic service) her to sit down and 'feed vpon' the 'Paschal Lamb' that the poet has 'prepar'd'.[154] She instructs the Countess of Kent to 'Receiue [her] Loue' whom she had 'sought so farre' and who 'presents himselfe within [her] view' in the pages of the poem.[155] Such articulations of presentation and display are standard in the dedicatory address; what is remarkable about Lanyer's expression is that she claims to be offering Christ to her readership. Such offerings are notably absent in the addresses of male poets. One could argue that the implication of such a gift is tacit in the dedication of a devotional poem. But, at most, Fletcher will only commend his 'broken lines' to the reader, and the dedicatee himself to 'the best Physitian, IESVS CHRIST'.[156] Breton will only claim 'to acquaint the honest mindes' with Herbert's 'heauenly Meditations'. The dedications of devotional works by men do not contain bald assertions that their representations of Christ are authentic. But Lanyer's poem itself opens space for such assertions. If the virtuous sight of her female readership is able to penetrate Christ's earthly guise, then

> it [is] no disparagement to you,
> To see your Sauiour in a Shepheards weed,
> . . . . . .
> Receiue him here by my vnworthy hand.[157]

While she appears to denigrate her work, what she is showing her female audience is a faithful depiction of the good shepherd of the Gospels.[158] Lanyer herself makes the suggestion that her representation is more genuine because she is a woman:

> And pardon me . . . though I presume,
> To doe that which so many better can;
> Not that I Learning to my selfe assume,
> Or that I would compare with any man:
> But as they are Scholers, and by Art do write,
> So Nature yeelds my Soule a sad delight.[159]

Here again, what at first appears pejorative is actually preferred. Lanyer seems to claim that her poetic efforts are inferior to men due to the limits of her education. But by underscoring the artifice by which men achieve their poetic effects, she renders the apprehension of Christ in their poems suspect. By contrast, the perfection of her art is derived from her own nature – and the syntax implies that men have moved away from this impulse as a result of rhetorical training. Of course this emphasis upon her level of education has a gendered inflection: Lanyer did not have the benefit of university training – nor did her female readership – and it is this distinction that she is highlighting. The artfulness which arrests the ability of men to fully render Christ in their poems was presumably learned within the enclosed walls of higher institutions that shut women out.

The gendered performance within Lanyer's poem is central to its formulations. The argument of *Salve Deus* suggests that women are better able to receive Christ – but this converts to a claim for the enhanced ability of the female poet to present the Christian story. Even the title of the work, with its alteration of the biblical salutation, recalls the impaired sight of men. In the context of the poem, Lanyer's ability to see Christ rightly ('Hail, God, King of the Jews') amounts to self-promotion. Her self-presentation as a superior conduit of Christian revelation is premised upon the gendered distinctions that are generated within her poem. Just as the 'eie of Faith' allows women to perceive Christ regardless of his outward form, it is the 'hand' of a female poet (the poem maintains) that is able to make him legible. By reading *Salve Deus* against *The Countesse of Penbrookes passion* we can begin to see what strain of contemporary discourse Lanyer's text opposes. The central features of her poetic argument – the allocation of blame, the conflation of past and present crimes, the lamentation of women (the daughters of Jerusalem) at the site of the Crucifixion, and the painful depiction of Christ's death that transforms into a spectacle to please the soul – are culled from Breton's poem and Calvin's interpretation of the Passion. Lanyer then refashions her poetic material, countering the patriarchal assumptions that organise Breton's text. (Even the patrilineal diction of Breton's central question – 'was it myne, or my forefathers deade?' – serves her counter-argument.) Noticing how the points of Lanyer's argument contradict Breton's formulations underscores the calculated nature of her poetic presentation. Breton was the most prolific religious poet of his time; Lanyer offers her own passion narrative as an alternative to female patrons of religious material.

Breton attempts his own strategies of identification: in *The soules harmony*, for example, he claims that the 'zealous loue to diuine studies' of Lady Sara Hastings 'haue brought forth these comfortable Meditations'; but the soul that speaks the poem expresses the devotion of poet and patron alike.[160] This demands that the female patron empathise with his poetic efforts. Lanyer tries to dissolve the links between male poet and female patrons by emphasising his sexual difference. *Salve Deus* is, as are most poems of the period, an exercise in literary imitation – but the imitative gestures of the poem call attention to the limits of Breton's work. The moral perspective of men is as inadequate in its assessment of female virtue as it is in the evaluation of Christ on earth. Thus the female poet is better equipped to administer devotional verse to a communion of female patrons.[161]

Given that Lanyer is arguably 'the first woman writing in English who clearly sought professional standing as a poet', nearly all of her critics have tried to understand the dynamics of the proto-feminist statements in her work.[162] It is legitimate to wonder what is added by the observation that these statements are the result of a poetic stratagem rather than the expression of a poet invigorated by a feminist energy. But once we locate the expression in the context of competitive circulation, we begin to see its origin and impulses – how it is developed and why. What becomes clear is that Lanyer's terms are forged in opposition – not to patriarchy *per se*, but to male poets of the middling sort who experience similar financial need. If the terms of Lanyer's poetic project respond to market pressures, it becomes an open question whether this expression would have been conceived absent the financial imperative that forces its claims. The lineaments of her stratagem, however, reveal a good deal about gender, class position, and the cultural evaluation of women's work. Lanyer writes against male poets in professional circulation; and presses the figure of an upper-class woman poet into the service of her professional aspirations. It becomes clear that the figure of the religious woman is a self-consciously developed marketing device – and one that is deployed in compound ways. Herbert forms part of the reason for Lanyer's emphasis upon gender: her use of Herbert as a vehicle for her work draws deliberate attention to a woman's role in the transmission of devotional verse.

Lanyer's appeal to female patrons distinguishes her service as a poet by virtue of her sex. Her petition, however, also relies upon her claim to poetic superiority in the devotional mode. 'The authors dreame' represents Herbert as the model that Lanyer follows. While the tactic plays upon the similar strategies of other contemporary devotional poets, Lanyer is better able to exploit its terms. Herbert 'Direct[s] all by [the] immortal light' of her verse; but the woman poet apprehends her song internally. The importance of Herbert to Lanyer's self-construction is partly revealed by the length of her 'dreame': the fantasy encounter between the two authors extends for over 200 lines before Lanyer begins her dedication. Hers is a dedication with a difference: it highlights female agency in the activation of religious lyric – and it implies that special attention should therefore be paid to the religious poetry of women. Lanyer's assumption of authority in a male-dominated profession is remarkable, but not for the reasons usually assumed: precisely what is noteworthy about it is that it trades upon the precedent of devotional writing by women. The bulk of the argument in *Salve Deus* affirms the spiritual acumen of women generally – this both flatters its audience, and advances the credentials of its author. But Herbert emerges from the lyric collection as the figure that authorises Lanyer's assertion that poetic apprehension of the religious subject is a female talent.

Afterword

In 1667, Abraham Cowley commemorates Katherine Philips in terms of her unique status as a female poet. In his elegy, she is solitary in her sex:

> She does no Partner with her see;
> Does all the Business there Alone which we
> Are forced to carry on by a whole company.[1]

Cowley sets her only in the company of Sappho, without a contemporary female precedent. Seventeenth-century representations of female poets, such as this one of Philips, have provoked speculation as to why the proliferation of women writers in the period seems to have paradoxically led to their diminished visibility.[2] Part of this impulse to write women out of history is commercial: female poets tended to emphasise singularity as a selling point for their work. Lanyer insists that 'A Womans writing of diuinest things' is a rare spectacle in spite of the devotional precedent of a woman poet whom she herself cites.[3] Margaret Cavendish wilfully ignores women writers of the past so as to not encounter writers of her sex who 'have out-done all the glory' that she could 'hope to attaine'.[4] Jeffrey Masten suggests that fewer companions and competitors than their male counterparts made it possible for seventeenth-century women poets to exploit emergent notions of authorship and author-genius.[5] But these women were obviously able to overlook, by accident or design, the example of women writers in the previous century. This oversight implies that women writers are effectively erased from English literary history by the seventeenth century.[6]

We need not take these women, or their advocates, at their word. Their language of solitude instead of solidarity, however, does indicate a shift in cultural attitudes concerning women writers in the seventeenth century. The profusion of printed texts by women from mid-century onward has been well documented.[7] The greatest expansion, however, lay in the range of subjects that women addressed in the public sphere, and the generic forms in which they expressed themselves. Narratives of personal experience and private letters, recipes and medicinal treatments became a staple of women's publications in the second half of the century. As religion increasingly became 'the common discourse and Table-talke' of the unordained and undereducated in ale-houses, taverns, and private homes, women increasingly became active in the propagation of sectarian positions.[8] Women's writing accounts for a healthy portion of the conversion narratives, spiritual autobiographies, prophetic writings, and pamphlets that voiced the beliefs of Protestant sectaries. None of these generic forms fits with standard conventions of the literary category. More than one critic has cited the forms in which seventeenth-century women predominantly wrote as the source of critical inattention to their work until very recently.[9] Cowley's statement that Philips 'Does all the Business there Alone which [men] / Are forced to carry on by a whole company' reveals a similar neglect. That Philips writes within the forms of literary convention – poetry and drama – causes her to *appear* isolated among her sex. Cowley's expression does not reflect the reduced visibility of women writers, but their reduced activity in recognisably orthodox religious and cultural practices.

The influence of women writers did not diminish in the seventeenth century; to the contrary, the proliferation of their published texts indicates a considerable market for their work. Women continued to be important in the advancement of non-traditional religious belief. But the sectarianism that they principally fostered remained fractured through the Interregnum. Non-conformity was obviously an influential religious movement in the mid-seventeenth century, but agreement among non-conformists resided only in their opposition to Church and State. Religious cohesion among the sectaries was never realised, even if their members formed part of a powerful political alliance, and sectarian positions did not inform the practices of the re-instituted Church of England after 1660. Consequently, the non-traditional religious beliefs that women promoted in print were not, over time, adopted as orthodox opinion or incorporated into mainstream Protestant thought.

Nor would women's participation in sectarianism encourage their composition in conventional literary forms. The iconoclasm that marked most of the radical religious sects of the seventeenth century made them hostile to figurative written forms (although the inspired speech of prophets such as Anna Trapnel did sometimes issue forth in verse). John Taylor pens his attack on the sectaries in prose because, he explains, 'nothing to any purpose either in Verse, poetry, Rime, or reason is for their stomacks'.[10]

Certainly women wrote in these forms: aside from Lanyer, Philips, and Cavendish, the work of Aphra Behn, Ann Bradstreet, Lucy Hutchinson, and Anna Weamys was published in print,[11] and aristocratic women such as Anne Southwell and Mary Wroth circulated their poetry in manu-script.[12] The women who wrote plays, poems, and prose fiction, in fact, increased in number in the seventeenth century. But the increased abun-dance of texts by women – there were 653 first edition printings of works by named female authors – overwhelmed the comparatively few texts by women poets.[13]

If the promotion of non-traditional religious belief had long been the office of women (in cultural terms), the status of their dissent changed in the seventeenth century. The rise in the number of women writing and publishing necessarily meant a decline in the social rank of practitioners. This partly accounts for the proliferation of forms. Poetry was an elite form, an index of acquired learning. But many women who wrote were very nearly hostile to an educated class. Both Anna Trapnel and Mary Cary, for example, cite the levelling of religious authority as a sign of the coming of the Lord. Furthermore, the involvement of women writers in the political and religious life of the nation was sufficiently vigorous to constitute a threat to social order. Cary's vision of *New Ierusalems glory* (1651) sounds like Stephen Gardiner's worst fears realised: '[N]ot onely men but women shall prophesie . . . not onely superiou[r]s, but inferiours; not onely those that have University-learning but those that have it not; even servants and handmaids'.[14] Women no longer merely signalled the egalitarian impulses of religious reform; instead, women writers were themselves vocal advocates, and examples, for the abolition of class and gender hierarchies.[15] Female authors of the previous century were clearly active reformers; but they were not, for the most part, activists in the area of social reform – except insofar as it was religious – in part because they were members of the social elite.[16] The increase in women writers from the lower ranks of society brought a political component to women's works – one that led to more concerted attempts to marginalise them.

Women were unruly spectacles in seventeenth-century English culture. The figure of the religious woman became a symbol of fractured religious authority and female self-government – a sign of the world turned upside-down. Patricia Crawford has shown the extent to which notions of 'female insubordination and [religious] separatism' combine in the examination of religious sects before the Civil War.[17] Women were allowed to join sects without the consent or knowledge of their husbands, and they outnum-bered men (according to the extant record) in sectarian congregations.

They taught, preached, and led meetings within the sects. This freedom of instruction and worship – outside of the sanctioned control of husbands – was correlated to the breakdown of ecclesiastical control.[18] The fact that sectarian meetings also frequently took place in domestic sites increased the identification of women with religious radicalism.[19] More threatening still, women defended their right to preach and prophesy in print, and argued for the diminution of state and ecclesiastical supervision. While religious radicals made up perhaps 5 per cent of the population,[20] the writing generated by women in the context of radical religious sects accounted for a disproportionate amount of women's writing during the Civil War and Interregnum.[21] Women were as active upon the religious and cultural environment as they had been the century before.[22] But the cultural influence of seventeenth-century women writers was more local-ised – in part because of the splintered nature of the religious sects that their published work supported.

Women's religious writings also did not remain relevant beyond a particular cultural moment. While separatism was more than a minority movement, the fact that the various sects never coalesced in anything other than political terms served the polemical purposes of their detractors. The diversity of religious opinion made it possible for opponents to assert the disorder of Church and State that sectarian activity had wrought ('Religion is made a Hotch potch', Taylor declares[23]). Women became the principal spectres of this disorder, as Thomas Jordan's 'The rebellion' indicates:

> Truth is the spell that made us rebell,
> And murder and plunder ding dong;
> Sure I have the truth, sayes *Numphs,*
> Nay, I have the truth, sayes *Clem,*
> Nay, I have the truth, sayes reverend *Ruth,*
> Nay, I have the truth, sayes *Nem.*[24]

The designation of 'reverend' gives Ruth special authority in this public sphere – and underscores how women were seizing authority for them-selves. In the political melee of the poem, women make up the majority of the voices. Clearly, this is not representative of actual political struggle, in which men were inevitably the primary agents; instead, it reveals the extent to which women – particularly religious women – became exemplary figures of chaos and social conflict.[25]

Jordan's poem also demonstrates that politics and religion became the subjects of popular literature. Susan Wiseman states that 'in the period of the Civil War what might be seen by twentieth-century critics as disparate and unrelated discourses', such as political theory and prose fiction, 'were interwoven and even interdependent'.[26] We should not, therefore, understand women's cultural activities in defence of religion and politics as isolated from their depiction in other areas of cultural production. In her analysis of the representation of women in seventeenth-century pamphlet literature, Sharon Achinstein concludes that 'the attempt to exclude women', in cultural practices, 'was a *response to* their vivid participation in the public sphere'.[27] A similar observation can be made about the representation of women in the literary mode. Critical methodology that has concentrated upon versified (canonical) literary texts has distorted the cultural values of the seventeenth century by marginalising the production of the literate non-elite.[28] At the same time, the methodology has failed to recognise the pressures that popular and polemical writing exerted upon elite culture.

'[W]hat seems to have happened in the 1640s and 1650s', Wiseman observes, 'is that ... women became visible in discourse as obstructions, channels which took virtue, semen, money out of the proper routes, no longer recombining these elements so as to fuel the patriarchal economy of status.'[29] We can witness male writers try to regain control of the public debate by implying the sexual availability of culturally productive women. A ribald rhyme, for example, implies the uncertain authorship of the work of Katherine Chidley:

> Oh Kate, O Kate, thou art unclean I heare,
> A man doth lye betweene thy sheetes, I feare.[30]

Even when sexual innuendo is not used to suggest a paternity for women's written work, doubts are cast upon their authorship. In Thomas Edward's *Gangraena*, for example, he also sets a man 'betweene [Chidley's] sheetes' – this time, her son. Chidley penned two sharp responses to Edward's *Reasons against the independent government of particular congregations* (1641), and *Antapologia* (1644).[31] In the third part of his *Gangraena*, however, Edwards removes her as the writer of her books, and instead cites them as a collaborative effort ('for the mother and son made them together, one inditing, and the other writing').[32] Edwards is specifically concerned with the social consequences of religious toleration – that such toleration would undermine patriarchal authority. It is this very authority that Chidley attacks.[33] The manner of Edwards's misattribution, then, is telling: Samuel Chidley is imagined as the author of his mother's works, but she incites his challenge to patriarchal values.[34] In a single gesture, Edwards manages to reclaim male proprietorship of knowledge while still figuring 'woman' as a destabilising force upon social order and homosocial bonds.

If the public discourse and popular literature of the mid-seventeenth century figured women as emblems of disordered arrangements of social power, their representation within elite cultural practices appears to be a remedial fantasy. The depiction of women in areas such as poetic composition is an index of the restoration of a class-based cultural order that is being mapped through the literary reputations of particular female authors. The resumption of male control over these cultural practices is registered in Cowley's declaration that Philips is alone in the enterprise of poetry. In Cowley's configuration, not only does Philips lack the collaboration of women in her artistic endeavour, she is also without a cohort of men. Which is to say that it is not her participation in literary activity, but the degree to which this involvement is portrayed as rare among her sex that defines her as a poet. For Cowley, this increases her value:

> The trade of Glory managed by the pen
> Though great it be, and every where is found,
> Does bring in but small profit to us men;
> 'Tis by the number of the sharers drown'd.[35]

This erasure of other contemporary women writers can be put to the service of promoting female poets (such as Cavendish). But even in Cowley's articulation, it mostly serves a reassertion of gender hierarchy, class hierarchy, and high culture. Philips is the 'exceptional' example of the female author: educated, socially privileged, and engaged in versification. And men are the arbiters of elite culture and its practitioners.

The disappearance of women from English literary history in the seventeenth century is a purely rhetorical vanishing act: by magnifying the reputations of certain women writers, male poets of the period caused others to disappear. At the same time, they reclaimed control of the terms that governed social and cultural relations. Those women who were able to pen pretty verse were confirmed as contributors to high culture; they were also set under glass as extraordinary spectacles. Through a cultural politic, men were able to ratify the education that enabled such versification as a source of social power. This authorised the practices of educated ladies and gentlewomen, and neatly excluded those women whose writing presented the most radical threat to social order. It also confirmed men as the proprietors of social and cultural values. Men controlled access to education, and while men of middling class position acquired significant educational advantages in the seventeenth century, women did not share equally in these gains.[36] The extent to which education was elevated as a mechanism of social power, then – over and above the privileges of rank – correspondingly affected the extent to which gender managed social relations.[37]

The success of the cultural strategy that I am describing is apparent in the well-known lines of Anne Finch:

> Alas! a woman that attempts the pen,
> Such an intruder on the rights of men.[38]

It is difficult to imagine Mary Sidney Herbert articulating such a view. But just over a century later, a woman possessed of rank and talent cedes the cultural field to men (even if she is willing to intrude upon it). The different attitudes of these two aristocratic women demonstrate the migration of cultural opinion concerning women writers over the course of one hundred-plus years: Finch's position is not the projection of a stable, male-dominated cultural order that uniformly prevailed throughout the early modern period; it is instead the product of a male revisionist project activated in the mid-seventeenth century. This is to posit a different scenario from critics who understand a masculine literary tradition emanating from a complex negotiation of the social conditions of literacy and education, rather than from actual exclusion.[39] The creation of the English canon is well outside of my purview here. But if an all-male writing tradition is inducted in the seventeenth century, as John Guillory and Jonathan Kramnick both suggest (even if they do not see it taking hold until the eighteenth), it is worth noting that such an invention might have found its initial impulse in a cultural backlash.[40]

When both the terms of religion and the terms of the literary category were under construction, women writers were able to shape these debates. But if women were vital participants in the cultural change of sixteenth-century England, we must admit that this was assisted by their acceptance of gendered assumptions. Indeed, it was the very habitation of the culturally constructed figure of the religious female that gave authority to the writing of women during the tumultuous period of English reform. The figure of the religious woman embodied the instabilities and ideals of the radical religious change that was taking place. Assumptions encoded in the sex/gender system could be traded upon to empower the writing of women in public and polemical discourse. Askew's figure is compelling in the context of early reform precisely because of the presumed physical and spiritual weakness of women. Anne Lok's deferral to male voices – ironically a marker of biographical experience – achieves a polyphonic subjectivity that (partly) resolves the problem of lyric in religious expression. Positioned outside of the orthodox institutions that governed rhetorical uses, women were able to speak differently, and, in the midst of the religious and cultural turmoil of the sixteenth century, catalytically.

As Protestantism became progressively codified and controlled by state apparatus, however, women increasingly became figures of religious – and therefore, political and social – dissent. The conditions that preceded and produced the English Civil War transformed the religious woman as a cultural sign. Far from being constituent in the operations of patriarchy, women of the middling sort began to insist that the equal state of individual souls before God must be reflected in social arrangements. They argued for ecclesiastical and civic self-determination, the equal moral state of men and women, the right to divorce, and the rise of the sovereign individual.[41] As actual women increasingly became advocates of populist causes in print, the figure of 'woman' came to be connected to class struggle and popular literacy. In the reconstruction of cultural order that followed the Civil War, these spectres of civil disorder were scrubbed from the record.

Notes

1. Early English women, such as Margery Kempe and Julian of Norwich, do not stand as part of this list, because it now seems clear that their texts were dictated to, and quite possibly altered by, male clergy. See *The book of Margery Kempe*, ed. S. B. Meech and H. E. Allen (Oxford: EETS, o.s. 212, 1940); and *Julian of Norwich's revelations of divine love*, ed. F. Beer (Heidelberg: Carl Winter, 1978).

2. The first wave of this criticism (and recovery) of women's writing in the early modern period came in the 1980s: *Silent but for the word: Tudor women as patrons, translators, and writers of religious works*, ed. M. Hannay (Kent, OH: Kent State University Press, 1985); E. Beilin, *Redeeming Eve: women writers of the English Renaissance* (Princeton: Princeton University Press, 1987); *Kissing the rod: an anthology of seventeenth-century women's verse*, ed. G. Greer *et al.* (London: Virago, 1988); *The paradise of women: writings by Englishwomen of the Renaissance*, ed. B. Travitsky (New York: Columbia University Press, 1988); E. Hobby, *Virtue of necessity: English women's writing, 1646–1688* (Ann Arbor: Michigan University Press, 1988); and T. Krontiris, *Oppositional voices: women as writers and translators of literature in the English Renaissance* (London: Routledge, 1992).

3. There were five editions of each versified work produced by the end of the century. With works of literature, printers often printed a first edition of about 500 copies. If that sold well, the next print run would usually be about 800 copies. Successive print runs (once the book's popularity was established) would be about 1,000 copies each. I owe these statistics to Mark Bland; see 'The London book trade in 1600', in *A companion to Shakespeare*, ed. D. S. Kastan (Oxford: Blackwell, 1999), 450–63.

4. I discuss the publication history of the works by Katherine Parr at length in the first chapter.

5. STC 848 and 850.

6. By Nicholas Hill (STC 851) and William Hill (STC 852).

7. William Hill's 1548 edition omits Bale's commentary. The *Examinations* saw two more early printings (without commentary) in 1550 (STC 852.5) and 1560 (STC 853).

8. There were five published editions of the *Acts and Monuments* in the sixteenth century (1563, 1570, 1576, 1583, 1596).

9. While I use the early modern spelling of the title in footnote citations, I will use the modern spelling in my text.
10. It was first used by Day for the 1548 pamphlet, *The confutation of xiii. articles wherunto N. Shaxton . . . subscribed* (STC 6083). See J. N. King, *English Reformation literature: the Tudor origins of the Protestant tradition* (Princeton: Princeton University Press, 1982), 439–40.
11. *The confutation*, K5r–v.
12. Ibid., H3r.
13. See C. Cross, '"Great reasoners in scripture": the activities of women Lollards 1380–1530', in *Medieval women*, ed. D. Baker (Oxford: Ecclesiastical History Society, 1978), 359–80, for a fuller discussion of the reorientation of women's place within the Lollard movement.
14. Ibid., 375.
15. In 'Women and the civil war sects', Keith Thomas explores the power of women in sectarian religion in England (and traces the roots of this back to the anti-clerical movements of the Middle Ages). Thomas's article was at the forefront of a renewed and important interest in women's religious writing of the seventeenth century – particularly that of women prophets; see *Crisis in Europe 1560–1660: essays from past and present 1952–1962*, ed. T. Aston (London: Routledge, 1965), 317–40.
16. See, for example, *The first examinacyon of Anne Askewe*, ♣4v–♣5r.
17. J. Summit, *Lost property: the woman writer and English literary history, 1380–1589* (Chicago, Chicago University Press, 2000), 141.
18. In the *The first examinacyon of Anne Askewe*, for example, Bale refers to the proclamation of 8 July 1546, which ordered the burning of books written by Frith, Tyndale, Wycliffe, Barnes, Coverdale, and himself (♣5v).
19. *A brefe chronycle concernynge the examinacyon and death of . . . syr Johan Oldecastell the lorde Cobham* (STC 1276); *A treatyse made by John Lambert unto kynge Henry the viii* (STC 15180).
20. *A brefe chronycle concernynge the examinacyon and death of . . . syr Johan Oldecastell*, A3v.
21. Ibid., A5v.
22. Summit, *Lost property*, 145.
23. Summit makes this point as well, and in this sense she is right to notice that Askew is handled differently from male martyrs in Bale's edited texts (ibid., 149).
24. *A brefe chronycle concernynge the examinacyon and death of . . . syr Johan Oldecastell*, A2r.
25. The extent to which Askew's body is displayed as a visible sign of her faith in the *Acts and Monuments* is something that I explore in detail in chapter 1.
26. *The first examinacyon of Anne Askewe*, ♣9v.
27. Ibid., ♣9r.
28. Important enough, in fact, that the excision of part of her *Examination* became necessary to preserve the political career of Secretary William Paget (see chapter 1, n. 83).
29. King, *English Reformation literature*, 84.
30. *The letters of Stephen Gardiner*, ed. J. A. Muller (Cambridge: Cambridge University Press, 1933), 278; quoted in *The examinations of Anne Askew*, ed. E. Beilin (Oxford: Oxford University Press, 1996), xxix.
31. *The lamentacion of a synner* (STC 4828), A2r; reproduced in *The early modern Englishwoman: Katherine Parr*, ed. J. Mueller (Aldershot: Scholar Press, 1996).

32. Margaret Ferguson cites this as the most dramatic feature of four books that in many ways established this as a critical concentration in the late 1980s and early 1990s: Hobby's *Virtue of necessity*; Margaret King's *Women of the Renaissance* (Chicago: Chicago University Press, 1991); Krontiris's *Oppositional voices*; and Barbara Lewalski's *Writing women in Jacobean England* (Cambridge: Harvard University Press, 1993). See Ferguson, 'Moderation and its discontents: recent work on Renaissance Women', *Feminist Studies* 20 (1994), 352.

33. E. Klotz, 'A subject analysis of printing, 1480–1640', *HLQ* 1 (1938), 417–19. See also H. S. Bennett, *English books and readers 1558–1603* (Cambridge: Cambridge University Press, 1965), 269; and P. Crawford, *Women and religion in England 1500–1720* (London: Routledge, 1993), 93.

34. J. Guillory, *Cultural capital: the problem of literary canon formation* (Chicago: Chicago University Press, 1993), 15.

35. B. Bowen, 'The rape of Jesus: Aemilia Lanyer's *Lucrece*', in *Marxist Shakespeares*, ed. J. Howard and S. C. Shershow (London: Routledge, 2001), 107.

36. Ibid.

37. S. Trill, 'Religion and the construction of femininity', in *Women and literature in Britain, 1500–1700*, ed. H. Wilcox (Cambridge: Cambridge University Press, 1996), 30–55.

38. David Cressy estimates that 'more than four-fifths of the women in the seventeenth-century could not write their names' (see *Literacy and the social order: reading and writing in Tudor and Stuart England* (Cambridge: Cambridge University Press, 1980), 59). Tables which calculate illiteracy among different social groups from the late sixteenth through the seventeenth century estimate illiteracy among women to be anywhere from 76 to 98 per cent depending upon the area scrutinised (ibid., 119–21). Since, as Margaret Ferguson points out, women did not routinely have access to the property transactions that would document their literacy, such statistics are inevitably subject to question (see 'Renaissance concepts of the "woman writer"', in *Women and literature*, ed. Wilcox, 147).

39. See in particular, J. Fleming, 'Review essay: writing women in Jacobean England', *HLQ* 57 (1994), 203–4. See also E. Hanson, 'Boredom and whoredom: reading Renaissance women's sonnet sequences', *Yale Journal of Criticism* 10 (1997), 171.

40. Mary Ellen Lamb, for example, asserts that 'the discourse of gender difference was generally, but not entirely, successful in its prevention of women's authorship of original works in the sixteenth and early seventeenth centuries' (*Gender and authorship in the Sidney circle* (Madison: Wisconsin University Press, 1990), 19). Suzanne Trill's important corrective undercuts Lamb's assumptions concerning 'original' work ('Sixteenth-century women's writing: Mary Sidney's Psalms and the "femininity" of translation', in *Writing and the English Renaissance*, ed. W. Zunder and S. Trill (London: Longman, 1996), 140–58). But I am not setting Lamb up as the straw man here – her extended study of Mary Sidney Herbert's poetic production demonstrates her recognition of the importance of (at least one) woman's work in the period. Her statement is, however, as Elizabeth Hanson points out, proleptic.

41. Hanson, 'Boredom and whoredom: reading renaissance women's sonnet sequences', 170–1.

42. Ibid., 171.

43. While Suzanne Trill notes the instabilities of gender codes in relation to religious reform ('Religion and the construction of femininity', 30–55), I am arguing that

the existing codes could be traded upon in order to empower women in Reformation discourse.

44. M. Bell, 'Women writing and women written', in *Cambridge history of the book in Britain, 1557–1695*, ed. J. Barnard and D. F. McKenzie (Cambridge: Cambridge University Press, 2002), IV: 431.

45. For an examination of how gender stigmas attached to print venues, see W. Wall, *The imprint of gender: authorship and publication in the English Renaissance* (Ithaca: Cornell University Press, 1993); for an argument that the figure of the 'woman writer' helped to formulate notions of public, canonical literary activity, see Summit, *Lost property*; and for an investigation of how the figure of 'woman' operated within the commerce of the book trade, see Bell, 'Women writing and women written'.

46. While the relationship between the number of editions produced and the influence of a work is by no means straightforward, it does provide some hard numbers on which to ground a discussion of cultural significance. Recent work by scholars such as Tessa Watt and Ian Green have made good and important use of publication figures: see Watt, *Cheap print and popular piety, 1550–1640* (Cambridge: Cambridge University Press, 1991); and Green, *Print and Protestantism in early modern England* (Oxford: Oxford University Press, 2000). Of course, these numbers are only useful gauges in relation to print culture. The ephemeral nature of manuscript renders reference, imitation, and echo the only convincing measures of influence.

47. D. Clarke, *The politics of early modern women's writing* (Harlow, Essex: Pearson Education, 2001), introduction; and *'This double voice': gendered writing in early modern England*, ed. D. Clarke and E. Clarke (Basingstoke: Macmillan, 2000), introduction. See also the excellent essay by Elizabeth Grosz, 'Sexual signatures: feminism after the death of the author', in her *Space, time, and perversion: essays on the politics of bodies* (London: Routledge, 1995), 9–24.

48. A notable exception to this are two recent anthologies: *Representing women in Renaissance England*, ed. C. J. Summers and T. Pebworth (Columbia: Missouri University Press, 1997); and *'This double voice'*, ed. Clarke and Clarke; but even the appearance of these anthologies – and how the editors represent their project – speaks to the absence of such critical work on women's writing in the early modern period.

49. *'This double voice'*, ed. Clarke and Clarke, 6.

50. Ibid., 2.

51. Those studies that do examine the operations of gender in material culture commonly understand 'woman' as a problematic term in the dissemination of texts (particularly in connection to print venues). Wendy Wall, for example, has produced finely nuanced analyses of the work of both Mary Sidney Herbert and Aemilia Lanyer in the context of material circulation. But the assumption that underpins her work is the liability of 'woman' in textual relations (see *The imprint of gender*; and 'Our bodies/our texts? Renaissance women and the trials of authorship', in *Anxious power: reading, writing, and ambivalence in narrative*, ed. C. J. Singley and S. E. Sweeney (Albany: State University of New York Press, 1993), 51–71).

52. In arguing that 'existing narratives of the relationship between women and printed text in the [early modern] period would benefit from a historicism sensitive to the material contexts of printing and publishing', Maureen Bell explores this issue at length (see 'Women writing and women written', 431–51).

53. Janel Mueller outlines the problems relating to the analysis of sixteenth-century religious texts in relation to other texts (intertextuality) when one's scope is confined to the triad of categories usually applied. Most problematic is that the

religious locutions of the early modern period tend to elide gender distinctions. Indeed, a positive lack of individuation can be expected within works that seek to affirm a universal Christian experience (see 'Complications of intertextuality: John Fisher, Katherine Parr and "The book of the crucifix"', in *Texts and cultural change in early modern England*, ed. C. C. Brown and A. F. Marotti (London: Macmillan Press, 1997), 15–36).

54. While historians have rightly cautioned that the use of the term 'class' is anachronistic in relation to the social formations of the early modern period, literary critics have nonetheless employed the vocabulary of class relationships in their discussions because it usefully articulates the social disparities that they are trying to describe and evaluate. For further analysis of the issues at stake, see P. Burke, 'The language of orders in early modern Europe', in *Social orders and social classes in Europe since 1500: studies in social stratification*, ed. M. L. Bush (London: Longman Publishing, 1992), 1–12; D. Cressy, 'Describing the social order of Elizabethan and Stuart England', *Literature & History* 3 (1976), 29–44; and D. S. Kastan, 'Is there a class in this (Shakespearean) text?', in his *Shakespeare after theory* (London: Routledge, 1999), ch. 8.

55. Guillory, *Cultural capital*, 41.

56. M. Quilligan, 'Completing the conversation', *Shakespeare Studies* 25 (1997), 42.

57. While Anne Lok surely took her husband's spelling ('Lock') of his surname, their son, Henry, adopted a different spelling. This might have been a personal idiosyncrasy, but it does reflect the fact that the orientation of the surname was a male prerogative. For the purposes of clarity, I use 'Lok' for both of them.

58. The twenty-six sonnets, collectively entitled 'A meditation of a penitent sinner', are attached to her translation of the *Sermons of John Caluin, vpon the songe that Ezechias made after he had bene sicke* (STC 4450).

59. The distinction between merely metrical psalm translations (of which there are many), and those that can be situated within the development of religious lyric in England, is explored at length over the course of chapters 3 and 4. Further, the assertion crucially relies upon a separation of public and private works: published devotional works of this period took pains to declare their faithful transmission of the scriptural word.

CHAPTER 1. THE DEATH OF THE AUTHOR (AND THE APPROPRIATION OF HER TEXT): THE CASE OF ANNE ASKEW'S *EXAMINATIONS*

1. C. Belsey, *The subject of tragedy: identity and difference in Renaissance drama* (London: Methuen, 1985), 190.

2. Belsey as much as says this in her careful analysis of the interrogation of witches – the distinction that she is making, then, might lie between public and published speech. See also K. Newman, *Fashioning femininity and English Renaissance drama* (Chicago: Chicago University Press, 1991), 69; and F. Dolan, '"Gentlemen, I have one more thing to say": women on scaffolds in England 1563–1680', *Modern Philology* 92 (1994), 157–78.

3. This irony is explored by Fran Dolan in '"Gentlemen, I have one more thing to say"', 161–2. Dolan, however, focuses exclusively on the pyre, and deals only with Foxe's representation of Askew's death.

4. The figure of six editions, while technically correct, includes the initial publication of *The first* [and] *lattre examinacyon* in separate editions (see introduction,

nn. 5–7). The vernacular *Actes and Monuments* (1563) was based upon the original *Rerum in ecclesia gestarum commentarii* (Basel, 1559) in which Askew's narrative also appeared. There is one more edition of the *Examinations* published after Foxe's martyrology appears in print (see n. 113).

5. Printers would only produce what they could sell – paper was a rare commodity, and there was no warehousing. By the estimate of initial print runs of 300–500 copies (which is a low-end figure), and subsequent runs of 1,000 copies, there were anywhere from 2,100 to 3,000 copies in circulation in England within the first two years of Edward's reign. Given the size of the reading public, even the low figure would make this book a terrific commercial success.

6. This woodcut appears in all of the sixteenth-century editions of the *Actes and Monuments* (1563, 1570, 1576, 1583, 1596).

7. According to Foxe's account 'When she was brought unto the stake, she was tied by the middle with a chayne, that held up her body' (*The first* [second] *volume of the ecclesiasticall history contaynyng the Actes and Monuments* ... etc. (STC 11223), 1420). Oddly, most art historians have seen only three figures in this picture, but the narrative and a careful analysis of the cut itself reveal four.

8. The question of whether the published *Examinations* are faithful to the papers that Bale maintains he received in Askew's 'owne hande writynge' (*The first examinacyon of Anne Askewe* (STC 848), ♣5r) is a problematic, and ultimately irresolvable, one. Adriaen van Haemstede printed a translation of the *Examinations* in his *De Ghe-schiedenisse ende den doodt de vromer Martelaren* (Emden, 1559). Thomas Freeman informs me that this text reproduces Bale's version with the exception of a single exchange between Bishop Gardiner and Anne Askew. As Haemstede's tendency is to abridge, not add, this suggests that Bale did tamper with Askew's manuscript – but it also indicates that he made few changes. (For a discussion of the questions that arise from Bale's editing practices, see L. P. Fairfield, *John Bale: mythmaker for the English Reformation* (West Lafayette, IN: Purdue University Press, 1976), 134–5.) Bale also publishes a ballad at the end of the second *Examination*, which he claims 'Anne Askewe made and sange whan she was in Newgate' (*The lattre exam-inacyon of Anne Askewe*, H7r–v). The authorship of this text is uncertain (see n. 131).

9. E. Hanson, 'Torture and truth in Renaissance England', *Representations* 34 (1991), 56. See also J. Mueller, 'Pain, persecution, and the construction of selfhood', in *Religion and culture in Renaissance England*, ed. C. McEachern and D. Shuger (Cambridge: Cambridge University Press, 1997), 161–87.

10. Mueller, 'Pain, persecution, and the construction of selfhood', 165.

11. For the purposes of this discussion, I will be focusing upon the 1546 and 1547 editions of Bale's *Examinacyons* printed in Wesel by Derek van der Straten, and the 1570 edition of the *Actes and Monuments*. When I refer to either work in the text, I use modern spelling.

12. Mueller, 'Pain, persecution, and the construction of selfhood,' 165.

13. *The examinations of Anne Askew*, ed. E. Beilin (Oxford: Oxford University Press, 1996), xix; see also S. Brigden, *London and the Reformation* (Oxford: Oxford University Press, 1989), 371.

14. City of London records confirm Askew's first detention on 10 Mar. 1545 (CLRO Repertory 11, fo. 174v).

15. C. Wriothesley, *A chronicle of England during the reigns of the Tudors. From A.D. 1485 to 1559*, ed. W. D. Hamilton (London: Camden Society, 1875–7), I: 155–6.

16. *A boke made by John Frith . . . answeringe unto M. Mores lettur* (STC 11381), A2v.
17. *The first examinacyon of Anne Askewe*, C5r.
18. *A boke made by John Frith*, A2v.
19. *The first examinacyon*, D7v.
20. Ibid., D3r–5r.
21. *Acts of the Privy Council of England*, ed. J. R. Dasent (London: Eyre and Spottiswoode, 1890–1964), I: 462.
22. See M. Matchinske, *Writing, gender and state in early modern England: identity formation and the female subject* (Cambridge: Cambridge University Press, 1998), 41–2, for a discussion of how Askew slips in and out of roles during questioning.
23. See in particular P. McQuade, '"Except that they had offended the lawe": gender and jurisprudence in *The examinations of Anne Askew*', *Literature & History*, 3rd ser. 3 (1994), 1–14; E. Mazzola, 'Expert witnesses and secret subjects: Anne Askew's *Examinations* and Renaissance self-incrimination', in *Political Rhetoric, Power, and Renaissance Women*, ed. C. Levin and P. Sullivan (Albany: State University of New York Press, 1995), 157–71; T. Betteridge, 'Anne Askewe, John Bale, and Protestant history,' JMEMS 27 (1997), 265–84; and Matchinske, *Writing, gender and state in early modern England*, ch.1.
24. S. Wabuda, 'The woman with the rock: the controversy on women and Bible reading', in *Belief and practice in Reformation England: a tribute to Patrick Collinson from his students*, ed. C. J. Litzenberger and S. Wabuda (Aldershot: Ashgate, 1998), 41–59.
25. *The first examinacyon*, B2r.
26. *The lattre examinacyon of Anne Askewe* (STC 850), G6r; my emphasis.
27. Ibid., C3v.
28. Ibid., H1v–H2r; my emphasis.
29. Ibid., D3r.
30. See R. O'Day, *Education and society 1500–1800: the social foundations of education in early modern Britain* (London: Longman Group, 1982), 179–95.
31. Vives began his treatise with the education of the Princess Mary in mind, and dedicated the finished work to Catherine of Aragon. However, he asserts that the whole book should be read 'by every class of woman' (see *The education of a Christian woman: a sixteenth-century manual*, ed. C. Fantazzi (Chicago: Chicago University Press, 2000), 46).
32. Ibid., 47.
33. M. Dowling, *Humanism in the age of Henry VIII* (London: Croom Helm, 1986), 222. See also M. E. Wiesner, *Women and gender in early modern Europe* (Cambridge: Cambridge University Press, 2000), 152–8.
34. D. Wilson, *A Tudor tapestry: men, women and society in Reformation England* (London: William Heinemann Ltd, 1972), 35.
35. Ibid., 33.
36. *The first examinacyon*, C5r.
37. *A boke made by John Frith*, L4v.
38. *Actes and Monuments*, 1556.
39. This image is seized on by many Protestant ecclesiastics (see, for example, the disputations of Cranmer and Ridley at Oxford in the *Actes and Monuments*, 1591–1622), but Frith introduces it.
40. *The lattre examinacyon*, C8v.
41. Ibid., C4v.

42. *A boke made by John Frith*, C2v–C3r. See *The examinations of Anne Askew*, ed. Beilin, xxv.
43. *The lattre examinacyon*, D7r–v.
44. *A boke made by John Frith*, B7r. This is an extension of the indistinguishability of consecrated and unconsecrated bread and wine which is often mentioned in Lollard writings (see, for instance, *Select English works of John Wyclif*, ed. T. Arnold (Oxford: Oxford University Press, 1869-71), III: 405); another variant on this is the point that consecrated wine can cause drunkenness just as unconsecrated (see *English Wycliffite sermons*, ed. A. Hudson and P. Gradon (Oxford: Oxford University Press, 1983–96), III: 229). The only reference to this specific idea that predates Frith is in John Wyclif's 'De apostasia' (see *Johannis Wyclif: tractatus de apostasia*, ed. Michael Henry Dziewicki (London: Wyclif Society, 1889), 189). My thanks to Professor Hudson for bringing these texts to my attention.
45. *A boke made by John Frith*, L6v–L7r.
46. *The lattre examinacyon*, G7v–G8r.
47. *A boke made by John Frith*, L7r.
48. It is also entirely possible that this phrase was inserted by John Bale – the same phrase is added to the published version of Princess Elizabeth's *THE glasse of the synnefull soule*, edited by Bale (*A godly medytacyon of the Christen sowle . . .* etc. (STC 17320), fo. 10r).
49. Askew's detainments and eventual execution must be viewed within the context of the struggles that were taking place. For detailed accounts of events, see Brigden, *London and the Reformation*, and C. Haigh, *English Reformations: religion, politics, and society under the Tudors* (Oxford: Oxford University Press, 1993), ch. 9. See also, 'Reminiscences of John Louth', in *Narratives of the days of the Reformation, chiefly from the manuscripts of John Foxe, the martyrologist*, ed. J. G. Nichols (London: Camden Society, 1859), 303–13; E. Trollope, 'Anne Askew, the Lincolnshire martyr', *Associated Architectural Societies Reports* 6 (1862), 117–35; J. K. McConica, *English humanists and Reformation politics under Henry VIII and Edward VI* (Oxford: Oxford University Press, 1965); Wilson, *A Tudor tapestry*; S. Brigden, 'Henry Howard, Earl of Surrey, and the "Conjured League"', *Historical Journal* 37 (1994), 507–37; McQuade, '"Except that they had offended the lawe"', 1–14; and *The examinations of Anne Askew*, ed. Beilin, xv–xlii.
50. *Actes and Monuments* (STC 11222), 733. All of the references to this correspondence will be taken from the 1563 *Actes and Monuments* because much of it is dropped in the 1570 edition.
51. See R. Weimann, '"Bifold authority" in Reformation discourse: authorization, representation, and early modern "meaning"', in *Historical criticism and the challenge of theory*, ed. J. L. Smarr (Chicago: Chicago University Press, 1993), 167–82.
52. *Statutes of the realm*, 31 Hen. 8 c. 14.
53. *Actes and Monuments* (1563), 739.
54. Weimann, '"Bifold authority" in Reformation discourse', 172.
55. *Actes and Monuments* (1563), 729.
56. *The lattre examinacyon*, C6v.
57. *Bondage of the will*, in *Martin Luther: selections from his writings*, ed. J. Dillenberger (New York: Doubleday, 1962), 191.
58. See A. Hudson, 'William Thorpe and the question of authority', in *Christian authority: essays in honour of Henry Chadwick*, ed. G. R. Evans (Oxford: Oxford University Press, 1988), 137. Anne Hudson makes this point in connection with

William Thorpe's demonstrated understanding of Christian authority in his examinations before Archbishop Arundel (1407). Two works in particular trace the narrative similarities between Askew's *Examinations* and *The examination of M. William Thorpe*: D. Watt, 'God's secretaries: studies of four women visionaries and prophets as writers in the late middle and early modern ages' (unpublished D.Phil. thesis, Oxford University, 1993), 267–87; and Betteridge, 'Anne Askewe, John Bale, and Protestant history', 277–9. The subject that emerges in each of these narratives is similarly positioned against ecclesiastical authority, but I want to highlight two crucial ways in which Thorpe and Askew differ. First, Thorpe's construction of the principle of *sola scriptura* insists that 'God's word and God are identical' (Hudson, 135); Askew is articulating something quite different here. Second, Thorpe clearly does locate himself centrally within the Lollard–Catholic religious polemic: he asserts his connection to other prominent Wycliffites (he says of John Aston, Philip Repingdon, Nicholas Hereford, and John Purvey that 'I was ofte homli & I comownede with hem long tyme & fele' (Bodleian MS Rawlinson C. 208, fo. 25r)); while he frequently cites scripture, he also uses patristic theology to support his claims (he deploys Augustine, Chrysostom, Gregory, and Jerome in his arguments). In short, Thorpe attempts to frame communal doctrine. His discourse is not the product of an individual whose place in the debate is marginal.

59. *The first examinacyon*, B4v. Sir William has not been identified. Dr Edward Crome recanted (for the third time during Henry's reign) at Paul's Cross 9 May 1546. (John Lascelles was detained for counselling Crome against recantation.) John Huntington was a zealous preacher for reform.
60. *The first examinacyon*, B5v–B6r. The 'course of scoles' refers to the rules of scholastic debate that governed Catholic scholarship; these rules were adopted as the order of disputation at the universities.
61. Ibid., B6r–v; my emphasis.
62. Bale is referring to two recent publications: Stephen Gardiner's *A detection of the devils sophistrie* (STC 11591); and William Peryn's *Three godlye and notable sermons* (STC 19785.5).
63. *The lattre examinacyon*, D7r.
64. *Actes and Monuments*, 1421.
65. Ibid.
66. *The first examinacyon*, A2v.
67. *The lattre examinacyon*, C8v–Dr.
68. Ibid., D2r–v.
69. Quoted in *The complete plays of John Bale*, ed. Peter Happé (Cambridge: D. S. Brewer, 1985–6), I: 4.
70. *The image of both churches*, in *Select works of John Bale*, ed. Henry Christmas (Cambridge: Cambridge University Press, 1849), 440.
71. D. S. Kastan, '"Holy wurdes" and "slypper wit": John Bale's *King Johan* and the poetics of propaganda', in *Rethinking the Henrician era*, ed. Peter Herman (Urbana: Illinois University Press, 1994), 275. See also E. Cameron, *The European Reformation* (Oxford: Oxford University Press, 1991), 140–2; E. Tribble, *Margins and marginality: the printed page in early modern England* (Charlottesville: Virginia University Press, 1993); C. McEachern, '"A whore at the first blush seemeth only a woman": John Bale's *Image of both churches* and the terms of religious difference in the early English Reformation', *Journal of Medieval and Renaissance Studies*

25 (1995), 263–5; and D. S. Kastan, '"The noyse of the new Bible": reform and reaction in Henrician England', in *Religion and culture in Renaissance England*, ed. McEachern and Shuger, 46–68.

72. *The lattre examinacyon*, B5r.

73. Ibid., B5v–B6r.

74. Bale does not feel compelled to add anything but a brief preface to *A treatyse made by Johan Lambert* (1548). Lambert's tract, however, is a learned work in which he interprets (and casts according to the terms of the debate) the meanings that he has derived from scripture.

75. *Actes and Monuments* (1563), 733.

76. Of course Cranmer is being reductive for the purpose of polemic – the idea that Catholics understood the sacrament in such stark and absolute terms allows their position to be made ridiculous. Moreover, such reduction allows Cranmer (and reformers like him) to polarise the different positions of what amounted to opposing sects of the same religion (a proximity that could not have been comfortable for anyone).

77. Mueller, 'Pain, persecution, and the construction of selfhood', *passim*.

78. *Actes and Monuments*, 1595.

79. Ibid., 1610.

80. I do not mean by this that Protestant conception emptied the Eucharist of spiritual matter, but rather that the course of these arguments concerning transubstantiation prompted Protestants to emphasise the material nature of the bread and wine itself. (Frith's point, borrowed from Wycliffe, concerning the mouldy bread is an example of this.) This in turn led to a concentration upon the acts themselves of eating and drinking – the reformers had to reconceptualise how these modes of physical activity were to be understood in spiritual terms (cf. Cranmer, above).

81. *Actes and Monuments*, 1231.

82. Ibid., 1937. The evidence suggests that Latimer never actually spoke these words (see T. Freeman, 'Texts, lies, and microfilm: reading and misreading Foxe's "Book of martyrs"', *Sixteenth Century Journal* 30 (1999), 42–5). But whether the source of the metaphor was Latimer or Foxe, the point is the same.

83. *Actes and Monuments*, 1417. Paula McQuade suggests that this passage is meant to imitate the literary model of Saul of Tarsus, 'in which moments of profound psychological transformation are thematically marked by episodes of extreme physical suffering' (McQuade, '"Except that they had offended the lawe"', 9). She argues that Askew articulates her tangible experience in order to mark a turning point in her text, since on the following day she goes before the Privy Council and denies the real presence in the sacrament. However, the first time that Askew openly denies Christ's presence in the sacrament it is just prior to this episode, when speaking to William Paget. Part of this conversation has been excised from several of the remaining copies of Bale's text (sigs. c6 and c7 have been pasted together) – as Paget survived the political upheavals following Henry's death to become Secretary of State – and the entire exchange does not appear at all in Foxe (see *Actes and Monuments* (1563), 739; *The latter examination* in *Select works of John Bale*, ed. Christmas, 205; and J. N. King, *English Reformation literature: the Tudor origins of the Protestant tradition* (Princeton: Princeton University Press, 1982), 79). Clearly the turning point for Askew is Gardiner's declaration, at which time she begins to state openly her own understanding of what is religiously true and real.

84. Askew's illegal torture was an attempt on the part of Richard Wriothesley and Richard Rich to extract information on the women around the queen: Catherine

Brandon, Duchess of Suffolk; Anne Radcliffe, Countess of Sussex; Anne Stan-hope, Countess of Hereford; Joan, Lady Denny; and Jane, Lady Fitzwilliam. See *Narratives of the days of the Reformation*, ed. Nichols, 303–13; Trollope, 'Anne Askew, the Lincolnshire martyr'; Haigh, *English Reformations*, 162–7; and *The examinations of Anne Askew*, ed. Beilin, xv–xlii.

85. *Actes and Monuments*, 1418. In the 1570 and 1576 editions, 'master Rich' is changed to 'Syr John Baker' (and is subsequently changed back).
86. Ibid.
87. E. Scarry, *The body in pain: the making and unmaking of the world* (Oxford: Oxford University Press, 1985).
88. Hanson, 'Torture and truth in Renaissance England', 56. Hanson is referring here to the practice of inflicting pain as a form of penance among certain Catholic orders. However, it seems clear to me that the predisposition of religious training is not required to produce this psychology, only the torture of the physical body in an attempt to make the conscience apostatise.
89. *Actes and Monuments*, 1419.
90. Ibid., 1231.
91. Ibid., 1418.
92. *A boke made by John Frith*, L6r.
93. *Actes and Monuments*, 1415.
94. Ibid., 1417.
95. Ibid.
96. Ibid., 1418.
97. Ibid., 1420.
98. I borrow Teresa de Lauretis's phrase in 'Eccentric subjects: feminist theory and historical consciousness', *Feminist Studies* 16 (1990), 115–50.
99. *Actes and Monuments*, 1419.
100. See McQuade, '"Except that they had offended the lawe"', 10.
101. *Actes and Monuments*, 1420.
102. Ibid.
103. J. Summit, *Lost property: the woman writer and English literary history, 1380 – 1589* (Chicago: Chicago University Press, 2000), 111.
104. Summit's central contention is a compelling one. I want only to clarify what is distinct about Bale's handling of Askew's narrative in relation to his other edited martyr writings.
105. *Scriptorum illustrium maioris Brytanniae . . . catalogus* (STC 1296 Variant), A2v–A3r. The translation is taken from J. C. Warner's excellent article in which he analyses Bale's complicated representation of his own antiquarian project. See 'Elizabeth I, savior of books: John Bale's Preface to the *Scriptorum illustrium maioris Brytanniae . . . catalogus* (1559)', in *John Foxe and his world*, ed. C. Highley and J. N. King (Aldershot: Ashgate, 2002), 91–101; the citation is from p. 95.
106. Warner, 'Elizabeth I, savior of books', 95.
107. In his preface to Lambert's treatise, Bale equates his project to that of Egesippus and Eusebius in that they record 'the d[e]scripcyon of that lyuely churche whych folowed immedyatly after the Apostles tyme' (*A treatyse made by Johan Lambert* (STC 15180) fo. 2r).
108. While Megan Matchinske makes a different argument from mine, we overlap in our contention that '[t]he resistant authority that Askew's text proclaims, an interiority that will, in fact, become synonymous with later Reformation

paradigms for *both men and women* finds at least one of its early voices in [a] ...
female exegesis' (*Writing, gender and state in early modern England*, 43).

109. King, *English Reformation literature*, 80.

110. See A. Ryrie, 'The unsteady beginnings of English Protestant martyrology', in
John Foxe: an historical perspective, ed. David Loades (Aldershot: Ashgate, 1999),
53.

111. Ibid., 54.

112. I need to be careful here: *Certein godly, learned, and comfortable conferences,
betwene ... Nicholas Ridley ... and ... Hughe Latimer* (STC 21047.3) was
published in 1556; but the primary source for Latimer's martyrdom was the
vernacular *Actes and Monuments*, printed seven years later. It is simply not possible
to gauge the impact of any particular martyr narrative in that collection. My
analysis, therefore, of how English book buyers responded to Askew's text over
other available martyr writings is only an attempt to question such assumptions.
Further, the popularity of a text (in this case, Askew's) to a reading public can only
be imperfectly related to its impact upon reform.

113. The *Actes and Monuments* made the printing of other martyr narratives virtually
obsolete. The closer the appearance of an individual martyr narrative to the first
printing of the vernacular *Actes and Monuments* (1563), the fewer the expected
number of printed editions. Still, there were seven editions of the *Examinations*
produced in the sixteenth century. The initial printing in two separate editions
obviously raises the number (see n. 4). Another edition was printed in 1585
(STC 549), after the first publication of the *Actes and Monuments*. Even if we
group the first two printings together, there are more editions of the *Examinations*
in the sixteenth century than that of any other martyr narrative.

114. D. MacCulloch, *The boy king: Edward VI and the Protestant Reformation* (New
York: Palgrave, 2001), 57.

115. There were two printed editions of the work: STC 1276 and STC 1278.

116. STC 11383 and 11384.

117. *The supplication made of doctour Barnes vnto ... Henrye the eyght* (STC 1472); *The
metynge of doctor Barns and doctor Powell at paradise gate* (STC 6083).

118. *Wicklieffes wicket. Faythfully ouerseene and corrected* (STC 25591).

119. *The lattre examinacyon*, A2v.

120. King, *English Reformation literature*, 80; see also n. 83.

121. See *The first [latter] examinacio[n] of Anne Askewe* (STC 851), J7r.

122. The 1585 edition (STC 549), which only reproduces *The first examinacyon*,
includes Bale's annotations.

123. See Ryrie, 'The unsteady beginnings of English Protestant martyrology', for
a good discussion of how the martyr story breaks down (51–66). See also
P. Crawford, 'Public duty, conscience, and women in early modern England',
in *Public duty and private conscience in seventeenth-century England*, ed. J. Morrill,
P. Slack, and D. Woolf (Oxford: Oxford University Press, 1993), 57–76; and
M. S. Robinson, 'Doctors, silly poor women, and rebel whores: the gendering of
conscience in Foxe's *Acts and Monuments*', in *John Foxe and his world*, ed. Highley
and King, 235–48.

124. See Crawford, 'Public duty, conscience, and women in early modern England',
67–76, for a discussion of how conscience was activated by women in the early
modern period, and how the concept was understood in gendered terms.

125. Ryrie, 'The unsteady beginnings of English Protestant martyrology', 55.

126. That large portions of the population were relatively unexposed to Protestantism, and remained untouched even after Edwardian reform, is clear from the writing of Christopher Haigh, J. J. Scarisbrick, and Eamon Duffy. See Haigh, *English Reformations*; Scarisbrick, *The Reformation and the English people* (Oxford: Blackwell, 1984); and Duffy, *The stripping of the altars: traditional religion in England c. 1400–c. 1580* (New Haven: Yale University Press, 1992).

127. STC 853.5 + Wing A3210B-14; see Ian Green, *Print and Protestantism in early modern England* (Oxford: Oxford University Press, 2000), 596.

128. See Tessa Watt, *Cheap print and popular piety, 1550–1640* (Cambridge: Cambridge University Press, 1991), 74–8; the citation is from p. 75.

129. We do know that it is mentioned in Nashe's *Have with you to Saffron-Walden* (1596). See *The works of Thomas Nashe edited . . . by Ronald B. McKerrow. Reprinted from the original edition with corrections and supplementary notes*, ed. F. P. Wilson (Oxford: Blackwell, 1958), III: 113; and *The examinations of Anne Askew*, ed. Beilin, lvi.

130. Watt, *Cheap print and popular piety*, 94. Watt points out that this reduction of martyrs to types was standard for the ballad form (90–6).

131. I have not included the ballad which Bale claims 'Anne Askewe made and sange whan she was in Newgate' (*The lattre examinacyon*, H7r–H7v) in my consideration because of the vexed question of its authorship. H. A. Mason was the first to observe that three stanzas of the ballad echo Henry Howard's poetic treatment of *Ecclesiastes* III (*Humanism and poetry in the early Tudor period* (London: Routledge, 1959), 243–4). Both Mason and Susan Brigden argue that Askew imitated Surrey's poem, having obtained a copy after her imprisonment (see Brigden, 'Henry Howard, Earl of Surrey, and the "conjured league"', 525). If, however, as Emrys Jones has suggested, Surrey wrote the piece during his final incarceration (December 1546–January 1547), this scenario would be impossible (see *Henry Howard, Earl of Surrey: poems*, ed. E. Jones (Oxford: Oxford University Press, 1964), 153).

132. Watt, *Cheap print and popular piety*, 94.

133. B. Makin, *An essay to revive the antient education of gentlewomen* (Wing M309), 28.

134. Ibid.

CHAPTER 2. REPRESENTING THE FAITH OF A NATION: TRANSITIONAL SPIRITUALITY IN THE WORKS OF KATHERINE PARR

1. For an interesting discussion of how Thomas Bentley uses the figure of Elizabeth as the Supreme Governor of the English Church to ratify prayer as 'the defining genre of the Protestant commonwealth', see J. Summit, *Lost property: the woman writer and English literary history, 1380–1589* (Chicago: Chicago University Press, 2000), 157–61.

2. *The lamentacion of a synner* (STC 4828), A1.

3. *The first examinacyon of Anne Askewe* (STC 848), ♣9v.

4. Janel Mueller first made the suggestion in 'Devotion as difference: intertextuality in Queen Katherine Parr's *Prayers or meditations* (1545)', *HLQ* 53 (1990), 176–7. Mueller, however, does not pursue the case of Parr's influence in her essay; rather, she confines herself to an analysis of the text at hand. Diarmaid MacCulloch, in his superb biography of Thomas Cranmer, examines the moment

of inception of the English Litany at length, without mention of Parr's participation in the larger supplication project (see *Thomas Cranmer* (New Haven: Yale University Press, 1996), 326–36).

5. E. Duffy, 'The spirituality of John Fisher', in *Humanism, reform and the Reformation: the career of Bishop John Fisher*, ed. B. Bradshaw and E. Duffy (Cambridge: Cambridge University Press, 1989), 205.

6. Fourteen editions were produced under the title of *Prayers or meditacions* (STC 4818-4826.7), and six were annexed to the *Psalmes or prayers* (see n. 15) – renamed *The king's prayers* – under the title of *The queen's prayers* (STC 3009-12). Four more editions were printed in the seventeenth century (STC 3012.3-3013.5).

7. In *Ecclesiastical memorials* (London: Samuel Bagster, 1816), John Strype writes: 'I am apt to think Queen Katharin herself might do one [chapter] at least, and perhaps that upon St. Matthew' (II.1: 47). The translator of the Book of Matthew has never been identified, and there is some reason to suppose that it was Parr.

8. This statistic only relates to the first volume – which went into five printings (see E. J. Devereux, 'The publication of the English paraphrases', *Bulletin of the John Rylands Library* 51 (1968-9), 358 n. 2). The second volume of the *Paraphrases* was not published until after the queen's death (London: E. Whitchurch, 1549) and did not have the success of the first.

9. Mueller 'Devotion as difference', 176. My debt to Mueller's work throughout this argument, is obvious and great.

10. *Works of Archbishop Cranmer*, ed. J. E. Cox (London: Parker Society, 1844-6), II: 494.

11. Ibid., II: 495.

12. *An exhortation vnto prayer* (STC 10620), BIv.

13. The English printing excluded Fisher's name – the bishop had been executed in 1535 for refusing to take the oath of supremacy – but he remained connected to the book in continental Europe.

14. *Psalmi sev precationes ex variis scriptvrae locis collectae* (STC 2994).

15. The *Psalmes or prayers* went into six editions under Henry VIII (STC 3001.7-3003), and were subsequently printed in every Tudor reign.

16. See the copy held at Exeter College, Oxford (STC 3001.7). A letter from Sotheby & Co. (2 Oct. 1932) gives a detailed description of the two other surviving copies. One (from the library of the Earl of Carysfort) contains an inscription from Henry VIII to the queen – the other two appear to have belonged to Edward Seymour, Duke of Somerset (and eventual Protector of England) and to William Herbert, first Earl of Pembroke (Katherine Parr's brother-in-law).

17. The first print run was evidently large, so a fair estimate of the circulation is about 9,000 copies that first year.

18. STC 10621.

19. STC 10623.3, bound with (*Psalmes*) 3002.3. There is one ostensible copy of STC 10623.5 housed at Stonyhurst College that breaks the pattern (it is bound with a Book of Hours). This copy is marked in the STC as a 'particular variant, issue, or edition ... which cannot or has not been determined'.

20. STC 10623 (printed by Petyt).

21. J. C. Warner, *Henry VIII's divorce: literature and the politics of the printing press* (Woodbridge: Boydell Press, 1998), 83.

22. Some recent studies of Parr's works have argued for, or simply assumed, her translation of Fisher's text: see S. James, *Kateryn Parr: the making of a queen*

(Aldershot: Ashgate, 1999), 200–8; and F. Howson, 'Queen Kateryn Parr's *Lamentacion of a synner* and the formularies', *Cahiers Elisabéthains* 57 (2000), 30.

23. *Ecclesiastical memorials*, II.1: 211. Strype's account of Parr's writing career is not always correct. He does not mention the *Lamentacion* at all; and his attribution of the translation of Savonarola's *An exposition after the maner of a contemplacyon upon the li psalme* to her is demonstrably wrong. The translator was certainly William Marshall, and the *Exposition* (STC 21789.3) was bound together with Marshall's 1534 *Prymer in Englyshe* (STC 15986). Parr was married to Lord Latimer, and a Catholic, at this time.

24. *The first tome or volume of the Paraphrase of Erasmus* (STC 2854.5), A2r.

25. Ibid., AAAv.

26. *Illvstrivm maioris Brittanniae scriptorvm, svmmarium* (STC 1295), fo. 238v.

27. In almost all cases – with the exception of one copy housed in the Bodleian – a full year separates the publication of the combined editions. The exception is Bodleian Douce B 231. But while the publication dates are 2 July 1545 for the *Psalmes*, and 6 Nov. 1545 for the *Prayers*, these works are bound with one of the first edition copies of the *Litany*. It is certainly possible that their gathering into a single volume was the work of a later collector, probably Francis Douce (because it was his custom to bind works in this way). However, it also seems possible that with the publication of the second prayer text (*Prayers or meditacions*) a year later, English book buyers added it to their collections.

28. See n. 6.

29. The names of Henry's offspring are interpolated in the king's prayer in subsequent reigns.

30. Roger Ascham praises her Latin aptitude, and there is no reason to doubt his sincerity (see M. A. Hatch, 'The Ascham letters: an annotated translation of the Latin correspondence' (unpublished Ph.D. thesis, Cornell University, 1948), 221–3). Prince Edward's oft-cited letter to his stepmother encouraging her progress in the study of Latin (10 June 1546) does not indicate that her grasp of the language was poor, only that it had acquired a further level of sophistication (one must bear in mind the extraordinary level of Edward's learning).

31. *Psalmes or prayers* (STC 3002), L6v.

32. One bill from Berthelet (probably written May 1544) records her having ordered a total of fourteen 'bokes of the Psalme prayers', twelve of which were delivered to George Day, the Bishop of Chichester (1543–51) and her almoner (see F. Rose-Troup, 'Two book bills of Katherine Parr', *The Library*, 3rd. ser. 2 (1911), 40–8). These were obviously quality-bound editions of the *Psalmes* which were intended as gift copies. But the king began this practice of presenting copies, and if the *Psalmes* were part of a crown project, her parcel to Day could have constituted copies for distribution among friends or prominent persons.

33. See n. 16.

34. J. Maltby, *Prayer book and people in Elizabethan and Stuart England* (Cambridge: Cambridge University Press, 1998), 4.

35. '[T]he role of liturgy as a means of persuasion', Maltby writes, is 'no less important than the English Bible, the Book of Homilies, sermons, or Foxe's *Book of Martyrs*' (ibid.).

36. See Ian Green, *Print and Protestantism in early modern England* (Oxford: Oxford University Press, 1991), 252–77, for a survey and discussion of this material.

37. Another edition was 'newly Imprinted at the request of mistres Elizabeth Rous' in 1587. No copies of this print run remain. See *A transcript of the registers of the Company of Stationers of London, 1154–1640*, ed. Edward Arber (New York: Peter Smith, 1950), II: 474; and M. White, 'Women writers and literary-religious circles in the Elizabethan West Country: Anne Dowriche, Anne Lock Prowse, Anne Lock Moyle, Ursula Fulford, and Elizabeth Rous', *Modern Philology* 103 (2005), 205.

38. See Green, *Print and Protestantism in early modern England*, 252, for a survey of the best-selling prayer collections (outside of the *Book of common prayer*) and the duration of their sales.

39. It saw slightly fewer: there were twenty-three editions of the *Psalmes* (later *The king's prayers*) – only one less than the *Prayers*. We should bear in mind, however, that the *Prayers* appeared a year later than the *Psalmes* (by which time three editions had already been printed). Further, the *Prayers* was also included in the *Monvment of matrones* (STC 1892), *The second lampe*, 80–98. I am not, however, really arguing for the popularity of one prayer book over the other (as they operate, in many ways, as a collection); I am only noting that royal status cannot entirely account for the sustained popularity of the *Prayers*.

40. D. Starkey, *Six wives: the queens of Henry VIII* (New York: Harper Collins Publishers, 2003), 753.

41. P. Lake, 'Religious identities in Shakespeare's England', in *A companion to Shakespeare*, ed. D. S. Kastan (Oxford: Blackwell, 1999), 57. See Lake's excellent discussion of this circumstance (and consequent religious polarisation), 57–84.

42. See P. C. Swensen, 'Noble hunters of the Romish fox: religious reform at the Tudor court, 1543–1564' (unpublished Ph.D. thesis, University of California, Berkeley, 1981), 77; and Mueller, 'Devotion as difference', 176.

43. Cranmer's marriage gave him family ties to the continental reformer Andreas Osiander.

44. C. F. Hoffman, 'Catherine Parr as a woman of letters', *HLQ* 23 (1959), 354. For the view that the English translation of the *Imitation* (under the title of *The folowyng of Chryste*) is not by Whytford, see G. Williams, 'Two neglected London-Welsh clerics: Richard Whitford and Richard Gwent', *Transactions of the Honourable Society of Cymmrodorion* (1961), 30–2.

45. Produced co-operatively by William Atkynson (Books 1–3) and Lady Margaret Beaufort (Book 4), it was first printed by Richard Pynson (STC 23954.7). For the pre-publication history of the *Imitatio*, see R. Lovatt, 'The *Imitation of Christ* in late medieval England', *Transactions of the Royal Historical Society* 18 (1968), 97–121.

46. 'The confutation of Tyndale's answer', in *The complete works of St. Thomas More*, ed. L. Schuster *et al.* (New Haven: Yale University Press, 1973), VIII: 1034.

47. 'Through ... systematic selections and alterations', she writes, 'the connotations of spirituality are wrenched from the perceptibly Catholic to those of an emergent Protestantism' (Mueller, 'Devotion as difference', 181).

48. MacCulloch, *Thomas Cranmer*, 329.

49. Green, *Print and Protestantism in early modern England*, 245. In fact, Cranmer had much of the work already done for him by William Marshall; see *A goodly prymer in Englyshe* (STC 15988). This primer is a revised and corrected version of the first English vernacular primer, which appeared in 1534 (see n. 23). See also C. C. Butterworth, *The English primers (1529–1545)* (Philadelphia: Pennsylvania University Press, 1953), 110–11; and MacCulloch, *Thomas Cranmer*, 328.

50. Mueller, 'Devotion as difference', 178–89.

51. *The folowyng of Christe* (STC 23963), fo. 77r.
52. Ibid., fo. 115r–v.
53. *Prayers or meditacions* (STC 4818.5), C3v–C4r.
54. *The folowyng*, fo. 79r.
55. *Prayers*, A4r.
56. *The folowyng*, fos. 81v–82r.
57. *Prayers*, A7r.
58. *The folowyng*, fo. 82r.
59. *Prayers*, A6r.
60. 'and by example of the & of thy holy sayntes' is amended to: 'and by example of the' (*The folowyng*, fo. 80r; *Prayers*, A5r). However, Parr does not excise reference to saints entirely (see *Prayers*, B1v).
61. Chapters 53 and 55 of *The folowyng* are fully incorporated (with minor emendations) into the concluding section of Parr's text (beginning at C4r). The *Prayers* breaks from chapter 55 at D5v, and shifts to the 'prayer to optayn the grace of deuocion' in chapter 4 of the third book of *The folowyng* (which is also completely incorporated).
62. *The folowyng*, fo. 77r. This sentence is reproduced in the *Prayers*, A2v–A3r.
63. *Prayers*, C1r.
64. The work of Christopher Haigh, J. J. Scarisbrick, and Eamon Duffy has done much to undermine these assumptions. Even so, while Duffy's early work in many ways provides the grounding for this present analysis (see 'The spirituality of John Fisher', 205–31), his critical attitudes seem to harden into more rigid categories in later work, such as *The stripping of the altars: traditional religion in England c. 1400–c. 1580* (New Haven: Yale University Press, 1992).
65. M. Questier, *Conversion, politics and religion in England, 1580–1625* (Cambridge: Cambridge University Press, 1996), 41.
66. See ibid., ch. 3, for a full discussion of 'the experience of change of religion'.
67. E. Jager, *The book of the heart* (Chicago: Chicago University Press, 2000), ch. 6.
68. Maltby, *Prayer book and people in Elizabethan and Stuart England, passim*; see also, R. Targoff, *Common prayer: the language of devotion in early modern England* (Chicago: Chicago University Press, 2001), 14–30.
69. L. Patterson, 'On the margin: postmodernism, ironic history, and medieval studies', *Speculum* 65 (1990), 87–108; and D. Aers, 'A whisper in the ear of early modernists; or, reflections on literary critics writing the "history of the subject"', in *Culture and history 1350–1600*, ed. D. Aers (Detroit: Wayne State University Press, 1992), 177–202. See also C. Taylor, *Sources of the self: the making of the modern identity* (Cambridge, MA: Harvard University Press, 1989).
70. W. Watts, *Saint Augustines confessions translated and with some marginall notes illustrated* (STC 912), 10.6 (quoted in Aers, 'A whisper in the ear of early modernists', 183).
71. More, 'The confutation of Tyndale's answer', 1034.
72. *The folowyng*, fo. 106r.
73. Patterson, 'On the margin', 99–100.
74. Roger Lovatt examines the evidence for the circulation of all three of these texts – in both manuscript and print forms – in 'The *Imitation of Christ* in late medieval England', 98–100.
75. STC 3259-67.
76. STC 14042-5.
77. See n. 45.

78. STC 23954.7-23964.7
79. Jager, *The book of the heart*, 104.
80. *The folowyng*, fo. 56v.
81. M. Luther, *Works*, ed. J. Pelikan (St Louis: Concordia Publishing, 1955–77), 40: 99–100; quoted in J. L. Koerner, *The reformation of the image* (Chicago: Chicago University Press, 2004), 160.
82. Koerner, *The reformation of the image*, 167.
83. Ibid., 160.
84. Ibid., 167. See the discussion of Luther's 'theology of the cross' at the end of the chapter.
85. 'It is the subject's all-too-human enunciation of something almost entirely other' (ibid., 190).
86. *Prayers*, c8v (cf. *The folowyng*, fo. 117v).
87. Mueller, 'Devotion as difference', 181.
88. *Prayers*, A5r–A5v (cf. *The folowyng*, fo. 80r). Parr makes two significant changes: she removes both a reference to saints as an example (see n. 60) and the specification that the path laid out is toward 'euerlasting lyfe'. Both of these alterations stress the role of Christ as the only mediator in our salvation.
89. *Prayers*, A5v (cf. *The folowyng*, fo. 82r).
90. *Prayers*, c1r. This is one of the few original sentences in the *Prayers*.
91. Ibid., B2r–v (cf. *The folowyng*, fo. 86r).
92. See Jager, *The book of the heart*, particularly 105–13.
93. *Prayers*, B7r (cf. *The folowyng*, fo. 101r–v).
94. Ibid., B2r (cf. *The folowyng*, fo. 84v).
95. See, for example, *The folowyng*, fo. 113r.
96. *Prayers*, c1v.
97. Ibid., A3v. While there is a similar consideration of God's withdrawal at this point in *The folowyng*, this is another rare instance of Parr's own written intervention in the text (cf. *The folowyng*, fo. 78v, end of ch. 18).
98. *Prayers*, c7v (cf. *The folowyng*, fo. 117v).
99. R. Williams, *Marxism and literature* (Oxford: Oxford University Press, 1977), 126.
100. Jager, *The book of the heart*, 139.
101. Ibid., 113.
102. Susan Felch was the first to point out to me just how remarkable the confessional mode of Parr's *Prayers* is in the context of the development of English prayer books. I am grateful to her for supplying me with a manuscript copy of the introduction to her edition of Elizabeth Tyrwhit's prayers (*Elizabeth Tyrwhit's morning and evening prayers*, forthcoming from Ashgate). See also 'The development of the English prayer book', in *Worship in medieval and early modern Europe: change and continuity in religious practice*, ed. K. Maag and J. D. Witvliet (Notre Dame: Notre Dame University Press, 2004), 132–61.
103. Felch, *Elizabeth Tyrwhit's morning and evening prayers*, introduction.
104. See n. 49 for the role of this revised primer in the composition of Cranmer's English *Litany*.
105. See, for example, George Joye's 1530 *Ortulus anime the garden of the soule* (STC 13828.4); and Marshall's *A goodly prymer in Englyshe*. See also, Butterworth, *English primers*, 28–46; Green, *Print and Protestantism in early modern England*, 244–6; and Felch, *Elizabeth Tyrwhit's morning and evening prayers*, introduction.

106. It is also important to bear in mind that at the time of Parr's composition of the *Prayers* she enjoyed the complete confidence of the king – as demonstrated by her Regency in his absence, and the favour that he showed her upon his return (an extravagant New Year's gift of 1,000 marks). She was marked as a political target – notably by Wriothesley and Gardiner – after the publication of the work.

107. Mueller, 'Devotion as difference', 186–7.

108. *The folowyng*, fo. 107v; *Prayers*, C2r.

109. Starkey, *Six wives: the queens of Henry VIII*, 757–8.

110. *Lamentacion*, A4r–v.

111. Ibid., A4v–A5r; my emphasis.

112. Janel Mueller, 'Complications of intertextuality: John Fisher, Katherine Parr and "The book of the crucifix"', in *Texts and cultural change in early modern England*, ed. C. C. Brown and A. F. Marotti (London: Macmillan Press, 1997), 15–36. I am not doing justice to Mueller's rich and complicated argument. It is an interrogation of critical practice and a discussion of linguistic change. But I am drawing out this feature of her analysis because it causes her to overlook some of the spiritual exchanges of Parr's text.

113. By 1546 we know that the queen was holding religious discussions in her rooms, and that the content of these was sensitive enough (or, at least, vocal enough) to warrant the admonition of Thomas Howard before the Privy Council:

> [T]he Lordes declared unto him the Kinges Majestes clemencie towardes him extended in willing [the council] to admonishe him of his indiscrete medling in Scripture things, and that if he did frankly confesse what wordes he hath uttred, aswell in disprove of the sermons this last Lent preached in the Courte, as also his other talke at large in the Quenes Chambre, and other places of the Courte, concerning Scripture, his Hieghnes would be Gratious Lord unto him. (*Acts of the Privy Council of England*, ed. J. R. Dasent (London: Eyre and Spottiswoode, 1890–1964), I: 408)

The racking of Anne Askew – only a month after Howard's warning – was an attempt to obtain information against Catherine Brandon, Anne Radcliffe, Anne Stanhope, Joan Denny, and Jane Fitzwilliam (cf. chapter 1, n. 84).

114. Jager, *The book of the heart*, 105.

115. Ibid., 105–6.

116. *The folowyng*, fo. 59v.

117. *The lattre examinacyon*, H2r.

118. The numbering of Donne's Holy Sonnets, throughout, is taken from *John Donne: a critical edition of the major works*, ed. J. Carey (Oxford: Oxford University Press, 1990).

119. Mueller, 'Complications of intertextuality', 15–36.

120. J. Fisher, *A spirituall consolation, written by Iohn Fyssher Bishoppe of Rochester* ... etc. [and] *A Sermon verie fruitfull, godly, and learned* ... *Preached vpon a good Friday* ... etc. (STC 10899).

121. See M. C. Spalding, *The Middle English Charters of Christ* (Bryn Mawr, PA: Bryn Mawr College, 1914). See also R. Woolf, *The English religious lyric in the Middle Ages* (Oxford: Clarendon Press, 1968), 210–14.

122. C. Brown, *Religious lyrics of the fourteenth century* (Oxford: Clarendon Press, 1952), 18–20.

123. *English writings of Richard Rolle*, ed. H. E. Allen (Oxford: Clarendon Press, 1968), 36.

124. BL MS Harl. 2382, fo. 111v (EETS 117, 637–57).

125. See, for example, BL MS Harl. 3954, fos. 87–94 (EETS 15, 271–8); see also EETS 117, 613–14.
126. Woolf, *English religious lyric*, 210. They occur, for instance, in *The meditations on the Passion* (Text 2), and *A meditacion of the fyue woundes of Ihesu Crist*, also attributed to Rolle (*Yorkshire writers: Richard Rolle of Hampole and his followers*, ed. J. C. Horstman (London: Library of Early English Writers, 1895–6), II: 440).
127. See, for example, *The Franciscan papers*, ed. A. G. Little (Manchester: Manchester University Press, 1943), 251–6. See also *Dives and pauper*, ed. P. H. Barnum (EETS, o.s., 275), 85; and J. Longland, *Sermones* (STC 16797), fo. 19a.
128. D. G. Selwyn, *The library of Thomas Cranmer* (Oxford: Oxford Bibliographical Society, 1996), 59–60. The works of Luther were presented to Cranmer by Justus Jonas Jr in 1548.
129. *The Newe Testament* (STC 2826), fo. 202v.
130. J. P. Carley, *The libraries of King Henry VIII* (London: British Library, 2000), 55.
131. This copy was Anne Boleyn's (BL C. 23.a.8) – technically part of Henry's library, but Henry had a habit of bestowing the goods of old wives upon the new (see James, *Kateryn Parr*, 125–6).
132. *Newe Testament*, fo. 209r–v.
133. *Lamentacion*, A1r–v.
134. The theology of Marguerite de Navarre, while not conventional in its observance of Catholic tenets, does not overthrow them. Hers is a brand of belief – neither traditionally Catholic nor strictly Lutheran – pervasive in the pre-reform period. See in particular H. Heller, 'Reform and reformers at Meaux, 1518–1525' (unpublished Ph.D. thesis, Cornell University, 1969); Heller, 'Marguerite of Navarre and the reformers of Meaux', *Bibliothèque d'Humanisme et Renaissance* 33 (1971), 271–310; and A. Winandy, 'Piety and humanistic symbolism in the works of Marguerite d'Angoulême, Queen of Navarre', *Yale French Studies* 47 (1972), 145–69.
135. *Newe Testament*, fo. 209v.
136. *Lamentacion*, A6r–v.
137. *Newe Testament*, fo. 210r.
138. *Lamentacion*, B5r.
139. *Newe Testament*, fo. 210v.
140. Ibid., fo. 211r.
141. *Lamentacion*, B5v.
142. Ibid., D6v, E6v.
143. *Newe Testament*, fo. 212v.
144. Ibid., fo. 212r–v.
145. Ibid., fo. 212v.
146. *Lamentacion*, C6v.
147. *Newe Testament*, fos. 215v–216r.
148. The *Praefatio methodica totius scripturae in Epistolam Pauli ad Romanos* (Mainz, 1524) reads: 'Tu uero, in ratione discendarum sacrarum rerum, sequere seriem et ordinem hic traditum ab Apostolo' (fo. 13v).
149. See C. R. Trueman, *Luther's legacy: salvation and English reformers, 1525–1556* (Oxford: Clarendon Press, 1994), 59–60.
150. *Lamentacion*, B8r.

151. Ibid., C2v.
152. Fisher, *A Sermon verie fruitfull, godly, and learned*, Evr.
153. *Lamentacion*, C2r.
154. Ibid., C4r.
155. *The New England primer: a history of its origin and development*, ed. P. L. Ford (New York: Dodd, Mead, and Co., 1897), 9.
156. Ibid., 70.
157. *Lamentacion*, D5v.
158. See Jager, *The book of the heart*, 139–56.
159. One full edition (STC 1892) and two excerpted editions (STC 1893 and 1894) of the *Monvment of matrones* were produced in 1582. It was not necessary to publish the *Lamentacion* itself once it was incorporated into this anthology (*The second lampe*, 37–79).
160. Unlike works of literature, which had a limited market (cf. Introduction, n. 3), religious books generally enjoyed larger initial print runs. Printers would frequently run off 700 copies, and then have subsequent runs of about 1,000 copies each (see also chapter 1, n. 5).
161. Questier, *Conversion, politics and religion in England*, 12–39.

CHAPTER 3. '[A] PEN TO PAYNT': MARY SIDNEY HERBERT
AND THE PROBLEMS OF A PROTESTANT POETICS

1. Articles and books that have considered the impact of Protestant prayer, sermonising, and martyrology upon the language of religious verse and fictional prose in England are too numerous to mention – particularly if one includes consideration of the specific diction of writers such as Donne, (George) Herbert, Vaughan, Traherne, Taylor, Milton, and Bunyon. Still, certain works bear mention: S. E. Fish, *The living temple: George Herbert and catechising* (Berkeley: California University Press, 1978); B. Lewalski, *Protestant poetics and the seventeenth-century religious lyric* (Princeton: Princeton University Press, 1979); J. N. King, *English Reformation literature: the Tudor origins of the Protestant tradition* (Princeton: Princeton University Press, 1982); J. Mueller, *The native tongue and the word: developments in English prose style 1380–1580* (Chicago: Chicago University Press, 1984); N. Smith, *Perfection proclaimed: language and literature in English radical religion 1640–1660* (Oxford: Oxford University Press, 1989); J. Stachniewski, *The persecutory imagination: English Puritanism and the literature of religious despair* (Oxford: Clarendon Press, 1991); D. Shuger, *The Renaissance Bible: scholarship, sacrifice, and subjectivity* (Berkeley: California University Press, 1994); E. Clarke, *Theory and theology in George Herbert's poetry: 'Divinitie, and poesie, met'* (Oxford: Clarendon Press, 1997); and R. Targoff, *Common prayer: the language of devotion in early modern England* (Chicago: Chicago University Press, 2001).
2. This paraphrases Margaret Ezell, 'The myth of Judith Shakespeare: creating the canon of women's writing', *New Literary History* 21 (1990), 580.
3. See E. Klotz, 'A subject analysis of printing, 1480–1640', *HLQ* 1 (1938), 417–19, for a breakdown of the subject categories of printed work.
4. Susan Wiseman's article, 'Unsilent instruments and the devil's cushions: authority in seventeenth-century women's prophetic discourse', in *New feminist discourses*, ed. I. Armstrong (London: Routledge, 1992), 176–96, also offers this explanation for the absence of women writers in our study of the sixteenth and seventeenth

centuries. See also H. Hinds, *God's Englishwomen: seventeenth-century radical sectarian writing and feminist criticism* (Manchester: Manchester University Press, 1996), ch. 1.

5. Margaret Hannay has suggested that Herbert intended (in Harold Love's phrase) to '[publish] through a single copy' by presenting a finished manuscript to Queen Elizabeth (see Hannay, '"Bearing the livery of your name": the Countess of Pembroke's agency in print and scribal publication', *Sidney Journal* 18 (2000), 8; see also Love, *Scribal publication in seventeenth-century England* (Oxford: Clarendon Press, 1993), 70).While the actual presentation never materialised, there are still indications – through the number of manuscripts that remain, and the wealth of local references to the work – that its manuscript circulation was extremely wide. See *The collected works of Mary Sidney Herbert, Countess of Pembroke*, ed. M. Hannay, N. Kinnamon, and M. Brennan (Oxford: Clarendon Press, 1998), II: 308–36, for a list of extant manuscripts. Gavin Alexander recently reported the discovery of one more manuscript in the sale of the library of William Foyle ('A new manuscript of the Sidney Psalms: a preliminary report', *Sidney Journal* 18 (2000), 43–54).

6. See in particular Israel Baroway, 'The Bible as poetry in the English Renaissance', *Journal of English and Germanic Philology* 32 (1933), 447–80; Baroway, '"The lyre of David": a further study in Renaissance interpretation of biblical form', *ELH* 8 (1941), 119–42; L. B. Campbell, *Divine poetry and drama in sixteenth century England* (Cambridge: Cambridge University Press, 1959), 51–4; A. D. Weiner, 'Moving and teaching: Sidney's *Defence of poesie* as a Protestant poetic', *Journal of Medieval and Renaissance Studies* 2 (1972), 259–78, and *Sir Philip Sidney and the poetics of Protestantism: a study of contexts* (Minneapolis: Minnesota University Press, 1978); G. F. Waller, '"This matching of contraries": Calvinism and courtly philosophy in the Sidney Psalms', *English Studies* 55 (1974), 22–31; A. Patterson, '*Bermudas* and *The coronet*: Marvell's Protestant poetics', *ELH* 44 (1977), 478–99; P. C. Herman, *Squitter-wits and muse-haters: Sidney, Spenser, Milton and Renaissance antipoetic sentiment* (Detroit: Wayne State University, 1996), 13–93; and Targoff, *Common prayer*, 73–84.

7. Lewalski, *Protestant poetics and the seventeenth-century religious lyric*, 241.

8. Hannibal Hamlin observes that the place of the Sidney–Pembroke Psalter 'in founding a broader tradition of devotional poetry has been appreciated for some time', but he maintains that the demonstration of its effect upon specific works (and writers) has still not been sufficiently appraised (*Psalm culture and early modern English literature* (Cambridge: Cambridge University Press, 2004), 120). Hamlin, however, assumes that the religio-cultural barriers to the poetic transcription of the Psalms (and the production of religious lyric generally) were relatively easy to release – and that the Psalter's effect upon later devotional literature was therefore largely artistic. I am arguing that the Psalter's intervention was both artistic *and* polemical – and that the cultural obstructions that it removed made possible the active production of devotional lyric that occurred in its wake.

9. E. ní Chuilleanáin, 'The debate between Thomas More and William Tyndale, 1528–33: ideas on literature and religion', *JEH* 39 (1988), 395.

10. John Frith, for example, cites More's 'jesting and bawdy tales' as a point of specific irritation (*Works of the English reformers Tyndale and Frith*, ed. Thomas Russell (London, 1828–30), III: 225.

11. See W. Tyndale, *An answer to Sir Thomas More's Dialogue*, ed. H. Walter (Cambridge: Parker Society, 1850), 61–2.

12. Ibid., 6, 122.

13. *A Reformation rhetoric*, ed. R. Rex (Cambridge: RTM Publications, 1999), 95.
14. STC 10766.3; STC 1540; Wing H441; Wing S4116A; Wing P3433. See Baroway, 'The Bible as poetry in the English Renaissance', 470.
15. This is partly due to the influence of Philip Melanchthon's *De rhetorica* (1519) and *Institutiones* (1521) both of which provide a model for a number of English rhetoric handbooks. See K. Meerhoff, 'The significance of Philip Melanchthon's rhetoric in the Renaissance', in *Renaissance rhetoric*, ed. P. Mack (New York: St Martin's Press, 1994), 46–62. Melanchthon, however, appears to have been less influential at Oxford than at Cambridge (cf. n. 98), as only eight copies of *Dialectica*, and four (possibly five) copies of *De rhetorica*, are included in 145 private libraries of Oxford academics and students inventoried between 1506 and 1589 (see *Private libraries in Renaissance England*, ed. R. J. Fehrenbach and E. S. Leedham-Green (Binghamton, NY: Medieval and Renaissance Texts and Studies, 1992–2004), II–VI).
16. I am, of course, only speaking of rhetoric textbooks in England; for a fuller discussion of rhetorics both in England and on the Continent, see Richard Rex's introduction (*A Reformation rhetoric*, 22–49).
17. H. Peacham, *The garden of eloquence conteyning the figures of grammer and rhetorick . . . for the better vnderstanding of the holy scriptures*, etc. (STC 19497); and Sherry, below.
18. R. Sherry, *A treatise of schemes [and] tropes* (STC 22428), A7v. Sherry actually does a more thorough job of treating biblical language in his subsequent work, *A treatise of the figures of grammer and rhetorike* (STC 22429).
19. *A Reformation rhetoric*, ed, Rex, 99–100. 'The letter killeth, but the spirit giveth life' (2 Cor. 3:6) was a biblical passage frequently invoked by Catholics to justify a figurative interpretation of scripture.
20. See, for example, Augustine, *De doctrina christiana*, ed. R. P. H. Green (Oxford: Clarendon Press, 1995), 2.10.15.
21. Ibid., 3.5.9, 3.10.14.
22. See R. Teske, 'Criteria for figurative interpretation in St. Augustine', in *De doctrina christiana: a classic of western culture*, ed. D. W. H. Arnold and P. Bright (Notre Dame: Christianity and Judaism in Antiquity, 1995), 109–22.
23. *De doctrina christiana*, ed. Green, 3.10.14. Teske has an extended discussion the implications of this maximising criterion (and why it should stand as the overarching law of Augustine's interpretative method).
24. I am indebted to Richard Rex's explication here (*A Reformation rhetoric*, 86–7).
25. Ibid., 88.
26. Ibid., 99. Cf.W. Tyndale, *Obedience of a Christian man*, in *Doctrinal treatises and introductions to different portions of the holy scripture*, ed. H. Walter (Cambridge: Parker Society, 1848), 308.
27. *A Reformation rhetoric*, ed. Rex, 165. Cf. Tyndale, *Obedience of a Christian man*, 305.
28. *A Reformation rhetoric*, ed. Rex, 103.
29. S. Gosson, *The s[c]hoole of abuse, conteining a pleasaunt inuectiue against poets, pipers, plaiers, iesters, and such like caterpillers of a commonwelth* (STC 12097).
30. Sidney addresses the charges against poetry in the following order: that 'a man might better spend his time' than in the composition of imaginative works; that poetry is the 'mother of lies'; that it is 'the nurse of abuse, infecting us with many pestilent desires'; that poets 'soften' men and make them effeminate; and lastly, that

'Plato banished [poets]' ('The defence of poetry', in *Miscellaneous prose of Sir Philip Sidney*, ed. K. Duncan-Jones and J. van Dorsten (Oxford: Oxford University Press, 1973), 101–2). Gosson's attack begins with charging poets (and poems) as 'fathers of lyes, Pipes of vanitie, & Schooles of Abuse'; he also asserts that 'Plato ... banished them quite from his common wealth, as effeminate writers, vnprofitable members, and vtter enimies to vertue (*S[c]hoole of abuse*, A2v–A3r).

31. Vives, Agrippa, Alley, Ascham, and Brasbridge are among many who published attacks.

32. Like Gosson's treatise, these pamphlets do not confine themselves to drama, but criticise poets and poetic works more generally.

33. Barnarbe Googe defends poetry briefly in the preface to his *Eglogs, epytaphes, and sonettes* (London, 1563); Thomas Lodge wrote a *Defence of poetry, music, and stage plays* (London, 1579), but the book was withdrawn immediately after publication. But written defences of poetry (both as treatises and in prefaces) become more common in print at the end of the century – Sidney's *Defence*, Thomas Nashe's *The anatomie of absurdite* (London, 1589), and George Puttenham's *Arte of English poesie* (London, 1589), notable among them.

34. A. Walsham, 'Godly recreation: the problems of leisure in late Elizabethan and early Stuart society', in *Grounds of controversy: three studies in late 16th and early 17th century English polemics*, ed. D. E. Kennedy (Melbourne: Melbourne University Press, 1989), 24.

35. C. M. Dent, *Protestant reformers in Elizabethan Oxford* (Oxford: Oxford University Press, 1983), 119.

36. D. Featley, 'The life and death of John Reinolds', in *Abel redevivus; or the dead yet speaking*, ed. William Nichols (London: William Tegg, 1867), II: 220.

37. Bodleian MS Auct. S.2.29. Laurence Green has published a full English transcription of the interleaved notations in *John Rainolds's Oxford lectures on Aristotle's rhetoric* (London and Toronto: Associated University Press, 1986).

38. *John Rainolds's Oxford lectures*, ed. and trans. Green, 389.

39. In the Aristotelian sense (*Rhetoric* 2: 12–14); see ibid., 67.

40. Ibid., 90. Bishop John Jewel committed his protégé Richard Hooker to Rainolds's tutelage – a further indication of just how normative Rainolds's religious thinking was at the time.

41. S. Gosson, *Playes confuted in fiue actions, prouing that they are not to be suffred in a Christian common weale* (STC 12095), B4v–B5r.

42. Sidney's reliance upon Aristotle for a definition of poetry (as idealistic counterfeit) as well as its rhetorical objectives ('to teach and delight') is widely acknowledged (*Miscellaneous prose of Sir Philip Sidney*, ed. Duncan-Jones and van Dorsten, 81–2).

43. See in particular J. P. McIntyre, 'Sidney's golden world', *Comparative Literature* 14 (1962), 356–65; and M. H. Partee, 'Anti-Platonism in Sidney's "Defence"', *English Miscellany* 22 (1971), 7–29.

44. Jan van Dorsten suggests that 'the most fundamental paragraph' in Sidney's *Defence* – which describes the capacity of the poet's imagination and establishes its efficacy in the instruction of virtue – is 'an essentially northern transformation of mannerist art theory in its heavily post-lapsarian Platonizing' (*Miscellaneous prose of Sir Philip Sidney*, ed. Duncan-Jones and van Dorsten, 64). See also F. G. Robinson, *The shape of things known: Sidney's* Apology *in its philosophical tradition* (Cambridge: Harvard University Press, 1972).

45. Weiner, 'Moving and teaching: Sidney's *Defence of poesie* as a Protestant poetic'.
46. D. H. Craig, 'A hybrid growth: Sidney's theory of poetry in *An apology for poetry*', *ELR* 10 (1980), 183–201. See also A. Sinfield, 'The cultural politics of the *Defence of poetry*', in *Sir Philip Sidney and the interpretation of Renaissance culture*, ed. G. Waller and M. D. Moore (London: Croom Helm, 1984), 124–43.
47. Herman, *Squitter-wits and muse-haters*, 66. I am indebted to Peter Herman for the outline of the *Defence* that follows.
48. *Miscellaneous prose of Sir Philip Sidney*, ed. Duncan-Jones and van Dorsten, 78.
49. Ibid., 79.
50. Herman, *Squitter-wits and muse-haters*, 67.
51. *The institutes of the Christian religion*, ed. J. T. McNeill (Philadelphia: Westminster Press, 1960), 1. 15. 7. This is the conclusion of an extended discussion in which Calvin interrogates the categories that profane philosophers assign: 'Therefore I admit in the first place that there are five senses, which Plato preferred to call organs, by which all objects are presented to common sense, as a sort of receptacle. There follows fantasy, which distinguishes those things which have been apprehended by common sense; then reason, which embraces universal judgment; finally understanding, which in intent and quiet study contemplates what reason discursively ponders' (1. 15. 6). His division of the 'understanding' and the 'will' is a revision of the Aristotelian distinction of 'reason' and 'appetite'.
52. Craig, 'A hybrid growth', 190–1.
53. *The institutes of the Christian religion*, ed. McNeill, 2. 2. 13.
54. *Miscellaneous prose of Sir Philip Sidney*, ed. Duncan-Jones and van Dorsten, 79.
55. Ibid., 2. 2. 12.
56. In the *Institutes* (2. 2. 18), Calvin states this in the clearest possible terms: 'Human reason . . . neither approaches, nor strives toward, nor even takes a straight aim at this truth: to understand who the true God is or what sort of God he wishes to be toward us' (cf. 1. 1. 2; 1. 10. 2; 3. 2. 6).
57. *John Rainolds's Oxford lectures*, ed. and trans. Green, 185.
58. *Miscellaneous prose of Sir Philip Sidney*, ed. Duncan-Jones and van Dorsten, 82.
59. *John Rainolds's Oxford lectures*, ed. and trans. Green, 151.
60. *Miscellaneous prose of Sir Philip Sidney*, ed. Duncan-Jones and van Dorsten, 76.
61. *John Rainolds's Oxford lectures*, ed. and trans. Green, 193. Rainolds is simply reiterating what any number of philosophers of discourse would have posited at the time. Most notable among these is Peter Ramus. It is with Ramus that we see a return to the earlier Platonic view of rhetoric as a means mainly to distort and mislead. Ramus assumes that 'the formation of a concept and the linguistic expression of it are, if not the same, simultaneous and, to all intents and purposes, inseparable processes' (J. P. Thorne, 'A Ramistical commentary on Sidney's *An apologie for poetrie*', *Modern Philology* 54 (1957), 159). In Ramism, poetry is not different from other kinds of discourse – what distinguishes it is simply that it is written in verse. The process by which poetry can be persuasive, then, is only by means of logical arguments – not imagination or rhetorical invention. Rainolds is following Aristotle's divisions – where demonstrative logic, dialectic, rhetoric, and poetry form separate operations – but he rejects lyric poetry on the grounds that it distorts.
62. *The institutes of the Christian religion*, ed. McNeill, 2. 2. 12.
63. Even though Rainolds allows for the impetus of emotions, he also insists that activity is ultimately controlled by the mind: 'In the inferior part of the soul, that is, the appetite, the emotions are implanted, like some stimulants which excite

a sluggish person, for performing things *which the mind has determined*' (*John Rainolds's Oxford lectures*, ed. and trans. Green, 141; my emphasis).

64. William Perkins, *A treatise of mans imaginations* (STC 19751), 21–2; quoted in Herman, *Squitter-wits and muse-haters*, 68. Peter Herman has an extended discussion of the status of the imagination in the mind of Elizabethan divines (67–9).

65. Cf. E. Dering, *A briefe and necessary catachisme or instruction* (STC 6679), A2r–A3v; and W. Alley, *The poore mans librarie* (STC 375), L11r–v.

66. *Miscellaneous prose of Sir Philip Sidney*, ed. Duncan-Jones and van Dorsten, 79.

67. *The institutes of the Christian religion*, ed. McNeill, 2. 2. 16.

68. See, for example, T. Elyot, *The boke named the gouernour* (London, 1531), 1. 13; and G. Puttenham, *The arte of English poesie* (London, 1589), 1. 1. See also C. D. Baker, 'Certain religious elements in the English doctrine of the inspired poet during the Renaissance', *ELH* 6 (1939), 300–23.

69. Weiner, 'Moving and teaching', 268.

70. *Miscellaneous prose of Sir Philip Sidney*, ed. Duncan-Jones and van Dorsten, 109; my emphasis.

71. Ibid., 79. See Weiner, 'Moving and teaching', 269. Weiner's article is incorporated into his much larger project of unpacking the inconsistencies of the *Defence* (*Sir Philip Sidney and the poetics of Protestantism*); but while his book is admirable in showing how some of these conflicts destabilise the work, Weiner ultimately seems to follow the trend that Alan Sinfield describes as a 'tendency among critics . . . still to seek and discover a final achieved coherence' in the *Defence* (see 'The cultural politics of the *Defence of poetry*', 124).

72. *The institutes of the Christian religion*, ed. McNeill, 2. 1. 5

73. Roy Battenhouse has written the most extended analysis of the congruence between Calvinism and Neoplatonic thought. But when evaluating the Neoplatonic idea that at the soul's zenith man's creative powers are comparable to God's, even Battenhouse concedes that 'Calvin . . . would have considered such views horrid blasphemy' ('The doctrine of man in Calvin and in Renaissance Platonism', *Journal of the History of Ideas* 9 (1948), 451).

74. *Commentary on Acts* 15:9; quoted in T. F. Torrance, *Calvin's doctrine of man* (Westport, CT: Greenwood Press, 1957), 82.

75. Calvin writes in the *Institutes* (2. 5. 15) that '[t]he Spirit cannot regulate without correcting, without reforming, without renewing. For this reason we say that the beginning of our regeneration is to *wipe out what is ours*' (my emphasis).

76. Ibid., 2. 2. 20.

77. Craig, 'A hybrid growth', 191; see also A. Sinfield, 'Sidney and Du Bartas', *Comparative Literature* 27 (1975), 8–20.

78. Sinfield, 'Sidney and Du Bartas', 9.

79. James VI, *The essayes of a prentise, in the divine art of poesie* (STC 14373), D4r. I am not suggesting that Sidney was acquainted with the work of Du Bartas when he composed the *Defence* – Alan Sinfield asserts, rightly, I think, that he was not (see 'Sidney and Du Bartas', 12–15).

80. In 'King David as a "right poet": Sidney and the Psalmist' (*ELR* 19 (1989), 131–51), Anne Lake Prescott compellingly argues that 'except for the crucial disability of his divine inspiration and authority, David makes a very presentable' model for the 'right poet' of Sidney's construction (34). I have been arguing that this model of inspiration is the very stumbling block of Sidney's *Defence* – and it is the problem that has particular bearing upon the Sidney–Pembroke Psalter.

81. *John Rainolds's Oxford lectures*, ed. and trans. Green, 349.
82. Craig, 'A hybrid growth', 193. See also D. P. Walker, 'Ways of dealing with atheists: a background to Pamela's refutation of Cecropia', *Bibliotheque d'Humanisme et Renaissance* 17 (1955), 252–77.
83. Lori Anne Ferrell, 'Transfiguring theology: William Perkins and Calvinist aesthetics', in *John Foxe and his world*, ed. C. Highley and J. N. King (Aldershot: Ashgate, 2002), 164–5. As Farrell notes, the date has been asserted by Patrick Collinson ('Protestant culture and cultural revolution', in *The Birthpangs of Protestant England: religious and cultural change in the sixteenth and seventeenth centuries* (London: Macmillan Press, 1988), 98), and supported by Christopher Haigh (*English Reformations: religion, politics, and society under the Tudors* (Oxford: Oxford University Press, 1993), 279–81).
84. Ibid., 165.
85. *John Rainolds's Oxford lectures*, ed. and trans. Green, 29.
86. P. Lake, *Moderate Puritans and the Elizabethan Church* (Cambridge: Cambridge University Press, 1982), 76.
87. See Lewalski, *Protestant poetics*, 214–31.
88. This does not mean that Rainolds fails to recognise metrical psalm translations as poetry; but he is following Aristotelian definitions. His emphasis upon the epic poets make his opposition to vernacular lyric poetry, the operation of which (according to Aristotle) involves invention, clear. His lectures demonstrate an enthusiasm for classical poetry (and he admits this appreciation in *Th'overthrow of stage-plays* (STC 20616), 59); but equally apparent is his resistance to the development of an English vernacular tradition based on these models.
89. Thorne, 'A Ramistical commentary on Sidney's *An apologie for poetrie*', 163.
90. *Miscellaneous prose of Sir Philip Sidney*, ed. Duncan-Jones and van Dorsten, 79.
91. Ibid., 78.
92. Ibid.
93. P. Munz, *The place of Hooker in the history of thought* (London: Routledge and Kegan Paul, 1952), 154.
94. Thorne, 'A Ramistical commentary on Sidney's *An apologie for poetrie*', 159.
95. See G. Harvey and E. Spenser, *Three proper and wittie, familiar letters: lately passed betvvene tvvo vniuersitie men: touching the earthquake in Aprill last, and our English refourmed versifying* (STC 23095); and A. Fraunce, *The sheapheardes logike* (BL MS Add. 34361), and *The Arcadian rhetorike* (STC 11338).
96. See W. S. Howell, *Logic and rhetoric in England, 1500–1700* (New York: Russell and Russell, 1961), 204–5.
97. Temple's *Analysis tractationis de poesi contextae a nobilissimo viro Philippe Sidneio equite a aurato* has been translated by John Webster (*William Temple's 'analysis' of Sir Philip Sidney's 'Apology for poetry': an edition and translation* (Binghamton, NY: Medieval and Renaissance Texts and Studies, 1984)).
98. Studies of the Cambridge curriculum reveal that Agricola, Melanchthon, Caesarius, Seton, and Ramus were the authors commonly employed in the teaching of dialectic at this time (see L. Jardine, 'The place of dialectic teaching in sixteenth-century Cambridge', *Studies in the Renaissance* 21 (1974), 50–1). However, the rhetorical philosophy of Ramus came to dominate Cambridge intellectual life after William Temple's public argument with Everard Digby in the early 1580s – resulting in Digby's ejection from St John's in 1588. See *Francisci Mildapetti Navarreni ad Everardvm Digbeium Anglvm admonitio de vnica P. Rami methodo*

(STC 23872); and *Pro Mildapetti de vnica methodo defensione contra diplodophilum commentatio Gvlielmi Tempelli* (STC 23874).

99. Cf. *William Temple's 'analysis'*, trans. Webster, 73–5.
100. *Miscellaneous prose of Sir Philip Sidney*, ed. Duncan-Jones and van Dorsten, 79.
101. *William Temple's 'analysis'*, ed. and trans, Webster, 79.
102. Ibid. (introduction), 31.
103. Ibid., 81.
104. Ibid.
105. Ibid. (introduction), 30.
106. Ibid.
107. *Miscellaneous prose of Sir Philip Sidney*, ed. Duncan-Jones and van Dorsten, 80.
108. *William Temple's 'analysis'*, ed. and trans. Webster, 83.
109. *Miscellaneous prose of Sir Philip Sidney*, ed. Duncan-Jones and van Dorsten, 91.
110. Ibid., 115.
111. Ibid., 35.
112. Thorne makes a similar observation in 'A Ramistical commentary on Sidney's *An apologie for poetrie*', 163.
113. See Howell, *Logic and rhetoric in England*, 163–4.
114. K. Meerhoff, '"Beauty and the beast": nature, logic and literature in Ramus', in *The influence of Petrus Ramus*, ed. M. Feingold, J. S. Freedman, and W. Rother (Basel: Schwabe, 2001), 209.
115. *The logike of the moste excellent philosopher P. Ramus, martyr* (STC 15246), 100. Moreover, in MacIlmaine's translation, all of the textual examples that Ramus provides from classical sources are scrubbed in favour of (mostly) scriptural citations. I am grateful to Gerard Passannante for alerting me to this fact.
116. D. K. McKim, *Ramism in William Perkin's theology* (New York: Peter Lang, 1987), 38.
117. Fenner, *The artes of logike and rethorike*, D1r (cf. n. 14); quoted in Howell, *Logic and rhetoric in England*, 221. Howell identifies *The artes of logike and rethorike* as 'an unacknowledged translation of the main heads of Ramus's *Dialecticae Libri Duo*' (219).
118. A. Fraunce, *The shepherd's logic*, English Linguistics (A Collection of Facsimile Reprints), ed. R. C. Alston (Menston, England: Scolar Press, 1969), fo. 3r; my emphasis.
119. Meerhoff, '"Beauty and the beast"', 210.
120. *The shepherd's logic*, ed. Alston, fo. 3r–v.
121. *The lawiers logike* (STC 11343), ¶r.
122. *The Arcadian rhetorike by Abraham Fraunce*, ed. Ethel Seaton (Westport, CT: Hyperion Press, 1979), xix. His *Arcadian rhetorike* is far more successful in realising this ambition – as Seaton points out – because he closely follows Omer Talon's *Rhetorica* (ix). However, Talon largely confines himself to examples from prose orators, whereas Fraunce takes the majority of his examples from poets (xviii–xx). As has been demonstrated, early modern English education drew a chalk line between the operations of oration and poetry (even if Ramism did not). Fraunce frequently has to discuss the distinction between poets and orators in the *Rhetorike* – an index of the difference between Talon's conception and his own (cf. 34–63; particularly the exception of 'conceited verses', 53–63).
123. *William Temple's 'analysis'*, ed. and trans. Webster, 75–7; my emphasis.
124. Ibid., 77.

125. Fraunce, *The shepherd's logic*, ed. Alson, fo. 3r.
126. Meerhoff, '"Beauty and the beast"', 210.
127. Like any Ramist, Fraunce rejects Aristotelian formulations. He therefore does not make Sidney's mistake regarding the affections: he denies that the emotions can ever be a cause in the process of acquiring knowledge: 'for that which is acause can neuer bee an effect in that same respect, vnlese that affection be chaunged, and that is in the argument, not in the art' (*The shepherd's logic*, ed. Alston, fo. 7r).
128. J. Webster, 'Temple's neo-Latin commentary on Sidney's *Apology*: two strategies for a defense', in *Acta Conventus neo-Latini bononiensis: proceedings of the Fourth International Congress of Neo-Latin Studies*, ed. R. J. Schoeck (Binghamton, NY: Medieval and Renaissance Texts and Studies, 1985), 323.
129. Howell, *Logic and rhetoric in England*, 228.
130. G. Passannante, 'The Lucretian Renaissance: ancient poetry and humanism in an age of science' (unpublished Ph.D. thesis, Princeton University, 2006), 95.
131. Ibid.
132. If Harvey's practice exposes a sceptical strain in Ramism itself – as Passannante claims it does – it also opposes the Ramism that he inherited from Scottish commentators such as MacIlmaine. Passannante argues that, while Ramus never completely abandons his Christian Plationism (that is, the conviction that humanist texts, and human logic, reflect the order of a universe that is divinely ordered), he is not without his own scepticism. Which is to say that Ramus also believed that the world and the text were in constant dialogue – that empirical experience would inflect the text. In the absence of empirical evidence with which to describe earthquakes, Harvey resorts to literary texts – and greatly magnifies the scepticism latent in Ramist philosophy.
133. Meerhoff, '"Beauty and the beast"', 211.
134. *Miscellaneous prose of Sir Philip Sidney*, ed. Duncan-Jones and van Dorsten, 77.
135. Katherine Duncan-Jones is perhaps the most notable opponent of the widely held belief that Sidney was a religious Calvinist as well as a political one; see *Sir Philip Sidney, courtier poet* (New Haven: Yale University Press, 1991), 126.
136. There are a number of recent critical challenges to the argument that I am making. Many of these revisions to our understanding of Sidney specifically, and early modern rhetoric generally, have been mounted through a revised understanding of the influence of Melanchthon (see in particular, K. Eden, *Hermeneutics and the rhetorical tradition* (New Haven: Yale University Press, 1997); R. Kuin, 'Querre-Muhau: Sir Philip Sidney and the New World', *Renaissance Quarterly* 51 (1998), 549–85; and R. E. Stillman, 'The scope of Sidney's *Defence of poesy*: the new hermeneutic and early modern poetics', *ELR* 32 (2002), 356–7). However, rhetoric handbooks that adopt Melanchthon's attitudes toward biblical material, and use scriptural language in the instruction of eloquence – such as Cox's *The art or crafte of rhetoryke* – draw particular fire from Calvin (see chapter 4).
137. W. Watts, *Saint Augustines Confessions translated and with some marginall notes illustrated* (STC 912), 10.33.
138. Patterson, '*Bermudas* and *The coronet*: Marvell's Protestant poetics', 480. This part of my argument draws heavily from Patterson's discussion, 479–81.
139. *Les Psaumes de Dauid, mis en rime Francoise par Clement Marot, & Theodore de Beze* (Geneva, 1576), fo. iiir–v). I am grateful to Anne Coldiron for translating this text.
140. Watts, *Saint Augustines Confessions*, 10.33.

141. Calvin's Commentaries were translated into English by Arthur Golding (*The Psalmes of Dauid and others. With M. Iohn Caluins commentaries* (STC 4395)).
142. *The Psalmes of Dauid, trvely opened and explaned by Paraphrasis*, trans. Anthony Gilby (STC 2033).
143. The Tremellius Bible has a separate section for the 'quinque libri poëtici': *Psalms, Canticles, Ecclesiastes, Proverbs*, and *Job*. It is from Tremellius that Sidney claims authority for his assertion that 'holy David's Psalms are a divine poem'. See *Testamenti Veteris Biblia sacra, sive, Libri canonici, priscae Judaeorum ecclesiae a Deo traditi* (STC 2058a), Aaa3r.
144. Gosson, *Playes confuted in fiue actions*, E5v.
145. *The forme of prayers and ministration of the sacraments ... vsed in the Englishe congregation at Geneua* (STC 16561).
146. For a list of all of the verse forms that this Psalter contains, see R. A. Leaver, '*Goostly Psalmes and spirituall songes': English and Dutch metrical Psalms from Coverdale to Utenhove, 1535–1566* (Oxford: Clarendon Press, 1991), 317–19.
147. See Rivkah Zim's excellent study, *English metrical Psalms: poetry as praise and prayer* (Cambridge: Cambridge University Press, 1987). For a list of metrical Psalms published during this period, see the appendix (211ff).
148. *The vvhole Psalter translated into English metre* (STC 2729), F2v.
149. Ibid., E2r.
150. Ibid., F3r.
151. *Miscellaneous prose of Sir Philip Sidney*, ed. Duncan-Jones and van Dorsten, 77.
152. *The institutes of the Christian religion*, ed. McNeill, I. 6. 3.
153. All citations are from *The collected works of Mary Sidney Herbert, Countess of Pembroke*, ed. Hannay *et al.*, II.
154. *Miscellaneous prose of Sir Philip Sidney*, ed. Duncan-Jones and van Dorsten, 77.
155. See, for example, Lewalski, *Protestant poetics*, 213–31.
156. M. Hannay, '"So may I with the *Psalmist* truly say": early modern English-women's psalm discourse', in *Write or be written: early modern women poets and cultural constraints*, ed. B. Smith and U. Appelt (Aldershot: Ashgate, 2001), 125.
157. Wyatt's *Certayne Psalmes chosen out of the Psalter of Dauid* was published in 1549 (STC 2726), and Surrey's translation of Psalm 88 (and possible translations of 31 and 51) found its way into *Certayne chapters of the Prouerbes of Salomon* (STC 2760), F1r–F2v. (Surrey's verse paraphrases of *Ecclesiastes* I-III are also published in this volume (E1r–F1r).) While George Gascoigne's lyric version of *Deprofundis* was published in 1575 (*The posies of George Gascoigne, Esquire* (STC 11636), xxvi–xxviii), more experimental poetic versions of the Psalms are rare in this period. William Hunnis's 1583 *Seuen sobs of a sorrowfull soule* (STC 13975) includes metrical versions of the Penitential Psalms that go beyond the usual plodding – but musical settings are helpfully included to direct their use (and they are written in common metre). So too, William Byrd's 1588 *Psalmes, sonets, & songs of sadnes and pietie* (STC 4253) are *made into musicke of fiue parts*. Since the body of psalm translation that precedes the Sidney–Pembroke Psalter requires further unpacking, I will discuss the more artistic interpretations of the Psalms – particularly the verse translation of Psalm 51 by Anne Vaughan Lok – at greater length in the next chapter.
158. L. Martz, *The poetry of meditation: a study in English religious literature of the seventeenth century* (New Haven: Yale University Press, 1954), 273–82; and Lewalski, *Protestant poetics*, 241–4. See also, *The Psalms of Sir Philip Sidney and*

the Countess of Pembroke, ed. J. C. A. Rathmell (New York: New York University Press, 1963), xviii–xix; and Hamlin, *Psalm culture and early modern English literature*.

159. Campbell, *Divine poetry and drama in sixteenth century England*. That this is a prevalent attitude at a certain point in English literary history is undeniably true; however, I am arguing that the shift can be rather precisely located around the intervention that the circulation of the Sidney–Pembroke Psalter performed.

160. *L'Vranie ov mvse celeste de G. de Saluste Seigneur du Bartas* (STC 21673).

161. Sinfield, 'Sidney and Du Bartas', 14; see *The essayes of a prentise, in the divine art of poesie* (1584), C3r (cf. n. 79). James's translation of *Vranie* runs from C4v to G1r in this collection.

162. *L'Vranie ov mvse celeste*, D3v.

163. None of the works of Du Bartas are included in the inventories that Fehrenbach and Leedham-Green have surveyed to date (see *Private libraries in Renaissance England*, II–VI; cf. n. 15).

164. Harvey, *Pierces supererogation* (STC 12903), 54. Du Bartas certainly influenced Sidney, Spenser, and Abraham Fraunce; but the full translation of the *Second weeke* was not published until 1598 (STC 21661), and his *Deuine weekes and workes* (also translated by Josuah Sylvester) did not appear until 1605 (STC 21649). The most authoritative and thorough account of Du Bartas's influence upon early modern English poetry is still Anne Lake Prescott's *French Poets and the English Renaissance: studies in fame and transformation* (New Haven: Yale University Press, 1978), ch. 5.

165. *Miscellaneous prose of Sir Philip Sidney*, ed. Duncan-Jones and van Dorsten, 79.

166. See H. R. Woudhuysen, *Sir Philip Sidney and the circulation of manuscripts 1558–1640* (Oxford: Clarendon Press, 1996), 234.

167. Ibid., 232–4.

168. Ibid., 234.

169. Debra Rienstra and Noel Kinnamon 'Circulating the Sidney–Pembroke Psalter', in *Women's writing and the circulation of ideas: manuscript publication in England, 1550–1800*, ed. G. L. Justice and N. Tinker (Cambridge: Cambridge University Press, 2002), 50–72. Margaret Hannay also argues that the fact that Herbert reserved the work for scribal – as opposed to print – publication cannot be attributed in any straightforward way to her gender (see '"Bearing the livery of your name"', *passim*).

170. Ibid., 52.

171. Ibid. I am not doing justice to Rienstra and Kinnamon's fine and subtle argument, but I am merely trying to plot the points at which we disagree. Although our arguments were developed independently (see 'Making sects: women as reformers, writers, and subjects in early Reformation England, 1534–1590' (unpublished D.Phil. thesis, Oxford University, 2002), ch. 3), they do much to confirm and support each other.

172. See n. 5. Michael Brennan has also shown that the initiative to print the complete Psalter was undertaken in the 1640s (although it is not certain by whom), as licence to print was granted by John Langley (see 'Licensing the Sidney Psalms for the press in the 1640s', *Notes and Queries* 31 (1984), 304–5). This intention was never realised.

173. *The Psalms of Sir Philip Sidney and the Countess of Pembroke*, ed. Rathmell, xxv–xxvi. See also T. Spencer, 'The poetry of Sir Philip Sidney', *ELH* 12 (1945), 251–78.

174. J. C. A. Rathmell, 'A critical edition of the Psalms of Sir Philip Sidney and the Countess of Pembroke' (unpublished Ph.D. thesis, University of Cambridge, 1964), 530. Rathmell does not include Psalm 34, which is an exact imitation of Beza's 34.

175. I owe these observations to Ellen St Sure Lifschutz; see 'David's lyre and the Renaissance lyric: a critical consideration of the Psalms of Wyatt, Surrey and the Sidneys' (unpublished Ph.D. thesis, University of California, Berkeley, 1980), 214–18, for her fine, and more detailed, discussion.

176. *Astrophil and Stella* was not published until 1591, but most editors put the time of its composition between 1581 and 1582 (See *The poems of Sir Philip Sidney*, ed. W. Ringler (Oxford: Clarendon Press, 1962), 438–9); Katherine Duncan-Jones and Jan van Dorsten argue that the *Defence* was composed between 1579 and 1580 (*Miscellaneous prose of Sir Philip Sidney*, 59–63).

177. Targoff notes the critical division which has grown up as a result of these two distinctive characteristics of the Psalter (see *Common prayer*, 77–8).

178. *The Psalms of Sir Philip Sidney and the Countess of Pembroke*, ed. Rathmell, xvii. Rathmell also cites Psalms 70 and 144 as an instance of repetition, but they do not, in fact, duplicate rhyme scheme.

179. In an oft-quoted phrase, Hallett Smith has called the Psalter a 'School of English Versification' (see 'English metrical psalms in the sixteenth century and their literary significance', *HLQ* 9 (1946), 269).

180. Mary's translation departs from Philip's in its rhyme scheme (P: ababccdd; M: ababbcbc – Philip's feminine endings are for the a and d rhymes; Mary's are all for the b rhymes).

181. Psalm 119 is a collection of twenty-two separate poems, each beginning (like the Hebrew original) with a different letter of the alphabet.

182. *The Psalms of Sir Philip Sidney and the Countess of Pembroke*, ed. Rathmell, xx.

183. *Miscellaneous prose of Sir Philip Sidney*, ed. Duncan-Jones and van Dorsten, 80.

184. Certainly, this is not true of all of the Psalms. Psalm 51 (in rhyme royal) and Psalm 130 are both preserved in musical settings in BL MS Add. 15117.

185. S. Weiner, 'The quantitative poems and the psalm translations: the place of Sidney's experimental verse in the legend', in *Sir Philip Sidney: 1586 and the creation of a legend*, ed. J. van Dorsten, D. Baker-Smith, and A. Kinney (Leiden: Sir Thomas Browne Institute, 1986), 211.

186. S. Woods, *Natural emphasis: English versification from Chaucer to Dryden* (San Marino: Huntington Library, 1984), 296.

187. *The vvhole Psalter translated into English metre*, HHIV (cf. n. 148).

188. Martz, *The poetry of meditation*, 273.

189. Cf. the Geneva Bible passage (*PS* 134: 1–3):

> Behold, prayse ye the Lord, all yee servants of the Lord,
> yee that by night stand in the house of the Lord.
>   Lift vp your hands to the Sanctuary, and prayse the
> Lord.
>   The Lord that hath made heaven and earth, blesse
> thee out of Zion.

190. G. Waller, *Mary Sidney, Countess of Pembroke: a critical study of her writings and literary milieu* (Salzburg: Institut für Anglistik und Amerikanistik, 1979), 198.

191. Cf. the Geneva lines (*PS* 45: 1): 'Mine heart will vtter foorth a good matter: I will intreat in my works of the king: my tongue is as the pen of a swift writer.'
192. J. Calvin, *Commentary on the Book of Psalms*, ed. J. Anderson (Grand Rapids, MI: Eerdmans Publishing, 1949), I: xlviii–xlix.
193. Ibid., V: 215.
194. Cf. Rathmell's discussion of this passage in his introduction (*The Psalms of Sir Philip Sidney and the Countess of Pembroke*, xx).
195. *The Psalmes of Dauid*, 274 (cf. n. 142).
196. Ibid., 276.
197. *The Psalms of Sir Philip Sidney and the Countess of Pembroke*, ed. Rathmell, xxvi. This is, in fact, the primary basis for assuming that Sidney's contribution predates *Astrophil and Stella*.
198. *Bel-vedére, or, The garden of the muses* (STC 3189), A4v. Francis Davison also includes her work – alongside that of Spenser, Sidney, and Donne – in his 1602 miscellany *A poetical rapsody* (STC 6373).
199. S. Daniel, *Delia and Rosamond augmented. Cleopatra* (STC 6243.4), H6r.
200. Quoted in *The collected works of Mary Sidney Herbert*, ed. Hannay *et al.*, II: 340.
201. In his *Treatise on playe* (not printed until 1779), John Harington claims that 'it is allready prophecied' that the 'precious leves' of the Psalter 'shall owtlast Wilton walls'; quoted in *The Psalms of Sir Philip Sidney and the Countess of Pembroke*, ed. Rathmell, xxvii.
202. Henry Constable's Catholic orientation presents a different case; however, as Constable is explicitly indebted to the work of the Sidneys – Constable wrote the introductory sonnets to the second edition of the *Defence, An apologie for poetrie* (STC 22534) – I include him in the list.
203. While I take up the influence of the Sidney–Pembroke Psalter upon Breton, Fraunce, and Giles Fletcher in chapter 5, the demonstration of its affect upon the work of Davison, Phineas Fletcher, Vaughan, and Milton has been done by Hamlin (see ch. 4 of *Psalm culture and early modern English literature*).
204. 'Upon the translation of the Psalms by Sir Philip Sidney, and the Countess of Pembroke his sister', *John Donne: a critical edition of the major works*, ed. J. Carey (Oxford: Oxford University Press, 1990), 304.
205. 'Abroad' in this line has sometimes been taken to mean 'outside of England'. But in the context in which Donne is speaking, as John Carey notes, it simply means 'outside the church' – in other words, the second line is a reiteration (or clarification) of the first.
206. Dering, *A briefe and necessary catachisme or Instruction*, A2v–A3r (cf. n. 65). Fifteen editions of Dering's *Instruction* appeared between 1572 and 1606.
207. Martz, *The poetry of meditation*, 278.

CHAPTER 4. A NEW JERUSALEM: ANNE LOK'S 'MEDITATION'
AND THE LYRIC VOICE

1. R. Greene, 'Sir Philip Sidney's *Psalms*, the sixteenth-century Psalter, and the nature of lyric', *SEL* 30 (1990), 27.
2. *Miscellaneous prose of Sir Philip Sidney*, ed. K. Duncan-Jones and J. van Dorsten (Oxford: Oxford University Press 1973), 77.
3. Rienstra and Kinnamon also point this out ('Circulating the Sidney–Pembroke Psalter', in *Women's writing and the circulation of ideas: manuscript publication in*

England, 1550–1800, ed. G. L. Justice and N. Tinker (Cambridge: Cambridge University Press, 2002),53).

4. Our sense of Calvin and his followers as 'Puritan' comes in the wake of late sixteenth- and early seventeenth-century polemics that converted certain tensions within the English Church into polar forces (with attendant terms of abuse). See P. Collinson, 'A comment: concerning the name of Puritan', *JEH* 31 (1980), 483–8.

5. B. Lewalski, *Protestant poetics and the Seventeenth-century religious lyrics* (Princeton: Princeton University Press, 1979), 237.

6. Hannibal Hamlin, *Psalm culture and early modern English literature* (Cambridge: Cambridge University Press, 2004), 120.

7. Lily Campbell initiates a historical narrative that downplays the effect of Calvin upon English religious lyric. Campbell openly declares that Calvin's theories concerning church music fall outside of her purview (*Divine poetry and drama in sixteenth century England* (Cambridge: Cambridge University Press, 1959), 37).

8. Buchanan's religious identity was Catholic, not Calvinist, when he first wrote his verse translation of the Psalms. Even so, he clearly did not reject the work, and continued to revise his *Paraphrasis Psalmorvm Davidis poetica* until its 1580 publication in England (STC 3983).

9. The versified psalms of Marcantonio Flaminio are included in three of the 145 private collections from Oxford (1506–89) that have been inventoried; two include the Marot–Beza Psalter; and one contains a copy of Buchanan's *Paraphrasis Psalmorvm* (see *Private libraries in Renaissance England*, ed. R. J. Fehrenbach and E. S. Leedham-green (Binghamton, NY: Medieval and Renaissance Texts and Studies, 1992–2004), II–VI.

10. There have been recent welcome counters to the prevalent critical construction, notably Ramie Targoff's argument in *Common prayer: the language of devotion in early modern England* (Chicago: Chicago University Press, 2001), 73–8; and Rienstra and Kinnamon, 'Circulating the Sidney–Pembroke Psalter', *passim*.

11. H. A. Mason was the first to observe Wyatt's departures from Aretino in favour of Campen (see 'Wyatt and the Psalms – I', *TLS* 27 Feb. 1953).

12. *Certayne Psalmes chosen out of the Psalter of Dauid* (STC 2726) (see chapter 3, n. 157).

13. *Certayne chapters of the Prouerbes of Salomon drawen into metre by Thomas Sterneholde* (STC 2760), E1r–F7v. The misattribution of the poems in *Certayne chapters of the Prouerbes of Salomon* to Sternhold is corrected in a subsequent 1550 edition of John Hall; however, none of Surrey's poems are reproduced in this volume (see *Certayne chapters taken out of the Prouerbes of Salomon* (STC 12631)). The translations of Psalms 31 and 51 were first attributed to Surrey by C. A. Hutter, 'Poems by Surrey and others in a printed miscellany circa 1550', *English Miscellany* 16 (1965), 9–18. See also, R. Zim, *English metrical Psalms: poetry as praise and prayer* (Cambridge: Cambridge University Press, 1987), 225–6.

14. F. Seagar, *Certayne Psalms select out of the Psalter of Dauid* (STC 2728), A3r–B6r. Seagar's intention in his metrical Psalter is explicitly to include *Notes to euery Psalme in iiii partes to synge*; it is possible, therefore, that the purpose of his revision was to set 'Sternhold's' metrical translations to music – as the erroneous volume would have been his only source for Surrey's poem(s). See M. Rudick, 'Two notes on Surrey Psalms', *Notes and Queries*, n.s. 22 (1975), 291–4; and Zim, *English metrical Psalms*, 228.

15. *The vvhole Psalter translated into English metre* (STC 2729), G2v.

16. See, in particular, T. Roche, *Petrarch and the English sonnet sequences* (New York: AMS Press, 1989), ch. 3.

17. J. Scanlon, 'Henry Lok's *Sundry Christian passions*: a critical edition' (unpublished Ph.D. thesis, Brown University, 1971), xxix.

18. While Roche was first to notice Anne Lok's precedent, he touches the subject lightly (*Petrarch and the English sonnet sequences*, 155). See also R. Greene, *Post-Petrarchism: origins and innovations of the western lyric sequence* (Princeton: Princeton University Press, 1991), 129, 132–4; and M. R. G. Spiller, *The development of the sonnet: an introduction* (London: Routledge, 1992), 93.

19. R. Greene, 'Anne Lock's *Meditation*: invention versus dilation and the founding of Puritan poetics', in *Form and reform in Renaissance England: essays in honor of Barbara Kiefer Lewalski*, ed. A. Boesky and M. T. Crane (Newark: Delaware University Press, 2000), 153. Greene's reading of Lok's work draws too radical a separation between her poetic objectives and the issues that occupy other contemporary translators of the Psalms (such as Parker and Sidney). '[Lok's] *Meditation*', he asserts, 'enacts a striking departure from what will become the consensus about poetry in the next generation, anticipating some of the issues that will come to figure [in seventeenth century devotional lyric]' (158). But it is this stark contrast between the concerns of sixteenth- and seventeenth-century devotional poets that I am trying to resist. The issues at stake are the same. This is not to say that the underlying assumptions of these translations are not different – but rather to say that they express the same anxiety, with different resolutions of the problem.

20. *Sermons of John Calvin, vpon the songe that Ezechias made after he had bene sicke* (STC 4450).

21. The preface to the New Testament was published as *An exhortation to the diligent studye of scripture* in 1529, and preceded Eramus's exposition of the seventh chapter of Paul's first letter to the Corinthians (STC 10493). The English *Exhortacyon to the study of readynge the Gospell* (the preface to the chapter of Matthew) was first published in 1534 (STC 10493.5). The two translations were subsequently printed with continuous signatures in 1534 (STC 10494).

22. *An exhortacyon to the dylygent study of scripture* (1534), B2r–v. A similar assertion, that he would have 'thy ploughman holdynge thy plough . . . synge som what of the mystycall Psalmes in his owne mother tonge', appears in *Exhortacyon to the study of readynge the Gospell* (G2r–v).

23. *The Psalter of Dauid newly translated into Englysh metre* (STC 2725). While the text bears Crowley's imprint, it was printed for him by Richard Grafton and Stephen Mierdman.

24. Ibid., ††1v.

25. Ibid.

26. Ibid., ††2r. The Psalms that Crowley used were the collaborative effort of Leo Jud and Theodore Bibliander (see *The Bible in the sixteenth century*, ed. D. C. Steinmetz (Durham: Duke University Press, 1990), 222). Heinrich Bullinger worked closely with Jud in the preparation of a large number of tracts designed to promote the reform cause in Switzerland. (Jud also collaborated in drafting the first Helvetic Confession.) Crowley's address to Ogelthorpe seems slightly impolitic – in that Ogelthorpe was accused by other fellows at Magdalen of opposing religious proceedings under Edwardian reform, particularly the Litany compiled by Cranmer (see A. Wood, *Athenæ Oxonienses* (New York and London: Johnson Reprint Corporation, 1967), II: 792). But Ogelthorpe apparently intervened on Crowley's behalf when poverty would have otherwise forced him to withdraw from Oxford; Crowley therefore attributes his scholastic abilities to Ogelthorpe.

27. *Goostly Psalmes and spirituall songes* (STC 5892), †4v; my emphasis.
28. Ibid.
29. *Philargyrie of Greate Britayne* (STC 6089.5), A2r. My thanks to Wade Razzi for bringing this citation to my attention.
30. P. W. White, *Theatre and Reformation: Protestantism, patronage, and playing in Tudor England* (Cambridge: Cambridge University Press, 1993).
31. See *The complete plays of John Bale*, ed. Peter Happé (Cambridge, D. S. Brewer, 1985–6); and D. S. Kastan, '"Holy wurdes" and "slypper wit": John Bale's *King Johan* and the poetics of propaganda', in *Rethinking the Henrician era*, ed. Peter Herman (Urbana: Illinois University Press, 1994), 267–82.
32. Bucer's defence is part of *De regno Christi*, a manuscript dedicated to Edward VI, and not fully translated into English during the early modern period; see *Melanchthon and Bucer*, Library of Christian Classics 19, ed. W. Pauck (Philadelphia: Westminster Press, 1969), 349–52.
33. *The schoole of vertue, and booke of good nurture, teaching children and youth their duties* (STC 22136), C7v–D7r.
34. There are certainly examples of Psalm versification under Henry VIII: John Croke translated thirteen Psalms, and Thomas Smith wrote metrical Psalms while a prisoner in the Tower. Neither of these psalm translations, however, appears to have circulated widely – Croke's were not printed until 1844, and Smith's never were (see R. A. Leaver, *'Goostly Psalmes and spirituall songes': English and Dutch metrical Psalms from Coverdale to Utenhore, 1535–1566* (Oxford: Clarendon Press, 1991), 117). Nor does there seem to be contemporary awareness of these projects. Dissemination is a crucial factor in the controversy (see n. 42, below).
35. A number of critics have attributed the metrical psalm which concludes *The first examinacyon of Anne Askewe* (STC 848), F7r, to her; however, as David Scott Kastan has pointed out (in connection to Elizabeth's *Godly medytacyon*), the metaphrase is isolated from Askew's text and appears in conclusion (see 'An early English metrical psalm: Elizabeth's or John Bale's?', *Notes and Queries* 21 (1974), 404–5). This would not itself establish that she did not write it. But the metrical pattern of all three of the psalm paraphrases included in texts either written or edited by Bale is identical; further, all three exhibit the habit of splitting the metrical line. This stylistic tic seems to indicate a single author – which could only be Bale. Cf. *A godly medytacyon of the christen sowle* (STC 17320), F7v–F8r; *A dialoge or communycacyon to be had at a table betwene two chyldren* (STC 1290), A1v; and *An expostulation or complaint against the blasphemyes of a franticke papyst of Hamshyre* (STC 1294), C6v–C7r.
36. *Certayne Psalmes chosen out of the Psalter of Dauid* (STC 2727). Hunnis makes clear in his preface that his poems are intended for the pleasure of the individual reader as well as the singer. But he also confesses 'that in som places' the poems are not 'eloquently turned' (A1v). This seems largely due to the limits of the form.
37. See n. 13. Hall includes metrical translations of Proverbs 1–11, as well as a translation of the Wisdom of Solomon 6 (from the Apocrypha), chapters of Ecclesiastes, and particular Psalms.
38. *Certayne chapters taken out of the Prouerbes of Salomon* (1550), D2r.
39. Ibid., A5r.
40. *The canticles or balades of Salomon* (STC 2768), A1v.
41. The first (and second) edition of Sternhold's English metrical psalm translations does not include musical settings. However, Sternhold obviously fit the words to

his own tunes, and his preface recounts how King Edward took 'pleasure to heare them song somtimes of me' (*Certayne Psalmes chosen out of the Psalter of Dauid* (STC 2419), A3r). Sternhold further declares his wish that Edward 'commaunde them to be song to you of others' (ibid.), suggesting that he hopes for official sanction of his work. Other translations of scriptural material, such as Seager's *Certayne Psalms select out of the Psalter of Dauid* (1553), are set to music (see n. 14).

42. These issues are engaged when a work is in print, or when manuscript copies are so widely disseminated that its circulation breaches the controlled environment of a coterie. This is the case with the Sidney–Pembroke Psalter (as I have argued in the previous chapter), but other works in manuscript fall into this category. Copies of Surrey's biblical translations, for example, were so widely available that John Case encounters them, and prints them, without apparent knowledge of their origin. Local references by Bale, Parker, and Puttenham make it clear that the paraphrases were well known (see Hutter, 'Poems by Surrey and others in a printed miscellany circa 1550', 11–12).

43. In the intervening years of 1551–8, only Thomas Becon's metrical translations of Psalms 103 and 112, written as songs of thanksgiving for his deliverance from prison, are printed (in Strasburg) without musical accompaniment (see *A confortable epistle too Goddes faythfull people in Englande* (STC 1716), D5v–D8r). Becon also composed metrical versions of Psalms 117 and 134, which are first printed in the 1561 *Psalmes of Dauid in Englishe metre, by Thomas Sternholde and others* (see n. 49, below).

44. Lewalski, *Protestant poetics*, 473 (n. 10).

45. Targoff, *Common prayer*, 75.

46. Ibid., 76.

47. S. Gosson, *Playes confuted in fiue actions prouing that they are not to be suffred in a christian common weale* (STC 12095), E5v.

48. *Les Psaumes de Dauid mis en rime Francoise par Clement Marot, & Theodore de Beze* (Geneva, 1576), fo. iiir.

49. It is included in the 1558 edition of *The forme of prayers* (STC 16561a), fos. 112v–13r. Day's 1561 *Psalmes of Dauid in Englishe metre, by Thomas Sternholde and others* (STC 2429) is an expansion of his earlier edition of 1560. *The whole booke of Psalmes, collected into Englysh metre* (STC 2430) is the first complete compilation of the Psalms and other parts of scripture adapted for church service and published in England. It includes the work of Thomas Becon, Richard Cox, Edmund Grindal, John Hopkins, William Kethe, John Marckant, Thomas Norton, John Pullain, William Samuel, Thomas Sternhold, William Whittingham, and Robert Wisdome. See Leaver, *'Goostly Psalmes'*, 194–249, for the evolution of this collection; and 248 and 252 for a complete list of the canticles and hymns contained within it.

50. See Leaver, *'Goostly Psalmes'*, 317–19, for a breakdown of the verse forms.

51. Cf. *Triplex, of songes* (STC 25584) and *The First booke of ayres* (STC 4546.5).

52. This project was first described in the preface to *Certayne chapters taken out of the Prouerbes of Salomon*, A5v.

53. Hall employs either common metre, or the following variations: 6686 (Pss. 34 and 54); 666666 (Ps. 113); 8888 (Pss. 114, 115, and 130). All of the variations have corresponding tunes in the volume (and all of the tunes are employed in the *Whole booke of Psalmes*). The only metrical variation in the volume not fitted to a corresponding tune (446446) is used in three 'songe[s] of prayse and thankesgeuinge' based on scripture (*The courte of vertue* (STC 12632), 44r–47v).

54. *Seuen sobs of a sorrowfull soule for sinne* (STC 13975). *A handfull of honisuckles, The poore widowes mite*, and the *Comfortable dialogs betwene Christ and a SINNER*, annexed to this work, do register the beginnings of a cultural shift – one that I will discuss later in connection to Byrd's *Psalmes, sonets & songs of sadnes and pietie* (1588) and *Songs of sundrie natures* (1589), and Michael Drayton's *The harmonie of the Church* (1591).

55. *The song of songs* (STC 2769).

56. In *Sermons of John Calvin*; and *The posies of George Gascoigne, Esquire* (STC 11636), respectively. The metrical paraphrase of Psalms 1–4 appended to the *First foure bookes of Virgil his Aeneis* translated by Richard Stanyhurst (STC 24806) was printed in Holland in 1582. This does not itself make it an exception; but Stanyhurst, an Irish Catholic, would not have been susceptible to the religio-cultural pressures that I have been tracking. Further, he may have had political motives underpinning his translation – motives connected to 'the establishment in Ireland of a new "Rome", based on the Roman Catholic Church' (Hamlin, *Psalm culture and early modern English literature*, 92). This gives a different inflection to his psalm translations.

57. As the sister of a (then) English Protestant martyr – whose profile as a major poet she raised – Herbert had considerable cultural clout. She was also the wife of one of the richest men in England. This combination made her uniquely powerful in political, cultural, and financial terms (Diane Purkiss has amusingly dubbed her the social equivalent of a 'Madame Microsoft'). For an excellent discussion of the particular experience of upper-class women (and the critical tendency to ignore this experience), see *Three tragedies by Renaissance women,* ed. D. Purkiss (London: Penguin, 1998), introduction.

58. C. Warley, '"An Englishe box": Calvinism and commodities in Anne Lok's *A meditation of a penitent sinner*', *Spenser Studies: A Renaissance Poetry Annual* 15 (2001), 205–41. See also C. Warley, *Sonnet sequences and social distinction in Renaissance England* (Cambridge: Cambridge University Press, 2005), ch. 3.

59. Warley '"An Englishe box"', 214 (cf. *Sonnet sequences and social distinction*, 52).

60. Warley notes that the compelling negotiation of the 'Mediation' is the balance between collective and individual claims ('"An Englishe box"').

61. Presbyterianism advocated a representative, versus a hierarchical, church structure. While this commitment does not animate collective religious agency *per se*, leaders of the church service were the congregants themselves. The responsibility for religious instruction was therefore collective – shared among the community of worshippers.

62. It is not clear if her departure was arranged for her own protection, or if her husband remained in London (if he accompanied the family to the continent, he did not go with them to Geneva). Hence, it is not clear if the separation represents a marital rift. What is clear is that she remained part of the exiled congregation in Geneva for two years. For a full discussion of this family history, see *The collected works of Anne Vaughan Lock*, ed. S. Felch (Tempe, AZ: Renaissance English Text Society, 1999), xxiii–xxvi.

63. P. Collinson, 'The role of women in the English Reformation illustrated by the life and friendships of Anne Locke', in *Studies in Church History*, ed. G. J. Cuming (London: Ecclesiastical History Society, 1965), 262.

64. See *John Knox's History of the Reformation in Scotland*, ed. W. Dickinson (London: Nelson, 1949), I: lxxxiii–lxxxv; and *The collected works of Anne Vaughan Lock*, ed. Felch, xxvi–xxix.

65. *Sermons of John Calvin*, A3r.
66. Ibid., A8r.
67. *The institvtion of Christian religion* (STC 4416), A1r.
68. Ibid., A1v.
69. While her dedication to Catherine Brandon only attaches her initials, this was not an unusual practice. The first edition of Norton's translation has no attribution on the title page at all (his initials are printed on the final page of text); the second transcribes his initials alone. His full name is added to the third edition (STC 4417).
70. 'A meditation of a penitent sinner', Aa1.
71. M. Hannay, '"Unlock my lipps": the *Miserere mei Deus* of Anne Vaughan Lok and Mary Sidney Herbert, Countess of Pembroke', in *Privileging gender in early modern England*, ed. J. R. Brink (Kirksville, MS: Sixteenth Century Journal Publishers, 1993), 21; and *The collected works of Anne Vaughan Lock*, ed. Felch, liv.
72. *The institvtion of Christian religion* (STC 4415), A1v.
73. *Sermons of John Calvin*, A3v. Calvin also frequently draws the comparison between the two kings in his *Sermons*.
74. See R. Smith, '"In a mirrour clere": Protestantism and politics in Anne Lok's *Miserere mei Deus*', *'This double voice': gendered writing in early modern England*, ed. D. Clarke and E. Clarke (Basingstoke: Macmillan, 2000), 41–60.
75. There was at least one other edition of the work printed in 1574 (STC 4451), but the remaining copy was destroyed in the bombing of the British Museum during World War II. An entry in Andrew Maunsell's 1595 *Catalogue of English printed bookes* suggests that another edition was produced in 1569 (see *The collected works of Anne Vaughan Lock*, ed. Felch, lxx).
76. *Of the markes of the children of God, and of their comforts in afflictions* (STC 23652), A3v–A4r.
77. Ibid., A3v.
78. See in particular, S. Amussen, *An ordered society: gender and class in early modern England* (Oxford: Blackwell, 1988); and B. J. Harris, *English aristocratic women, 1450–1550: marriage and family, property and careers* (Oxford: Oxford University Press, 2002).
79. This ethic commonly relied upon a passage from the Ephesians (5:22–4) for support; this biblical passage equates the love of Christ for his church with the love of a man for his wife – and demands the wife's subordination to her husband.
80. *The institvtion of Christian religion*, A1r.
81. Ibid.
82. Indeed, the 'friend' who supplied the sonnets was assumed by critics to be Knox until very recently (see, for example, Collinson, 'The role of women in the English Reformation', 265). Thomas Roche was the first to attribute the work to Lok (see n. 18).
83. See M. R. G. Spiller, 'A literary "first": the sonnet sequence of Anne Locke (1560)', *Renaissance Studies* 11 (1997), 48–9, for a complete reconstruction of the stylistic patterns that exhibit Lok's debt to this specific poem.
84. Ibid., 46–8.
85. Even if she used a manuscript copy, an echo in her final sonnet suggests that her version paralleled the print copy. In the Blage MS, towards the end of the poem, Wyatt's Psalm 51 reads:

Make Syon, lord, according to thy will,
Inward Syon, the Syon of the ghost:
Off hertes Hierusalem strength the walles still.

(*The collected poems of Sir Thomas Wyatt*, ed. K. Muir and P. Thompson (Liverpool: Liverpool University Press, 1969), 115). In the printed *Certayne psalms*, the second line is altered to 'Inward Syon, the Syon of the *hoste*' (my emphasis). Lok's sonnet 21 contains the lines: 'Thou shalt behold vpon thine altar lye / Many a yelden host of humbled hart' ('A meditation of a penitent sinner', Aa8r). There is no corresponding phrase in the biblical psalm.

86. Warley, '"An Englishe box"', 215.
87. *Songes and sonettes, written by the ryght honorable Lorde Henry Haward late Earle of Surrey, and others* (STC 13860), D2r.
88. Ibid.
89. Greene, 'Sir Philip Sidney's *Psalms*', 22.
90. Warley, '"An Englishe box"', 211.
91. For an analysis of Lok's source for the biblical translation, see S. Felch, 'The Vulgate as Reformation Bible: the sonnet sequence of Anne Lock', in *The Bible as book: the Reformation*, ed. O. O'Sullivan and E. N. Herron (London: British Library, 2000), 65–88. Her decision to split verses 1 and 4, as Spiller notes, is prompted by Wyatt's poem ('A literary "first"', 46).
92. Greene, 'Anne Lock's *Meditation*', 164. Greene builds upon the critical work of Patricia Parker in *Literary fat ladies: rhetoric, gender, property* (London: Methuen, 1987).
93. *Sermons of John Calvin*, D2r–v.
94. Wilson's *Arte of rhetorique* (STC 25799) does not dwell much on the subject of preaching, but it does make pointed reference to the dullness of oration in the church (see, for example, fo. 75).
95. *The art or crafte of rhetoryke* (STC 5947), A2v (see chapter 3, n. 136).
96. *Sermons of John Calvin*, D2r.
97. Ibid., D4r–v.
98. 'A meditation of a penitent sinner', Aa3r.
99. Both Susan Felch and Christopher Warley notice this progression (although only Felch attributes it to the exercise of penitence): see *The collected works of Anne Vaughan Lock*, ed. Felch, lv; and Warley, '"An Englishe box"', 224.
100. *Sermons of John Calvin*, F6r.
101. 'A meditation of a penitent sinner', A[a]2r.
102. *Sermons of John Calvin*, F8r.
103. 'A meditation of a penitent sinner', Aa3v.
104. Ibid., Aa7r.
105. *Sermons of John Calvin*, A6v.
106. *The institutes of the Christian religion*, ed. T. McNeill (Philadelphia: Westminster Press, 1960), 2. 2. 20.
107. *The collected works of Anne Vaughan Lock*, ed. Felch, lv.
108. 'A meditation of a penitent sinner', Aa5r.
109. See Spiller, 'A literary "first"', 47.
110. *Certayne Psalmes chosen out of the Psalter of Dauid*, C6v. Obviously, the addition of 'inwarde' at line 460 spoils the rhyme; the printer moved it from the subsequent line: 'For loo, thou louest the truthe of the [inward] harte' (cf. *The*

collected poems of Sir Thomas Wyatt, ed. Muir and Thompson, 114). It seems clear, however, that Lok used the printed version of Wyatt's *Psalmes* (see n. 85).

111. 'A meditation of a penitent sinner', Aa5r–v.
112. *Certayne Psalmes chosen out of the Psalter of Dauid*, C7r–v.
113. J. Donne, 'Holy Sonnet 2', *John Donne: a critical edition of the major works*, ed. J. Carey (Oxford: Oxford University Press, 1990), 174.
114. 'A meditation of a penitent sinner', Aa6v–Aa7r.
115. Ibid., Aa7r–v.
116. Greene, 'Anne Lock's *Meditation*', 161.
117. *Sermons of John Calvin*, E5v.
118. Greene, for example, asserts that Lok was 'obliged to confront for herself, by herself, what will shortly become a widely recognized issue in English devotional poetics' ('Anne Lock's *Meditation*', 161). But Lok's sequence is a complex negotiation of – and response to – a very current and contested cultural problem (cf. n. 19).
119. *Songes and sonettes*, Bb4r.
120. STC 2429.5; see Leaver, *'Goostly Psalmes'*, 251.
121. *The primer, set foorth by the kynges maiestie and his clergie* (STC 16034); and *The Byble in Englyshe* (STC 2068). Felch has collated the fourteen Psalter versions (including four Latin Psalters, two of which are versions of the Vulgate) most commonly available to the English readership; see 'The Vulgate as Reformation Bible', 78–88.
122. For notable exceptions, see n. 145, below.
123. *The whole booke of Psalmes*, 121 (cf. n. 49).
124. 'A meditation of a penitent sinner', Aa3v–Aa4r.
125. *The Byble in Englyshe*, 'The Psalmes of Dauid', fo. 10v.
126. 'A meditation of a penitent sinner', Aa5r.
127. *The whole booke of Psalmes*, 118.
128. Ibid., 121.
129. 'The Psalmes of Dauid', fo. 10v.
130. 'A meditation of a penitent sinner', Aa5r.
131. *The whole booke of Psalmes*, 122.
132. 'A meditation of a penitent sinner', Aa5v.
133. 'The Psalmes of Dauid', fo. 10v.
134. *Certayne Psalmes chosen out of the Psalter of Dauid* (1550), A3r.
135. *The whole booke of Psalmes*, 122.
136. 'A meditation of a penitent sinner', Aa6r.
137. *Dauids Psalter, diligently and faithfully tra[n]slated by George Ioye* (STC 2372), K4r.
138. Ibid., K4v.
139. *The whole booke of Psalmes*, 122.
140. 'A meditation of a penitent sinner', Aa6v.
141. *The whole booke of Psalmes*, 122.
142. The first quotation is from *The primer*, K1r; the second is Whittingham's translation in *The whole booke of Psalmes*, 120.
143. *Certayne Psalmes chosen out of the Psalter of Dauid*, C8r.
144. 'A meditation of a penitent sinner', Aa7r.
145. There are two echoes in his translation that seem to come from these sources: line 21 refers to 'the truthe in inward partes', that has a correspondence in verse 6 of

the Great Bible ('The Psalmes of Dauid', fo. 10v); the final line of Norton's translation offers 'calues' on the altar of God, which is found in only certain versions of the Psalter, *The primer* among them (K1r).

146. Compare, for example, the widely divergent translation of Whittingham to that of Norton.

147. Not much should be made of the poems by Dering and Lok contained in a manuscript at Cambridge (CUL MS ii.5.37). The manuscript seems to have had a political intention – but it was, in any case, clearly transcribed for an elite, educated, and tightly controlled coterie (cf. n. 42). The secular nature of the poems in praise of Bartholo Sylva, as well as their composition in Latin (Lok) and Greek (Dering) set them in another context entirely (see *The collected works of Anne Vaughan Lock*, ed. Felch, lviii–lix, and 73).

148. *Of the markes of the children of God* (1590), s1r.

149. *The posies of George Gascoigne, Esquire*, ¶ iir.

150. Ibid., xxvi–xxviii.

151. Ibid., ¶ iiir–iiiir.

152. Buchanan, Dante, Flamineo, and Petrarch all composed lyric translations of the Psalms. (Claiming Buchanan as a Continental source might seem confusing; however, Buchanan's Latin translation of the Psalms had only been published on the Continent by 1575.) The extent to which any of these individual authors was read in England at this time is subject to question. Two copies of the paraphrases of Flamineo do show up in scholastic libraries catalogued before 1570 (see n. 9). Du Bartas's *La muse chrestiene* had only been recently published in France at the time of Gascoigne's first edition of *The posies*.

153. Buchanan's *Psalmorum Dauidis paraphrases poetica* was first published in Paris in 1556. M. A. Shaaber records two extant copies: one held in the library of the University of Edinburgh; and the other at the Hunterian Museum, Glasgow University (see *Check-list of works of British authors printed abroad, in languages other than English, 1641* (New York: Bibliographical Society of America, 1975), 36). The second edition of Buchanan's *Psalmorum Dauidis* was published in Geneva c. 1565 with appended psalm translations by Beza (*Psalmi aliquot à Th. B. V. versi*), and subsequently published many times (see *Catalogue of the books printed on the Continent of Europe, 1501–1600 in Cambridge libraries*, ed. H. M. Adams (Cambridge: Cambridge University Press, 1967), I: 145). Beza's French play, *Abraham sacrifiant* (1550), also treats a religious topic, but this topic is not sustained in his Latin lyric poems; his *Poemata* was first published in Paris c. 1555 (ibid., I: 122).

154. *The vvhole woorkes of George Gascoigne* (STC 11638), 26–8.

155. Roy T. Eriksen has persuasively argued that Gascoigne's poetic translation influenced Herbert's own Psalm 130 (see 'George Gascoigne's and Mary Sidney's versions of Psalm 130', *Cahiers Elisabéthains* 36 (1989), 1–9).

156. *Baptistes, sive calvmnia, tragoedia, avctore Georgio Buchanao Scoto* (STC 3969); and *A tragedie of Abrahams sacrifice* (STC 2047). Vautrollier published a subsequent edition of *Baptistes* in 1578 (STC 3970).

157. *Paraphrasis Psalmorvm Davidis poetica* (STC 3983, 3983.5, and 3984 respectively). The second 1580 edition was farmed out to Henry Denham.

158. *Paraphrasis Psalmorvm Davidis poetica* (STC 3985).

159. Contrary to the assertion of J. E. Phillips, the publication of *Baptistes* does not appear to have been motivated by people around Sidney and Leicester – as a letter introducing Vautrollier to Buchanan came later (cf. I. D. McFarlane, *Buchanan* (London: Duckworth, 1981), 264).

160. See J. E. Phillips, 'George Buchanan and the Sidney circle', *HLQ* 12 (1948), 25–7, 40–49; and McFarlane, *Buchanan*, 264.

161. There are variants of the paraphrases in the English edition(s) not found in previous editions. This has caused I. D. McFarlane to speculate that Buchanan himself supplied the material (McFarlane, *Buchanan*, 264).

162. See 'Carminvm genera', in *Paraphrasis Psalmorvm Davidis poetica*, 305–11.

163. *Miscellaneous prose of Sir Philip Sidney*, ed. Duncan-Jones and van Dorsten, 110. Harvey also cites the 'Psalmes of King Dauid, royally translated by *Buchanan*' (*Fovre letters, and certaine sonnets* (STC 12900.5), 48).

164. Daniel Rogers did not compose religious verse, but his Latin poetry is collected into a manuscript held at the Huntington Library (HM 31188). The date of composition of Henry Constable's *Spirituall sonnettes* remains unclear, although it seems certain that he wrote them sometime after 1593 (see *The poems of Henry Constable*, ed. Joan Grundy (Liverpool: Liverpool University Press, 1960), 59).

165. Sidney's 'translation of Salust de Bartas' was entered into the Stationer's Register in 1588, but was never printed. As Anne Lake Prescott observes, the action has left only questions as to why the publication was held back by Sidney's family. I am suggesting that the later publishing strategies of Mary Sidney Herbert (particularly the circulation of the Sidney–Pembroke Psalter in manuscript) provide some answers. See Prescott, *French poets and the English Renaissance: studies in fame and transformation* (New Haven: Yale University Press, 1978), 178.

166. The only evidence we have of this body of work is an account of it in the printer's preface to Spenser's 1591 *Complaints containing sundrie small poemes of the worlds vanitie* (STC 23078), A2v. The psalm translations and devotional poems are claimed to be in 'Pamphlets looselie scattered abroad' – but it is not clear if this is print or manuscript circulation, or how broad the circulation is. (In any case, despite announcing his determination to obtain the works – from Spenser or another source – William Ponsonbie was apparently unable to do so.)

167. McFarlane, *Buchanan*, 272.

168. *The historie of Iudith in forme of a poeme* (STC 21671); and *The essayes of a prentise, in the divine art of poesie* (STC 14373), C4v–G1r.

169. J. Doelman, 'The accession of King James I and English religious poetry', *SEL* 34 (1994), 19–40.

170. Sidney also cites the poetic vocation of King James in his *Defence* (*Miscellaneous prose of Sir Philip Sidney*, ed. Duncan-Jones and van Dorsten, 110).

171. W. Webbe, *Discourse of English poetrie* (STC 25172); T. Nashe, *The anatomie of absurdite* (STC 18364 and 18365); and G. Puttenham, *The arte of english poesie* (STC 20519 and 20519.5).

172. *The monvment of matrones*, II: 213. The translation of verses from Psalm 119 by Dorcas Martin may have had a public intent. Martin's poem prefaces her translation of *An instruction for Christians* (II: 221). It seems possible that she was preparing this translation for a public venue. But her short psalm poem is rendered in common metre, and therefore does not fit among the exceptions.

173. *The poore widowes mite* was first printed in *The monvment of matrones* (V: 173). Bentley probably obtained a copy from Henry Denham, who published both works.

174. See, for example, 'A meditation to be said of women with child', and 'A mediation to be deliuered from sinne', in *A handfull of honisuckles*, 22–5.

175. See *Comfortable dialogs betwene Christ and a SINNER*, 51–62.

176. *Psalmes, sonets & songs of sadnes and pietie* (STC 4253), D1v–D2r. Byrd does employ a more adventurous rhyme scheme in his ballad psalms; Psalms 12, 13, 15, 112, and 119 rhyme abcb (B2v–C3v).

177. Drayton often opts for pentameter lines of rhyming couplets. But his first 'Song of Moses' (Deuteronomy 32), for example, is rhymed ababcc; his second 'Song of Moses' (Exodus 25) is rhymed abba. See *The harmonie of the Church* (STC 7199), A4r–B3r.

178. Ibid., A1r.

179. *Svndry Christian passions contained in two hundred sonnets* (STC 16697).

180. *Ecclesiastes, othervvise called The preacher* (STC 16696).

181. Lewalski, *Protestant poetics*, 239.

182. Ibid., 239–40; and Roche, *Petrarch and the English sonnet sequences*, ch. 3. See also Scanlon, 'Henry Lok's *Sundry Christian passions*: a critical edition', introduction; and Greene, *Post-Petrarchism*, 129–33.

183. Although none of her literary work survives, Anne Lok's daughter, Anne Moyle, is praised for her literary skill in Charles FitzGeffrey's *Affaniae, sive epigramatum libri tres* (STC 10934), 123–4; see M. White, 'Women writers and literary-religious circles in the Elizabethan West Country: Anne Dowriche, Anne Lock Prowse, Anne Lock Moyle, Ursula Fulford, and Elizabeth Rous', *Modern Philology* 103(2005) 205–8.

184. *Svndry Christian Passions*, A5r.

185. Ibid.

186. Ibid., 1, 53.

187. Lewalski, *Protestant poetics*, 240.

188. *Svndry Christian passions*, 31.

189. For Roche's superb analysis of this poem, see *Petrarch and the English sonnet sequences*, 158–61.

190. *Svndry Christian passions*, 52.

191. Roche, *Petrarch and the English sonnet sequences*, 160.

192. *Svndry Christian passions*, 19.

193. Ibid., A5r.

194. The second section adopts a sonnet form of abbaaccacbbcdd, and rhymes the twelfth line and the middle word, at the caesura, in the thirteenth.

195. *Ecclesiates, othervvise called The preacher*, A5r.

196. Lewalski, *Protestant poetics*, 240.

197. *A divine centvrie of spiritvall sonnets* (STC 1467). Thomas Roche has made the most explicit case for the influence of Lok upon Barnes (see *Petrarch and the English sonnet sequences*, 166–85). Aside from Barnes's structure of 100 sonnets, there are also sonnets within his collection that suspiciously echo Lok (cf. *DC* sonnet 4 and *SCP* III. 114; *DC* sonnet 23 and *SCP* II. 33; and *DC* sonnet 61 and *SCP* I. 54).

198. Greene makes this assertion in connection to the poetry of Anne Lok. Greene was the first to advance the case that Anne formulated what can be described as

a 'Puritan poetics' (see Greene, 'Anne Lock's *Meditation*', *passim*). But because he does not fully recognise the interruption of devotional lyric production in England – and its cause – he understands her poetry as a model for later 'reformed poet[s]' rather than as one means by which the religious lyric tradition in England is itself initiated.

199. See J. Doelman, 'Seeking "the fruit of favour": the dedicatory sonnets of Henry Lok's *Ecclesiastes*', *ELH* 60 (1993), 1–15. Lok also composed a commendatory sonnet for James's 1591 *Poetical exercises at vacant houres* (STC 14379).

200. Vivianus's *Ecclesiastes Solomonis* was not printed in England until 1662 (Wing V669).

201. Almost certainly the most influential translation would have been Gabriel Lermeus's Latin *Hebdomas*, published in England in 1591. This translation carried a commendatory Latin poem by Beza, which, while it emphasised the learned aspect of Du Bartas's work (Beza addresses him by the elevated term 'docte'), nonetheless hailed the *Premiere sepmaine* as a second creation. See *Gvilielmi Salvstii Bartassii Hebdomas* (STC 21656), A5r; see also Prescott, *French poets and the English Renaissance*, 179–83, for a complete list of translations published in England from 1589 to 1600.

202. The citation of Du Bartas in the work of Fraunce and Barnes, not to mention Henry Lok's unavoidable familiarity with his verse, would seem to disprove this. But while, for example, Barnes invokes the 'holy fire' that is Du Bartas's model of inspiration (see *A divine centvrie of spirituall sonnets*, A2v), the work of Roche, and Lewalski, shows Barnes to be replicating models that he finds in English poetry. The first notable imitation of Du Bartas in extant English religious lyric, I would argue, is found in Giles Fletcher's *Christs victorie, and triumph in heauen, and earth* (1610). This, of course, does not discount the influence of Du Bartas upon the poetry of men like Sidney or Spenser – as Sidney's translation of *Premiere sepmaine* is lost (see A. Sinfield, 'Sidney and Du Bartas', *Comparative Literature* 27 (1975), 12–15).

CHAPTER 5. 'A WOMANS WRITING OF DIUINEST THINGS':
AEMILIA LANYER'S PASSION FOR A PROFESSIONAL
POETIC VOCATION

1. *Salve Devs Rex Ivdæorvm* (STC 15227), a3.

2. See in particular, B. Lewalski, 'Of God and good women: the poems of Aemilia Lanyer', in *Silent but for the word: Tudor women as patrons, translators, and writers of religious works*, ed. M. Hannay (Kent, OH: Kent State University Press, 1985), 203–24; A. B. Coiro, 'Writing in service: sexual politics and class position in the poetry of Aemilia Lanyer and Ben Jonson', *Criticism* 35 (1993), 357–76; and L. Schnell, '"So great a difference is there in degree": Aemilia Lanyer and the aims of feminist criticism', *Modern Language Quarterly* 57 (1996), 23–35.

3. See L. Hutson, 'Why the lady's eyes are nothing like the sun', in *Women, texts, and histories 1575–1760*, ed. C. Brent and D. Purkiss (London: Routledge, 1992), 13–38; and S. F. Ng, 'Aemilia Lanyer and the politics of praise', *ELH* 67 (2000), 433–51.

4. Notable examples of the analysis of gender – or of gender and class – in Lanyer's poem are: Coiro, 'Writing in service'; J. Mueller, 'The feminist poetics of "Salve

Deus Rex Judaeorum"', in *Aemilia Lanyer: gender, genre, and the canon*, ed.
M. Grossman (Lexington: Kentucky University Press, 1998), 99–127; M.
Schoenfeldt, 'The gender of religious devotion: Amelia Lanyer and John Donne',
in *Religion and culture in Renaissance England*, ed. C. McEachern and D. Shuger
(Cambridge: Cambridge University Press, 1997), 209–33; and H. Wilcox,
'"Whom the Lord with love affecteth": gender and the religious poet, 1590–
1633', in *'This double voice': gendered writing in early modern England*, ed. D.
Clarke and E. Clarke (Basingstoke: Macmillan, 2000), 185–207.

5. L. McGrath, '"Let us have our libertie againe": Amelia Lanier's 17th-century
feminist voice', *Women's Studies* 20 (1992), 331–48. Other critical analyses of
Lanyer's feminism include L. McGrath, 'Metaphoric subversions: feasts and mirrors in Amelia Lanier's *Salve Deus Rex Judaeorum*', *Literature, Interpretation, Theory*
3 (1991), 101–13; W. Wall, *The imprint of gender: authorship and publication in
the English Renaissance* (Ithaca: Cornell University Press, 1993), 319–30; and
Mueller, 'The feminist poetics of "Salve Deus Rex Judaeorum"'. Early works that
analyse Lanyer's opposition to patriarchy – but do not apply the term 'feminist' –
include: Lewalski, 'Of God and good women', 203–24; E. Beilin, *Redeeming Eve:
women writers of the English Renaissance* (Princeton: Princeton University Press,
1987), 177–207; and T. Krontiris, *Oppositional voices: women as writers and
translators of literature in the English Renaissance* (London: Routledge, 1992),
103–20. The interrogation of Lanyer's oppositional voice has been the subject
of many other subsequent investigations of her work: see, in particular, B. Lewalski,
'Re-writing patriarchy and patronage: Margaret Clifford, Anne Clifford, and
Aemilia Lanyer', *Yearbook of English Studies* 21 (1991), 87–106; *Writing Women
in Jacobean England* (Cambridge: Harvard University Press, 1993), 213–41; and
'Seizing discourses and reinventing genres', in *Aemilia Lanyer: gender, genre, and the
canon*, ed. Grossman, 49–59; and in the same volume, S. Woods, 'Vocation and
authority: born to write', 83–98; and N. Miller, '(M)other tongues: maternity and
subjectivity', 143–66.

6. The analysis that best situates Lanyer's work within a market economy – one that
exerts pressure upon the formulations of the text itself – is Lorna Hutson's fine
article 'Why the lady's eyes are nothing like the sun'. But a recent article by Mary
Ellen Lamb decries the fact that so many discussions of *Salve Deus* 'have bracketed
off financial motives as somehow extraneous to the work' (see 'Patronage and class
in Aemilia Lanyer's *Salve Deus Rex Judaeorum*', in *Women, Writing, and the Reproduction of Culture in Tudor and Stuart Britain*, ed. M. E. Burke, J. Donawerth,
L. L. Dove, and K. Nelson (Syracuse: Syracuse University Press, 2000), 38–57).

7. Mueller touches on the issue of Lanyer's source material, but makes 'no pretense of
offering . . . a full treatment' of what she herself notes is a 'scarcely opened question'
in critical terms ('The feminist poetics of "Salve Deus Rex Judaeorum"', 107).

8. *Salve Devs Rex Ivdæorvm*, c2.

9. Quoted in S. Woods, *Lanyer: a Renaissance woman poet* (Oxford: Oxford University Press, 1999), 15.

10. Ibid., 9.

11. L. Barroll, 'Looking for patrons', in *Aemilia Lanyer: gender, genre, and the Canon*,
ed. Grossman, 29–48.

12. Bod. MS Ashmole 226, fo. 110v. As Susanne Woods and Leeds Barroll recount,
this MS has received a thorough going-over – and the reviewing of Woods,
Katherine Duncan-Jones, and the Bodliean paleographer has failed to positively

determine what Forman's notation reads. This, however, has been concluded by all
to be the most likely meaning (see Woods, *Lanyer*, 167 n. 23; and Barroll,
'Looking for patrons', 43–4 n. 11).

13. Woods, *Lanyer*, 14. Woods outlines the course of study that a young charge in
Kent's household could be expected to follow (see 9–14).

14. Bod. MS Ashmole 226, 201. Also quoted in Woods, *Lanyer*, 24–5.

15. Although, as David Bevington points out, these arrangements could extend beyond
the marriage (see 'A. L. Rowse's dark lady', in *Aemilia Lanyer: gender, genre, and the
Canon*, ed. Grossman, 20). What is clear is that Lanyer gave birth to a son, Henry,
in early 1593.

16. Quoted in *The poems of Aemilia Lanyer: Salve Deus Rex Judæorum*, ed. S. Woods
(Oxford: Oxford University Press, 1993), xxviii.

17. PRO Chancery Case, C2/James I L11/64.

18. Although I must say that I disagree with Susanne Woods that the structural
organisation of certain parts of Lanyer's work itself actually verifies her classical
education (see *Lanyer*, 11–13). While the examples that she cites are compelling, I
think that these rhetorical forms are readily available in vernacular works.

19. There is some difficulty in talking about the *Salve Deus*, in that it is the title of both
a collection and a long poem. Throughout this chapter, I will refer to the central
poem as *Salve Deus*, and to the other poems in the collection by their individual
titles.

20. In 'Writing in service' Anne Baynes Coiro emphasises the context of Lanyer's social
class, and argues that the 'politics of current literary criticism in Renaissance studies
and feminist studies in particular' has imagined a female community around
Aemilia Lanyer, and failed to notice the more disruptive class tensions in Lanyer's
work (358). The influence of Coiro's important corrective can be immediately felt
in the arguments of, for example, Schnell ('"So great a difference is there in degree"') and Ng ('Aemilia Lanyer and the politics of praise').

21. Hutson, 'Why the lady's eyes are nothing like the sun', 23.

22. J. Rogers, 'The passion of a female literary tradition: Aemilia Lanyer's *Salve Deus
Rex Judæorum*', *HLQ* 63 (2000), 436.

23. Ibid., 435.

24. *The copy of a letter, lately written in meeter, by a yonge gentilwoman: to her vnconstant
louer* (STC 25439); and *A sweet nosgay, or pleasant posye* (STC 25440). Moreover,
so much of the work of Christine de Pizan was circulated in English translation that
Lanyer had a good example of a woman poet with a professional career.

25. Margaret Ezell has highlighted the particular problem that making rigid distinc-
tions between print and scribal publication in the study of women's texts creates
(see, 'The myth of Judith Shakespeare: creating the canon of women's writing',
New Literary History 21 (1990), and *Writing Women's Literary History* (Baltimore:
Johns Hopkins University Press, 1993)). See also, the work of Harold Love, *Scribal
publication in seventeenth-century England* (Oxford: Clarendon Press, 1993);
Arthur Marotti, *Manuscript, print, and the English Renaissance lyric* (Ithaca: Cornell
University Press, 1995); and Peter Beal, *In praise of scribes: manuscripts and their
makers in seventeenth-century England* (Oxford: Oxford University Press, 1998).

26. Lewalski, *Writing women in Jacobean England*, 223.

27. K. B. McBride, 'Remembering Orpheus in the poems of Aemilia Lanyer', *SEL* 38
(1998), 94–5.

28. Rogers, 'The passion of a female literary tradition', 443.

29. Rogers points to Fletcher as a 'poetic forebear' in 'The passion of a female literary tradition', 443. The idea of Fletcher and Breton as models was first suggested by Lewalski in *Writing women in Jacobean England*, 227; Janel Mueller subsequently posits Fletcher's *Christs victorie* as the prototype in 'The feminist poetics of "Salve Deus Rex Judaeorum"', 107–8.
30. D. Rienstra, 'Dreaming authorship: Aemilia Lanyer and the Countess of Pembroke', in *Discovering and (re)covering the seventeenth century religious lyric*, ed. E. R. Cunnar and J. Johnson (Pittsburgh: Duquesne University Press, 2001), 87.
31. *Salve Devs Rex Ivdæorvm*, iv.
32. Ibid., d2r.
33. G. Fletcher, *Christs victorie, and truimph in heauen, and earth* (STC 11058), ¶¶r.
34. See F. Kastor, *Giles and Phineas Fletcher* (Boston: Twayne Publishers, 1978), 41–3.
35. See Hannibal Hamlin, *Psalm culture and early modern English literature* (Cambridge: Cambridge University Press 2004), 134–6, for an exposition of Phineas's use of Sidney's Psalm 42 in his own translation.
36. *Salve Devs Rex Ivdæorvm*, d1v.
37. The marginalia cites 'The Psalms written newly by the Countesse Dowager of Penbrooke.'
38. Ibid., d2r.
39. Ibid., d1r.
40. Ibid., d1v.
41. Ibid., d3r.
42. Ibid., d1v.
43. See n. 29.
44. Rienstra's careful reconstruction of the pastiche of psalm passages in *Salve Deus* (which she identifies as running from lines 57–143 in the poem) further suggests Lanyer's indebtedness. Lanyer uses psalm passages from the *Book of common prayer*, not the Sidney–Pembroke Psalter (as both Rienstra and Rogers observe). But she is nonetheless locating her work within a tradition that the verse Psalter initiated (see Rienstra, 'Dreaming authorship', 80–103; and Rogers, 'The passion of a female literary tradition', 443).
45. *Salve Devs Rex Ivdæorvm*, d3r.
46. See Mark Bland, 'The London book-trade in 1600', in *A companion to Shakespeare*, ed. D. S. Kastan (Oxford: Blackwell, 1999), 461, for a discussion of how evidence of the London book-trade can help us to reorient our assumptions about the literary values of early modern English culture.
47. Two of these printed works – *A diuine poeme, diuided into two partes* and *The pilgrimage to paradise* – are actually collections of two long poems (see n. 50, below). *The soules heavenly exercise* (STC 3700.5) is a composition that is written in both verse and prose – and is dedicated to William Rider, the mayor of London.
48. While *The Countesse of Penbrookes passion* (which will be the subject of much of the discussion that follows) was printed by Thomas East under the title *The passions of the spirit* (STC 3682.5), and dedicated to Mrs Mary Houghton (the wife of one of the Sheriffs of London), there is no indication that Breton was responsible for this presentation (see M. Brennan, 'Nicholas Breton's *The passions of the spirit* and the Countess of Pembroke', *RES* 38 (1987), 221–5). East printed the work without attribution, and attached his own dedication. The two poetic works not presented

to women are: *An excellent poeme, vpon the longing of a blessed heart* (STC 3649), dedicated to Lord Dudley North; and *The soules immortall crowne* (STC 3701), dedicated to James I.

49. As James Doelman points out, Henry Lok served as secretary to Lord Hunsdon sometime in the early 1590s ('Seeking "the fruit of favour: the dedicatory sonnets of Henry Lok's *Ecclesiastes*"', *ELH* 60 (1993), 6). As Lanyer was Hunsdon's mistress until 1592, it is possible that their respective services overlapped. Lanyer's previous acquaintance with Anne Lok's work, as Woods has argued, is entirely possible given her connection to the Vaughan family (see 'Anne Lock and Aemilia Lanyer: a tradition of Protestant women speaking', in *Form and reform in Renaissance England: Essays in Honor of Barbara Kiefer Lewalski*, ed. A. Boesky and M. T. Crane (Newark: Delaware University Press), 171–84).

50. See N. Breton, *A diuine poeme, diuided into two partes: the rauisht soule, and the blessed vveeper* (STC 3648); *The pilgrimage to paradise, ioyned with the Countesse of Penbrookes loue* (STC 3683); and A. Fraunce, *The Countesse of Pembrokes Emanuel* (STC 11338.5). See also Breton, *The Countesse of Penbrookes passion* (BL Sloane MS 1303).

51. Cf., for example, the opening stanzas of *The Countesse of Penbrookes loue* and those of 'The authors dreame'.

52. Coiro, 'Writing in service', 358.

53. Mary Ellen Lamb, *Gender and authorship in the Sidney circle* (Madison: Wisconsin University Press, 1990), 47–50.

54. *An excellent poeme vpon the longing of a blessed heart* (1601), C2r. Cf. 'Let me not listen to the sinners songes, / But to the Psalmes thy holy saints doe sing', *A solemne passion of the soules loue* (STC 3665), G7v.

55. Suzanne Trill makes a similar observation in 'Engendering penitence: Nicholas Breton and "the Countesse of Penbrooke"', in *Voicing women: gender and sexuality in early modern writing*, ed. K. Chedgzoy, M. Hansen, and S. Trill (Keele: Keele University Press, 1996), 37–8.

56. Lamb has greatly reduced the imagined proportions of Pembroke's circle, but lists Breton and Fraunce among the satellites (see Lamb, 'The Countess of Pembroke's patronage', *ELR* 12 (1982), 167).

57. For the publication history of Stanyhurst's *First foure bookes of Virgil his Aeneis* (1582), see chapter 4, n. 56.

58. *The lawiers logike* (STC 11343), B3v.

59. *The Arcadian rhetorike* (STC 11338), A1v.

60. For an analysis of how Fraunce's translations of the Psalms are indebted to Herbert's quantitative verse, see Hamlin, *Psalm culture and early modern English literature*, 100–2 (for Pembroke's quantitative practice, see 92–100).

61. G. Harvey, *Fovre letters, and certaine sonnets* (STC 12900.5), 48; cited in *Richard Stanyhurst. Translation of the first four books of the Æneis . . . 1582*, ed. E. Arber (London, 1880), vii.

62. See chapter 4, n. 56.

63. See Lamb, 'The Countess of Pembroke's patronage', 171.

64. I. Baroway, 'The Hebrew hexameter: a study in Renaissance sources and interpretation', *ELH* 2 (1935), 71.

65. See *Richard Stanyhurst. Translation of the first four books of the Æneis . . . 1582*, ed. Arber, 124.

66. Hamlin, *Psalm culture and early modern English literature*, 104–5.

67. *Piers Gaveston* (STC 7214.5), F4v.
68. Jean Robertson, 'Drayton and the Countess of Pembroke', *RES* 16 (1965), 49.
69. Fraunce, *The Countesse of Pembrokes Emanuel*, A2r.
70. The introduction to Gascoigne's psalm translation first appears in his 1573 *A hundredth sundrie flowres* (STC 11635), 373; but the Psalm itself is not published in this volume. *The posies of George Gascoigne, Esquire* (STC 11636) reprints the verse introduction, and Psalm 130 is included in the 'Flowers' section of the work (xxv–xxviii). There was one more edition of the *Posies* published in 1575, and *Deprofundis* is reprinted in Gascoigne's *VVhole woorkes* in 1587.
71. *The pilgrimage to paradise, ioyned with the Countess of Penbrookes loue*, ¶3r.
72. Lamb, *Gender and authorship*, 48.
73. *The soules harmony* (STC 3699), A3r.
74. Trill, 'Engendering penitence', 37.
75. *Countess of Penbrookes loue*, 13v.
76. While Lamb has assumed that the speaker of *The Countesse of Penbrookes passion* is represented as Herbert, I do not agree with her reading (see *Gender and authorship*, 49). Where Breton *does* ventriloquise Herbert's voice, he figures himself in the text as overhearing her private meditation. Further, as Lamb observes, representing Pembroke as the penitent in the *Passion* would have been a serious breach in decorum – one that I do not think that Breton would have risked (cf. 51–2). Trill also assumes a 'female' voice in devotional texts that Breton dedicates to women (particularly those dedicated to Herbert), but the voice of the soul, typically gendered female, complicates such a reading (see 'Engendering penitence', in particular 43 n. 16).
77. Trill, 'Engendering penitence', 38. Cf. M. Hannay, *Philip's phoenix: Mary Sidney, Countess of Pembroke* (Oxford: Oxford University Press, 1990), where Hannay declares that Breton attributed to Herbert 'an inappropriate asceticism that denied poetry' (136).
78. *Auspicante Iehoua. Maries exercise* (1597), which is not versified; and *A diuine poeme, diuided into two partes: the rauisht soule, and the blessed vveeper* (1601). While the date of composition of *The Countesse of Penbrookes passion* is unknown, it was published in 1599 under a different title (*The passions of the spirit*). *Marie Magdalens loue* with its appended verse meditation, *A solemne passion of the soules loue* (1595) bears no dedication; however, Herbert is strongly identified with Mary Magdalene in *Auspicante Iehoua* – and Breton's title of the previous work is therefore suggestive.
79. Breton's dedication of *The soules harmony* (1602) to Lady Sara Hastings serves as a useful index of the strategy.
80. See 'The "diffrence ... in degree": social rank and gendered expression', in *The impact of feminism in English Renaissance studies*, ed. Dympna Callaghan (London: Palgrave, 2007), 150–70.
81. Although Barbara Lewalski does not name *The Countess of Penbrookes passion* as a source for Lanyer's work, she does include Breton's *The rauisht soule*, *The blessed vveeper*, *The pilgrimage to paradise*, and *The Countess of Penbrookes loue* in a list of suggestive Protestant analogues for Lanyer's work. Lewalski also cites Fletcher and Fraunce as possible models (see *Writing women in Jacobean England*, 227).
82. *The passions of the spirit* (see n. 48). East also printed Breton's *Auspicante Iehoua. Maries exercise*, and *A trve description of vnthankfulnesse* (1602).

83. In Bodleian Tanner 221, the poem is transcribed into a collection of Breton's printed works (fos. 3–18v).

84. The British Library copy (Sloane MS 1303) is entitled *The Countesse of Penbrookes passion.*

85. This MS was previously housed in the Plymouth Library. The Plymouth MS (entitled 'A devout, ffrutefull, ande Godly remembraunce of the Passion off oure Savyoure Chryst Jesu') was transcribed by James Halliwell-Phillipps in *A brief description of the ancient and modern manuscripts preserved in the public library, Plymouth* (London: C. and J. Adlard, 1853). Halliwell-Phillips presented Plymouth with the manuscript after he had completed his edition. A submission to *Notes and Queries* trying to identify the author of a poem suggests a fourth manuscript copy in private hands ('Poem by Nicholas Breton', *Notes and Queries* 5 (1852), 487). However, the signature of the anonymous author ('H'), and the date, indicate that it might have been Halliwell-Phillipps himself attempting to attribute the poem in the manuscript he had purchased. Another extant manuscript in the Bodleian (MS Rawl. poet. 186) is a 1641 transcription of East's printed edition by Mary Matthews; it does not ascribe the poem to Breton.

86. See *Alumni Cantabrigienses*, ed. J. Venn and J. A. Venn (Cambridge: Cambridge University Press, 1922–54), I: 185.

87. See D. Shuger, *The Renaissance Bible: scholarship, sacrifice, and subjectivity* (Berkeley: California University Press, 1994), 226 n. 3, for a complete list of Calvinist passion narratives.

88. Sloane MS 1303, fo. 60r.

89. Ibid.

90. *Salve Devs Rex Ivdæorvm*, C4r.

91. See *The Covntesse of Pembrokes Arcadia* (STC 22540), III. 159; and V. 230.

92. *Salve Devs Rex Ivdæorvm*, B2r.

93. Cf. Sloane MS 1303, fo. 68r (stanza 93), and *Salve Devs Rex Ivdæorvm*, B2r (stanza 40).

94. Sloane MS 1303, fo. 63v.

95. *Salve Devs Rex Ivdæorvm*, Cr.

96. Debora Shuger has identified and analysed this group of texts in chapter 3 ('The death of Christ') of *The Renaissance Bible*, 89–127. The argument that follows concerning the passion narratives relies heavily upon Shuger's analysis.

97. B. Bowen, 'The rape of Jesus: Aemilia Lanyer's *Lucrece*', in *Marxist Shakespeares*, ed. J. Howard and S. C. Shershow (London: Routledge, 2001), 108. While Bowen makes the observation, she does not examine the grounds for the claim. Erica Longfellow has recently published a study that does trace the influence of the Calvinist passion narratives upon *Salve Deus*. While these arguments were developed independently, Longfellow's research offers welcome support to my findings (see *Women and religious writing in early modern England* (Cambridge: Cambridge University Press, 2004), ch. 2).

98. J. Calvin, *A harmonie vpon the three euangelists, Matthew, Mark and Luke* (STC 2962).

99. Shuger, *The Renaissance Bible*, 92–3.

100. Sloane MS 1303, fo. 62r.

101. See Shuger, *The Renaissance Bible*, 91.

102. J. Calvin, *Commentary on a harmony of the evangelists: Matthew Mark, and Luke*, trans. William Pringle (Grand Rapids, MI: Eerdmans Publishing, 1956), III: 317.

103. Ibid., III: 253, 278.
104. Ibid., III: 256, 281.
105. Sloane MS 1303, fo. 65v.
106. *Salve Devs Rex Ivdæorvm*, C3v; see also B4v (stanza 63).
107. Shuger, *The Renaissance Bible*, 91.
108. Calvin, *Commentary on a harmony of the evangelists*, III: 240.
109. Ibid., III: 317.
110. Shuger, *The Renaissance Bible*, 93. This transfer of responsibility, and its effect upon subjectivity in these texts, is carefully analysed by Shuger (91–104).
111. Sloane MS 1303, fo. 65r.
112. Shuger, *The Renaissance Bible*, 96.
113. Calvin, *Commentary on a harmony of the evangelists*, III: 290 (my emphasis).
114. Shuger, *The Renaissance Bible*, 96.
115. *Salve Devs Rex Ivdæorvm*, D4v, C3v.
116. See Sloane MS 1303, fo. 65r (stanza 51), and passages below.
117. Ibid., fos. 62r, 63v.
118. *Salve Devs Rex Ivdæorvm*, E3r. (Notice how Lanyer's stanza mirrors the progression of Breton's.)
119. Calvin, *Commentary on a harmony of the evangelists*, III: 259.
120. Shuger, *The Renaissance Bible*, 97–8.
121. Ibid.
122. Sloane MS 1303, fos. 64v, 65r.
123. *Salve Devs Rex Ivdæorvm*, F1v.
124. Shuger, *The Renaissance Bible*, 89.
125. See, for example, *A diuine poeme, diuided into two partes: the rauisht soule, and the blessed vveeper*, and the prose work, *Marie Magdalens loue* (STC 3665).
126. While various critics have made this point, I am concentrating upon how this formulation is driven by Lanyer's self-representation as a female poet in contradistinction to male competitors. See, in particular, Wall, *The imprint of gender*, 320–1; and Mueller, 'The feminist poetics of "Salve Deus Rex Judaeorum"', 109–16.
127. *Salve Devs Rex Ivdæorvm*, A4r.
128. Ibid.
129. See *The poems of Aemilia Lanyer*, ed. Woods, 60–1; see also Mueller, 'The feminist poetics of "Salve Deus Rex Judaeorum"', 105.
130. *Salve Devs Rex Ivdæorvm*, C4v.
131. Ibid., D4r.
132. Wendy Wall was the first critic to notice this construction (see *The imprint of gender*, 320).
133. *Salve Devs Rex Ivdæorum*, D2r.
134. Ibid.
135. That Pilate is informed that Christ is the Saviour is consistent with the moral blindness that Calvin describes. Christ's persecutors know him for who and what he is, but a kind of insanity grips them: 'their minds were darkened, so that, *seeing they did not see*'.
136. See, for example, Lewalski, 'Re-writing patriarchy and patronage', 103; Hutson, 'Why the lady's eyes are nothing like the sun', 32; and McGrath, '"Let us have our libertie againe"'.

137. Mueller, 'The feminist poetics of "Salve Deus Rex Judaeorum"', 123.
138. Ibid.
139. J. Donne, 'Holy Sonnet 7', in *John Donne: a critical edition of the major works*, ed. J. Carey (Oxford: Oxford University Press, 1990), 176.
140. *Salve Devs Rex Ivdæorvm*, D4r.
141. Beilin, *Redeeming Eve: women writers of the English Renaissance*, 183.
142. *Salve Devs Rex Ivdæorvm*, D4r.
143. Mueller, 'The feminist poetics of "Salve Deus Rex Judaeorum"', 112.
144. Ibid.
145. Calvin does praise their fortitude in staying with Christ until the end (*Commentary on a harmony of the evangelists*, III: 328).
146. Ibid., III: 292.
147. *Salve Devs Rex Ivdæorvm*, D4v.
148. Ibid., E3r.
149. Ibid., F1v.
150. Ibid., b3r.
151. See in particular W. Wall, 'Our bodies / our texts? Renaissance women and the trials of authorship', in *Anxious power: reading, writing, and ambivalence in narrative*, ed. C. J. Singley and S. E. Sweeney (Albany: State University of New York Press, 1993), 64–7; and J. Goldberg, *Desiring women writing: English Renaissance examples* (Stanford: Stanford University Press, 1997), 34–8.
152. Wall, 'Our bodies / our texts?', 64; see also N. Vickers, 'Diana described: scattered women and scattered rhyme', in *Writing and sexual difference*, ed. E. Abel (Chicago: Chicago University Press, 1986), 95–109.
153. Goldberg, *Desiring women writing*, 34.
154. *Salve Devs Rex Ivdæorvm*, a4v.
155. Ibid., c2v.
156. Fletcher, *Christs victorie*, ¶2v.
157. *Salve Devs Rex Ivdæorvm*, d3v.
158. Longfellow notices that Margaret Clifford is able to discern Christ on earth even when he comes to her disguised (*Salve Deus*, F2r). Clifford's '[t]rue interpretation' in this passage 'is a sign of [her] election' (see *Women and religious writing*, 80–1).
159. *Salve Devs Rex Ivdæorvm*, b1v.
160. *The soules harmony*, A3r.
161. Much has been made of the fact that Lanyer's pursuit of patronage does not appear to have yielded financial success, and that there were only two editions of her work in print (STC 15227 and 15227.5). But it was not unusual for works of devotional verse at this time to receive single issues. Most of Breton's devotional verse saw only single printings; the exceptions to this are: *The passion of a discontented minde* (two editions (STC 3680 and 3681)); and *A solemne passion of the soules loue* (six editions (STC 3665; and 3696–3698.3)).
162. Woods, *Lanyer*, vii. Isabella Whitney's venture into print troubles this claim. While Whitney does not work within patronage systems, there is certainly evidence that she wrote for payment (see *The copy of a letter, lately written in meeter, by a yonge gentilwoman: to her vnconstant louer* (1567?); and *A sweet nosgay* (1573)). Other previous instances of women's poetic work in circulation – in print and manuscript – do not exhibit signs of expectation for financial remuneration.

AFTERWORD

1. 'On the death of Mrs Katherine Philips', in *Poems by the most deservedly admired Mrs. Katherine Philips, the matchless Orinda* (Wing P2033), f2v.
2. See in particular, J. Summit, *Lost property: the woman writer and English literary history, 1380–1589* (Chicago: Chicago University Press, 2000), 203–9.
3. Lanyer was also obviously aware of other female precedents besides Herbert; see S. Woods, 'Anne Lock and Aemilia Lanyer: a tradition of Protestant women speaking', in *Form and Reform in Renaissance England: Essays in Honor of Barbara Kiefer Lewalski*, ed. A. Boesky and M. T. Crane (Newark Delaware University Press), 171–84.
4. M. Cavendish, *Natures Pictures drawn by fancies pencil to the life* (Wing N855), c1r.
5. See Masten's discussion of how Cavendish constructs her authorship as a solitary endeavor. 'Her language', he observes, 'emphasizes the organicism and "natural" self-inspiration that will become the hallmarks of the author-genius in subsequent English culture' (*Textual intercourse: collaboration, authorship, and sexualities in Renaissance drama* (Cambridge: Cambridge University Press, 1997), 161).
6. The implication has been provocatively pursued by several critics, notably Jennifer Summit. Summit's thesis is that the narratives that understand the woman writer as 'lost' within or 'oppositional' to literary tradition are embedded in the tradition itself. She argues that the figure of the woman writer was inscribed as 'lost' in order to formulate notions of public, canonical, *male* literary activity. The argument, while compelling, is problematic because it consigns the production of written culture, and the terms by which it operates, to the activities of men – even while it asserts the value of women writers in the sixteenth century.
7. See P. Crawford, 'Women's published writings 1600–1700', in *Women in English society, 1500–1800*, ed. Mary Prior (London: Methuen, 1985), 211–82; *A biographical dictionary of English women writers, 1580–1720*, ed. M. Bell, G. Parfitt, and S. Shepherd (Boston: G. K. Hall, 1990); and *Women and the literature of the seventeenth century*, ed. H. Smith and S. Cardinale (Westport, CT: Greenwood Press, 1990).
8. J. Taylor, *Religions enemies* (Wing T503), 6; quoted in K. Gillespie, *Domesticity and dissent in the seventeenth century: English women's writing and the public sphere* (Cambridge: Cambridge University Press, 2004), 24, n. 88.
9. See Wiseman, 'Unsilent instruments and the devil's cushions: authority in seventeenth-century women's prophetic discourse' in *New Feminist Discourses*, ed. I. Armstrong (London: Routledge, 1992); and H. Hinds, *God's Englishwomen: seventeenth-century radical sectarian writing and feminist criticism* (Manchester: Manchester University Press, 1996), *passim*.
10. Taylor, *Religions enemies* (1641), 1.
11. The first five cantos of Lucy Hutchinson's *Order and disorder: or, the world made and undone* were printed anonymously in 1679 (Wing A3594). Long attributed to Hutchinson's brother, Sir Allen Apsley, the poem was first reattributed to Hutchinson by David Norbrook in 'A devine Originall: Lucy Hutchinson and the "woman's version"', *TLS* 19 Mar. 1999, 13–15.
12. Erica Longfellow argues that Southwell's scribal publication of her work might well have been an attempt to elevate her social standing after her second marriage (see *Women and religious writing in early modern England* (Cambridge: Cambridge University Press, 2004), ch. 3).

13. Patricia Crawford has analysed the number of first editions by women in the seventeenth century in 'Women's published writings 1600–1700', 214, and Appendix 2, Figure 7.3 (270).

14. *New Ierusalems glory*, in *The little horns doom* (Wing C737), 238; Cf. A. Trapnel, *A defiance to all reproachfull . . . defaming speeches* in *Anna Trapnel's report and plea* (Wing T2033), 55.

15. Again, while 'class' is an anachronistic term for the early modern period, it most accurately represents the social tensions that I am trying to describe (see introduction, n. 54).

16. Even Anne Lok's membership in the merchant class constitutes a higher social sphere than that of many of the women writing in the seventeenth century.

17. P. Crawford, *Women and religion in England 1500–1720* (London: Routledge, 1993), 123.

18. Ibid., 129–30. The passage from Ephesians 5:22–4 that was often used to secure women's subordination to their husbands makes this parallel between domestic and ecclesiastical control: 'Wiues, submit your selues vnto your husbands, as vnto the Lord. For the husband is the wiues head, euen as Christ is the head of the Church . . . Therefore as the Church is in subiection to Christ, euen so *let* the wiues *be* to their husbands in euery thing' (Geneva Bible).

19. See, in particular, Gillespie, *Domesticity and dissent in the seventeenth century* (cf. n. 8).

20. Crawford, *Women and religion in England 1500–1720*, 130.

21. Crawford, 'Women's published writings 1600–1700', 213, 224.

22. As Nigel Smith has pointed out, sectarianism in the seventeenth century cannot properly be termed 'marginal' in either political or cultural terms:

   > Many religious radicals were at the centre of political power during the Interregnum. Oliver Cromwell was one of their number. 'Marginal' is often taken to mean 'non-orthodox', but the extent of unorthodoxy if we take by all of those who at some point between 1558 and 1685 voiced an unorthodox or unofficial belief, including Recusants, Protestant sectaries and atheists, is hardly a 'marginal' phenomenon. A particular prophet active in early seventeenth-century London may have seemed 'marginal' if considered by him or herself: add them all together and the picture is very different ('Non-conformist voices and books', *Cambridge History of the Book in Britain, 1557–1695*, ed. J. Barnard and D. F. McKenzie (Cambridge: Cambridge University Press, 2002), IV: 412).

23. Taylor, *Religions enemies*, 6.

24. *Rump, or An exact collection of the choicest poems . . . anno 1639 to anno 1661* (Wing B4851), 291–2; quoted in S. Achinstein, 'Women on top in the pamphlet literature of the English Revolution', in *Feminism & Renaissance studies*, ed. L. Hutson (Oxford: Oxford University Press, 1999), 342.

25. Achinstein, 'Women on top in the pamphlet literature of the English Revolution', 342–3.

26. S. Wiseman, '"Adam, the father of all flesh", porno-political rhetoric and political theory in and after the English Civil War', in *Pamphlet wars: prose in the English Revolution*, ed. J. Holstun (London: Frank Cass & Co., 1992), 134.

27. Achinstein, 'Women on top in the pamphlet literature of the English Revolution', 343.

28. Wiseman makes this point in '"Adam, the father of all flesh"', 135. The recent work of critics such as Katherine Gillespie and Hilary Hinds has gone a long way in

correcting this misapprehension: see Gillespie, *Domesticity and dissent in the seventeenth century*; and Hinds, *God's Englishwomen: seventeenth-century radical sectarian writing and feminist criticism.*

29. Wiseman, '"Adam, the father of all flesh"', 146.
30. BL Harl. MS 4931, fo. 9; quoted in Crawford, *Women and religion in England 1500–1720*, 129.
31. Wing E233 and E222.
32. *The third part of Gangraena. Or, A new and higher discovery of the errors, heresies, blasphemies, and insolent proceedings of the sectaries of these times* (Wing E237), 170. While Chidley and her son may have collaborated on other pamphlets (*The ivstification of the independent chvrches of Christ* (Wing C3832); and *A new-yeares-gift* (Wing C3833)), there is no indication that Samuel was co-author of Katherine's ripostes to Edwards. The pamphlet that Edwards cites, *Lanseters launce*, is no longer extant (and it is not clear if the Chidleys composed it).
33. She writes that 'Taylors, Felt-makers, Button-makers, Tent-makers, shepherds or ploughmen' are more qualified to erect a church than are 'ill-meaning priests' (*The ivstification of the independent chvrches of Christ*, 22).
34. This gesture is even more revealing when we are aware of how humiliated Edwards actually was by Chidley's attack; Hezekiah Woodward records that the response to his works by a woman was like 'a spetting in his face' (*A short letter modestly intreating a friends judgement upon Mr Edwards his booke* (Wing 3502), 5.)
35. *Poems by the most deservedly admired Mrs. Katherine Philips*, f2v.
36. The benefits of higher education (which went beyond basic literacy) were still largely the privilege of upper-class women.
37. See, in particular, H. L. Smith, *Reason's disciples: seventeenth-century English feminists* (Urbana: Illinois University Press, 1982), ch. 1.
38. *The poems of Anne Countess of Winchilsea*, ed. M. Reynolds (Chicago: Chicago University Press, 1903), 4.
39. J. Guillory, *Cultural capital: the problem of literary canon formation* (Chicago: Chicago University Press, 1993).
40. Jonathan Brody Kramnick argues that 'restriction' in the gender and social class of canonical authors was, for some eighteenth-century critics, 'precisely the point'. Kramnick demonstrates how women writers and readers serve as an index of rising popular literacy. While he sees a cultural negotiation that is far more complicated than straightforward exclusion, he also understands the restriction of the canon as a reaction to the 'opening up of culture to women and commoners' (*Making the English canon: print-capitalism and the cultural past, 1700–1770* (Cambridge: Cambridge University Press, 1998), 9).
41. See, in particular, Gillespie, *Domesticity and dissent in the seventeenth century.*

Index